Advanced Metaheuristic Methods in Big Data Retrieval and Analytics

Hadj Ahmed Bouarara
Dr. Moulay Tahar University of Saïda, Algeria

Reda Mohamed Hamou
Dr. Moulay Tahar University of Saïda, Algeria

Amine Rahmani
Dr. Moulay Tahar University of Saïda, Algeria

A volume in the Advances in
Computational Intelligence and
Robotics (ACIR) Book Series

Published in the United States of America by
    IGI Global
    Engineering Science Reference (an imprint of IGI Global)
    701 E. Chocolate Avenue
    Hershey PA, USA 17033
    Tel: 717-533-8845
    Fax: 717-533-8661
    E-mail: cust@igi-global.com
    Web site: http://www.igi-global.com

Library of Congress Cataloging-in-Publication Data

Names: Bouarara, Hadj Ahmed, 1990- editor. | Hamou, Reda Mohamed, 1967-
   editor. | Rahmani, Amine, 1991- editor.
Title: Advanced metaheuristic methods in big data retrieval and analytics /
   Hadj Ahmed Bouarara, Reda Mohamed Hamou, and Amine Rahmani, editors.
Description: Hershey, PA : Engineering Science Reference, [2019] | Includes
   bibliographical references.
Identifiers: LCCN 2018024574| ISBN 9781522573388 (hardcover) | ISBN
   9781522573395 (ebook)
Subjects: LCSH: Big data. | Metaheuristics.
Classification: LCC QA76.9.B45 A34 2019 | DDC 005.7--dc23 LC record available at https://lccn.
loc.gov/2018024574

This book is published in the IGI Global book series Advances in Computational Intelligence and Robotics (ACIR) (ISSN: 2327-0411; eISSN: 2327-042X)

British Cataloguing in Publication Data
A Cataloguing in Publication record for this book is available from the British Library.

All work contributed to this book is new, previously-unpublished material.
The views expressed in this book are those of the authors, but not necessarily of the publisher.

For electronic access to this publication, please contact: eresources@igi-global.com.

Advances in Computational Intelligence and Robotics (ACIR) Book Series

ISSN:2327-0411
EISSN:2327-042X

Editor-in-Chief: Ivan Giannoccaro, University of Salento, Italy

MISSION

While intelligence is traditionally a term applied to humans and human cognition, technology has progressed in such a way to allow for the development of intelligent systems able to simulate many human traits. With this new era of simulated and artificial intelligence, much research is needed in order to continue to advance the field and also to evaluate the ethical and societal concerns of the existence of artificial life and machine learning.

The **Advances in Computational Intelligence and Robotics (ACIR) Book Series** encourages scholarly discourse on all topics pertaining to evolutionary computing, artificial life, computational intelligence, machine learning, and robotics. ACIR presents the latest research being conducted on diverse topics in intelligence technologies with the goal of advancing knowledge and applications in this rapidly evolving field.

COVERAGE

- Computational Intelligence
- Synthetic Emotions
- Computer Vision
- Artificial life
- Brain Simulation
- Computational Logic
- Fuzzy systems
- Adaptive and Complex Systems
- Algorithmic Learning
- Cognitive Informatics

IGI Global is currently accepting manuscripts for publication within this series. To submit a proposal for a volume in this series, please contact our Acquisition Editors at Acquisitions@igi-global.com or visit: http://www.igi-global.com/publish/.

Titles in this Series

For a list of additional titles in this series, please visit:
https://www.igi-global.com/book-series/advances-computational-intelligence-robotics/73674

Handbook of Research on Predictive Modeling and Optimization Methods in Science...
Dookie Kim (Kunsan National University, South Korea) Sanjiban Sekhar Roy (VIT University, India) Tim Länsivaara (Tampere University of Technology, Finland) Ravinesh Deo (University of Southern Queensland, Australia) and Pijush Samui (National Institute of Technology Pata, India)
Engineering Science Reference • ©2018 • 618pp • H/C (ISBN: 9781522547662) • US $355.00

Handbook of Research on Investigations in Artificial Life Research and Development
Maki Habib (The American University in Cairo, Egypt)
Engineering Science Reference • ©2018 • 501pp • H/C (ISBN: 9781522553960) • US $265.00

Critical Developments and Applications of Swarm Intelligence
Yuhui Shi (Southern University of Science and Technology, China)
Engineering Science Reference • ©2018 • 478pp • H/C (ISBN: 9781522551348) • US $235.00

Handbook of Research on Biomimetics and Biomedical Robotics
Maki Habib (The American University in Cairo, Egypt)
Engineering Science Reference • ©2018 • 532pp • H/C (ISBN: 9781522529934) • US $325.00

Androids, Cyborgs, and Robots in Contemporary Culture and Society
Steven John Thompson (University of Maryland University College, USA)
Engineering Science Reference • ©2018 • 286pp • H/C (ISBN: 9781522529736) • US $205.00

Developments and Trends in Intelligent Technologies and Smart Systems
Vijayan Sugumaran (Oakland University, USA)
Engineering Science Reference • ©2018 • 351pp • H/C (ISBN: 9781522536864) • US $215.00

Handbook of Research on Modeling, Analysis, and Application of Nature-Inspired...
Sujata Dash (North Orissa University, India) B.K. Tripathy (VIT University, India) and Atta ur Rahman (University of Dammam, Saudi Arabia)
Engineering Science Reference • ©2018 • 538pp • H/C (ISBN: 9781522528579) • US $265.00

For an entire list of titles in this series, please visit:
https://www.igi-global.com/book-series/advances-computational-intelligence-robotics/73674

701 East Chocolate Avenue, Hershey, PA 17033, USA
Tel: 717-533-8845 x100 • Fax: 717-533-8661
E-Mail: cust@igi-global.com • www.igi-global.com

Editorial Advisory Board

Table of Contents

Detailed Table of Contents

Under uncertainty, understanding and controlling complex environments is only possible with an ability to use distributed computing by the way of information exchange between devices to be able to understand the response of the system to a particular problem. From transformation of raw data in a huge distribution of network into the meaningful information, to use the understood knowledge to make rapid decisions needs to have a network composed of smart devices. Internet of things (IoT) is a novel approach, where these smart devices can communicate with each other by using key technologies of artificial intelligence (AI) in order to make timely autonomous decisions. This emerging technical advancement and realization of horizontal and vertical integration caused the fourth stage of industrialization (Industry 4.0). The objective of this chapter is to give detailed information on both IoT based on key AI technologies and Industry 4.0. It is expected to shed light on new work to be done by providing explanations about the new areas that will emerge with this new technology.

Computer modeling of ecological systems is the activity of implementing computer solutions to analyze data related to the fields of remote sensing, earth science, biology, and oceans. The ecologists analyze the data to identify the relationships between a response and a set of predictors, using statistical models that do not accurately describe the main sources of variation in the response variable. Knowledge discovery techniques are often more powerful, flexible, and effective for exploratory analysis than statistical techniques. This chapter aims to test the use of data mining in ecology. It will discuss the exploration of ecological data by defining at first data mining, its advantages, and its different types. Then the authors detail the field of bio-inspiration and meta-heuristics. And finally, they give case studies from where they applied these two areas to explore ecological data.

Chapter 3
Abdelkrim Tabti, Dr. Tahar Moulay University of Saida, Algeria
Mohammed Djellouli, Dr. Tahar Moulay University of Saida, Algeria

In this chapter, the authors define the context of the person in social networks. Subsequently they introduce modeling and context of the development process of a person. Then they work on analyzing and feeling defined analysis technique, the sour feelings tweets and their characteristics, and method of how to recuperate data from Twitter by using API extraction.

Chapter 4
Frederic Jack, University of Grenoble, France

We live in a world of information. It is everywhere, but it is sometimes difficult to find and know that data first. In today's digital society, it's easy to find texts to plagiarize. These texts may come from the internet, publishers, or other content providers. Plagiarism is considered a serious fault. Throughout the world, universities are making significant efforts to educate students and teachers, offering guides and tutorials to explain the types of plagiarism, to avoid plagiarism. Internet contains easy to get texts the people can use in their newsrooms simply using copy and paste. This chapter shows the various types of plagiarism and the different techniques of automatic plagiarism detection and related work that addresses the topic.

Chapter 5
Salvia Praga, Poland University of Worcester, Poland

The automatic construction of ontologies from texts is usually based on the text itself, and the domain described is limited to the content of the text. In order to design semantically richer ontologies, the authors propose to extend the classical methods of ontology construction (1) by taking into account the text from the point of view of its structure and its content to build a first nucleus ontology and (2) enriching the ontology obtained by exploiting external resources (general texts and controlled vocabularies of the same domain). This chapter describes how these different resources are analyzed and exploited using linked data properties.

Chapter 6

The phenomenon of big data (massive data mining) refers to the exponential growth of the volume of data available on the web. This new concept has become widely used in recent years, enabling scalable, efficient, and fast access to data anytime, anywhere, helping the scientific community and companies identify the most subtle behaviors of users. However, big data has its share of the limits of ethical issues and risks that cannot be ignored. Indeed, new risks in terms of privacy are just beginning to be perceived. Sometimes simply annoying, these risks can be really harmful. In the medium term, the issue of privacy could become one of the biggest obstacles to the growth of big data solutions. It is in this context that a great deal of research is under way to enhance security and develop mechanisms for the protection of privacy of users. Although this area is still in its infancy, the list of possibilities continues to grow.

Chapter 7

Cardiovascular diseases (CVDs) have turned out to be one of the life-threatening diseases in recent times. The key to effectively managing this is to analyze a huge amount of datasets and effectively mine it to predict and further prevent heart-related diseases. The primary objective of this chapter is to understand and survey various information mining strategies to efficiently determine occurrence of CVDs and also propose a big data architecture for the same. The authors make use of Apache Spark for the implementation.

Chapter 8

Damian Alberto, Indian Institute of Technology Bombay, India

The manual classification of a large amount of textual materials are very costly in time and personnel. For this reason, a lot of research has been devoted to the problem of automatic classification and work on the subject dates from 1960. A lot of text classification software has appeared. For some tasks, automatic classifiers perform almost as well as humans, but for others, the gap is still large. These systems are directly related to machine learning. It aims to achieve tasks normally affordable only by humans. There are generally two types of learning: learning "by heart," which consists of storing information as is, and learning generalization, where we learn from examples. In this chapter, the authors address the classification concept in detail and how to solve different classification problems using different machine learning techniques.

Chapter 9

Souria Ortiga, Mente Argentina University, Argentina

During the 1980s, and despite its maturity, the search information (RI) was only intended for librarians and experts in the field of information. Such tendentious vision prevailed for many years. Since the mid-90s, the web has become an increasingly crucial source of information , which has a renewed interest in IR. In the last decade, the popularization of computers, the terrible explosion in the amount of unstructured data, internal documents, and corporate collections, and the huge and growing number of internet document sources have deeply shaken the relationship between man and information. Today, a great change has taken place, and the RI is often used by billions of people around the world. Simply, the need for automated methods for efficient access to this huge amount of digital information has become more important, and appears as a necessity.

Chapter 10

Yasmin Bouarara, Dr. Tahar Molay University of Saida, Algeria

In today's world of globalization and technology without borders, the emergence of the internet and the rapid development of telecommunications have made the world a global village. Recently, the email service has become immensely used, and the main means of communication because it is cheap, reliable, fast, and easy to access. In addition, it allows users with a mailbox (BAL) and email address to exchange messages (images, files, and text documents) from anywhere in the world via the internet. Unfortunately, this technology has become undeniably the original source of malicious activity, in particular the problem of unwanted emails (spam), which has increased dramatically over the past decade. According to the latest report from Radicati Group, which provides quantitative and qualitative research with details of the e-mail, security, and social networks, published in 2012, 70-80% of email traffic consists of spam. The goal of the chapter is to give a state of the art on spam and spam techniques and the disadvantages of this phenomenon.

Chapter 11
Mekelleche Fatiha, University of Oran 1 Ahmed Ben Bella, Algeria
Haffaf Hafid, University of Oran 1 Ahmed Ben Bella, Algeria
Ould Bouamama Belkacem, University of Lille 1, France

A wireless sensor network (WSN) is a special ad hoc network. It consists of a large number of sensors communicating with wireless links to monitor the real-world environment. They have limited energy, computational power, memory, and transmission range. They are widely used in different fields like military operations, environmental monitoring, and healthcare applications. However, the openness and hostility of the deployment space and the resources limitations make these networks vulnerable to several types of attacks and intrusions. So, the WSN security becomes a real challenge. Principally, the attacks in the network aim at damaging the smooth running of the legitimate nodes and cause a dysfunction of the network. Sybil attack is one of the perilous attacks which affects the WSN networks and poses threats to many security goals. This attack makes the sensor node into Sybil node and illegitimately takes and claims multiple identities.

Chapter 12
Lavika Goel, Birla Institute of Technology and Science (BITS), India
Lavanya B., Birla Institute of Technology and Science (BITS), India
Pallavi Panchal, Birla Institute of Technology and Science (BITS), India

This chapter aims to apply a novel hybridized evolutionary algorithm to the application of face recognition. Biogeography-based optimization (BBO) has some element of randomness to it that apart from improving the feasibility of a solution could reduce it as well. In order to overcome this drawback, this chapter proposes a hybridization of BBO with gravitational search algorithm (GSA), another nature-inspired algorithm, by incorporating certain knowledge into BBO instead of the randomness. The migration procedure of BBO that migrates SIVs between solutions is done between solutions only if the migration would lead to the betterment of a solution. BBO-GSA algorithm is applied to face recognition with the LFW (labelled faces in the wild) and ORL datasets in order to test its efficiency. Experimental results show that the proposed BBO-GSA algorithm outperforms or is on par with some of the nature-inspired techniques that have been applied to face recognition so far by achieving a recognition rate of 80% with the LFW dataset and 99.75% with the ORL dataset.

Foreword

The Big Data phenomenon (excavation of mass data) refers to the exponential growth in the volume of data available on the web. In view of this remarkable development, data analyzers have focused on this treasure to benefit to improve the daily lives of users. However, Big Data has its limits in terms of ethical issues and risks that cannot be ignored, such as finding relevant and useful information to meet users' needs and queries.

In order to meet the challenges of the explosion of data volume and the variety of documents being processed, retrieving information in big data has become an opportunity to ensure scalable, efficient and fast access to relevant information everywhere and at any time. Except behind this task lies a complicated process that has three main axes: the indexing of documents, correspondence (relevance) and finally the interrogation that includes the representation, analysis and reformulation of requests. Information retrieval systems are used in different fields such as medical, marketing, education, government, etc. At this stage, developing approaches and solutions to process those challenges has become a major issue in today's digital world for large research studies.

In this context this book aims mainly to collect and offer the scientific community new advancement of exploration, creation and development of solutions in the information retrieval field over big data challenges. We intended to discuss and share existed and original research works and practical experiences by providing the latest and most innovative contributions in such complex and huge environments like Big Data and IoT domains. Globally, this book touches a variety of issues and concerns such as, spam filtering, supervised classification, bio-inspiration, networks security, sensor networks, internet of things, private and clear retrieval social works analysis, etc.

Zakaria Bendaoud
University of Saida, Algeria

Preface

Recently with the arrival of big data and internet of things, the modern digital world was photographed as an "ocean" fueled by Google searches, social networks, blogs and commercial websites. This ocean has led to renewed interest and enthusiasm for Information Retrieval (IR) technology. One of the strengths of this technology is its ability to help users find the desired needle in a haystack of digital data. The meaning of the term IR in big data can be very broad and often used in an imprecise content. Just taking out an ID card from my wallet so that I can type the number of this card is a form of IR. This dynamic domain is focused mainly on the design and implementation of computer systems that process the representation, storage, and organization of data elements such as textual documents, web pages, catalogs line or multimedia objects to provide users with easy access to relevant information.

Information Retrieval (IR) is a well-established discipline that has been providing solutions for users for more than three decades, but is still an active area of research. This suggests that although much works have been done in this area, much remains to be done. In terms of scope, IR in big data is related to multidisciplinary and interdisciplinary applications including modeling, web-based research, text classification, systems architecture, user interfaces, visualization, filtering, research multilingual, grouping and searching for multimedia information. As a result, as long as information exists, the search for information is ubiquitous.

In the last decade, the WWW has become a vital commodity used on a daily basis by a growing number of users. It is an extremely versatile and cost-effective way to perform tasks such as communication, commerce and business, entertainment and recreation, cultural outreach, and access to information, etc. The amount of data stored and shared on the Web and other document repositories is steadily increasing. Unfortunately, this growth results from well-known difficulties and problems when it comes to finding the relevant information. Recently, we can say that getting relevant information from the web is like taking a drink from a fire hydrant. There are several arguments why IR on the web is so inefficient. First of all, the web is vast, distributed, an accessible space for the general public and essentially contains unstructured data that greatly complicates IR's tasks.

Many applications that manage information on the web would be totally insufficient without the support of IN technology. How could we find information on the web if there were no search engines? How could we manage our emails without spam filtering? How could we protect our homes and stores remotely without video surveillance systems across the web? In the light of the foregoing, the researchers try to find solutions through the imitation of biological phenomena found in nature to model artificial algorithms to solve different problem related to information retrieval spot in the big data as classification supervised, clustering, plagiarism, spam, sensor networks, medical problems, etc.

Meta-heuristics techniques are an important alternative for solving complex and optimization problems that is not treatable by deterministic methods. In our life they are literally as many ideas as there are organisms. Bio-mimicry, considered as a sub-class of meta-heuristics, represents innovation that seeks durable solutions to human challenges by emulating the proven models and strategies of nature. For example, mimicking termites to create sustainable buildings, imitating humpback whales to create efficient wind energy, and imitating dolphins to send underwater signals, or imitate ants to look for the shortest path in a graph. . . etc. With a simple analysis we can clearly notice that IR and bio-mimicry may seem like they do not have many properties in common. However, recent studies suggest that they can be used together for several application problems in big data and internet of things (IOT) especially when conventional methods would be too expensive or difficult to implement.

By regrouping the previously detailed parts, we go out with the major objective of this chapter which is to reveal the links between the mystique of bio-inspired metaheuristic techniques and the development of solutions to the different problems related to IR tasks in Big Data. The target of this book is intended for a wide audience, in particular academic researchers, engineers, and PhD students wishing to have a general overview of new trends in information retrieval over big data and a detailed study of different approaches existed in literature.

BOOK ORGANISATION

The book content is organized as follow:

The first chapter discusses the objects connected and the position of artificial intelligence in industry 4.0 because the IoT is a novel approach, where these smart devices can communicate with each other by using key technologies of artificial intelligence (AI) in order to make timely autonomous decisions. This emerging technical advancement and realization of horizontal and vertical integration is caused by the fourth stage of Industrialization (Industry 4.0). The objective of this chapter is to give details of the information on the key AI Technologies and Industry 4.0. Besides, it is expected to shed light on new work to be done by providing explanations about the new areas that will emerge with this new technology.

In The second chapter, the authors try to test the use of data mining in ecology; firstly they discuss the exploration of ecological data by defining at first data mining, its advantages and its different types. Then they have detailed the field of bio-inspiration and meta-heuristics. And finally, we give case studies from where they applied these two areas to explore ecological data.

The content of the Third chapter present the context of people in social networks, why they start by defining the context of a person which will enable them subsequently to introduce the modeling of development processes and analytical techniques feelings in the micro blog such as twitter.

The principal objective of the fourth chapter was to allocate researchers and phD student in the various types of plagiarism and the different techniques of automatic plagiarism detection and related work that addresses the topic by giving the process of some technique like genetic algorithm, naïve Bayes and k means in external detection of textual plagiarism detection.

The fifth chapter proposed by Salvia Praga which has proposed to extend the classical methods of ontology construction by taking into account the text from the point of view of its structure and its content to build a first nucleus and enriching the ontology obtained by exploiting external resources (general texts and controlled vocabularies of the same domain). Finally, describes how these different resources are analyzed and exploited using linked data properties.

Turning now to a very interesting chapter number sixth where the authors aim to study and implement new techniques for the protection of privacy in the Big Data context.

In the seventh chapter the primary objective is to understand and survey various information mining strategies to efficiently determine occurrence of CVDs and an also propose a bigdata architecture for the same we are making use of Apache Spark for the implementation.

The goal of the eighth chapter proposed by Damian Alberto was to carry-out a study concerning the different supervised and unsupervised learning algorithms that exist in the literature such as k means, KNN, ascending and descending hierarchical classification, etc. By studying some application problems related to the task of the classification in general.

In the last few years, the challenge in the IR was the evaluation of an SRI consists in measuring its performance with respect to the user's needs, for this purpose the evaluation methods widely adopted in IR are based on a model that provides a basis for comparative evaluation of the efficiency of different systems through common resources. The purpose of the ninth chapter was to propose a new evaluation measure for the evaluation of IRT approach in the big data.

In today's world of globalization and technology without borders, the emergence of the internet and the rapid development of telecommunications have made the world a global village. Recently, the email service has become immensely used, and the main means of communication because it is cheap, reliable, fast and easy to access. In addition, it allows users with a mailbox (BAL) and email address to exchange messages (images, files, and text documents) from anywhere in the world via the Internet. Unfortunately, this technology has become undeniably the original source of malicious activity in particular the problem of unwanted emails (SPAM), which has increased dramatically over the past decade. According to the latest report from Radicati Group published in 2012, which provides quantitative and qualitative research with details of the e-mail, security, and social networks. It has been shown that 70-80% of email traffic consists of spam. The goal of the tenth chapter is to give a state of the art on spam filtering and spam techniques.

As we know Wireless Sensor Network (WSN) is a special ad hoc network. It consists of large number of sensors communicating with wireless links to monitor the real-world environment. They have limited energy, computational power, memory and transmission range. They are widely used in different fields like military operations, environmental monitoring, and healthcare applications. However, the openness and hostility of the deployment space and the resources limitation, make these networks vulnerable to several types of attacks and intrusions. So, the WSN security becomes a real challenge. Principally, the attacks in the network aim at damaging the smooth running of the legitimate nodes and cause a dysfunction of the network. Sybil attack is one of the perilous attacks which affects the WSN networks and poses threats to many security goals. Indeed, in this attack, a malicious node uses multiple identities simultaneously or non-concurrently to disrupt the operation of the network. In conducting such an attack, the attacker's goal is to gain more resources if they are allocated per node, falsifying the neighborhood information, or controlling the network in whole or in part. In the eleventh chapter, Mekelleche Fatiha aims to detect the Sybil attacks and ignore it from the network. For that, in the first time, the security problem in WSNs is discussed where the main attacks are systematically introduced. However, in the second time, Sybil attack are detailed and the most relevant works proposed to detect it and avoid it are mentioned.

Lavika Goel in his twelfth chapter aims to apply a novel hybridized evolutionary algorithm to the application of face recognition. Biogeography-Based Optimization (BBO) has some element of randomness to it that apart from improving the feasibility of a solution could reduce it as well. In order to overcome this drawback, this work proposes a hybridization of BBO with Gravitational Search Algorithm (GSA) another nature inspired algorithm by incorporating certain knowledge into BBO instead of the randomness. The proposed BBO-GSA algorithm overcomes the problem of infeasible solution generation and late convergence of the BBO algorithm by eliminating the randomness associated with it. The migration procedure of BBO that migrates SIVs between solutions is done between solutions only if the migration would lead to the betterment of a solution. BBO-GSA algorithm is applied to Face Recognition with the LFW (Labelled Faces in the Wild) and ORL datasets in order to test its efficiency. Experimental results show that the proposed BBO-GSA algorithm outperforms or is in par with some of the nature inspired techniques that have been applied to face recognition so far by achieving a recognition rate of 80% with the LFW dataset and 99.75% with the ORL dataset.

Acknowledgment

I have taken effort in this project. However it would not have been possible without the support of many individuals. I would like to extend my sincere thanks to all of them.

First and foremost, I would like to thank the reviewers for their help comments and suggestions as well as the teachers of the university Dr. Molay Tahar Saida Algeria, and my colleagues of the laboratory GeCoDe who helped me in order to finalize this project.

I would like to express my gratitude to the global manager team of IGI global for their suggestions and helps in order to make our work much less painful than it could be.

Thank you finally to the authors who will recognize themselves here, for their participation so precious and especially for their availability which allowed me to realize in good conditions this project.

Hadj Ahmed Bouarara
Dr. Tahar Moulay University of Saida, Algeria
June 2018

Chapter 1

A Comprehensive Study on Internet of Things Based on Key Artificial Intelligence Technologies and Industry 4.0

Banu Çalış Uslu
Marmara University, Turkey

Seniye Ümit Fırat
Marmara University, Turkey

ABSTRACT

Under uncertainty, understanding and controlling complex environments is only possible with an ability to use distributed computing by the way of information exchange between devices to be able to understand the response of the system to a particular problem. From transformation of raw data in a huge distribution of network into the meaningful information, to use the understood knowledge to make rapid decisions needs to have a network composed of smart devices. Internet of things (IoT) is a novel approach, where these smart devices can communicate with each other by using key technologies of artificial intelligence (AI) in order to make timely autonomous decisions. This emerging technical advancement and realization of horizontal and vertical integration caused the fourth stage of industrialization (Industry 4.0). The objective of this chapter is to give detailed information on both IoT based on key AI technologies and Industry 4.0. It is expected to shed light on new work to be done by providing explanations about the new areas that will emerge with this new technology.

DOI: 10.4018/978-1-5225-7338-8.ch001

INTRODUCTION

With the rapid advancement of technology and science, IT technology has paved new ways of research and discoveries on computational intelligence regarding large data set come from things or objects in a distributed environment. These varieties of things or objects is a network of interconnected, integrated and organized objects (Liu et al. 2017) which allows to communication between things to human, human to human, and things to things in order to analyze large amount of data to produce needed information generated by IoT to reach a certain goal (Madakam et al. 2015). In other words, instead of traditional centralized applications, IoT utilize advanced information analytics via smart devices (things or objects) to be able to integrate various components of network connected as a collaborative way to improve productivity, service ability and flexibility of companies. Based upon the analyzed literature, Figure 1 is generated to demonstrate main architecture of IoT covering basically three different levels.

The first level of IoT determined as level of Big Data that is an ability to turn data into meaningful value (**Value**). In this level, decision makers deal with vast amounts of data (**Volume**) with huge diversity (**Variety**) to control messiness or trustworthiness of data (**Veracity**) that need to analyze while it is being generated (**Velocity**). In the second level of IoT architecture is defined as AI level where each node represents an integrated things or objects which can sensing, processing, reacting and control the environment to understand current situation of the system and based on the learned knowledge providing necessary information to utilize future decisions. In the Figure 1, data exchange between Big Data level and AI level is illustrated by bi-directional arrow.

The state of environment may change at any time so each thing or object needs to have an ability to adapt to changes and learn from the experience. In this dynamic environment, intelligent and autonomous system is crucial technology in order to obtain integration is managed, coordination is provided and distributed computing is enabled. To utilize and understand intelligent system, need to focus on AI technology that encompasses wide spectrum of research field like *machine learning, deep learning, natural language processing, machine reasoning, visual processing, robotics* and *neural networks*. AI application range seems like unlimited. It is possible to see AI –based applications from assistance system for healthcare to smart customer service systems. In section 2 this components, applications, and issues of AI explained in detail. In third level of IoT, each node is linked into a network that composed of set of things or objects working together to make real-time, accurate and coherent decision when a specific input arrive the system.

Rising applications of the IoT caused a sweeping change that will fundamentally reconfigure industry and the Fourth Industrial Revolution is emerged. In many case, these two word are accepted as interchangeable. Mainly this two approaches focus on the ways to constant high quality by making system faster and secure at the same time but industry 4.0 is a primarily government and academic-based movement that aims to make process and products intelligent (Brettel et al., 2014). Although IoT takes place in the business world, it is one of the most important effect that trigger the fourth industrial revolution. When the previous industrial revolutions is examined; after usage of steam and steam engines, world was confronted with first industrial revolution in 18th century. Electrification was the main cause to second industrial revolution in 19th century and usage of computers and robots led to third industrial revolution in 20th century.

Today, Connecting Cyber-Physical systems (CPS) to physical and digital systems is the main idea of fourth industrial revolution (Fırat, 2016). IoT provides connection

Figure 1. Main Architecture of the Internet of Things

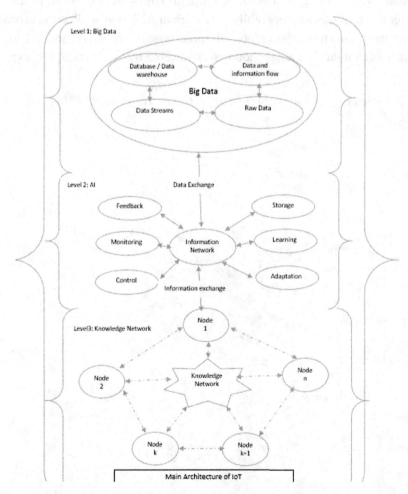

and information transfer between physical entity and its cyber twins so that control and monitoring the outcome of physical entity is possible. Other technologies related to Industry 4.0 is illustrated in Figure 2. These technologies and relations between the IoT is explained in detail in section 2.

AI-based applications employ artificial intelligence techniques into things in order to control system complexity through autonomy. In order to build an autonomous system there is strong need an infrastructure that consists of sensors and actuators that interact autonomously to handle created and replicated data that grown exponentially. Autonomy gives decision makers an ability to cope with vast amounts of data with huge diversity to analyze while it is being generated. Extremely large data sets that need to be analysed computationally refers to the concept of Big Data. AI layer that is used to construct the necessary infrastructure for the coordination, cooperation and integration required to produce meaningful information from data obtained from things or objects in a distributed environment is defined as information network where data is monitored, controlled and stored. Knowledge network is stated as third layer that provides interoperability of different AI-based application in order to create a meaningful knowledge. When this three-layer structure is examined, IoT can be defined as an industrial adaptation that is powered by automation. It is expected

Figure 2. Technologies related to Industry 4.0 (Guerreiro et al, 2018)

that AI-based IoT applications with automation features will contribute significantly to solving problems such as minimum cost, minimum energy consumption, time saving, less resource and less memory usage. The objectives of the IoT almost coincide with the objectives of Industry 4.0. Therefore, this study also referred to Industry 4.0 and its components.

Main objective of this chapter is to deeply analyze IoT technology and its components to find out main challenges and advantages of this novel technology, Also, is to provide detailed literature review of applications of IoT technology to emphasis importance of IoT for Industry 4.0. Besides, it is expected to shed light on new work to be done by providing explanations about the new areas that will emerge with this new technology. The rest of this chapter is organized as follows. In Section 2, the main characteristics of IoT are further discussed in detail. Industry 4.0 and big data are briefly explained. In Section 3, AI techniques are discussed and AI applications of IoT are pointed out. Beneficial outcomes for IoT applications are stated from the business point of view. Then, Main challenges of IoT designs are listed in Section 4. Finally, the conclusions and future work are given in Section 5.

IOT AND MAIN CHARACTERISTICS

Basically, IoT composed of two words that are "Internet" and "Things". The first word "Internet" represents the network structure of the technology, while the second word represents "objects" that can be integrated into one another in a distributed environment (Atzori et al. 2010). In the tremendous network including public and private business systems and personal computers that are connected in order to exchange data, IoT can be define as the new information technology that enables the interconnection (physical and virtual) between things or humans based on connected and interoperable systems (Huxtable & Schaefer, 2016). Concept of IoT is emerged in a presentation by Kevin Ashton (1999) *"The Internet of Things has the potential to change the world, just as the Internet did. Maybe even more so"*, however officially it took place in the literature by the report published by International Telecommunication Union (ITU, 2005). Later on, based on this phenomenon, companies started becoming more intelligent in order to increase their efficiency by applying features of IoT technologies in their business processes (Santora et al. 2017).

IoT consists of sensors and actuators that interact autonomously to handle created and replicated data that grown exponentially. By 2025, expected interaction for an average person in the world with a connected device is 18 seconds, it means that nearly 4.800 times per day (Reinsel et al., 2017). Generated data from many applications and services are expected to reach 50 billion devices in next year (Sharma et al. 2018).

In this environment, autonomous data collection, processing, contextual inference, collaborating with other IoT objects and decision making should be supported by any IoT infrastructure (Sarkar et al., 2015). This infrastructure should have characteristics including "self-configuration, self-optimization, self-protection, and self-healing" (Kephart & Chess, 2003; Kortuem et al. 2010) that satisfy an ability to collaborate and interact in order to create new functionality that individual devices cannot provide (Ornato et al. 2017). These characteristics defines the intelligent devices that employ artificial intelligence techniques into things and communication networks (Arsénio et al., 2014) in order to create autonomous systems that enables to control system complexity through the achievement of self-governance (autonomy) and self-management (autonomicity) (Sterritt & Hinchey, 2005). For this systems, design of effective interaction between both between humans and things and between things is only possible with the better if "intelligent" interfaces and infrastructure (Atzori et al, 2017) in order to get real-time data processing.

To satisfy this integration and connection between smart devices there is a need of an architecture that is not as simple as to explain as the word structure and equipped with powerful features on the backplane. There are many approaches in the literature but there isn't any standard form in order to define IoT architecture. In this study, IoT is identified based on the three main layer that are; Big Data Layer, AI Layer, and Knowledge Network. It is not technically possible to distinguish these three interlocking layers from one another and examine them separately, but it is possible to explain how the characteristics of the IOT are reflected in what layer. In order to do this analysis, based on the literature reviewed, the five main characteristics of IoT are illustrated in Figure 2. ((Tien, 2017; Yadav et al, 2017; Miorandi et al 2012; Patel et al.2009; Banerjee et al.2014; Le-Phuoc et al., 2010);

These five characteristics are discussed in following sections based on the related layers

1. **Sensing:** Sensing is one of the key characteristic of IoT especially work on Big data that represents vast amounts of data (Volume) with huge diversity (Variety) and uncertainty or imprecision (Veracity) that need to analyse while it is being generated (Velocity) in order to produce meaningful decision (Value). Datasets became so large and complex, it can be obtained from different sources such as Radio Frequency Identification (RFID) sensors, web applications, unstructured data (pictures, documents etc.), radar, navigation sequences, smart watches, Wi-Fi, and telephonic data services etc. (Tien, 2017; Huda et al, 2018; Perry, 2015; Gubbi et al, 2013). In other word, sensing gives an ability to understand around the physical world (Yadav et al, 2017) by using some sensors when an event occurred. This event can be discrete (producing data after an event), continuous (e.g. temperature sensor) (Patel et al.2009), or can be produced

Figure 3. Key Characteristics of IoT

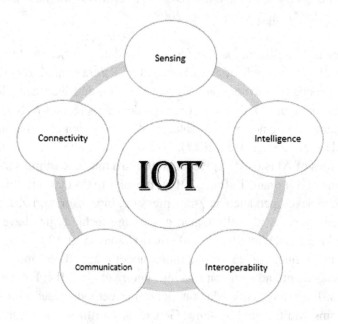

by interaction between smart devices (Miorandi et al, 2012). In addition to handle big data, sensing is also important to integrate sensor data together in order to create new knowledge (Banerjee et al., 2014) in the system. Analysis of big data, in the dynamic and complex environment caused the insufficiency of traditional data processing approaches and increase in the use of artificial intelligence techniques.

AI techniques have been used for a long time in the process of creating applications in the analysis of non-structural data, classifying or structuring these data, and transforming data into meaningful information. AI techniques gives an ability to users in order to monitoring the systems by smart devices and controlling through Machine to Machine (M2M) communications where data are generated and finally collected (Sadowski et al., 2016). In other words, AI employ intelligent analysis to create value by providing capturing structured interpretations and it is necessary in order to obtain patterns and make timely automated decisions (Gubbi et al., 2013).

Some of the new solution approaches that are generated to handle big data are listed below;

1.   Cloud computing (Cheng et al.,2014)
2.   Distributed File Systems (Segatori et al., 2018)

3.   Data Mining (C4.5, C5.0,ANNs, DLANNS (Alam et al., 2016)
4.   MapReduce (Dean & Ghemawat, 2008).

2.   **Intelligence:** Intelligence is transformation of data into meaningful information in order to get the application of knowledge (Perera et al., 2014) that enables accurate recognition functions, correct thinking and judgment (Ritter et al, 2011) to make or enable context related decisions (Sintef & Norvay, 2014). This characteristic not only to make right decision but also making adaptive and real time decision (Tien, 2017). Sensing, processing, learning and reacting capabilities of AI is used to give an ability to a machine mimics the cognitive functions of a human (Lafrate, 2018). In order to do that, intelligent sensors have been developed such as γ-ray, pressure, biosensor, and X-ray (Li et al., 2015) and various algorithms and computing technologies have been used that make a device intelligent and smart (Yadav et al. (2017) by collecting, providing an intelligence for planning, modelling, and reasoning the context for management and decision making (Perera et al., 2014; Patel et al, 2016). Such as; Expert systems, Machine learning methods based on evolutionary algorithms, Multi Agent Systems, Genetic Algorithms, and Neural networks.
3.   **Connection:** Network accessibility and compatibility are provided through the connectivity. In other words, IoT enable things to be connected that allows the interoperability of IoT devices at any time and in anyplace by using a path/ network. (Patel et al, 2016). These characteristics can be accept as foremost requirement of the IoT because the users of the IoT network are devices (De Poorter et al., 2011). Figure 4 summarizes the evolution of connectivity from connecting two computers to interconnected devices. Technologies that are used to satisfy IoT connectivity that make "Internet of Things" applications possible are; Ethernet, WI-FI, Bluetooth, ZigBee, GSM, and GPRS, wireless sensor networks, sensor networks etc. Perera et al. (2014) defined evaluation connectivity from network without the internet to interconnected objects that defines the IoT (see Figure 4)

In order to satisfy necessary connection between IoT devices, Khan et al. (2017) defined the connectivity requirements of the IoTs in two groups based on the radio range;

1.   Low Power Wide Area Network (LPWAN) connectivity that includes a large number of distributed devices.
2.   Low Power Short Range Network (LPSRN) connectivity that includes devices in short range. ıt requires low power and suitable for small networks such as home automation.

Figure 4. Evolution of Connectivity (Perera et al., 2014)

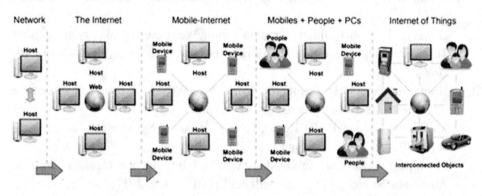

Today, huge amount of devices with different capabilities are connected in order to support the interaction between the constrained devices. Due to resource constraints such as insufficient wireless bandwidth, power supply or computing capabilities, IoT devices need to standardization of connection in order to have an ability to communicate. Bello and Zeadally (2016) identified the constrained networks as follows;

1. Short-range wireless network
2. Low-power loss network
3. Delay-tolerant network
4. WSNs:
5. Cellular networks
6. WiMAX

4. **Communication:** IoT devices can communicate among themselves not only within the same network (intra-domain) but also across heterogeneous networks (inter-domain) (Bello & Zeadally 2013). Communication means that exchange of information between devices in the network that must support devices using different protocol (De Poorter et al., 2011). Common technologies to enable communication between devices are RFID and WiFi. Also Web of Thing (WoT) technology is developed to solve communication problem between IoT devices by using same languages but security and scalability problem is remained unchained (Hakiri et al, 2015).

IoT connectivity can be classified into four categories based on interactions that are;

1. Human to Human; Cellular Communication, Web based speaker systems, Blue Tooth Communication etc. (Tien, 2017; Zelenkauskaite et al., 2012, Crockford, 2006)
2. Human to Machine; E-Commerce, World Wide Web, Automatic Teller Machine etc. (Tien, 2017; Shelby et al., 2014; Guinard et al., 2010)
3. Machine to Human; RFID, Radio, Television, Alarm Systems etc. Kushalnagar et al., 2007; Tien 2017; Ishaq et al., 2013)
4. Machine to Machine; Embedded Artificial Intelligence Devices, Drones, Automatic Vehicles etc. (Paganelli et al., 2013; Tien, 2017;

Other solutions for the communication of IoT devices are;

1. LinkSmart (Kostelnik et al., 2011)
2. Open IoT (Kim & Lee, 2014)
3. Data Distribution Service (DDS) (OMG, 2015)

Bandyopadhyay& Sen, (2011) defines some of communication issues and parameters need to be taken into consideration as follows;

1. Deployment
2. Mobility
3. Cost, size, resources, and energy
4. Heterogeneity
5. Communication modality
6. Infrastructure
7. Network topology
8. Coverage
9. Connectivity.
10. Network size
11. Lifetime
12. QoS requirements

4. **Interoperability:** After the connectivity and communication is utilized, another characteristic must be taken into consideration that is the interoperability of IoT devices in order to make possible cooperation of these devices due to design and communication capabilities of each device. Interoperability basically exchanging information in a way that other IoT devices can use it for improving

system performance (Cousin et al., 2015) Vandaele et al. (2015) proposed four main characteristic of interoperability platform;

a. Monitor
b. Configure
c. Automatically install
d. Diagnose

CPS is one of the important technology that enables the interoperability by satisfying real-time information exchange (Yue et al, 2015). Cousin et al. (2015) provide most common challenges for interoperability as; Integration of multiple data sources, unique ontological point of reference, and P2P (peer to peer) communication. Some existing integration platforms are given in Table 1.

AI on IoT and Technological Advancement on Way of Working

With technological advancement, several hugely and positively disruptive changes are taking place and way of working is getting simpler and easier by using automated systems in all aspects of the life. Smart devices equipped with powerful sensing, connectivity, communication, and intelligent data processing capabilities resulted in enhance capabilities of real-time information extraction, data analysis, decision making, and data transmission.

Artificial intelligence plays a key role on these technological advancements by giving an ability of cognition to the IoT devices that means increasing intelligence at all stages from the decision of which data to be collected to the analysis to be presented to the user. Three important characteristic features of artificial intelligence are of great importance in increasing the intelligence of the objects, these are perception, cognition and reaction capabilities

The use of Artificial Intelligence Technology in the design and application areas of manufacturing systems is gaining more popularity day by day. The intelligence mentioned here is the decision-making mechanism that will find the best solution to a problem. For a system that made up of various functions such as design, planning, monitoring, testing and storage it is necessary to convert these functions into intelligent autonomous systems in order to shortening the time, reducing costs, increasing the competences, and strengthening the control mechanisms. In other words, Artificial Intelligence is intelligent software that enable machine learning and decision-making skills to be gained for solutions to problems.

Key Characteristics of AI are (Rzevski,1993);

Table 1. Some Existing integrating platforms (Vandaele et al., 2015)

Platform	Platform installation	Add new technology	Detect new device	Install app
openHAB	Command Line	Config Files + OSGi bundles	Config Files	Config Files
Open Remote	Command Line	Command Line	Manual in GUI	Manual config in GUI
Zodianet	App Store, Sync with web server	Automated	Config via GUI, Partially automated	App Store
HomeOS	Build from source	Manual config in GUI	Our device not detected	App Store
DYAMAND	Start Scrip	Automatic, At Runtime	Automatic Detection	Developer API

1. ***Adaptability:*** To have the ability to behave in a way that is appropriate and desired in a predefined manner when unforeseen changes in the external environment occur.
2. ***Self-Maintenance:*** To have an ability to diagnose its own situation in the face of unexpected changes (errors) and an ability to perform the necessary repairs at operational speed.
3. ***Communication:*** To have an ability to connection with other systems it is connected to, and to have an ability to receive or transmit necessary information, control, reporting and calculations.
4. ***Autonomy:*** To have a capability (at a certain level) that operates independently of other systems.
5. ***Learning:*** To have ability to self-develop based on past experience, other factors, or the in human management when it conducts a particular task.
6. ***Anticipation:*** To have an ability to predict changes that may affect the operation it performs.
7. ***Goal-Seeking:*** To have an ability to formulate and modify sub-objectives to achieve a defined strategic goal.

When the above-described properties are examined, these properties are peculiar to IoT devices. In other words, IoT devices can be defined as artificial intelligence assisted devices. The basic application techniques involved in the development of artificial intelligence technology can be summarized as follows;

1. ***Knowledge Based Systems:*** Knowledge-based systems that are defined as If-Then rules in a computer in advance to solve a particular problem. A

knowledge-based system may perform close to the logic of a highly informed decision-maker

2. ***Expert Systems:*** This area of artificial intelligence is focused on creating high-performance programs in a matter of expertise. (Öz and Baykoç, 2004)

3. ***Neural Networks:*** This method is one of the most widely used technique both for optimizations and classifications. Historical data is used for training in a network that automatically identifies the most appropriate configuration of a hidden network (Mehrotra et al. 1997).

4. ***Genetic Algorithms:*** This method uses population genetics to solve complex global optimization problems

Today, AI based IoT advancement caused to positively disruptive changes in many areas, some of them are listed in Table 2.

Table 2. Some AI-based IoT studies

Research Area	Studies
Home monitoring systems for elderly care in their homes and smart hospital applications	Gluhak et al, 2011; Luo et al., 2010; Alemdar & Ersoy, 2010; Pang et al., 2013; Dhariwal & Mehta, 2017; Park et al., (2017)
Describing open collaborative work space using pool of "GenMobile" employees	Venkatesh, 2017; Nothhaft, 2018
Open learning systems that enables active learning for millions of users worldwide	O'Sullivan et al, 2018; Gülbahar, 2017 ; Anshari et al., (2017); Ma, 2017
Using IoT in transportation and rela-time logistics to improve demand response	Conner, 2018; Su et al., 2017; Sreelatha et al., 2018; Pawar & Bhosale, 2017; Atzori et al, 2010; Yue et al, 2010
Supply Chain Controls and Managements	Leng et al., (2018); Accorsi et al., 2017; Majeed & Rupasinghe, 2017; Witkowski, 2017; Pang et al., 2015; Aung & Chang, 2014; Verdouw et al., 2016
Intelligent Vehicle Design and Vehicle Monitoring Systems	Rao, 2017; Wang & Luo, 2017 ; Qin et al, 2013 ; Zhang et al., 2011; Desai & Phadke, 2017; Goyal et al., 2018; Balid et al., 2017; Kuppusamy et al., 2018
Mine safety and energy industries in order to make early warning by using intelligent communications technology	Han, 2017; Qiuping et al, 2011; Jo et al., 2017; Dong et al., 2017; Mohamed et al., 2015; Ma et al., 2016
High-Risk Environment and Risk Management	Montoya et al., 2018 ; Tupa et al., 2017; Ji & Anwen, 2010; Zhang & Yu 2013; Hiromoto et al., 2017; Aung & Chang, 2014
Intelligent manufacturing / Smart Manufacturing applications	Guo & Zhang, 2009; Tao et al; 2014; Chen, 2017; Jeschke et al., 2017; Zheng et al., 2018; Ye et al., 2018
Smart Cities	Rathore et al., 2016; Mohanty et al., 2016; Ejaz et al., 2017; Hui et al., 2017; Montori et al., 2018

As can be seen in Table 2 IoT-based applications that can be define as the connected network between things in order to make enable real-time decision making, are rather widespread in many industries. To be able to satisfy cooperation and coordination among different objects intelligent tools are compulsory in order to get reliable and efficient solutions.

MAIN CHALLENGES OF IOT

Based on the literature examined in this study, several issues and parameters should be taken into consideration for the implementation of the IoT architecture; some of them are listed below

1. *Internet:* Internet is one of the key parameter for the communication and interoperability
2. *Standardization:* Different IoT devices with different communication ability caused to lack of interoperability so there is a need a standardize architecture that includes mobility, availability, manageability and scalability for easy and natural information exchange.
3. *Scalability:* Every day more and more IoT devices will be connected to the network so data processing and data transfer will become more complex.
4. *Security and Privacy:* Controlling of information security and data privacy protection also another issue for IoT devices.
5. *Energy Saving:* IoT devices needs to be connected to a power supply so sufficient energy source is needed to sustainable device smartness.
6. *Heterogeneous Network:* It includes managing heterogeneous applications and devices in a network and it is accepted as a major challenge for many authors.

IoT has become one of the most popular technological advancement of business today. Every production or service systems require intelligent solutions in order to get the most economically feasible solutions for their systems. For analysing, interpreting and forming solutions to the information generated by multiple sources in a distributed environment, it is necessary to take into consideration the 6 basic challenges described above.

DISCUSSIONS AND CONCLUSION

This chapter provides a comprehensive overview on the introduction of IoT and its' key characteristics. In addition to given introduction, IoT applications are listed based on each characteristics in section 2. Role of AI on IoT and applications generated based on AI is stated in section 3 and main challenges in order to create an IoT infrastructure are listed in section 4. Main motivation of this study is to provide a good basis for researchers and practitioners who want to learn about the components of the IoT and the general architecture of communication and collaboration protocols. In addition, current IoT applications and fundamental issues are discussed in the interaction of large data analytics, artificial intelligence technology and network infrastructure.

Based on this study, following conclusions can be made;

1. Huge amount of devices with different capabilities are connected in order to support the interaction between the constrained devices so there is a strong need for a standard architecture in order to satisfy connection between these IoT devices.
2. In order to monitoring the systems by smart devices and controlling through Machine to Machine (M2M) communications there is a strong need for a standard architecture in order to satisfy communication between these IoT devices.
3. Various algorithms and computing technologies have been used in order to increase level of intelligence however especially concept of deep learning one of the key important issues for IoT devices.
4. Cyber Physical Systems is one of the most important technology that enables the interoperability by satisfying real-time information exchange so there is a strong need for a standard architecture in order to satisfy P2P (peer to peer) communication.

REFERENCES

Accorsi, R., Bortolini, M., Baruffaldi, G., Pilati, F., & Ferrari, E. (2017). Internet-of-things paradigm in food supply chains control and management. *Procedia Manufacturing*, *11*, 889–895. doi:10.1016/j.promfg.2017.07.192

Alam, F., Mehmood, R., Katib, I., & Albeshri, A. (2016). Analysis of eight data mining algorithms for smarter Internet of Things (IoT). *Procedia Computer Science*, *98*, 437–442. doi:10.1016/j.procs.2016.09.068

Alam, S., Chowdhury, M. M., & Noll, J. (2010, November). Senaas: An event-driven sensor virtualization approach for internet of things cloud. In *Networked Embedded Systems for Enterprise Applications (NESEA), 2010 IEEE International Conference on* (pp. 1-6). IEEE.

Alemdar, H., & Ersoy, C. (2010). Wireless sensor networks for healthcare: A survey. *Computer Networks*, *54*(15), 2688–2710. doi:10.1016/j.comnet.2010.05.003

Anshari, M., Almunawar, M. N., Shahrill, M., Wicaksono, D. K., & Huda, M. (2017). Smartphones usage in the classrooms: Learning aid or interference? *Education and Information Technologies*, *22*(6), 3063–3079. doi:10.100710639-017-9572-7

Arora, S., Sharma, S., Dua, R., & Sharma, A. (2017). Internet of things, artificial intelligence, automation. *Technology*.

Arsénio, A., Serra, H., Francisco, R., Nabais, F., Andrade, J., & Serrano, E. (2014). Internet of intelligent things: Bringing artificial intelligence into things and communication networks. In *Inter-cooperative Collective Intelligence: Techniques and Applications* (pp. 1–37). Berlin: Springer. doi:10.1007/978-3-642-35016-0_1

Ashton, K. (2009). That 'internet of things' thing. *RFiD Journal*, *22*(7), 97–114.

Atzori, L., Iera, A., & Morabito, G. (2010). The internet of things: A survey. *Computer Networks*, *54*(15), 2787–2805. doi:10.1016/j.comnet.2010.05.010

Atzori, L., Iera, A., & Morabito, G. (2017). Understanding the Internet of Things: Definition, potentials, and societal role of a fast evolving paradigm. *Ad Hoc Networks*, *56*, 122–140. doi:10.1016/j.adhoc.2016.12.004

Aung, M. M., & Chang, Y. S. (2014). Traceability in a food supply chain: Safety and quality perspectives. *Food Control*, *39*, 172–184. doi:10.1016/j.foodcont.2013.11.007

Balid, W., Tafish, H., & Refai, H. H. (2017). Intelligent Vehicle Counting and Classification Sensor for Real-Time Traffic Surveillance. *IEEE Transactions on Intelligent Transportation Systems*.

Bandyopadhyay, D., & Sen, J. (2011). Internet of things: Applications and challenges in technology and standardization. *Wireless Personal Communications*, *58*(1), 49–69. doi:10.100711277-011-0288-5

Banerjee, P., Friedrich, R., Bash, C., Goldsack, P., Huberman, B., Manley, J., ... Veitch, A. (2011). Everything as a service: Powering the new information economy. *Computer*, *44*(3), 36–43. doi:10.1109/MC.2011.67

Bello, O., & Zeadally, S. (2013). Communication issues in the Internet of Things (IoT). In *Next-Generation Wireless Technologies* (pp. 189–219). London: Springer. doi:10.1007/978-1-4471-5164-7_10

Bello, O., & Zeadally, S. (2016). Intelligent device-to-device communication in the internet of things. *IEEE Systems Journal, 10*(3), 1172–1182. doi:10.1109/JSYST.2014.2298837

Brettel, M., Friederichsen, N., Keller, M., & Rosenberg, M. (2014). How virtualization, decentralization and network building change the manufacturing landscape: An Industry 4.0 Perspective. *International Journal of Mechanical, Industrial Science and Engineering, 8*(1), 37–44.

Chen, Y. (2017). Integrated and Intelligent Manufacturing: Perspectives and Enablers. *Engineering, 3*(5), 588–595. doi:10.1016/J.ENG.2017.04.009

Cheng, X. Q., Jin, X. L., Wang, Y. Z., Guo, J., Zhang, T., & Li, G. (2014). Survey on big data system and analytic technology. *Journal of Software, 25*(9), 1889–1908.

Conner, M. K. (2018). *Dynamic Logistics Enabled by IoT*. Academic Press.

Cousin, P., Serrano, M., & Soldatos, J. (2015). Internet of things research on semantic interoperability to address manufacturing challenges. *Enterprise Interoperability: Interoperability for Agility, Resilience and Plasticity of Collaborations (I-ESA 14 Proceedings), 280*.

Crockford, D. (2006). *The application/json media type for javascript object notation (json)*. Academic Press.

Da Xu, L., He, W., & Li, S. (2014). Internet of things in industries: A survey. *IEEE Transactions on Industrial Informatics, 10*(4), 2233–2243. doi:10.1109/TII.2014.2300753

De Poorter, E., Moerman, I., & Demeester, P. (2011). Enabling direct connectivity between heterogeneous objects in the internet of things through a network-service-oriented architecture. *EURASIP Journal on Wireless Communications and Networking, 2011*(1), 61. doi:10.1186/1687-1499-2011-61

Dean, J., & Ghemawat, S. (2008). MapReduce: Simplified data processing on large clusters. *Communications of the ACM, 51*(1), 107–113. doi:10.1145/1327452.1327492

Desai, M., & Phadke, A. (2017, February). Internet of Things based vehicle monitoring system. In *Wireless and Optical Communications Networks (WOCN), 2017 Fourteenth International Conference on* (pp. 1-3). IEEE. 10.1109/WOCN.2017.8065840

Dhariwal, K., & Mehta, A. (2017). Architecture and plan of smart hospital based on Internet of Things (IOT). *Int. Res. J. Eng. Technol, 4*(4), 1976–1980.

Dong, L., Mingyue, R., & Guoying, M. (2017). Application of Internet of Things Technology on Predictive Maintenance System of Coal Equipment. *Procedia Engineering, 174*, 885–889. doi:10.1016/j.proeng.2017.01.237

Ejaz, W., Naeem, M., Shahid, A., Anpalagan, A., & Jo, M. (2017). Efficient energy management for the internet of things in smart cities. *IEEE Communications Magazine, 55*(1), 84–91. doi:10.1109/MCOM.2017.1600218CM

Etzion, O. (2015, June). When artificial intelligence meets the internet of things. In *Proceedings of the 9th ACM International Conference on Distributed Event-Based Systems* (pp. 246-246). ACM. 10.1145/2675743.2774216

Fırat, S. Ü. (2016). *Sanayi 4.0 dönüşümü nedir? belirlemeler ve beklentiler*. Global Sanayici: Ekonomi ve İş Dünyası Dergisi ÇOSB Yayını.

Fırat, S. Ü., & Fırat, O. Z. (2017). Sanayi 4.0 Devrimi Üzerine Karşılaştırmalı Bir İnceleme: Kavramlar, Küresel Gelişmeler ve Türkiye. *Toprak İşveren Dergisi,* (114), 10-23.

Fırat, S. Ü., & Fırat, O. Z. (2017). Dördüncü sanayi devriminde riskler robotlar ve yapay zekanin yönetişim sorunlari. *Global Sanayici: Ekonomi ve İş Dünyası Dergisi, 8*(81), 66-70.

Frey, C. B., & Osborne, M. A. (2017). The future of employment: How susceptible are jobs to computerisation? *Technological Forecasting and Social Change, 114*, 254–280. doi:10.1016/j.techfore.2016.08.019

Gluhak, A., Krco, S., Nati, M., Pfisterer, D., Mitton, N., & Razafindralambo, T. (2011). A survey on facilities for experimental internet of things research. *IEEE Communications Magazine, 49*(11), 58–67. doi:10.1109/MCOM.2011.6069710

Goyal, R., Kumari, A., Shubham, K., & Kumar, N. (2018). IoT and XBee Based Smart Traffic Management System. *Journal of Communication Engineering & Systems, 8*(1), 8–14.

Gubbi, J., Buyya, R., Marusic, S., & Palaniswami, M. (2013). Internet of Things (IoT): A vision, architectural elements, and future directions. *Future Generation Computer Systems, 29*(7), 1645–1660. doi:10.1016/j.future.2013.01.010

Guerreiro, B. V., Lins, R. G., Sun, J., & Schmitt, R. (2018). Definition of Smart Retrofitting: First steps for a company to deploy aspects of Industry 4.0. In *Advances in Manufacturing* (pp. 161–170). Cham: Springer. doi:10.1007/978-3-319-68619-6_16

Guinard, D., Mueller, M., & Pasquier-Rocha, J. (2010, November). Giving rfid a rest: Building a web-enabled epcis. In Internet of Things (IOT), 2010 (pp. 1-8). IEEE.

Gülbahar, Y. (2017). E-öğrenme. *Pegem Atıf İndeksi*, 1-410.

Guo, Q., & Zhang, M. (2009). A novel approach for multi-agent-based intelligent manufacturing system. *Information Sciences*, *179*(18), 3079–3090. doi:10.1016/j. ins.2009.05.009

Hakiri, A., Berthou, P., Gokhale, A., & Abdellatif, S. (2015). Publish/subscribe-enabled software defined networking for efficient and scalable IoT communications. *IEEE Communications Magazine*, *53*(9), 48–54. doi:10.1109/MCOM.2015.7263372

Han, Z. (2017). Study on safety management information system of coal mine based on internet of things. *Coal Economic Research, 3*, 15.

Hiromoto, R. E., Haney, M., & Vakanski, A. (2017, September). A secure architecture for IoT with supply chain risk management. In *Intelligent Data Acquisition and Advanced Computing Systems: Technology and Applications (IDAACS), 2017 9th IEEE International Conference on* (Vol. 1, pp. 431-435). IEEE. 10.1109/IDAACS.2017.8095118

Huda, M., Maseleno, A., Atmotiyoso, P., Siregar, M., Ahmad, R., Jasmi, K. A., & Muhamad, N. H. N. (2018). Big Data Emerging Technology: Insights into Innovative Environment for Online Learning Resources. *International Journal of Emerging Technologies in Learning*, *13*(01), 23–36. doi:10.3991/ijet.v13i01.6990

Hui, T. K., Sherratt, R. S., & Sánchez, D. D. (2017). Major requirements for building Smart Homes in Smart Cities based on Internet of Things technologies. *Future Generation Computer Systems*, *76*, 358–369. doi:10.1016/j.future.2016.10.026

Huxtable, J., & Schaefer, D. (2016). On Servitization of the Manufacturing Industry in the UK. *Procedia CIRP*, *52*, 46–51. doi:10.1016/j.procir.2016.07.042

Ishaq, I., Carels, D., Teklemariam, G. K., Hoebeke, J., Abeele, F. V. D., Poorter, E. D., ... Demeester, P. (2013). IETF standardization in the field of the internet of things (IoT): A survey. *Journal of Sensor and Actuator Networks*, *2*(2), 235–287. doi:10.3390/jsan2020235

Jeschke, S., Brecher, C., Meisen, T., Özdemir, D., & Eschert, T. (2017). Industrial internet of things and cyber manufacturing systems. In *Industrial Internet of Things* (pp. 3–19). Cham: Springer. doi:10.1007/978-3-319-42559-7_1

Ji, Z., & Anwen, Q. (2010, November). The application of internet of things (IOT) in emergency management system in China. In *Technologies for Homeland Security (HST), 2010 IEEE International Conference on* (pp. 139-142). IEEE.

Jo, B. W., & Khan, R. M. A. (2017). An Event Reporting and Early-Warning Safety System Based on the Internet of Things for Underground Coal Mines: A Case Study. *Applied Sciences*, *7*(9), 925. doi:10.3390/app7090925

Kephart, J. O., & Chess, D. M. (2003). The vision of autonomic computing. *Computer*, *36*(1), 41–50. doi:10.1109/MC.2003.1160055

Khan, M., Wu, X., Xu, X., & Dou, W. (2017, May). Big data challenges and opportunities in the hype of Industry 4.0. In *Communications (ICC), 2017 IEEE International Conference on* (pp. 1-6). IEEE.

Kim, J., & Lee, J. W. (2014, March). OpenIoT: An open service framework for the Internet of Things. In *Internet of Things (WF-IoT), 2014 IEEE World Forum on* (pp. 89-93). IEEE.

Kortuem, G., Kawsar, F., Sundramoorthy, V., & Fitton, D. (2010). Smart objects as building blocks for the internet of things. *IEEE Internet Computing*, *14*(1), 44–51. doi:10.1109/MIC.2009.143

Kostelnik, P., Sarnovsk, M., & Furdik, K. (2011). The semantic middleware for networked embedded systems applied in the internet of things and services domain. *Scalable Computing: Practice and Experience*, *12*(3), 307–316.

Kuppusamy, P., Kamarajapandian, P., Sabari, M. S., & Nithya, J. (2018). Design of Smart Traffic Signal System Using Internet of Things and Genetic Algorithm. In *Advances in Big Data and Cloud Computing* (pp. 395–403). Singapore: Springer. doi:10.1007/978-981-10-7200-0_36

Kushalnagar, N., Montenegro, G., & Schumacher, C. (2007). *IPv6 over low-power wireless personal area networks (6LoWPANs): overview, assumptions, problem statement, and goals* (No. RFC 4919).

Lafrate, F. (2018). *Artificial Intelligence and Big Data: The Birth of a New Intelligence*. John Wiley & Sons. doi:10.1002/9781119426653

Lasi, H., Fettke, P., Kemper, H. G., Feld, T., & Hoffmann, M. (2014). Industry 4.0. *Business & Information Systems Engineering*, *6*(4), 239–242. doi:10.100712599-014-0334-4

Le-Phuoc, D., Parreira, J. X., Hausenblas, M., Han, Y., & Hauswirth, M. (2010, September). Live linked open sensor database. In *Proceedings of the 6th International Conference on Semantic Systems* (p. 46). ACM.

Lee, I., & Lee, K. (2015). The Internet of Things (IoT): Applications, investments, and challenges for enterprises. *Business Horizons, 58*(4), 431–440. doi:10.1016/j. bushor.2015.03.008

Leng, K., Jin, L., Shi, W., & Van Nieuwenhuyse, I. (2018). Research on agricultural products supply chain inspection system based on internet of things. *Cluster Computing*, 1–9.

Li, S., Da Xu, L., & Zhao, S. (2015). The internet of things: A survey. *Information Systems Frontiers, 17*(2), 243–259. doi:10.100710796-014-9492-7

Liu, M., Ma, J., Lin, L., Ge, M., Wang, Q., & Liu, C. (2017). Intelligent assembly system for mechanical products and key technology based on internet of things. *Journal of Intelligent Manufacturing, 28*(2), 271–299. doi:10.100710845-014-0976-6

Luo, H., Ci, S., Wu, D., Stergiou, N., & Siu, K. C. (2010). A remote markerless human gait tracking for e-healthcare based on content-aware wireless multimedia communications. *IEEE Wireless Communications, 17*(1), 44–50. doi:10.1109/MWC.2010.5416349

Ma, X., Pan, Y. J., Chen, F., Ding, X., & Tseng, S. P. (2017, November). A Constructive Problem-Based Course Design for Internet of Things. In *International Conference on Smart Vehicular Technology, Transportation, Communication and Applications* (pp. 397-402). Springer.

Ma, Y. W., Chen, J. L., & Chang, Y. Y. (2016, January). Cloud computing technology for the petroleum application. In *Advanced Communication Technology (ICACT), 2016 18th International Conference on* (pp. 101-104). IEEE.

Madakam, S., Ramaswamy, R., & Tripathi, S. (2015). Internet of Things (IoT): A literature review. *Journal of Computer and Communications, 3*(05), 164–173. doi:10.4236/jcc.2015.35021

Majeed, A. A., & Rupasinghe, T. D. (2017). Internet of things (IoT) embedded future supply chains for industry 4.0: An assessment from an ERP-based fashion apparel and footwear industry. *International Journal of Supply Chain Management, 6*(1), 25–40.

Malewicz, G., Austern, M. H., Bik, A. J., Dehnert, J. C., Horn, I., Leiser, N., & Czajkowski, G. (2010, June). Pregel: a system for large-scale graph processing. In *Proceedings of the 2010 ACM SIGMOD International Conference on Management of data* (pp. 135-146). ACM.

Mehrotra, K., Mohan, C. K., & Ranka, S. (1997). *Elements of Artificial neural networks*. The MIT Press. doi:10.1145/1807167.1807184

Miorandi, D., Sicari, S., De Pellegrini, F., & Chlamtac, I. (2012). Internet of things: Vision, applications and research challenges. *Ad Hoc Networks*, *10*(7), 1497–1516. doi:10.1016/j.adhoc.2012.02.016

Mohamed, A., Hamdi, M. S., & Tahar, S. (2015, August). A machine learning approach for big data in oil and gas pipelines. In *Future Internet of Things and Cloud (FiCloud), 2015 3rd International Conference on* (pp. 585-590). IEEE. 10.1109/FiCloud.2015.54

Mohanty, S. P., Choppali, U., & Kougianos, E. (2016). Everything you wanted to know about smart cities: The internet of things is the backbone. *IEEE Consumer Electronics Magazine*, *5*(3), 60–70. doi:10.1109/MCE.2016.2556879

Montori, F., Bedogni, L., & Bononi, L. (2018). A collaborative internet of things architecture for smart cities and environmental monitoring. *IEEE Internet of Things Journal*, *5*(2), 592–605. doi:10.1109/JIOT.2017.2720855

Montoya, G. N., Junior, J. B. S. S., Novaes, A. G., & Lima, O. F. (2018, February). Internet of Things and the Risk Management Approach in the Pharmaceutical Supply Chain. In *International Conference on Dynamics in Logistics* (pp. 284-288). Springer. 10.1007/978-3-319-74225-0_38

Nothhaft, C. (2018). Understanding China's Consumers. In *Made for China* (pp. 3–20). Cham: Springer. doi:10.1007/978-3-319-61584-4_1

O'Sullivan, C., Wise, N., & Mathieu, P. P. (2018). The Changing Landscape of Geospatial Information Markets. In *Earth Observation Open Science and Innovation* (pp. 3–23). Cham: Springer. doi:10.1007/978-3-319-65633-5_1

OMG. (2015). *Object Management Group*. DDS. Retrieved from http://www.omg.org/spec/DDS/1.4/PDF/

Ornato, M., Cinotti, T. S., Borghetti, A., Azzoni, P., D'Elia, A., Viola, F., & Venanzi, R. (2017). Application system design: Complex systems management and automation. In *IoT Automation* (pp. 317–352). CRC Press. doi:10.1201/9781315367897-10

Öz, E., & Baykoç, Ö.F. (2004). Expert System Approach Supported by Decision Theory on Supplier Selection Problem. *Gazi Univ. Eng. Faculty, 19*(3).

Paganelli, F., Turchi, S., Bianchi, L., Ciofi, L., Pettenati, M. C., Pirri, F., & Giuli, D. (2013). *An information-centric and REST-based approach for EPC Information Services*. Academic Press.

Pang, Z., Chen, Q., Han, W., & Zheng, L. (2015). Value-centric design of the internet-of-things solution for food supply chain: Value creation, sensor portfolio and information fusion. *Information Systems Frontiers*, *17*(2), 289–319. doi:10.100710796-012-9374-9

Pang, Z., Chen, Q., Tian, J., Zheng, L., & Dubrova, E. (2013, January). Ecosystem analysis in the design of open platform-based in-home healthcare terminals towards the internet-of-things. In *Advanced Communication Technology (ICACT), 2013 15th International Conference on* (pp. 529-534). IEEE.

Park, A., Chang, H., & Lee, K. J. (2017). Action research on development and application of Internet of Things services in hospital. *Healthcare Informatics Research*, *23*(1), 25–34. doi:10.4258/hir.2017.23.1.25 PMID:28261528

Patel, K. K., Patel, S. M., & Professor, P. S. A. (2016). Internet of Things-IOT: Definition, characteristics, architecture, enabling technologies, application & future challenges. *International Journal of Engineering Science and Computing*, *6*(5).

Patel, P., Jardosh, S., Chaudhary, S., & Ranjan, P. (2009, September). Context aware middleware architecture for wireless sensor network. In *Services Computing, 2009. SCC'09. IEEE International Conference on* (pp. 532-535). IEEE. 10.1109/SCC.2009.49

Pawar, V., & Bhosale, N. P. (2017). *SMART local bus transport Management System using IoT*. Academic Press.

Perera, C., Zaslavsky, A., Christen, P., & Georgakopoulos, D. (2014). Context aware computing for the internet of things: A survey. *IEEE Communications Surveys and Tutorials*, *16*(1), 414–454. doi:10.1109/SURV.2013.042313.00197

Poniszewska-Maranda, A., & Kaczmarek, D. (2015, September). Selected methods of artificial intelligence for Internet of Things conception. In *Computer Science and Information Systems (FedCSIS), 2015 Federated Conference on* (pp. 1343-1348). IEEE. 10.15439/2015F161

Qin, E., Long, Y., Zhang, C., & Huang, L. (2013, July). Cloud computing and the internet of things: Technology innovation in automobile service. In *International Conference on Human Interface and the Management of Information* (pp. 173-180). Springer. 10.1007/978-3-642-39215-3_21

Qiuping, W., Shunbing, Z., & Chunquan, D. (2011). Study on key technologies of Internet of Things perceiving mine. *Procedia Engineering*, *26*, 2326–2333. doi:10.1016/j.proeng.2011.11.2442

Rao, Y. R. (2017). Automatic smart parking system using Internet of Things (IOT). *Int J Eng Technol Sci Res, 4*(5).

Rathore, M. M., Ahmad, A., Paul, A., & Rho, S. (2016). Urban planning and building smart cities based on the internet of things using big data analytics. *Computer Networks, 101*, 63–80. doi:10.1016/j.comnet.2015.12.023

Reinsel, D., Gantz, J., & Rydning, J. (2017). *Data Age 2025: The Evolution of Data to Life-Critical*. Don't Focus on Big Data.

Reis, M. S., & Gins, G. (2017). Industrial Process Monitoring in the Big Data/ Industry 4.0 Era: From Detection, to Diagnosis, to Prognosis. *Processes, 5*(3), 35. doi:10.3390/pr5030035

Ritter, N., Kilinc, E., Navruz, B., & Bae, Y. (2011). Test review: Test of nonverbal intelligence-4 (TONI-4). *Journal of Psychoeducational Assessment, 29*(5), 384–388.

Rzevski, G. (1993). On Behaviour and Architectures of Autonomous Intelligent Agents: An Engineering Perspective. First International Round-Table on Abstract Intelligent Agents, Rome, Italy.

Sadowski, B., Nomaler, O., & Whalley, J. (2016). *Technological Diversification of ICT companies into the Internet of things (IoT): A Patent-based Analysis*. Academic Press.

Santoro, G., Vrontis, D., Thrassou, A., & Dezi, L. (2017). The Internet of Things: Building a knowledge management system for open innovation and knowledge management capacity. *Technological Forecasting and Social Change*. doi:10.1016/j. techfore.2017.02.034

Sarkar, C., SN, A. U. N., Prasad, R. V., Rahim, A., Neisse, R., & Baldini, G. (2015). DIAT: A scalable distributed architecture for IoT. *IEEE Internet of Things Journal, 2*(3), 230-239.

Sharma, M. L., Kumar, S., & Mehta, N. (2018). *Internet of things application, challenges and future scope*. Academic Press.

Shelby, Z., Hartke, K., & Bormann, C. (2014). *The constrained application protocol (CoAP)*. Academic Press.

Singh, D., Tripathi, G., & Jara, A. J. (2014, March). A survey of Internet-of-Things: Future vision, architecture, challenges and services. In Internet of things (WF-IoT), 2014 IEEE world forum on (pp. 287-292). IEEE.

Singh, M. P., & Chopra, A. K. (2017, June). The Internet of Things and Multiagent Systems: Decentralized Intelligence in Distributed Computing. In *Distributed Computing Systems (ICDCS), 2017 IEEE 37th International Conference on* (pp. 1738-1747). IEEE.

Sintef, O. V., & Norway, P. F. (2014). *Internet of Things–From Research and Innovation to Market Deployment*. Academic Press.

Sreelatha, B., Alakananda, E., Bhavya, B., & Prasad, S. H. (2018). *IoT applied to logistics using intelligent cargo*. Academic Press.

Sterritt, R., & Hinchey, M. (2005, August). Autonomicity-an antidote for complexity? In Computational systems bioinformatics conference, 2005. Workshops and poster abstracts (pp. 283-291). IEEE. doi:10.1109/CSBW.2005.28

Su, J. P., Wang, C. A., Mo, Y. C., Zeng, Y. X., Chang, W. J., Chen, L. B., . . . Chuang, C. H. (2017, May). i-Logistics: An intelligent Logistics system based on Internet of things. In *Applied System Innovation (ICASI), 2017 International Conference on* (pp. 331-334). IEEE.

Tao, F., Zuo, Y., Da Xu, L., & Zhang, L. (2014). IoT-based intelligent perception and access of manufacturing resource toward cloud manufacturing. *IEEE Transactions on Industrial Informatics, 10*(2), 1547–1557. doi:10.1109/TII.2014.2306397

Tien, J. M. (2017). Internet of Things, Real-Time Decision Making, and Artificial Intelligence. *Annals of Data Science, 4*(2), 149–178. doi:10.100740745-017-0112-5

Tupa, J., Simota, J., & Steiner, F. (2017). Aspects of Risk Management Implementation for Industry 4.0. *Procedia Manufacturing, 11*, 1223–1230. doi:10.1016/j.promfg.2017.07.248

Vandaele, H., Nelis, J., Verbelen, T., & Develder, C. (2015, October). Remote management of a large set of heterogeneous devices using existing IoT interoperability platforms. In *International Internet of Things Summit* (pp. 450–461). Cham: Springer.

Venkatesh, A. N. (2017). *Connecting the Dots: Internet of Things and Human Resource Management*. Academic Press.

Verdouw, C. N., Wolfert, J., Beulens, A. J. M., & Rialland, A. (2016). Virtualization of food supply chains with the internet of things. *Journal of Food Engineering, 176*, 128–136. doi:10.1016/j.jfoodeng.2015.11.009

Wang, L., & Luo, H. (2017, December). Design of intelligent vehicle for distribution system based on speech recognition. In *Computer and Communications (ICCC), 2017 3rd IEEE International Conference on* (pp. 2807-2811). IEEE. 10.1109/CompComm.2017.8323044

Wang, S., Wan, J., Li, D., & Zhang, C. (2016). Implementing smart factory of industrie 4.0: An outlook. *International Journal of Distributed Sensor Networks, 12*(1), 3159805. doi:10.1155/2016/3159805

Witkowski, K. (2017). Internet of Things, Big Data, Industry 4.0–Innovative Solutions in Logistics and Supply Chains Management. *Procedia Engineering, 182,* 763–769. doi:10.1016/j.proeng.2017.03.197

Yadav, J., Yadav, R., & Monika, M. (2017). A Study on Internet of Things. *International Journal (Toronto, Ont.), 8*(1).

Ye, Y., Hu, T., Yang, Y., Zhu, W., & Zhang, C. (2018). A knowledge based intelligent process planning method for controller of computer numerical control machine tools. *Journal of Intelligent Manufacturing,* 1–17.

Yue, X., Cai, H., Yan, H., Zou, C., & Zhou, K. (2015). Cloud-assisted industrial cyber-physical systems: An insight. *Microprocessors and Microsystems, 39*(8), 1262–1270. doi:10.1016/j.micpro.2015.08.013

Zelenkauskaite, A., Bessis, N., Sotiriadis, S., & Asimakopoulou, E. (2012, September). Interconnectedness of complex systems of internet of things through social network analysis for disaster management. In *Intelligent Networking and Collaborative Systems (INCoS), 2012 4th International Conference on* (pp. 503-508). IEEE. 10.1109/iNCoS.2012.25

Zhang, Y., Chen, B., & Lu, X. (2011, August). Intelligent monitoring system on refrigerator trucks based on the internet of things. In *International Conference on Wireless Communications and Applications* (pp. 201-206). Springer.

Zhang, Y. C., & Yu, J. (2013). A study on the fire IOT development strategy. *Procedia Engineering, 52,* 314–319. doi:10.1016/j.proeng.2013.02.146

Zheng, P., Sang, Z., Zhong, R. Y., Liu, Y., Liu, C., Mubarok, K., ... Xu, X. (2018). Smart manufacturing systems for Industry 4.0: Conceptual framework, scenarios, and future perspectives. *Frontiers of Mechanical Engineering,* 1–14.

Zhong, N., Ma, J., Huang, R., Liu, J., Yao, Y., Zhang, Y., & Chen, J. (2016). Research challenges and perspectives on Wisdom Web of Things (W2T). In *Wisdom Web of Things* (pp. 3–26). Cham: Springer. doi:10.1007/978-3-319-44198-6_1

Chapter 2
Ecological Data Exploration

Mohamed Elhadi Rahmani
Dr. Tahar Moulay University of Saida, Algeria

Abdelmalek Amine
Dr. Tahar Moulay University of Saida, Algeria

ABSTRACT

Computer modeling of ecological systems is the activity of implementing computer solutions to analyze data related to the fields of remote sensing, earth science, biology, and oceans. The ecologists analyze the data to identify the relationships between a response and a set of predictors, using statistical models that do not accurately describe the main sources of variation in the response variable. Knowledge discovery techniques are often more powerful, flexible, and effective for exploratory analysis than statistical techniques. This chapter aims to test the use of data mining in ecology. It will discuss the exploration of ecological data by defining at first data mining, its advantages, and its different types. Then the authors detail the field of bio-inspiration and meta-heuristics. And finally, they give case studies from where they applied these two areas to explore ecological data.

INTRODUCTION

Several statistical methods exist to explore a large search space when knowledge exists are not sufficient to create a single parametric model. One of these methods is popular among ecologists, it is called the multi-model inference based on the use of Akaike information criteria from which a small number of Model (Burnham, 2011). To analyze a large number of models, the Monte Carlo techniques with reversible Markov chain were found (King, 2004). Other approaches appear when

DOI: 10.4018/978-1-5225-7338-8.ch002

the predictive variables are specified, the weak point of these variables is that the relations between the predictive variables and the response variables are complex (Wood, 2006). All these techniques offer confirmatory analysis of ecological data with analytical flexibility designed to test the model parameters and the assumptions represented, but they remain insufficient if knowledge is minimal or not clearly represented. However, exploratory analysis presents the best solution for analyzing ecological data and generating new hypotheses.

Exploratory analysis techniques have proved to be better than statistical techniques (John, 2010).

The power of exploratory analysis can be summed up in three points:

- Automatic and accurate prediction of data.
- The identification of important predictive variables from a large number of variables.
- The ability to process data without making assumptions about the relationships between predictive variables and response variables.

That is, unlike the statistical techniques from which the user must specify as parameters to enter the important predictive variables and the formal representation of the relations between variables, data mining techniques do not take these parameters but they do it automatically. These advantages guide ecological researchers to develop powerful exploration techniques (Hochachka, 2007)(Anderson, 2006). With the advancement of exploratory techniques, researchers have founded many approaches to this task, giving rise to the domain of data mining with different approaches and a single goal, Extraction of hidden knowledge in the data. This area in turn has been expanded more and more to reveal another area called bio-inpiration and meta-heuristics, the latter considers nature as a source of inspiration for new approaches dedicated to the Data mining.

In this chapter, the exploration of ecological data will be discussed by defining data mining, its advantages and its different types at the beginning, and the field of bio-inspiration and meta-heuristics will be detailed in order to give case- Studies where they applied these two domains to explore ecological data.

Data Mining

"Data mining is the core stage of the knowledge discovery process that is aimed at the extraction of interesting—nontrivial, implicit, previously unknown and potentially useful—information from data in large databases." (Caruana, 2006)

Data mining is a multidisciplinary domain, and for that we find several definitions of this term, even the expression data mining does not present all the main components of this domain. Data mining is a reduced expression, which means the search of knowledge from the data. In addition, we can find several terms that have the same meaning as knowledge extraction from data. Several people see data mining and knowledge extraction as a front for a part, others see data mining as a knowledge extraction step.

Knowledge extraction consists of seven essential steps:

1. **Data Cleaning:** It consists of eliminating noise and inconsistent data.
2. **Data Integration:** Where multiple data sources can be combined.
3. **Data Selection:** Where the relevant data for the analysis are selected from the database.
4. **Data Transformation:** Where the data is transformed to be adaptable to the operation.
5. **Data Mining:** Where intelligent methods are applied to extract knowledge.
6. **Model Evaluation:** To identify relevant models that represent knowledge based on evaluation measures.
7. **Knowledge Representation:** Where representation techniques are used to represent knowledge.

Steps from 1 to 4 are considered pre-processing steps from which the data are prepared to adapt them to the exploratory technique used for data analysis. Data mining is the most important step in the process of knowledge extraction. However, in the literature, data mining is a term used to refer to the extraction of knowledge. Therefore, data mining can be defined as a process of discovering interesting profiles and knowledge from a large amount of data. An essential advantage of data mining techniques is that they are applicable on any type of data

Figure 1 – Process of knowledge extraction provided that the data must be meaningful to the field of application. In general, the data most processed by data mining methods are databases, data warehouses, and transactional data recorded from commercial systems such as items purchased from a supermarket, but it does not prevent researchers from adapting these methods for processing other types of data such as sequential or time-bound data, multimedia data (text, images, audio, or video), network data, spatial data or scientific data. The data can be described to classes and concepts which are summarized, concise and precise terms. They can be derived using the data characterization to summarize the data characteristics for a target class specified by the user in a query to collect the data. The class/concept description can be obtained by comparing the characteristics of the objects of a target class with the characteristics of the other objects of several classes by a method called the discrimination of the data. The data obtained by these two methods are represented by statistical measures and summarizing diagrams.

Figure 1. Presents the process of knowledge extraction

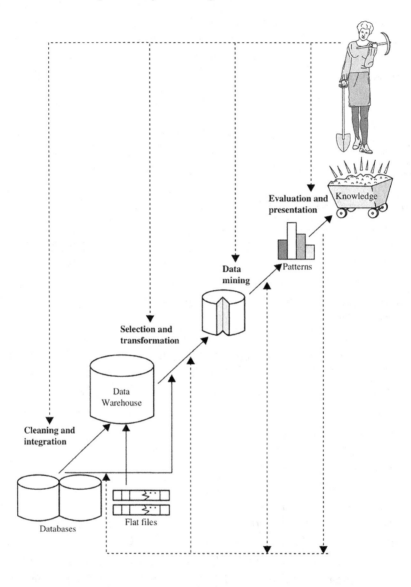

Machine Learning

Before we delve in machine learning and its details, let's step back and think what learning actually is, the key concept that we will need to think about for our machines is learning from data, because data size augment day after day, we talk here about very large data (terabytes of it), we all agree that humans and animals can display behaviors that we label as intelligent by learning from experience. Learning is remembering, adapting and generalizing, and that's based on the ability to adjust and adapt to circumstances, and learn new tricks, that last what gives us the flexibility in our life. It's the recognition of what we did last time in a situation and do it again if it worked before or try something else. Therefore, we can say that generalizing is about recognizing similarity between different situations, so that things that applied in one place can be used in another. This is what makes learning useful, because we can use our knowledge in lots of different places (Fayyad, 1996).

What's Machine Learning?

In computer science, there are a lot of problems that we don't have any algorithm to solve it such as the most famous one: spam/ham filtering, when we speak about an algorithm, we talk about a set of instructions that should be carried out to transform input to output. Backing to the problems, those last have a data (very large examples), and here where can machine learning can solve these problems by collect data and hope to extract the answers to these and similar questions from it.

Looking for techniques that explain the observed data, although the identification of the procedures underlying the data generation is very difficult, researchers are trying to find approximations that can explain a piece of data instead of the whole set. These approximations can detect certain patterns or regularity, it is the niche of digital learning. The models obtained help to understand the process for predicting new cases in the future (Cios, 2007). A model can be predictive to make future, or descriptive predictions to gain knowledge from the data, or both at the same time. It is defined by a set of parameters then the goal of the learning is the optimization of these parameters using the data of past experience, these data are called learning data (Alpaydin, 2014). Machine learning is considered also as a part of artificial intelligence. Intelligence means the ability to learn, and artificial intelligence means that a system is in a changing environment should have that ability to learn and adapt to such changes, what means that the system designer need not foresee and provide solution for possible situation. Machine learning uses the theory of statistics in building mathematical models, because the core task is making inference from a sample. The role of computer science is twofold: First, in training, we need efficient algorithms to solve the optimization problem, as well as to store and process the massive amount of data we generally have. Second, once a model is learned, its representation and algorithmic solution for inference needs to be efficient as well. In certain applications, the efficiency of the learning or inference algorithm, namely, its space and time complexity, may be as important as its predictive accuracy.

The relation between machine learning and data mining is summarized in "each one is a part of the other one". ". Data mining uses many machine learning methods for many goals, for this we can say machine learning is a part of data mining. On the other hand, machine learning employs data mining as unsupervised learning or as pre-processing step to improve learner accuracy, and here we find that data mining is a part of machine learning. This relation make these two terms commonly confused, because they can be roughly defined as follows:

- Machine learning focuses on prediction, based on known properties learned from the training data.
- Data mining focuses on the discovery of (previously) unknown properties in the data.

This is the analysis step of Knowledge Discovery in Databases.

So maybe you ask, how can they be confused? In machine learning, there is a performance that's usually evaluated with respect to the ability to reproduce known knowledge, here, an unsupervised method will easily outperform by supervised method. While in data mining, there an important task, it's the main task, the discovery of previously unknown knowledge, in this case, supervised methods cannot be used due to the unviability of training data. These two basic assumptions that machine learning and data mining work with make the confusion.

Types of Machine Learning

- **Learning Associations:** for example, in a supermarket chain, we can use a machine learning application based on basket container analysis for each customer, this application finds associations between products bought by customers: If people who buy X typically also buy Y, and if there is a customer who buys X and does not buy Y, he or she is a potential Y customer. Once we find such customers, we can target them for cross-selling. This type of machine learning try to find rules that help to find deduction, these rules called association rule. In finding an association rule, we are interested in learning a conditional association rule probability of the form P(Y |X), suppose it was found 0.7, this means that 70% of customers who buy product X also purchase product Y. This probability is called support and represents the percentage of customers who purchase X and Y products at the same time in all purchases:

Totalpurchasesof X andY productsatthesametime

$$\text{Support} = \frac{Total\ purchases\ of\ X\ and\ Y\ products\ at\ the\ same\ time}{Total\ purchases}$$

(1)

Totalpurchases

We also compute for a rule confiance ce qui représente la chance d'acheter un produit Y lorsque les clients achètent le produit X:

Totalpurchasesof X andY productsatthesametime

Confiance =

$$\frac{Total\ purchases\ of\ X\ and\ Y\ products\ at\ the\ same\ time}{Total\ purchases\ of\ X} \qquad (2)$$

Totalpurchaseof productX

Based on these two measures and two thresholds fixed at the beginning for each, we define the set of rules of final association, this set called Frequent Items Set (Lai, 2009).

- **Supervised Classification:** Supervised classification is a task based on the analysis of a set of data objects for which the class labels are known called training data, and try to find a model that describes and distinguishes data classes or concepts, this model allow to predict the class label of objects. The techniques in this case differ according to the principle of each. There are those based on mathematical formulas from where to classify each new instance, it calculates a measure of similarity with the whole set of learning data, or calculates probability of belonging to a class. There is that based on the creation of models such as classification rules (IF-THEN), decision trees, mathematical formulae, or neural networks (see figure 2). A decision tree is a flowchart like tree structure, where each node denotes a test on an attribute value, each branch represents an outcome of the test, and tree leaves represent classes or class distributions. Decision trees can easily be converted to classification rules. A neural network, when used for classification, is typically a collection of neuron like processing units with weighted connections between the units.
- **Regression:** In the following we will define the regression as a type of data mining. Regression problems are supervised classification problems, the difference between this type and the supervised classification discussed in the previous paragraph lies in the class type. In the supervised classification, we have a small number of classes, in contrast to the regression from which the class is a variable that represents a projection of a set of variables and a numerical class. More formally, the regression tries to find a hyperplane $f(x)$ which for each set of values of the attributes x, $f(x) = y$, y is the desired class.

33

Figure 2. A classification model can be represented in various forms: (a) IF-THEN rules

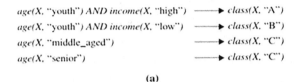

(a)

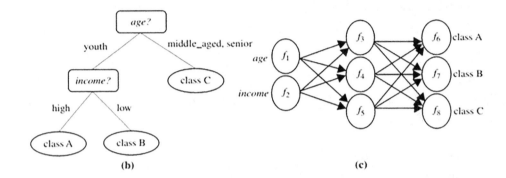

(b)   **(c)**

The regression model attempts to "capture" most data through the area of the highest data density. The quality of the model depends on the nature of the data and its functional form (Cios, 2007). The regression has proved a good efficiency by representing the dependencies between the input and output variables. Several cases are presented in figure 3: (a) linearly distributed data with a very limited dispersion an excellent fit (b) a decision tree, or (c) a neural network offered by some linear model; (b) linearly distributed data with significant dispersion; no model could result in acceptable fit; (c) nonlinearly distributed data well captured by the corresponding nonlinear model yet leading to poor performance of any linear model.

- **Unsupervised Classification (Clustering):** Unlike classification and regression, which analyse training data sets and create a model (supervisor). In unsupervised learning, there is no such supervisor and we only have input data. The aim is to find the regularities in the input. There is a structure to the input space such that certain patterns occur more often than others, and we want to see what generally happens and what does not. In statistics, this is called density estimation. Clustering can be used to generate class labels for a group of data. The objects are clustered or grouped based on the principle of maximizing the intraclass similarity and minimizing the interclass similarity. That is, clusters of objects are formed so that objects within a cluster have high similarity in comparison to one another but are rather dissimilar to objects

Figure 3. Examples of regression models with single input and single output and their relationships with data (Cios, 2007)

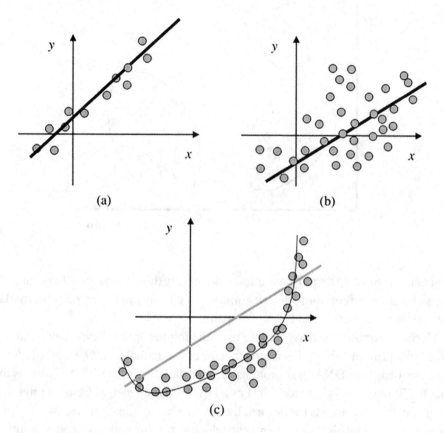

(a)

(b)

(c)

in other clusters. Each cluster so formed can be viewed as a class of objects, from which rules can be derived. Clustering can also facilitate taxonomy formation, that is, the organization of observations into a hierarchy of classes that group similar events together. Figure 4 presents a simple example of clustering of some data in 3 clusters (Cios, 2007).

In the case of a company with a data of past customers, the customer data contains the demographic information as well as the past transactions with the company, and the company may want to see the distribution of the profile of its customers, to see what type of customers frequently occur. In such a case, a clustering model allocates customers similar in their attributes to the same group, providing the company with natural groupings of its customers; this is called customer segmentation. Once such groups are found, the company may decide strategies, for example, services and products, specific to different groups; this is known as customer relationship

Figure 4. Simple example of clustering (Cios, 2007)

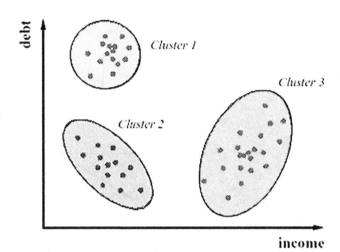

management. Such a grouping also allows identifying those who are outliers, namely, those who are different from other customers, which may imply a niche in the market that can be further exploited by the company.

Machine learning methods are also used in bioinformatics. DNA in our genome is the "blueprint of life" and is a sequence of bases, namely, A, G, C, and T. RNA is transcribed from DNA, and proteins are translated from the RNA. Proteins are what the living body is and does. Just as a DNA is a sequence of bases, a protein is a sequence of amino acids (as defined by bases). One application area of computer science in molecular biology is alignment, which is matching one sequence to another. This is a difficult string matching problem because strings may be quite long, there are many template strings to match against, and there may be deletions, insertions, and substitutions. Clustering is used in learning motifs, which are sequences of amino acids that occur repeatedly in proteins. Motifs are of interest because they may correspond to structural or functional elements within the sequences they characterize. The analogy is that if the amino acids are letters and proteins are sentences, motifs are like words, namely, a string of letters with a particular meaning occurring frequently in different sentences.

• Reinforcement Learning: The technique of reinforcement learning was introduced by (Preux, 2009). The goal of these methods is to find a set of appropriate actions to take given situations in order to maximize a reward. A supervised learning algorithm takes as input a set of actions and states in which it interacts with its environment. Performing an action affects not only the immediate reward, but also the rewards of all subsequent states. (Sutton, 1998) have proved that the use of reinforcement learning with a neural network can teach the latter to play the backgammon game at a high level. Here the network must learn to take a board position as input, along with the result of a dice throw, and produce a strong move as the output. This is done by having the network play against a copy of itself for perhaps a million games. A major challenge is that a game of backgammon can involve dozens of moves, and yet it is only at the end of the game that the reward, in the form of victory, is achieved. The reward must then be attributed appropriately to all of the moves that led to it, even though some moves will have been good ones and others less so. This is an example of a credit assignment problem. A general feature of reinforcement learning is the trade-off between the exploitation and the exploration. in which the system makes use of actions that are known to yield a high reward. Too strong a focus on either exploration or exploitation will yield poor results.

Reinforcement learning continues to be an active area of machine learning research.

One of the major areas for applying reinforcement learning is the field of robotics. The idea in this case is that a robot can learn a correct sequence of actions in order to reach a target location after a certain number of tests, so at the end it can move from an initial place to a final location quickly and without touching any of the obstacles.

According to (Cios, 2007), One factor that makes reinforcement learning harder is when the system has unreliable and partial sensory information. For example, a robot equipped with a video camera has incomplete information and thus at any time is in a partially observable state and should decide taking into account this uncertainty; for example, it may not know its exact location in a room but only that there is a wall to its left. A task may also require a concurrent operation of multiple agents that should interact and cooperate to accomplish a common goal. An example is a team of robots playing soccer.

Bio-Inspiration and Meta-Heuristics

Data mining is not only a matter of grouping or classifying data but optimizing exploration itself is an area of major importance in engineering fields in general. The problems NPHard Are difficult problems to be solved by conventional techniques. The increase of such kinds of problems has created an active research topic, from which researchers try to develop mathematical techniques to find the best possible solutions for a given problem. Optimization methods are divided into two categories: deterministic methods that are the oldest. These methods require a great effort to make calculations, which gives a greater limit in terms of complexity when the size of the problem increases. This gives the motivation to invent new techniques which consist in using a random computation and a local search to solve an optimization problem based on iterative improvements of a population of solutions or a unique solution. These methods have been brought together in a field called Bio-inspiration and meta-heuristics.

Bio-Inspiration and Meta-Heuristics

Meta-Heuristics

A heuristic is a method that finds good solutions to a problem without proving that they are correct or optimal solutions (Brownlee, 2011). The interest of heuristic methods is to improve the early success, accuracy and quality of the results in favor of temporal and spatial complexity. They can work under some conditions, which leads to a higher level called meta-heuristics. These are methods that can be applied to several optimization problems by modifying them relatively to adapt them to each problem (Michalewicz, 2013)(Glover, 2006). The word meta refers to a combination of one or more heuristics using a higher-level policy. Meta-heuristics contains a component of diversification that is used to explore the global search space, and a intensification component that is used to demonstrate the right solutions in a part by a local search (Binitha, 2012). (Thomas, 2009) identified nine characteristics of meta-heuristics:

1. Meta-heuristics are strategies that guide the research process.
2. The objective is to effectively explore the research space in order to find optimal solutions.
3. The techniques that constitute meta-heuristic algorithms range from simple local search procedures to complex learning processes.
4. Meta-heuristic algorithms are approximate and usually non-deterministic.
5. They can integrate mechanisms to avoid being trapped in confined areas of the research space.
6. The basic concepts of meta-heuristics allow an abstract level description.
7. Meta-heuristics are not problem-specific.
8. Meta-heuristics can use domain-specific knowledge in the form of heuristics controlled by the higher-level strategy.
9. The most advanced meta-heuristics of today use a research experiment (incorporated into some form of memory) to guide research.

Bio-Inspiration

The term bio-inspiration comes from the inspiration of the principles of algorithms. These algorithms are inspired by nature, bio means biology, then the word bio-inspiration means inspiration of natural biology. (Tesauro, 1994) mentioned: "The true beauty of nature-based algorithms lies in the fact that it receives its unique inspiration from nature and has the ability to describe and solve complex relationships from Initial conditions intrinsically very simple and rules with little or no knowledge of the search space ". Nature contains many characteristics and phenomena that if studied, optimal solutions and strategies to address the complex interaction between organisms are always found, even if the strategy is simple, the results are incredible. All conceptions of nature and its capabilities motivate researchers to imitate nature in technology, especially since modern computer science can have many problems that nature has already encountered and solved, then bio-inspired algorithms A new era in technological development, they affect almost all computer domains, including computer networks, security, robotics, biomedical engineering, control systems, parallel processing, data exploration, power systems, production engineering and much more.

Problem solving algorithms are divided into two types: algorithms based on exact calculations (such as logical programming), and heuristics. The latter have proved effective in solving complex problems in relation to exact methods. A bio-inspired algorithm is a heuristic that presents an artificial image of a strategy of nature as long as this strategy can be considered as a constrained optimization process. The inspiration of an algorithm passes through several stages, beginning with a problem formulation and the choice of an adequate representation of this problem, and then a definition of the operators is carried out by imitating the various natural factors in order to evaluate the quality Solutions through a fitness function. The literature of bio-inspired algorithms is very rich in approaches to solve an impressive array of problems, a number of studies have reported the success of these techniques to solve difficult problems in all key areas of computing (Tesauro, 1994). Bio-inspired algorithms are divided into two main categories: evolutionary algorithms based on natural evolution, and algorithms based on swarms based on the collective behavior of animals. (Binitha, 2012). In this section, we will discuss the two main categories of bio-inspired algorithms by giving examples of the best-known algorithms for each category.

The Evolutionary Bio-Inspired Algorithms

Population growth, development, reproduction, selection and survival are phenomena that represent the evolutionary process of organisms, this process is responsible for survival strategies and interaction between living beings. In artificial intelligence, these phenomena are a source of inspiration for evolutionary algorithms, using a powerful design to find solutions to problems, they are based on costs, and their main characteristic is that they are non-linear algorithms Deterministic (Baeza-Yates, 1999). There are several evolutionary algorithms that share the same principle of stochastic research, starting with the creation of an initial population, and generating generations of population iteratively based on physical exercises (fitness function) of the previous population, the function of Fitness is determined according to the field of application of the algorithm, the best solutions are selected to survive the next iteration.

One of the most successful evolutionary algorithms is the genetic algorithms. They are suggested by (Back, 1996) and are inspired by Charles Darwin's survival principles. The three main operations of the genetic algorithms are: selection, crossing, and mutation. They begin by selecting a set of solutions called chromosome, its solutions must be represented in binary vectors, then they evaluate each chromosome by the fitness function to choose the best solutions, in the next iteration, the selected population goes through a mating process, where the solutions undergo crossings and mutations in order to generate a new population of chromo-

2. Bio-Inspiration and Meta-Heuristics

somes. Genetic algorithms are useful when the search space is large or complex, or when no mathematical analysis or traditional method is available. But this does not prevent genetic algorithms from having disadvantages such as convergence towards the local optimum if the fitness function is poorly defined, so genetic algorithms cannot solve constraint optimization problems.

An extension of the genetic algorithms is proposed by (Holland, 1973) called the genetic programming, this kind of algorithms follows the same steps as the genetic algorithms, the difference is summarized in the representation of the solutions, they use a tree Like indirect encoding to apply the search directly to the solution, the solutions can be computer programs. Genetic programming is based on four essential steps:

1. Generation of an initial population of computer programs including functions.
2. Running each program on the population in order to assign it a fitness value.
3. After choosing the best programs, they undergo mutations.
4. A crossing is made between the generated programs.

The algorithms based on the mutation and crossing principles continue to appear with the algorithm called differential evolution proposed by (Koza, 1992). The difference between the latter and the genetic algorithms is in the mutation principle which is a result of an individual's gene perturbations in genetic algorithms, whereas it is the result of the arithmetic combinations of individuals in the algorithm of Differential evolution. According to (Storn, 1997), noise can adversely affect the performance of the differential evolution algorithm because of its greedy nature, and the specification of the control parameters is done manually by the user dependent on the problem studied, these two ideas present the limits of differential evolution algorithms. But the ease of implementation and the exposure of rapid convergence, present the strengths of these algorithms, which makes them reliable, accurate, robust and fast optimization techniques.

The most recent evolutionary algorithm was invented in 2009 by (Krink, 2004), it is called Paddy Field. This algorithm is very different from the others, it is inspired by the phenomenon of reproduction of plant populations, its principle is dependent on proximity to the overall solution and population density. It consists of the following five steps:

1. It diffuses an initial population (seeds) randomly.
2. It selects the best solutions (plants) by a threshold method.
3. According to a fitness function, it determines the highest plants in the population, hence each plant develops a number of seeds that fall in different places, so the highest plants are the only ones that come from the most favorable places.
4. Pollination is the primary factor in increasing population density.
5. Dispersal is the second factor, its goal is to avoid local minima, the seeds are scattered and develop into new plants that produce other seeds.

Swarm-Based Algorithms

Swarm Intelligence is a type of bio-inspired algorithms that are based on the collective behavior of organisms (Premaratne, 2009). According to the definitions, swarm-based algorithms mimic the collective intelligence of groups of organisms, it is the source of nomination of this type of problem solving algorithms. A swarm-based algorithm is an algorithm from which the solutions present particles with irregular movements in the search space. These algorithms are decentralized and self-organized processes in food research (Brownlee, 2011). They can be described by the following five principles:

1. **Proximity Principle:** Calculations must be simple in terms of time and space.
2. **Principle of Quality:** The quality of the solutions is controlled by factors in the environment.
3. **Multiple Response Principle:** The solutions are several agents that search in space, which gives multiple answers for a query.
4. **Principle of Stability:** The search principle does not change every time the environment changes.
5. **Principle of Adaptability:** Agents seeking solutions can adapt to a new behavior when it is worth.

The most famous swarm-based algorithm is inspired by the flocking of birds by searching for food, invented by (Kennedy, 2001) and called the Particle Swarm

Optimization (PSO) . It is an algorithm based on a population (set of particles) initialized at the beginning randomly (Hu, 2004), each particle is associated with a speed that is dynamically adjusted according to the flight history, based on this history, the particles fly To the best research areas by imitating a process of searching for foods by birds (Theodoridis, 1999). The birds follow the closest to the food to find it. In the artificial model, birds are solutions (particles), they fly in the search space by following the best solutions that are determined by a speed assessment using a fitness function, the purpose in all this is research of the optima by updating the population in each iteration (Topchy, 2004).

The algorithms of colony of ants are also algorithms based on swarms which have proved an efficiency of resolution of problems of optimization. Invented by (Abraham, 2007), (Dorigo, 2005), (Dorigo, 1999), ant colony algorithms are inspired by the behavior of ants' social life, knowing that they are interested in the survival of the colony rather than individual survival. The collaborative behavior of ants to find the shortest path from their nest to food is the main source of inspiration. The ants first explore the surroundings of the nest randomly by leaving a pheromone that guides them by its smell. If an ant finds a source of food, it leaves more pheromone dependent on food quality, based on the smell of pheromone, the ants follow the shortest path to the best food. (Dorigo, 1997) defined artificial ant colony algorithm model:

1. Pheromone path initialization.
2. Pheromone solution construction: each ant seeks the best solutions (food) according to a probability (pheromone concentration).
3. Transition Rule: An ant constructs a movement rule that guides other ants.
4. Pheromone Update: An ant can update the concentration of pheromone every time it creates a transition rule. This update is made in two phases, a phase of evaporation of pheromone, and a phase of reinforcement of pheromone (Toksari, 2006).

These four steps are iterated until a stopping criterion is reached.

The social life of bees is a set of behaviors that contain collective tasks, such as eating behavior, bees seek nectar around the hive, if a bee finds the nectar, it communicates with the other bees by a dense indicating Direction, distance and quality of food in the way it took. This behavior is an excellent source of inspiration for an algorithm called algorithm of bees, which is classified under the category of swarm-based algorithms. The natural behavior follows the following steps: Scouts of the hive locate the pieces of flowers by randomly moving around the hive and then return and inform the other bees of the path and quality of the food. Scouts then return with other bees to the path to collect the nectar, while other scouts continue to look for other paths. On the other hand, the bee algorithm mimics this behavior from which the Scouts are randomly initialized, then they exploit the random search space to find good sites that present optimal solutions to optimization problems, they rely on a Local search for good sites, where there are sites that are exploited more than others, and in each iteration, other scouts are sent to exploit additional sites (Dorigo, 2000).

Ecological Data Exploration

In the 1950s and 1960s, researchers began the analysis of lakes data by nonlinear regression. This statistical approach has become a basic model for analyzing ecological data. With the technological inventions in computer science, and the appearance of new data mining techniques and bio-inspired calculations with a good performance of discovering knowledge in complex databases, analysis of ecological data was influenced by these inventions. In this section, some examples of application of data mining techniques and bio-inspired techniques for exploring ecological data will be discussed, these works were collected by (Blum, 2003).

Prediction and Elucidation of Stream Ecosystems

(Recknagel, 2006) developed classification systems based on decision trees and artificial neural networks to predict macro-invertebrate communities in the Zwalm Basin in Belgium. Based on structural characteristics and physico-chemical characteristics, classification models were used to predict the presence of macro-invertebrate taxa. The attributes of the collected data are presented in the table 1:

The results obtained were varied according to the species to be predicted, for example for prediction of the Tubificide species, the decision tree correctly classified 93% of the data of this species, whereas the neural networks predicted 93.3% correctly, however for prediction of the species Asellidae, decision trees gave an early success of 63% and neural networks classified 43.3% of Asellidae species correctly. The cause of this difference is the distribution of species (Tubificide species appear in 93% of the Zwalm surface, whereas the Asellidae species appear in 43% of the area studied).

(Goethals, 2006) studied the application of different neural networks for the detection of important variables to describe the non-linear relationships between abiotic elements and biotic elements in a marine ecosystem. The studies were carried out on two datasets from the Hesse, Germany:

Table 1. Variables (attributes) monitored in the Zwalm river basin (Recknagel, 2006)

Attribute	Unit
PH	-
Temperature	°C
Dissolved oxygen	mg/l
Conductivity	μS/cm
Suspended solids	mg/l
Water level	cm
Fraction of pebbles	%
Shadow	%
Water plants	2 classes: 0 = absent; 1 = present
Width	cm
Flow velocity	m/s
Meandering	6 classes (1 = well developed to 6 = absent)
Hollow river beds	6 classes (1 = well developed to 6 = absent)
Pools/Riffles	6 classes (1 = well developed to 6 = absent)
Artificial embankment structures	3 classes (0 = absent; 1 = moderate; 2 = intensive

- A set of organic pollution data that contains 248 macrozoobenthos taxa and physical, chemical and hydromorphological variables. This set has been presented by (Schleiter, 2006) (Schleiter, 1999).
- Thirty-year records of environmental variables (precipitation, landfills, water temperature) and aquatic insects of a near-immaculate stream (Schleiter, 2000).

Neural networks were used to model and visualize the relationships between the different organic elements in these two sets. A non-supervised model based on Kohonen (Schleiter, 2001) maps was used to explore ecological data in this ecosystem. Other supervised systems have been developed for: prediction of environmental variables based on the multilayered perceptron (MLP) (Kohonen, 2001) neural network, prediction of aquatic insects by sensory neural networks (Rumelhart, 1985), regression of Anthropogenic emissions altered by the general regression neural network (NRG) (Dapper, 1998), and the prediction of the indicator variables by the motorized feature maps (MFM) (Dapper, 1998), all these supervised models are neural networks Modified multilayer perceptron. Radial base (RBF) (Specht, 1991) neural networks were also presented as a tool for visualizing the properties of marine ecosystems.

(Bishop, 1995) implemented a set of neural networks to predict benthic macroinvertebrate communities in running waters. The first neural network implemented was based on Kohonen maps combined with the adaptive theory resonance model (Chon, 2006) (Carpenter, 1987) in order to regroup the changes in the community. These clusters help to make short-term predictions of community abundance by multilayer neural networks or recurrent networks (Pao, 1989). Fully connected recurring networks have proved to be the best solutions for analyzing the temporal development of communities. The counter-proparagation (Elman, 1990) is another neural network approach implemented by (Bishop, 1995) to describe the relationship models between different hierarchical levels in the benthic macroinvertebrate community. This approach was based on a hybridization of Kohonen maps and the multilayer perceptron.

(Hoang, 2006) developed neural networks based on clean water data (Hoang, 2001) to predict fauna on the studied sites, and other models were developed based on data from the dirty water (Hoang, 2001) to identify the variables that influence the prediction of ecological consequences. This study was conducted on data from the Queensland River in Australia, where they used 39 physical variables and 17 environmental variables to represent 40 macro-invertebrate species. This data set was used to model different models of multilayer neural networks under different scenarios, with a sensitivity analysis for each model, validate the models and detect the relationships between the environmental variables and physical variables of each species.

Prediction and Elucidation of River Ecosystems

In the study by (Jeong, 2006), annual dynamics of two algal species in the lower Nakdong River in South Korea were modeled by recurrent neural networks, both associated with flowers, Microcystis aeruginosa during hot summers and Stephanodiscus hantzschii from winter to early spring. The objective of the study was to understand the factors that control the formation of algal blooms in regulated river systems. To represent the data, (Ha, 1999) used 16 attributes as input for predicting the quantities of the two species. The attributes were divided into five categories: meteorological, physical, chemical, hydrological, and biological. Table 2 demonstrates the attributes of river data:

The results obtained in this study have shown that recurrent neural networks are a very good tool for conducting sensitivity analyzes of variables important for complex ecosystems such as river ecosystems.

(Bowden, 2003) is another work from where they used neural networks to analyze data from river ecosystems. They compared three techniques for reducing the dimensionality of the input space, one based on prior knowledge, one based

Table 2. The attributes of the Nakdong River used as input and output variables in the neural network (Ha, 1999)

	Category	Attribute	Unit
Inputs	**Meteorological**	Irradiation	$MJm^{-2}d^{-1}$
	Hydrological	Precipitation	mmd^{-1}
		Discharge	$CMSd^{-1}$
		Evaporation	mmd^{-1}
	Physical	The temperature of the water	°C
		Secchi depth	cm
		Turbidity	NTU
	Chimical	PH	-
		DO	mgL^{-1}
		Nitrate-N	mgL^{-1}
		Ammoniac-N	μgL^{-1}
		Phosphate-P	μgL^{-1}
		Silica dissolved	mgL^{-1}
	Biological	Rotifera	$Ind.L^{-1}$
		Cladocera	$Ind.L^{-1}$
		Copepoda	$Ind.L^{-1}$
Outputs	**Biological**	Microcystis aeruginosa	$\mu m^3 mL^{-1}$
		Stephanodiscus hantzschii	$\mu m^3 mL^{-1}$

on self-organizing maps (SOM) (Kohonen, 2001), and one based on principal components analysis (PCA) (Masters, 1995). Then, they classified their data using two techniques, one based on a neural network implementation, and one based on a hybridization of the genetic algorithms (Goldberg, 2006) and neural networks using the NeuroGenetic Optimizer (NGO) (ASCE, 2000). The objective of this study was to select the optimal input variables to predict the concentration of a bacterium called Anabaena Spp in the Murray River at Morgan for 4 weeks. Comparative techniques have proven to be effective in analyzing river ecosystem data.

(Gevrey, 2006) have compared two methods for analyzing the main factors influencing the richness of riparian fishes on a global scale. Both methods are based on multi-linear regression, one called profile algorithm presented by Lek et al. In (Lek, 1996)(Lek, 1996b), and one called the derivative profile (Dimopoulos, 1995) (Dimopoulos, 1999). These two techniques consist in analyzing each variable successively in order to define the important variables that affect the richness of the riparian fish. They applied its methods on data collected across different rivers in the world, after determining important variables, they used neural networks to predict the richness of fish. The results obtained demonstrated a high performance of multi-linear regression techniques to determine the explanatory variables in a river ecosystem.

Prediction and Elucidation of Lake and Marine Ecosystems

(Karul, 2003) compared two regression methods to estimate the amount of chlorophyll-a in Turkish lakes. They applied neural network models presented in (Karul, 1999)(Karul, 2000) based on multilayer neural networks. The second method implemented in this study is the multiple linear regression (Kutner, 2004) where they used the MatLab tool for the (Demuth, 2000) implementation. These methods have been applied to analyze data from three Turks lakes, the Keban Dam reservoir, whose data are collected in a study project named Environmental Basin Project to study water quality in The data contains the following chemical characteristics: PO4, NO3, alkalinity, suspended solids, pH, temperature, electrical conductivity, dissolved oxygen, depth Secchi, density of species Daphnia only And apparent densities of species belonging to Cladocera and Copepoda, Lake Mogan and Lake Eymir (Altınbilek, 1995) which include total phosphorus, NO3, NH3, suspended solids, temperature, electrical conductivity, pH, turbidity, Secchi depth. (Karul, 2003) also used the water properties of these lakes in the data representation as presented in the table 3

(Karul, 2003) concluded that neural networks, with their properties and their ability to process complex non-linear data, can be a modeling tool for estimating eutrophication parameters such as Chlorophyll-a and also for other environmental variables.

(Recknagel, 2006) is a study from which they applied recurrent neural networks introduced by (Pineda, 1997) to predict a 7-day seasonal succession of Microcystis and Cyclotella for Kasumigaura Lake, and species of Anabaena and Asterionella for the lake of Soyang in Japan. Data from these two lakes were represented by 12 attributes including chemical and physical characteristics. This study has shown that recurrent neural networks can be used to analyze complex time series data for the prediction of short- and long-term water quality changes and also to analyze the relationships between the environmental variables of lakes.

Evolutionary algorithms were also applied to predict population dynamics of diatoms and algae in the two lakes of Kasumigaura and Soyang, this study was carried out by (Cao, 2006). They implemented a hybrid evolutionary algorithm from which they used genetic programming to formulate rules in the form IF-THEN-ELSE and then optimized the parameters of these rules by a genetic algorithm. The results obtained demonstrated that evolutionary algorithms can be a tool for formulating

Table 3. Properties of freshwater lakes (Karul, 2003)

Property	Eymir	Mogan	Keban Dam
Formation of the lake	Formed by the deposit of alluvial material carried by lateral tributaries.	Formed by the deposit of alluvial material carried by lateral tributaries.	Artificial reservoir mainly for the production of energy.
Shape	A riparian pattern characterized by a riparian profile by a long and narrow morphology.	Looks like extended riverbeds.	Irregular plan view.
Depth	Shallow	Shallow	Deep
Hydrographic area	970 Km²	970 Km²	64 100 Km²
Average width	300 m	1350 m	-
Center line length	4.5 Km	6 Km	151 Km
Average high water (sea level)	968.5 m	972 m	845 m
Average area	22 Km²	5.43 Km²	191 Km² at maximum water level
Average volume	3.5 Million m³	11.63 Million m³	30.6 * 10⁹ Million m³
Average depth	3 m	2.2 m	21.7 m at the maximum altitude
Trophic status	Eutrophic-dominated by suspended algae	Eutrophic - Dominated by the macrophyte	Oligotrophic to eutrophic (No macrophytes)
Secchi depth	0.25-0.70 m	0.2-3.75 m	0.22-5.64 m
Cholorophyl-a	9.02-87.20 µg/lt	0.0-23.8 µg/lt	1-33.36 µg/lt
P	0.05-0.57 mg/l as ortho-P	0.021-0.81 mg/l as total-P	0.001-0.081 mg/l as phosphate

classification rules to predict and represent the relationships between environmental variables and lake populations. Also, the structure of rules formed by arithmetic operators makes it possible to control the complexity of analysis of ecological data.

Lake Kasumigaura is a rich site that attracts researchers to explore the different species. (Atanasova, 2006) is another work that involved finding ordinary differential equations to predict chlorophylla in this lake. They based on a library of lacustrine domains to discover its predictive equations. The proposed approach is the core of a tool called LAGRAMGE which allows a user to provide domain knowledge to construct mathematical models of complex real-world ecological systems.

Neural networks are the most widely applied algorithms in the exploration of ecological data. (Reick, 2006) is another job of applying neural networks to environmental variables in order to predict time series. These are difficult to analyze due to several reasons such as uncontrollable environmental conditions, complexity and data sampling costs. (Reick, 2006) gave an example of this data from where they applied neural network models for zooplankton predictions to automate the learning process, so they proved that the major problem in this case is How to automatically stop the learning process.

The fuzzy logic (Klir, 1995) is a data mining algorithm that has also been present in the field of ecological data mining. (Chen, 2003) is an example of this application, from which the authors applied a fuzzy logic model with a hybrid global learning algorithm to explore and represent the relationships between stock and recruitment in different regimes for environmental management and fisheries management. To estimate the lack of uncertainty in the learning methods, they proposed a resampling approach based on a technique called bootstrap. This study was applied at two sites, southeast of Alaska in the US (Quinn, 1999), and the west coast of Vancouver Island in British Columbia, Canada. The proposed model has proved to be a useful tool for the analysis of stock recruitment to the fish population.

Classification of Ecological Images at Micro and Macro Scale

Analytical flow cytometry is a valuable research tool in marine science that helps to promote the composition, distribution and abundance of species in the oceans of the world using electronics to capture analog data to collect statistics Summaries for each impulse. (Wilkins, 2003) is a job that used neural networks to analyze the data of an analytical flow tool called CytoBuoy (Dubelaar, 1999) (Dubelaar, 2000). They went through a pre-processing process which consisted of: extracting the characteristics and then sampling pulses of variable length and the converts has a more compact representation. The next step in the pre-treatment was a separation of the particle size information and the global maximum pulse intensity using a discrete cosine transformation (Press, 1992), and finally they investigated the discrimination of different categories from the shape of the pulse alone by an algorithm of the principal components analysis(PCA) (Jolliffe, 1986). The resulting pretreatment data were used as inputs to the RBF (Specht, 1991) neural networks which proved to be a very good tool for analyzing large-scale ecological data.

(Robertson, 2003) presented another application of probabilistic neural networks, their approach consists in identifying the age of three species of fish based on thin layers of visible sagittal otoliths with transmitted light and on the number of opaque increments. This study was carried out on the species of Pagrus Auratus with 987 samples (Francis, 1992), the species of Acanthopagrus Butcheri with 913 samples (Morison, 1998), and species Macruronus Novaezelandiae with 1531 samples (Kalish, 1997)(Punt, 2001). The information was collected from the gray-level species images and was represented by 6 attributes as shown in the table 4:

Table 4. Summary of input variables used for learning neural networks (Robertson, 2003)

Category	Attributes	Type
Biological	Weight of Otolith (g)	Numeric
	Length of fish (cm)	Numeric
	Gender	Categorical
	Date of capture	Numeric
	Transect length (pixels)	Numeric
Signal	The first 21 Harmonics of the fast Fourier transform	Numeric

The results obtained were compared with the results obtained using the backpropagation neural networks presented in (Robertson, 1999) where they proved that the probabilistic neural networks improved the recognition of The age of the fish from their images, but they always remain inferior to the performance of human readers.

(Foody, 2003) discussed a general topic that is the application of neural networks for the classification of remote sensing data. They have introduced the application of multilayer neural networks, RBF neural networks and probabilistic neural networks. Then they gave as examples of these applications, the application of the neural networks to the data of the multi-spectral images acquired by an airborne thematic mapping sensor of an agricultural site in the United Kingdom. This dataset is presented in (Foody, 1997). They used 11 spectral wavebands for 600 pixels to detect the data set using an extraction technique using a stratified random sampling design, they extracted 100 pixels for each of the six main species grown in the Site studied. The results demonstrated a high efficiency of neural networks for the analysis of remote sensing data for agriculture.

Other Applications

(Salski, 2003) presented a state-of-the-art to show that application of fuzzy logic algorithms is a powerful tool for analyzing heterogeneous and imprecise ecological data. In this study, they presented a variety of works that used fuzzy logic for ecosystem modeling. There are some works that have implemented fuzzy logic approaches for the grouping of ecological data such as (Friederichs, 1996) which have grouped chemicals based on their ecotoxicological structure. (Piotrowski, 1996) is a study discussed in (Salski, 2003) where they applied fuzzy logic for spatial interpolation of geological data. The construction of knowledge-based models using fuzzy logic is also discussed in this paper from which they gave (Bock, 1998) as an example of such applications.

Qualitative reasoning is to construct knowledge-based models that capture the knowledge of the domain in order to analyze the functioning of the systems. (Bredeweg, 2003) discussed the application of such algorithms for ecosystem modeling. They have detailed the principle of qualitative reasoning, they have given some examples of application of this kind of algorithms to analyze the ecological data. (McIntosh, 2003) is a work discussed by (Bredeweg, 2003), it is one of the more recent work of applying qualitative reasoning for ecological data, McIntoch et al. have described a modeling language to address partial and imprecise ecological knowledge. (Salles, 2003) is a model development study to understand marine ecosystems, to restore proactive management actions by combining them with the predicted environmental variables.

(Giraudel, 2003) developed a methodology for a learning process of a non-supervised neural network that helps analyze the data set of upland forests at Winscosin in the US (Peet, 1977). In this study, the authors represented the data in a matrix of units in order to use it as input to train the self-organizing maps of the Kohonen neural networks, this technique proved a great efficiency to analyze the data of the ecosystems in forests.

Another algorithm is also known in the field of ecosystem modeling. Genetic algorithms have been very successful in modeling ecosystems in terms of number of publications, although they have only been applied since the 1990s. (Morrall, 2003) discussed the success of genetic algorithms for the analysis of ecological data by giving an overview on the principle of these algorithms and then presented some major works in the literature, such as (Ludvigsen, 1997) which used genetic algorithms to seek the optimal combination of bacterial phospholipid fatty acid biochemical parameters. And (Reynolds, 1999) who developed an approach based on genetic algorithms to generate the optimal parameters of an ecological data structure evaluation model.

Evolutionary algorithms are considered solutions for ecosystem modeling, which is summarized in (Whigham, 2003) where the authors presented the basic approaches to ecological modeling and evolutionary algorithms, and then illustrated the relationship between these two areas by citing work of applying evolutionary algorithms in real ecological problems. (Whigham, 1999) is one of the works discussed that have applied evolutionary algorithms to construct equations that can predict Chlorophyll-a in rivers. The use of evolutionary algorithms for prediction habitat density was a research topic presented by (Whigham, 2000) who developed classification rules based on a grammar of a genetic programming system.

When we talk about data mining, we talk about adaptive agents that are individuals of an algorithm that can adapt to several situations according to states defined in the system studied (Glass, 2008), and since ecological systems are known by their dynamic states, the adaptive agents take a good place in the modeling of the ecosystems. One of the works that proved this idea is that of Recknagel (Recknagel, 2003) who developed individual adaptive agents for microbial and terrestrial ecosystems. They proposed an approach for simulating the evolution of species abundance and succession in aquatic ecosystems of nine lakes based on adaptive agents.

One of the most recent work in exploring ecological data is presented by (Memmah, 2015) where they discussed the use of meta-heuristics for optimization of agricultural land. They presented 50 articles that applied different meta-heuristics, and they drew four main conclusions summarized in: the choice and success of meta-heuristics depends on the problems to be solved. For land use, (Memmah, 2015) claimed that for multi-stakeholder decision-making methods to be needed to optimize land use based on the hybridization of optimization methods and meta-heuristics, And by developing parallelization techniques.

CONCLUSION

Learning automatically performs tasks that humans perform well but difficult to specify algorithmically is how they are based on creating high-performance information processing systems. It refers to a system capable of automatically acquiring and integrating knowledge. The ability of systems to draw from experience, training, analytical observation and other means leads to a system that can continuously improve and thus show efficiency and effectiveness.

An automatic learning system usually begins with a certain knowledge and a corresponding knowledge organization so that it can interpret, analyze and test the acquired knowledge. Bio-inspired algorithms present a revolution in computer science. The scope of this field is really vast because, in relation to nature, computer problems are only a subset, opening up a new era to the next generation of computing, modeling and engineering, algorithms (Michalewicz, 2013).

Recently, the analysis, synthesis, and prediction of ecological data have been influenced by data mining methods. In this chapter, the importance of exploring ecological data for ecosystem modeling has been presented. Different studies have been discussed that have applied techniques for integrating data into ecosystem categories and levels of ecosystem complexity, inference of the data model to ecological processes and adaptive simulation and prediction of different ecological real-world data. Neural networks present the majority of ecological data mining applications. Bio-inspiration has also been very successful in the field of ecological data analysis.

REFERENCES

Abraham, A., Grosan, C., & Ramos, V. (2007). *Swarm intelligence in data mining* (Vol. 34). Springer.

Alpaydin, E. (2014). *Introduction to machine learning*. MIT Press.

Altınbilek, D. (1995). Water Resources and Environmental Management Plan for Mogan and Eymir Lakes. Final Report prepared by METU Civil Eng. Dept. to The General Directorate of Ankara Municipality Water and Sewage Administration (ASKI), Ankara, Turkey.

Anderson, P. R. (2006). Novel methods improve prediction of species' distributions from occurrence data. *Ecography*, *29*(2), 129–151. doi:10.1111/j.2006.0906-7590.04596.x

ASCE Task Committee on Application of Artificial Neural Networks in Hydrology. (2000). Artificial Neural Networks in Hydrology. II, BioComp Systems, I. (1998) NeuroGenetic Optimizer (NGO). Redmond, WA: Hydrologic Applications. *Journal of Hydrologic Engineering*, *5*(2), 124–137. doi:10.1061/(ASCE)1084-0699(2000)5:2(124)

Atanasova, N. (2006). Computational assemblage of ordinary differential equations for chlorophyll-a using a lake process equation library and measured data of Lake Kasumigaura. In *Ecological Informatics* (pp. 409–427). Springer. doi:10.1007/3-540-28426-5_20

Back, T. (1996). *Evolutionary algorithms in theory and practice: evolution strategies, evolutionary programming, genetic algorithms*. Oxford university press.

Baeza-Yates, R., & Ribeiro-Neto, B. (1999). Modern information retrieval (Vol. 463). ACM Press.

Binitha, S., & Sathya, S. S. (2012). A survey of bio inspired optimization algorithms. *International Journal of Soft Computing and Engineering*, *2*(2), 137–151.

Bishop, C. M. (1995). *Neural networks for pattern recognition*. Oxford University Press.

Blum, C., & Roli, A. (2003). Metaheuristics in combinatorial optimization: Overview and conceptual comparison *ACM Computing Surveys*, *35*(3), 268–308. doi:10.1145/937503.937505

Bock, W., & Salski, A. (1998). A fuzzy knowledge-based model of population dynamics of the yellow-necked mouse (Apodemus flavicollis) in a beech forest. *Ecological Modelling, 108*(1), 155–161. doi:10.1016/S0304-3800(98)00026-X

Bowden, G. J., Dandy, G. C., & Maier, H. R. (2003). An evaluation of methods for the selection of inputs for an artificial neural network based river model. In *Ecological Informatics* (pp. 215–232). Springer. doi:10.1007/978-3-662-05150-4_11

Bredeweg, B., Salles, P., & Neumann, M. (2003). Ecological applications of qualitative reasoning. In *Ecological Informatics* (pp. 15–47). Springer.

Brownlee, J. (2011). *Clever algorithms: nature-inspired programming recipes.* Jason Brownlee.

Burnham, K. P., Anderson, D. R., & Huyvaert, K. P. (2011). AIC model selection and multimodel inference in behavioral ecology: Some background, observations, and comparisons. *Behavioral Ecology and Sociobiology, 65*(1), 23–35. doi:10.100700265-010-1029-6

Cao, H. (2006). Hybrid evolutionary algorithm for rule set discovery in time-series data to forecast and explain algal population dynamics in two lakes different in morphometry and eutrophication. In *Ecological informatics* (pp. 347–367). Springer. doi:10.1007/3-540-28426-5_17

Carpenter, G. A., & Grossberg, S. (1987). ART 2: Self-organization of stable category recognition codes for analog input patterns. *Applied Optics, 26*(23), 4919–4930. doi:10.1364/AO.26.004919 PMID:20523470

Caruana, R., & Niculescu-Mizil, A. (2006). An empirical comparison of supervised learning algorithms. In *Proceedings of the 23rd international conference on Machine learning.* ACM. 10.1145/1143844.1143865

Chen, D. G. (2003). Classification of fish stock-recruitment relationships in different environmental regimes by fuzzy logic with bootstrap re-sampling approach. In *Ecological Informatics* (pp. 329–351). Springer. doi:10.1007/978-3-662-05150-4_17

Chon, T. S. (2006). Non-linear approach to grouping, dynamics and organizational informatics of benthic macroinvertebrate communities in streams by Artificial Neural Networks. In *Ecological Informatics* (pp. 187–238). Springer. doi:10.1007/3-540-28426-5_10

Cios, K. J. (2007). *Data mining: a knowledge discovery approach.* Springer Science & Business Media.

Dapper, T. (1998). *Dimensionsreduzierende Vorverarbeitungen für neuronale Netze mit Anwendungen in der Gewässerökologie*. Shaker.

Demuth, H., & Beale, M. (2000). Neural network toolbox user's guide. Academic Press.

Dimopoulos, I., Chronopoulos, J., Chronopoulou-Sereli, A., & Lek, S. (1999). Neural network models to study relationships between lead concentration in grasses and permanent urban descriptors in Athens city (Greece). *Ecological Modelling*, *120*(2), 157–165. doi:10.1016/S0304-3800(99)00099-X

Dimopoulos, Y., Bourret, P., & Lek, S. (1995). Use of some sensitivity criteria for choosing networks with good generalization ability. *Neural Processing Letters*, *2*(6), 1–4. doi:10.1007/BF02309007

Dorigo, M., & Blum, C. (2005). Ant colony optimization theory: A survey. Theoretical Computer Science, 344(2-3), 243–278. doi:10.1016/j.tcs.2005.05.020

Dorigo, M., Bonabeau, E., & Theraulaz, G. (2000). Ant algorithms and stigmergy. *Future Generation Computer Systems*, *16*(8), 851–871. doi:10.1016/S0167-739X(00)00042-X

Dorigo, M., Di Caro, G., & Gambardella, L. M. (1999). Ant algorithms for discrete optimization. *Artificial Life*, *5*(2), 137–172. doi:10.1162/106454699568728 PMID:10633574

Dorigo, M., & Gambardella, L. M. (1997). Ant colony system: A cooperative learning approach to the traveling salesman problem. *IEEE Transactions on Evolutionary Computation*, *1*(1), 53–66. doi:10.1109/4235.585892

Dubelaar, G. B. J., & Gerritzen, P. L. (2000). CytoBuoy: A step forward towards using flow cytometry in operational oceanography. *Scientia Marina*, *64*(2), 255–265. doi:10.3989cimar.2000.64n2255

Dubelaar, G. B. J., Gerritzen, P. L., Beeker, A. E. R., Jonker, R. R., & Tangen, K. (1999). Design and first results of CytoBuoy: A wireless flow cytometer for in situ analysis of marine and fresh waters. *Cytometry*, *37*(4), 247–254. doi:10.1002/(SICI)1097-0320(19991201)37:4<247::AID-CYTO1>3.0.CO;2-9 PMID:10547609

Elman, J. L. (1990). Finding structure in time. *Cognitive Science*, *14*(2), 179–211. doi:10.120715516709cog1402_1

Fayyad, U., Piatetsky-Shapiro, G., & Smyth, P. (1996). From data mining to knowledge discovery in databases. *AI Magazine*, *17*(3), 37.

Foody, G. M. (2003). Pattern Recognition and Classification of Remotely Sensed Images by Artificial Neural Networks. In *Ecological Informatics* (pp. 383–398). Springer. doi:10.1007/978-3-662-05150-4_20

Foody, G. M., & Arora, M. K. (1997). An evaluation of some factors affecting the accuracy of classification by an artificial neural network. *International Journal of Remote Sensing*, *18*(4), 799–810. doi:10.1080/014311697218764

Francis, R. I. C. C., Paul, L. J., & Mulligan, K. P. (1992). Ageing of adult snapper (Pagrus auratus) from otolith annual ring counts: Validation by tagging and oxytetracycline injection. *Marine & Freshwater Research*, *43*(5), 1069–1089. doi:10.1071/MF9921069

Friederichs, M., Fränzle, O., & Salski, A. (1996). Fuzzy clustering of existing chemicals according to their ecotoxicological properties. *Ecological Modelling*, *85*(1), 27–40. doi:10.1016/0304-3800(95)00009-7

Gevrey, M., Lek, S., & Oberdorff, T. (2006). Utility of sensitivity analysis by artificial neural network models to study patterns of endemic fish species. In *Ecological Informatics* (pp. 293–306). Springer. doi:10.1007/3-540-28426-5_14

Giraudel, J. L., & Lek, S. (2003). Ecological Applications of Non-supervised Artificial Neural Networks. In *Ecological Informatics* (pp. 49–67). Springer. doi:10.1007/978-3-662-05150-4_2

Glass, A., McGuinness, D. L., & Wolverton, M. (2008). Toward establishing trust in adaptive agents. In *Proceedings of the 13th international conference on Intelligent user interfaces*. ACM.

Glover, F. W., & Kochenberger, G. A. (2006). *Handbook of metaheuristics* (Vol. 57). Springer Science & Business Media.

Goethals, P. (2006). Development and application of predictive river ecosystem models based on classification trees and artificial neural networks. Ecological Informatics, 151–167. doi:10.1007/3-540-28426-5_8

Goldberg, D., Deb, K., & Korb, B. (1989). Messy genetic algorithms: Motivation, analysis, and first results. *Complex Systems*, *3*, 493–530.

Ha, K., Cho, E.-A., Kim, H.-W., & Joo, G.-J. (1999). Microcystis bloom formation in the lower Nakdong River, South Korea: Importance of hydrodynamics and nutrient loading. *Marine & Freshwater Research*, *50*(1), 89–94. doi:10.1071/MF97039

Hoang, H. (2006). Elucidation of hypothetical relationships between habitat conditions and macroinvertebrate assemblages in freshwater streams by artificial neural networks. In *Ecological Informatics* (pp. 239–251). Springer. doi:10.1007/3-540-28426-5_11

Hoang, H., Recknagel, F., Marshall, J., & Choy, S. (2001). Predictive modelling of macroinvertebrate assemblages for stream habitat assessments in Queensland (Australia). *Ecological Modelling, 146*(1), 195–206. doi:10.1016/S0304-3800(01)00306-4

Hoang, H. T. T. (2001). *Predicting Freshwater Habitat Conditions by the Distribution of Macroinvertebrates Using Artificial Neural Network*. University of Adelaide, Department of Soil and Water.

Hochachka, W. M., Caruana, R., Fink, D., Munson, A., Riedewald, M., Sorokina, D., & Kelling, S. (2007). Data-mining discovery of pattern and process in ecological systems. *The Journal of Wildlife Management, 71*(7), 2427–2437. doi:10.2193/2006-503

Holland, J. H. (1973). Genetic algorithms and the optimal allocation of trials. *SIAM Journal on Computing, 2*(2), 88–105. doi:10.1137/0202009

Hu, X., Shi, Y., & Eberhart, R. (2004). Recent advances in particle swarm. In Evolutionary Computation, 2004. CEC2004. Congress on (vol. 1, pp. 90-97). IEEE.

Jeong, K. S., Recknagel, F., & Joo, G. J. (2006). Prediction and elucidation of population dynamics of the blue-green algae Microcystis aeruginosa and the diatom Stephanodiscus hantzschii in the Nakdong River-Reservoir System (South Korea) by a recurrent artificial neural network. In Ecological Informatics. Springer. doi:10.1007/3-540-28426-5_12

John Lu, Z. Q. (2010). The elements of statistical learning: Data mining, inference, and prediction. *Journal of the Royal Statistical Society. Series A, (Statistics in Society), 173*(3), 693–694. doi:10.1111/j.1467-985X.2010.00646_6.x

Jolliffe, I. T. (1986). Principal component analysis. Springer Verlag.

Kalish, J. M., Johnston, J. M., Smith, D. C., Morison, A. K., & Robertson, S. G. (1997). Use of the bomb radiocarbon chronometer for age validation in the blue grenadier Macruronus novaezelandiae. *Marine Biology, 128*(4), 557–563. doi:10.1007002270050121

Karul, C., & Soyupak, S. (2003). A comparison between neural network based and multiple regression models for chlorophyll-a estimation. In *Ecological Informatics* (pp. 249–263). Springer. doi:10.1007/978-3-662-05150-4_13

Karul, C., Soyupak, S., Çilesiz, A. F., Akbay, N., & Germen, E. (2000). Case studies on the use of neural networks in eutrophication modeling. *Ecological Modelling*, *134*(2), 145–152. doi:10.1016/S0304-3800(00)00360-4

Karul, C., Soyupak, S., & Yurteri, C. (1999). Neural network models as a management tool in lakes. In *Shallow Lakes' 98* (pp. 139–144). Springer. doi:10.1007/978-94-017-2986-4_14

Kennedy, J. F. (2001). *Swarm intelligence*. Morgan Kaufmann.

King, R., & Brooks, S. P. (2004). Bayesian analysis of the Hector's Dolphin data. *Animal Biodiversity and Conservation*, *27*(1), 343–354.

Klir, G., & Yuan, B. Fuzzy sets and fuzzy logic (vol. 4). Prentice Hall.

Kohonen, T., Schroeder, M. R., & Huang, T. S. (2001). Maps, Self-Organizing. doi:10.1007/978-3-642-56927-2

Koza, J. R. (1992). *Genetic programming: on the programming of computers by means of natural selection* (Vol. 1). MIT Press.

Krink, T., Filipic, B., & Fogel, G. B. (2004). Noisy optimization problems-a particular challenge for differential evolution? In Evolutionary Computation, 2004. CEC2004. Congress on (Vol. 1). IEEE. doi:10.1109/CEC.2004.1330876

Kutner, M. H., Nachtsheim, C., & Neter, J. (2004). *Applied linear regression models*. McGrawHill/Irwin.

Lai, C., Doong, S., & Wu, C. (2009). Machine Learning. In *Wiley encyclopedia of computer science and engineering*. John Wiley.

Lek, S., Belaud, A., Baran, P., Dimopoulos, I., & Delacoste, M. (1996). Role of some environmental variables in trout abundance models using neural networks. *Aquatic Living Resources*, *9*(1), 23–29. doi:10.1051/alr:1996004

Lek, S., Delacoste, M., Baran, P., Dimopoulos, I., Lauga, J., & Aulagnier, S. (1996). Application of neural networks to modelling nonlinear relationships in ecology. *Ecological Modelling*, *90*(1), 39–52. doi:10.1016/0304-3800(95)00142-5

Ludvigsen, L. (1997). Correlating phospholipid fatty acids (PLFA) in a landfill leachate polluted aquifer with biogeochemical factors by multivariate statistical methods. FEMS Microbiology Reviews, 20(3-4), 447–460. doi:10.1111/j.1574-6976.1997.tb00329.x

Masters, T. (1995). *Neural, novel and hybrid algorithms for time series prediction*. John Wiley & Sons, Inc.

McIntosh, B. S. (2003). Qualitative modelling with imprecise ecological knowledge: A framework for simulation. *Environmental Modelling & Software, 18*(4), 295–307. doi:10.1016/S1364-8152(03)00002-1

Memmah, M. M., Lescourret, F., Yao, X., & Lavigne, C. (2015). Metaheuristics for agricultural land use optimization. A review. *Agronomy for Sustainable Development, 35*(3), 975–998. doi:10.100713593-015-0303-4

Michalewicz, Z., & Fogel, D. B. (2013). *How to solve it: modern heuristics.* Springer Science & Business Media.

Morison, A. K., Robertson, S. G., & Smith, D. C. (1998). An integrated system for production fish aging: Image analysis and quality assurance. *North American Journal of Fisheries Management, 18*(3), 587–598. doi:10.1577/1548-8675(1998)018<0587:AISFPF>2.0.CO;2

Morrall, D. (2003). Ecological applications of genetic algorithms. Ecological Informatics, 35–48. doi:10.1007/978-3-662-05150-4_3

Pao, Y. (1989). Adaptive pattern recognition and neural networks. Academic Press.

Peet, R. K., & Loucks, O. L. (1977). A gradient analysis of southern Wisconsin forests. *Ecology, 58*(3), 485–499. doi:10.2307/1938999

Pineda, F. J. (1987). Generalization of back-propagation to recurrent neural networks. *Physical Review Letters, 59*(19), 2229–2232. doi:10.1103/PhysRevLett.59.2229 PMID:10035458

Piotrowski, J. A., Bartels, F., Salski, A., & Schmidt, G. (1996). Geostatistical regionalization of glacial aquitard thickness in northwestern Germany, based on fuzzy kriging. *Mathematical Geology, 28*(4), 437–452. doi:10.1007/BF02083655

Premaratne, U., Samarabandu, J., & Sidhu, T. (2009). A new biologically inspired optimization algorithm. In *Industrial and Information Systems (ICIIS), 2009 International Conference on.* IEEE.

Press, W. H. (1992). *Numerical Recipes in C: The Art of Scientific Computing.* Cambridge Univ. Press.

Punt, A. E., Smith, D. C., Thomson, R. B., Haddon, M., He, X., & Lyle, J. M. (2001). Stock assessment of the blue grenadier Macruronus novaezelandiae resource off south-eastern Australia. *Marine & Freshwater Research, 52*(4), 701–717. doi:10.1071/MF99136

Quinn, T. J., & Deriso, R. B. (1999). *Quantitative fish dynamics*. Oxford University Press.

Recknagel, F. (2006). *Ecological Informatics–Scope*. Technique and Applications. doi:10.1007/3-540-28426-5

Recknagel, F. (2006). Artificial neural network approach to unravel and forecast algal population dynamics of two lakes different in morphometry and eutrophication. In *Ecological informatics* (pp. 325–345). Springer. doi:10.1007/3-540-28426-5_16

Recknagel, F. (2003). Ecological applications of adaptive agents. Ecological Informatics, 73–88. doi:10.1007/978-3-662-05150-4_5

Reick, C. H., Grünewald, A., & Page, B. (2006). Multivariate Time Series Prediction of Marine Zooplankton by Artificial Neural Networks. In *Ecological Informatics* (pp. 369–383). Springer. doi:10.1007/3-540-28426-5_18

Reynolds, J. H., & Ford, E. D. (1999). Multi-criteria assessment of ecological process models. *Ecology*, *80*(2), 538–553. doi:10.1890/0012-9658(1999)080[0538:MCAOEP]2.0.CO;2

Robertson, S. G., & Morison, A. K. (1999). A trial of artificial neural networks for automatically estimating the age of fish. *Marine & Freshwater Research*, *50*(1), 73–82. doi:10.1071/MF98039

Robertson, S. G., & Morison, A. K. (2003). Age Estimation of Fish Using a Probabilistic Neural Network. In *Ecological Informatics* (pp. 369–382). Springer. doi:10.1007/978-3-662-05150-4_19

Rumelhart, D. E., Hinton, G. E., & Williams, R. J. (1985). *Learning internal representations by error propagation. Tech. rep*. DTIC Document. doi:10.21236/ADA164453

Salles, P., & Bredeweg, B. (2003). Qualitative reasoning about population and community ecology. *AI Magazine*, *24*(4), 77.

Salski, A. (2003). Ecological applications of fuzzy logic. In *Ecological informatics* (pp. 3–14). Springer. doi:10.1007/978-3-662-05150-4_1

Schleiter, I. M. (2000). Prediction of running water properties using radial basis function self-organising maps combined with input relevance detection. In *Second International Conference on Applications of Machine Learning to Ecological Modelling*, Adelaide, Australia.

Schleiter, I. M., & ... . (2006). Modelling ecological interrelations in running water ecosystems with artificial neural networks. In *Ecological informatics* (pp. 169–186). Springer. doi:10.1007/3-540-28426-5_9

Schleiter, I. M., Borchardt, D., Wagner, R., Dapper, T., Schmidt, K.-D., Schmidt, H.-H., & Werner, H. (1999). Modelling water quality, bioindication and population dynamics in lotic ecosystems using neural networks. *Ecological Modelling, 120*(2), 271–286. doi:10.1016/S0304-3800(99)00108-8

Schleiter, I. M., Obach, M., Borchardt, D., & Werner, H. (2001). Bioindication of chemical and hydromorphological habitat characteristics with benthic macro-invertebrates based on artificial neural networks. *Aquatic Ecology, 35*(2), 147–158. doi:10.1023/A:1011433529239

Specht, D. F. (1991). A general regression neural network. *IEEE Transactions on Neural Networks, 2*(6), 568–576. doi:10.1109/72.97934 PMID:18282872

Storn, R., & Price, K. (1997). Differential evolution–a simple and efficient heuristic for global optimization over continuous spaces. *Journal of Global Optimization, 14*(4), 341–359. doi:10.1023/A:1008202821328

Sutton, R. S., & Barto, A. G. (1998). Reinforcement learning: An introduction (Vol. 1). MIT Press.

Tesauro, G. (1994). TD-Gammon, a self-teaching backgammon program, achieves masterlevel play. *Neural Computation, 6*(2), 215–219. doi:10.1162/neco.1994.6.2.215

Theodoridis, S., & Koutroubas, K. (1999). Feature generation II. *Pattern Recognition, 2*, 269–320.

Thomas, Fowler, & Hunt. (n.d.). *Programming Ruby 1.9: The Pragmatic Programmers' Guide, Pragmatic Bookshelf.* Tech. rep.

Toksari, M. D. (2006). Ant colony optimization for finding the global minimum. *Applied Mathematics and Computation, 176*(1), 308–316. doi:10.1016/j.amc.2005.09.043

Topchy, A., Jain, A. K., & Punch, W. (2004). A mixture model for clustering ensembles. In *Proceedings of the 2004 SIAM International Conference on Data Mining.* SIAM. 10.1137/1.9781611972740.35

Whigham, P. A. (2000). Induction of a marsupial density model using genetic programming and spatial relationships. *Ecological Modelling, 132*(2-3), 299–317. doi:10.1016/S0304-3800(00)00248-9

Whigham, P. A., & Fogel, G. B. (2003). Ecological applications of evolutionary computation. In *Ecological Informatics* (pp. 49–71). Springer. doi:10.1007/978-3-662-05150-4_4

Whigham, P. A., & Recknagel, F. (1999). Predictive modelling of plankton dynamics in freshwater lakes using genetic programming. Academic Press.

Wilkins, M. F., Boddy, L., & Dubelaar, G. B. J. (2003). Identification of marine microalgae by neural network analysis of simple descriptors of flow cytometric pulse shapes. In *Ecological Informatics* (pp. 355–367). Springer. doi:10.1007/978-3-662-05150-4_18

Wood, S. (2006). *Generalized additive models: an introduction with R*. CRC Press.

Chapter 3
Context of the Person in Social Networks

Abdelkrim Tabti
Dr. Tahar Moulay University of Saida, Algeria

Mohammed Djellouli
Dr. Tahar Moulay University of Saida, Algeria

ABSTRACT

In this chapter, the authors define the context of the person in social networks. Subsequently they introduce modeling and context of the development process of a person. Then they work on analyzing and feeling defined analysis technique, the sour feelings tweets and their characteristics, and method of how to recuperate data from Twitter by using API extraction.

INTRODUCTION

The various advances in IT have created the need for systems dependent on context. The purpose of these systems is to provide information which depend on the user's environment to improve its interaction with different systems they use every day.

social networks in the internet are web services that allow individuals to build a linked public or semi-public profile with a list of other profiles that requires bi-directional confirmation for the hacker, but some networks do not, these Unidirectional links are sometimes labeled as fans or subscribers, with these friends he has relationships and he shares with them information.

The notion of context was used in linguistics and psychology before being adopted in computing, but also has a distant origin and a long history in philosophy. Mobility has given an important dimension to the context that touched many areas of IT application as computer ubiquitous artificial intelligence, processing of natural language (cognitive computing), ... etc.

DOI: 10.4018/978-1-5225-7338-8.ch003

We can define the context as any information that can be used to characterize the situation of an entity. An entity is a place, person, or object that is considered relevant to the interaction between a user with social media. The context may include the location, the person's identity, the people around person, activities or products of interest.

In this chapter we first define the notion of context of a person, and then do a study on the sentiments analysis in micro-blogs by detailing different techniques existed in literature.

Social Network Analysis

Social network analysis is a process of quantitative and qualitative analysis of a social network. it measures and maps the flow of relationships and changes in the relationships between entities with knowledge. these simple and complex entities of the websites can be people, groups, organizations and nations. We can see different methods in the literature that help to understand the relationships that people establish between themselves through the study of the intensity of their interactions, both in the world of work and in their private social community.

The analysis of sentiment (or tonality), also called opinion mining, is a concept that is often mentioned but often misunderstood. It is the process of determining the emotional tone behind a series of words. This analysis is used to better understand the perception, opinions and emotions expressed in an online statement. The purpose of this section is to understand the sentiment analysis: what is it and what is it for?

The Uses of Sentiment Analysis

Sentiment analysis is extremely useful in social media it provides an overview of public opinion about certain topics. The standby tools make this process faster and easier than ever thanks to their real-time scanning capabilities. The uses of sentiment analysis are both vast and powerful. The ability to extract insights from social web data is a practice that is widely adopted by companies around the world. It has been shown that tone changes on social media correlate with changes in the stock market. For example, the Barack Obama administration used sentiment analysis to measure public opinion against various reforms and campaigns in preparation for the 2012 presidential elections. Being able to quickly understand and react to consumer attitudes has also been extremely helpful to Expedia's Canadian team, who has seen a surge in negative reviews of music used in one of their TV commercials.

The analysis of the feeling then led by the group revealed that the music used in their advertising became annoying after several broadcasts. Consumers turned to social media to express their dissatisfaction. A few weeks after the first broadcast, more than half of the social web discussions about the campaign were negative. Rather than resigning to failure, Expedia was able to respond in an informed and entertaining manner by releasing a new version of the ad that showed the culprit, a violin, being destroyed.

CONTEXTUAL UNDERSTANDING AND TONE

But the analysis of feeling remains an inexact science because the Human language is complex. Teaching a machine how to analyze grammatical and / or cultural nuances, slang and spelling mistakes that are common things online is a difficult process. Teaching a machine how the context can influence the tone is even more difficult.

Humans are relatively intuitive when it comes to interpreting the tone of a text. Take this sentence for example: "My flight was canceled. Great ! " Most of us will know that the person is sarcastic. We know that as a rule the delay or cancellation of a flight is an unpleasant experience. By applying this contextual understanding to this sentence, we can easily identify the associated negative feeling. Without contextual understanding, a machine that analyzes this sentence will take into account the word "Super" and identify it as a positive mention.

What Procedures Exist for Sentiment Analysis?

Human language evolves, so the dictionary used by machines to understand the feeling continues to evolve as well. With the growing use of social media, language is evolving faster than ever before. One of the possible methods is to use rules that help the software better understand how the context can impact the feeling. For example by taking all the words and phrases that imply a positive or negative feeling, and by applying rules that take into account the context and its impact on the feeling. The software can then know that the first part of the next sentence is positive and the second negative: "I want a burger too much. I am serious ! "

Predictions for the Future of Sentiment Analysis

Although it is difficult to speculate on the evolution of a relatively immature system, the majority agrees that the sentiment analysis must go beyond a two-dimensional scale: positive or negative. Just like the positions of policies that cannot always be described as right or left, there are certain feelings that cannot be placed on a mere barometer. In the future, to truly understand and capture the full range of human emotions that can be expressed by words, a more sophisticated multidimensional dimension is needed. Is it possible to measure skepticism, hope, anxiety, enthusiasm or lack of it? Until this is possible, sentiment analysis is and will remain one-dimensional.

Businesses will become increasingly aware of the different uses of sentiment analysis in their respective industries. This will contribute to the growth of the market for services and technologies to apply sentiment analysis to business practices (eg intelligence tools that help analysts and traders make better decisions). We will observe a turning point in the perception of sentiment analysis and its reliability. Users will become more familiar with the idea that it is difficult to replicate human performance with automatic text analysis.

The insights that can be obtained from the large amounts of information (millions of Tweets) will become more important than concerns about the relevance of the analysis of a single mention (a Tweet). Instead, the focus will be on methods to make the results interpretable and actionable.

MODELING OF A USER CONTEXT OF THE DEVELOPMENT PROCESS

It is Crucial to help the user to easily access the information that meets their specific needs. For over a decade, the design of the context of a person in information systems has become a major issue for improving the quality of services provided to users. The context of those built from social networks are then used in various systems such as personalization systems, adaptive systems, recommender systems, systems of behavioral analysis ... etc. Its application may interest search engines. E-Commerce. E-Learning digital libraries. Medicine, telecommunications, security etc .... The use of the context of a person in these systems involves the steps:

- Development context of users who require data collection on the trail of user activities and the use of machine learning techniques on these data (data mining) especially when we have to do with incomplete profiles or user information is inadequate.
- Representation of the context of users constructed that involves the structuring of data collected seen their quantity and diversity (the most popular activities, the most popular people, psychological characteristics, the most visited places ... etc.).

We can say that the context of the development process of a user from the social network is similar to any knowledge extraction process from data. We distinguish four main steps in this process: the collection of data, the structuring of data, data analysis and data representation.

Theory of the Five Major Personality Factors (Big Five)

The "Big Five" technique is one of the methods used to make the behavior or personality of the user, ie his psychological profile. It involves analyzing the five (5) major personality traits illustrated clatis [Figure] that come from bringing all the traits of a human being. Here are the 5 items of the Big Five:

- **Introvert or Extrovert:** An extroverted person is sociable, knows assertive, energetic and active (Kouloumpis, 2011).
- **Degree of Agreeableness:** A person with high agreeableness is selfless, sensitive, full of compassion. Modest and like the collective dimension in action.
- **Degree of Neuroticism:** A person with high neuroticism tend to experience negative emotions such as anxiety, tension. mood swings. Depression, emotional instability and to be very impulsive ... In contrast, with a low degree of neuroticism, one is emotionally stable, positive, good about yourself.

Figure 1. Development process in the context of a person

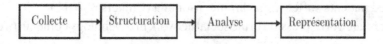

Figure 2. 5 major personality traits (Feldman, 2013)

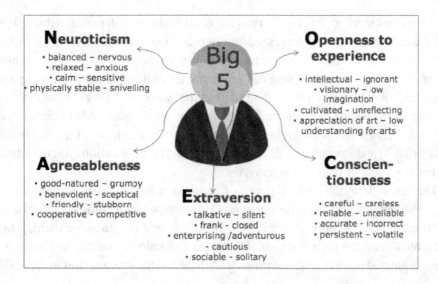

- **The Degree of Openness to Experience:** If it's high, the person is curious. imaginative, original, inventive, ingenious mind. bright and artistic trends.
- **Conscientiousness:** When a person has such character to a high degree, it's an organized person. effective, responsible, able to resist the impulse of the moment and invest in a task with relatively distant rewards.

We have seen that the area of analysis of context in social networks and wide so we said we work on sentiment analysis of tweets on the side if the person depressed or not.

THE DEPRESSION PSYCHOLOGY

Depression Research in Psychology

Depression is the fourth largest disease in the world and is in second place in 2020 according to statistics from the World Health Organization (Bartz, 2011) The main clinical symptom of depressed patients is sustainable depressed mood and lack of positive emotions . They prefer to be alone rather than with others. Moreover, most depressed patients suffer from chronic insomnia (Chikersal, 2015).

The research of depression in the social network in psychology comes in two types:

- One is to uncover the disciplines of a crowd of depressed users. (Bergman, 2003)
- The other is to scrutinize a particular case. (Khatoon, 2019)

Literature (Moreno, 2011) observed linguistic markers of depression through the collection of messages by depressed and non-depressed people Internet forum. It analyzes the text with LIWC a counting tool computer words, and shows that online writers use more depressed singular pronouns in the first person, but less plural pronouns, more negative emotion words but the words of 'less positive emotion. The literature (Khan, 2015) discusses the relationship between SNS behavior and depression levels based on events. It is established by the tools of questionnaires and statistics, and reveals that the results of the initial publications might indicate depressive levels of micro-bloggers. Also.

The research on the characteristics of depression in view of psychology found any reliable knowledge base for our study. However, when it comes to information analytical problems, only a simple statistical tools are designed for them, which undoubtedly limited their research. Therefore, a technique specific data mining to detect depressed users is designed in this study based on their results (Bergman, 2003).

Sentiment Analysis Techniques

As the cardinal symptom of depression is severe negative emotions and lack of positive emotions, sentiment analysis is the most important step in detecting depression. Sentiment analysis is the opinions and feelings of the users most of the texts they published (Khan, 2015). Recently, many advances have been made in sentiment analysis on Twitter data. This research includes two aspects:

- Independent analysis of the subject, namely the judgment of the polarity of tweets

Regardless of whether it is relevant to a subject. The main approaches Are based on hashtags, smilies and some abstract features (Guellil, 2015).

- Dependent analysis of the subject, namely judged polarity tweets

On the given subject. Feelings tweets are positive, negative or neutral, depending on not only the abstract characteristics but also dependent features of the target, which refer to the comments on the target itself and related things, which are defined as extended targets .

Research sentiment analysis on the texts is in the process of development. The Few studies have been made to solve problems in a specific field, although the analysis strategy is very different for different fields. For example, the sweat of depression tend to think about the "death", so it kind of words should be given special attention when building vocabulary. Micro-blogs are often written in a colloquial style, which also brings new challenges when establishing the linguistic rules in the proposed method.

The problem addressed in this topic is the analysis of feelings depending on micro-blogs. Inspired by the work in the literature (Jiang, 2011), the abstract features and dependent features of the target are taken into account. This study emphasizes the particularity of depression and content of micro-blog, and the entire model is specifically tailored to them. As shown in Figure 3 a sentiment analysis method is firstly proposed to use the vocabulary and artificial rules for calculating the inclination of each micro-blog FIG. (AT). The vocabulary and rules in human sentiment analysis method are constructed on the basis of French and English syntax rules, the special feature of depression and micro-blogging. Then, as shown in Fig. (B), a depression detection model is built on the basis of the method and 10 characteristics of depressed users from psychological research proposal. Finally, the meaning of each characteristic is analyzed and simplified. Model is proposed for application in micro-blog.

SENTIMENT ANALYSIS OF THE MICRO-BLOG CONTENT

The most direct expression of depressive mood is the content of micro-blog users, so the feelings of the analysis method in this section helps understand the polarity of each piece of micro-blog, which highlights the inclination depression reflected in the content. A vocabulary is built on the basis of **HowNet**And sentence structure patterns and calculation rules are derived according to Rules of French or English syntax. As described above, the feature of depression and micro-blogging pay particular attention to the whole process (Wang, 2013).

Building Vocabulary

The most essential feature of depression and micro-blogging is the use of words. A vocabulary for the detection of depression is built on the basis of HowNet A complete vocabulary of French and English words, as shown in the table (Chung, 2011).

HowNet contains most popular emotion words and degree modifiers. The degree of weight modifiers are quantified into six levels based on their intensities.**HowNet**is designed for the analysis of the general feeling. To make it to calculate the tilt by depression, several adjustments were made as follows:

Figure 3. Technical sentiment analysis suggest in this work (Jiang, 2011)

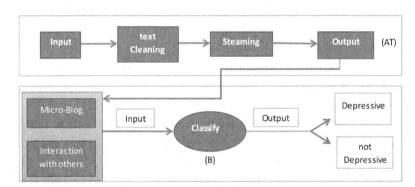

Table 1. Words in HowNet vocabulary (Dong, 2003).

2 Item		Num.	Example
Emotion	Positive	4566	pretty, love, like, happy, good
Words	Negative	4370	ugly, sad, depressed, unhappy, bad
Degree Modifiers		219	most(2), over(1.75), very(1.5), more(1), -ish(0.75),insufficient(0.5)

The words of emotion, the cyberspeaks, modal particles and negative words are added:

1. Depressed users tend to use more words of emotion, especially negative emotions. instruction words, some are not even for them. For example, "bye" is a neutral word for normal people, but this is a typical negative depressed for users. So these words typical emotion for depression are added.
2. Whereas cyberspeaks are widespread on the Internet, they are important in micro-blogs. Therefore, these words are also added, for example, "smilence" which means "smile silently" in the vocabulary.
3. Such as micro-blogs are often written in a colloquial style, modal particles often occurs in micro-blogs to express feelings directly, such as "ha-ha" and "a-ha", so these modal particles are also added to the vocabulary.

The part of speech of each word is recognized:

The proposed calculation rules are derived from French and English syntax rules are defined by the parts of speech. Thus, the part of speech of each word is recognized denied and also imported as an attribute in the vocabulary.

Language Construction Rules

The meaning of a sentence can not be decided only by the words she uses, but also by word order, called the sentence structure. For example (a bit unfortunate) "(very unhappy)," the two sentences share the same word, but have obvious different scope of how happy is the case, so the sentence structure should be taken into account in the process of calculating the polarity. Sentence structure could be described as linguistic rules, reflecting the complexity of the language in one aspect. In this section, the linguistic rules based on the proposed vocabulary are built taking into account the familiar style of the micro-blog.

FEELINGS AND DATA TWITTER

Data Set

Twitter contains all data and tweets that we will automatically recover with the Twitter API. These tweets were annotated automatically depressed and not depressed. Those containing both, have not been kept. The drive assembly is annotated into two classes (depressive and non depressive), while the test set is annotated by hand on two different classes (depressive, not depressed). For our experiments, we use only the depressed classes and not depressed in the test set. Each line of the file contains a single updates containing a maximum of 140 characters and can contain several sentences (according to length). Because tweets were collected directly on the twitter API, so they can contain HTML addresses, # hashtags and usernames (preceded by @).

1. The polarity of the updates (eg, $0 = 1 =$ depressed non depressive)
2. The id of the updates (eg, 4510)
3. THE date of the tweet (eg Sat May 16 23: 58: 44 UTC 2009)
4. the name of the user who posted the tweet (eg, robotickilldozr)
5. The text of the tweet (eg "I must think positive about.")

Characteristics of Tweets

We quickly present in this Subpart the main features of a tweet and Twitter.

Length

The maximum length of a message posted on Twitter is 140 characters. According Go et al. (Alec, 2009), the average length of tweets is 14 words or 78 characters on that corpus. This length is very Short unlike those used in other body for the classification of feelings (such as film reviews).

Availability of Data and Models of Language

The topics on Twitter are very diverse and twitter API allows to reap millions of messages. Indeed, the number of tweets posted each day is huge. Users can post messages from any location and with different devices. Please note that updates may contain spelling mistakes related to the use of smartphones and the restriction of characters. In addition, the register of language used may be familiar.

CONCLUSION

In this chapter we have defined the context of the person in social networks Subsequently we introduced modeling and context of the development process of a person, then we said we worked on analyzing and feeling defined analysis technique the sour feelings tweets and their characteristics.

To conclude, it is important to recognize that human communication does not only fall into three categories: positive, negative and neutral; the notion of feeling can be much more complex.

REFERENCES

Bartz, J. A., Zaki, J., Bolger, N., & Ochsner, K. N. (2011). Social effects of oxytocin in humans: Context and person matter. *Trends in Cognitive Sciences, 15*(7), 301–309. PMID:21696997

Bergman, L. R., Magnusson, D., & El Khouri, B. M. (2003). *Studying individual development in an interindividual context: A person-oriented approach.* Psychology Press.

Chikersal, P., Poria, S., & Cambria, E. (2015). SeNTU: sentiment analysis of tweets by combining a rule-based classifier with supervised learning. In *Proceedings of the 9th International Workshop on Semantic Evaluation (SemEval 2015)* (pp. 647-651). Academic Press. 10.18653/v1/S15-2108

Chung, C. K., & Pennebaker, J. W. (2011). Using computerized text analysis to assess threatening communications and behavior. *Threatening communications and behavior: Perspectives on the pursuit of public figures*, 3-32.

Dong, Z., & Dong, Q. (2003). HowNet: A Hybrid Language and Knowledge Resource. In *Proceedings of International Conference on Natural Language Processing and Engineering* (pp. 820-824). Los Alamitos, CA: IEEE Press.

Feldman, R. (2013). Techniques and applications for sentiment analysis. *Communications of the ACM, 56*(4), 82–89. doi:10.1145/2436256.2436274

Go, A., Bhayani, R., & Huang, L. (2009). Twitter sentiment classification using distant supervision. CS224N Project Report, Stanford, 1(12).

Guellil, I., & Boukhalfa, K. (2015, April). Social big data mining: A survey focused on opinion mining and sentiments analysis. In *Programming and Systems (ISPS), 2015 12th International Symposium on* (pp. 1-10). IEEE. 10.1109/ISPS.2015.7244976

Jiang, L., Yu, M., Zhou, M., Liu, X., & Zhao, T. (2011, June). Target-dependent twitter sentiment classification. In *Proceedings of the 49th Annual Meeting of the Association for Computational Linguistics: Human Language Technologies-Volume 1* (pp. 151-160). Association for Computational Linguistics.

Khan, A. Z., Atique, M., & Thakare, V. M. (2015). Combining lexicon-based and learning-based methods for Twitter sentiment analysis. *International Journal of Electronics, Communication and Soft Computing Science & Engineering*, 89.

Khatoon, M., Banu, W. A., Zohra, A. A., & Chinthamani, S. (2019). Sentiment Analysis on Tweets. In *Software Engineering* (pp. 717–724). Singapore: Springer. doi:10.1007/978-981-10-8848-3_70

Kouloumpis, E., Wilson, T., & Moore, J. D. (2011). Twitter sentiment analysis: The good the bad and the omg! *ICWSM*, *11*(538-541), 164.

Moreno, M., Jelenchick, L. Egan, K. Cox, E. Young, H., & Gannon, K. (2011). Feeling Bad on Facebook: Depression Disclosures by College Students on Social Networking Site. *Depression and Anxiety, 28*, 447-455.

Pang, B., & Lee, L. (2008). Opinion mining and sentiment analysis. *Foundations and Trends® in Information Retrieval, 2*(1–2), 1-135.

Wang, X., Zhang, C., Ji, Y., Sun, L., Wu, L., & Bao, Z. (2013, April). A depression detection model based on sentiment analysis in micro-blog social network. In *Pacific-Asia Conference on Knowledge Discovery and Data Mining* (pp. 201-213). Springer. 10.1007/978-3-642-40319-4_18

Chapter 4
Study on the Different Forms of Plagiarism in Textual Data and Image:
Internal and External Detection

Frederic Jack
University of Grenoble, France

ABSTRACT

We live in a world of information. It is everywhere, but it is sometimes difficult to find and know that data first. In today's digital society, it's easy to find texts to plagiarize. These texts may come from the internet, publishers, or other content providers. Plagiarism is considered a serious fault. Throughout the world, universities are making significant efforts to educate students and teachers, offering guides and tutorials to explain the types of plagiarism, to avoid plagiarism. Internet contains easy to get texts the people can use in their newsrooms simply using copy and paste. This chapter shows the various types of plagiarism and the different techniques of automatic plagiarism detection and related work that addresses the topic.

INTRODUCTION

The information filter (FI) also called multicast information (DSI), is one of the RI field of spots that controls large amounts of information dynamically generated. The aim is to deliver the items of information to the user in an intelligent manner, using a predefined user profile derived from its list and interests. Unlike RA, FI system is a model for long-term preferences of the user whose requests (information

DOI: 10.4018/978-1-5225-7338-8.ch004

needs built by the user) remain relatively static. It is applied to an incoming data stream (can be a message, an image, text ... ..etc.) That changes over time and simply indicates information that could be of interest to the user and delete the irrelevant from the inflows data. In this case the documents are delivered to the system one by one; the system then calculates their similarity to the user profile and decide the relevant ones (will be presented to the user) and those that are not. The classification of filtered documents is not expected since no algorithm can be applied to judge which document is more relevant than the other (McGregor, 2005).

The construction of an information filtering system (IFC) is more complex than building a model of ad-hoc research (MRA), as an SFI is built based on a huge database of profiles of data rather that on the basis of a simple query in a MRA. A generic IFC includes four basic components (see figure): (a) data analyzer; (B) filtering component; (C) a user model component; (D) a learning component (Si, 1997).

- The data analyzer (a): this component as input data elements (e.g., a message, an image, video ... etc.) From an information provider. The data elements are scanned and displayed in a suitable format (eg vector terms). This representation will be the input of the filter component (b).
- The user model (c) collects explicitly and / or implicitly information about users and their information needs, and built a model user (user profile). the model constructed will be the filter input component (b).
- The filtering component (b): it is the heart of an IFC for comparing the user profile with the data elements represented by the component (a) and decides whether a data item is relevant to the user or not (eg spam message or messages Ham). FI process is applied to a single data item (for example an incoming e-mail message). The user receives the relevant data item is the final and ultimate determinant of its relevance. his / her assessment is returned to the learning component.
- The learning component (d) is necessary to improve the filtering, due to difficulties in modeling user profiles and their changing information needs, filtering systems must include a process of learning to detect changes in the interests of users to update the user model and ensure the production of an effective user model.

In the Web exist many IR applications related to information filtering task. In our thesis, we discussed two most popular issues that are FI spam filtering and plagiarism detection.

Figure 1. Generic model of information filtering systems (FI)

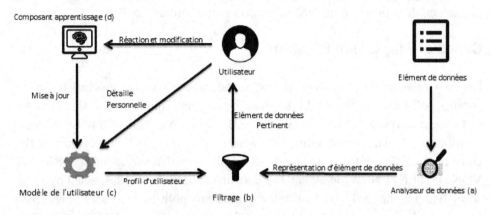

Textual Plagiarism Detection

In recent years, it has become very difficult to estimate the amount of text data created each month in the government, enterprises, institutions, or the amount of scientific publications in various fields of research. This resolution gave birth to a big problem called plagiarism that has received much attention from the academic and business communities. The basics of this are many and Crusaders. Recent advances in technology have facilitated plagiarism. For example, the Google search engine claims to index more than 3 billion web pages providing a wide variety of source texts on a wide range of topics in many different languages. Word processors have also become more sophisticated,

Instead of producing original work, some students and researchers prefer to directly take ideas, words or passages from someone else from books, encyclopedias, newspaper articles submitted by previous work of others or cheat many sites available on the internet recently, whether intentional or unintentional without putting it in quotes and / or without citing the source. Lancaster and Culwin say that plagiarism is theft of intellectual property, it is not only dishonest, but also an offense that can lead to sanctions. It is considered one of the biggest problems in publishing, science and education. (Potthast, 2010)

A study was conducted on 18,000 students made by McCabe shows that about 70% of students admit plagiarizing foreign documents (Werner, 1993). According to a new recent US study, published in the journal of academic ethics says that plagiarism had been paid before the arrival of today's digital age. In this study, 184 doctoral works published before 1994 and after 2012 were randomly selected from universities that put theses online. The result shows that over 50% of the manuscripts contain plagiarized passages. For these reasons the development of an automatic plagiarism detection tool has become a necessity (Potthast, 2010).

Cases of Plagiarism Popular

Recently, plagiarism phenomenon has spread, where he even touched the most popular politicians in the world designed by German ministers like the Minister of Defense, atypical KARL-THEODOR ZU GUTTENBERG who resigned after accusations plagiarism concerning the writing of his doctoral thesis in law at the University of Bayreuth (Bavaria). In 2014 also the defense minister URSULA VON DER LEYEN considered an heiress Angela Markel, was suspected by a site specializing in the analysis of written arguments by politicians to have plagiarized a number of passages in his dissertation of Medicine. Without forgetting also the Minister of Education and Research ANNETTE SCHAVAN who resigned in 2014 because the Düsseldorf University revoked his doctoral contains too many passages borrowed from others. In a country where the doctor title is a value, they do not joke with plagiarism.

Plagiarism

Plagiarism is derived from the Latin word "Plagiarius" meaning kidnapper. it is defined as the unlawful abuse of stealing thoughts, images, ideas or words from the original work of someone else or external source, in the same language or in another language and the presented as his own. (Zu Eissen, 2006) Often plagiarists modify or rewrite sections they copy so as to mask plagiarism. According to the behavior of plagiarism, we can distinguish several forms of plagiarism, such as:

- **The Verbatim Copy (Verbatim):** Is when someone uses the text as is, which involves copying sentences directly or pieces of sentence of the work of another person.
- **Paraphrase:** When the syntax of sentences copied is changed.
- **Plagiarism Secondary Sources:** Sources are cited, but taken from a secondary source (not added).
- **Plagiarism of Ideas:** Reuse of a thought / original idea (independent of the form) from a source. reuse of an original thought or idea (independent of the form) from a source.
- **Plagiarism Blunt (Author of Plagiarism):** Stealing the work of another and put another name.
- **Plagiarism With Translation:** This is to reuse the work of another person in another language using machine translation technology.

Figure 2. Taxonomy of plagiarism types

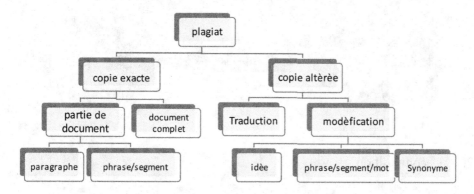

- **Plagiarism Synonymous With:** Copy the words of someone else and replace them with their synonyms.
- **Recycling Text (Self Plagiarism):** When an author reuses portions of his article already published in another article.

THE AUTOMATIC PLAGIARISM DETECTION

For the purpose of detecting whether a document is plagiarized or not, and identify different plagiarism cases, several techniques have been introduced that can be classified into two major families:

External Plagiarism Detection

When we compare a suspect document against a collection of external source documents (registration document), it is attempted to identify the sentences, paragraphs or ideas that have been copied. This is called external plagiarism detection.

The figure above clearly shows the general operation of external plagiarism analysis, given a set of original documents (documents can be source of plagiarism) "O" and a document "S" suspect the problem is find phrases pairs (P, Ps) as Po and Ps $\in$ O $\in$ S and what is "Ps" plagiarized Po The general principle of this family can be grouped into three main stages.:

1. Heuristic

This is a phase of finding a solution to reduce the size of source documents by choosing only documents which candidates are more likely to be sources of plagiarism.

Figure 3. External Plagiarism Detection

2.   Decomposition

This phase consists in cutting out the text into a set of fragment or sequence (which may be phrases, sequence of words, paragraphs, character set ... etc.)

3.   Analysis and Comparison

This step is to identify the plagiarized passages for each suspect document and source documents plagiarized each pass.

Procedure

The general structure of the technical following the principle that family is defined in the pseudo code:

Nickname II.7 Code: External Plagiarism Detection

{DC} subset of source documents that are likely to be sources of plagiarism
     {PP}: the list of plagiarizing passages of the suspect document with the source document of each passage; LS { }: list of suspect document fragment; LD { } list of candidate source document fragment;
     Sun: candidate document number i which is more likely to be a source of plagiarism (D SD { } $\in$

```
Entrance:
-   SD {} documents Source
-   S: Suspect paper
beginning
                / * // heuristic
     select DC} to {S from SD {}
              /* decomposition*/
```

```
For each new document to S
    For each document Di SD∈
                ←LS {} decompose (S)
                ←LD} {decompose (Di)
                ←PP PP {} {} + analyze and compare (LS {}, {}
LD)
    end
    End
Output: PP {}
```

ADVANTAGES AND DISADVANTAGES

- Able to demonstrate a paragraph or part of a document is copied.
- Requires external information such as original documents (designated by an expert) for comparison.
- Calculation time: the systems following this approach are time calculation because a comparison going to be performed between the suspect document and every original document.
- Quality result: effective because this approach is independent of the author's style.

EXTERNAL PLAGIARISM DETECTION TECHNIQUES

The techniques according to the external plagiarism detection principle are detailed below:

Detector Inverted Index

This detector was proposed by Kasprzak et al in (Clough, 2003):

1. Bag of Words Representation (Decomposition)

The authors selected as the word processor or text each will be converted to a list of words using the word bag method (see section).

2. The Construction of Inverted Index (Analysis)

The words are then joined by piece, we use overlapping sequences of several words. The pieces are then chopped by a hash function[1]. After, an inverted index is calculated by mapping the track ID in the list of structures containing the following attributes (the document identifier, the track sequence number, the first character of the song, and the last character of piece).

3.   Detection of Pieces Plagiarized (Comparison)

Calculating the inverted index is used to examine the suspect documents (the inverted index of its tracks is calculated in the same way as for the source documents). We seek the common ID into pieces for each pair (source document suspicious document). We discard the source documents with less than 20 bits in common with the suspect document.

For each pair of documents (source and suspect) with more than 20 songs in common, we test the passage between two each piece of base. If this passage contains less than 50 pieces in both the suspect document and the source document, then this passage is flagged as plagiarized.

Encoplot Detector

The detector has been proposed by Grozea et al in (Liu, 2006) based on the correspondence between the two sequences in linear time:

1.   Representation by N-Gram Characters (Decomposition)

We translate documents (source and suspect) to a list of units using the n-gram characters with $N = 16$.

2.   Ranking (Analysis)

In this phase a similarity matrix is calculated between the suspect document and the source document through a kernel function and a distance measurement. Then we classify the source documents in descending order according to their similarity to the suspect document. Finally we set a similarity threshold and we select the documents with a higher similarity threshold.

3.   Detection (Comparison)

In this step a technique called Encoplot is used where each pair (suspect document and paper source selected in the previous step) is studied in order to extract specific positions and lengths of the passages copied.

SCF Detector (Selection, Correspondence and Merger)

This detector is proposed by Chiara Basile et al in (Basile, 2009):

1.   Selection (Heuristic)

Each suspect documents, we first identify a small subset of source documents. After, we start by calculating a distance between each suspect document and a source document using the n-gram for representation. Then, for each suspect text 10 adjacent first source material ordered according to the distance are stored for later analysis.

2.   T9 Coding (Decomposition)

For the decomposition of the texts they used the T9 coding or alphabets are coded with a specific formula such letters {a, b, c} are encoded by 1 and {D, E, F} by 2 and so on each three successive letters. The new alphabet for encoding text is composed of 10 symbols: {0, 1, 2, ..., 9}. The symbol 0 is used for the new line and white space.

3.   Search Correspondence and Merging (Analysis and Comparison)

In this step we seek the common passages between each pair of documents (source and suspect) and we calculate their lengths. If the length exceeds a fixed threshold the channel is stored in a list. In the end a merger algorithm to bring together selected correspondence (the passages stored in the list).

PDLK Detector

This detector was proposed by Abdi et al in (Kasprzak, 2009) based on the language skills:

1.   Pretreatment (Decomposition)

This step is based on three functions: segmentation to transform documents into a set of sentences using sentence bag; disposal of empty words to expedite the processing of the system; Stemming to reduce the words to their roots.

2.   Similarity and Outlines (Analysis and Comparison)

This step will calculate the similarity between sentences the suspect document and the sentences of the source document. The authors used the semantic similarity and similarity of word order between sentences. Finally, the sentence pairs with greater than a threshold similarity are considered plagiarism and source of plagiarism.

Detector Base of Fuzzy Semantics

This technique was proposed by Gupta et al in (Potthast, 2011):

1.   Representation (Decomposition)

The authors tested the different techniques of natural language processing that exists in the literature for representing documents.

2.   The fuzzy Semantic (Analysis and Comparison)

For THE comparison between documents, a similarity method based on the semantics of fuzzy logic has been used to detect plagiarism source documents and plagiarized passages for each suspect document.

Internal Plagiarism Detection

When we compare the texts on a reference set of possible sources, the complication is to choose the right set. Unfortunately, now with the possibilities of the internet for plagiarists, this task becomes more complex to achieve because it requires a lot of computing time. For this Internal plagiarism detection has recently been introduced in 2006 by Meyer zu Eissen & Stein in 2006 (Zu Eissen, 2006). This internal plagiarism analysis is similar to the external analysis, but the source documents are not supported. This approach analyzes the suspect document, which does not take into consideration all references. For example we are dealing with a suspect documents "dq" the goal is to find phrases or passages "p" where "p" "dq" and "p" are plagiarized passages. $\in$

General Process

To manage the internal plagiarism detection task must detect plagiarized passages of a suspect paper exclusively with irregularities or inconsistencies in the document. Such inconsistencies or anomalies are mainly stylistic. methods of internal plagiarism detection are constructed to characterize the author's style then compare his style to the characteristics of the style of suspect documents "dq" to set a criterion to determine whether the style of the suspect document has changed enough to identify possible cases of plagiarism. For example, if a student copy a paragraph from the Web. It is possible that the student's writing style does not match the style of the paragraph copied. By identifying this difference, it is possible to say that the student plagiarized. The author's style can be analyzed in the document because every author in his own style (Uzuner, 2005).

Advantages and Disadvantages

The internal plagiarism detection task has received less attention than the external plagiarism detection because:

- She is unable to demonstrate that a paragraph or a document is copied part because there is no reference to compare.
- It is purely indicative and should be used in conjugation with human supervision.
- following this approach systems require little calculations to find the result.
- It is not convincing for the style of an author can change with time and a document to another.

Internal Plagiarism Detection Techniques

The various sensors internal plagiarism that exist in the literature will be detailed later:

Sensor Profile N-Gram

The entrance to this approach is the suspect documents "SD" only. The basic idea is to take passages from "SD" and compare them with the whole document "SD". For this function which quantifies the change of style in the document should be set to detect passages that are dissimilar with the entire document (the plagiarized passages). Stamatatos et al have used a copyright identification method called N-gram profile to detect the author's writing style in (MATALLAH, 2011). The different steps of this technique are detailed below:

1. Initially the passages and the entire document are converted to vectors using the n-gram character representation (see section) with $N = 3$, which shows the optimum value, and the coding by the normalized frequency weighting. The vectors are profiles either for the full text or text passages. Then, to calculate

the dissimilarity between the vector of each pass and the vector of the full text (two text with different sizes), the authors used the following formula:

$$nd_1\left(A,B\right) = \frac{\sum_{g\in P(A)}\left[\frac{2\left(f_A\left(g\right)-f_B\left(g\right)\right)}{f_A\left(g\right)+f_B\left(g\right)}\right]^2}{4\left|P\left(A\right)\right|} \quad \textbf{(II.22)}$$

$f_B\left(g\right)$: The normalized occurrence frequency of the N-gram g in the portion of the entire text B.

$f_A\left(g\right)$: Normalize the frequency of occurrence of the N-gram g in the text passage A.

| P (A) |: is the size of the text profile of the passage A.

2.   A The size window'll move throughout the text A step by step and movement is size S. In other words, every time the window moves to the right by S characters then the characters of The profile will be extracted. Then we can define the style change function (sc) of the text of the passage i in the document B as follows:

sc (i, B) = nd1 (wi, B), i = 1 ... | w | (II.23)

| W |: the total number of windows depends on the length of the text.

X: the length of the text which is equal to the number of characters in the full text.

3.   When a document is written by the same author, the function of the style change remains relatively stable. On the other hand, if the plagiarized sections, function, style change will be characterized by peaks that differ significantly from the average value. The existence of these peaks is indicated by the standard deviation. Let S be the standard deviation of the change in style function. If S is less than a predefined threshold, the document is not considered plagiarism. In the first international competition in 2009 on the plagiarism detection, this method was the first winner with precision and recall = 0.2321 = 0.4607.

Plag-Inn Detector

The inn-Plag detector was proposed by Tschuggnall (Berry, 2004) based on a syntactic function based on the grammar used by an author to identify the passages that might have been plagiarized. The assumption is that how to construct sentences is significantly different from one author to another because two phrases can be semantically equivalent, but syntactically different. For this, the authors proposed an idea to calculate the syntactical changes in the suspect document to quantify the differences between sentences and identify the plagiarized passages. This detector is modeled following the steps below:

1. Analyze the document and divide it into a set of sentences using an algorithm to detect the beginning and end of sentences.
2. Analyze each sentence according to grammar and words of each sentence will be tagg by labels that called morphosyntactic labeling. For this they used the analyzer stanford[2] which is an automatic processing tool open source language that extracts the grammatical features of a sentence and also generates a grammar tree for each sentence of the document.
3. In this step the distance between the shafts of each grammatical two sentences of SD is calculated and stored by using a distance measurement sensitive to structural changes[3].
4. To detect plagiarized sentences, the authors applied the standard Gaussian distribution algorithm on the comparison results of the previous phase.

Style Deviation Detector Bag-Of-Words Model

This approach was proposed in Oberreuter et al. (Ashworth, 1997) In the 3rd International Competition in plagiarism detection in 2011, she was the first winner with precision of 0.34 and recall of 0.31. The general operation of this technique is detailed in the following steps:

1. The entrance of this approach is a suspect documents "SD". Initially we remove special characters and numbers. All characters are united in lowercase and the text is converted to a list of words. In the final text will be indexed to a vector "V" where each component of the vector represents the frequency of words in the text.
2. This step allows the clustering of words in the document "C" groups. cC these groups are created through a sliding window size "m" or each group is composed of m words. After each group a frequency vector Vc is created that is used in

the next step to compare if a cluster has deviated from the style of the whole document. ∈

3.   3. The deviation of each cluster or segment c is calculated according to the frequency of the word W in the vector Vc and the cluster in the vector V of the entire document using the following function:

$$dc\ (Vc,\ V) = (II.24) \sum_{W \in V_c} \frac{\left|fréquence\left(W,V\right) - fréquence\left(W,V_c\right)\right|}{fréquence\left(W,V\right) + fréquence\left(W,V_c\right)}$$

dc (Vc, V): vector of the deflection Vc cluster c with respect to the vector V of the total document SD.

$fréquence\left(W,V\right)$: Frequency of the word W in the document c.

$fréquence\left(W,V_c\right)$: Frequency of the word W in the vector Vc cluster c.

4.   The style of the SD document is represented by the average of all branches calculated for each cluster (segment). The deviation of each cluster or segment c is compared to the SD document style and if DC (V, V) <style (SD), while the C-segment is considered plagiarized.

5.   In this study, the problem of the plagiarism detection was considered one of

6.   most forms publicized text reuse around us today. In particular, he

7.   demonstrated in this study how the plagiarism problem can be handled using various techniques and tools. However, there's still some weaknesses and shortages in these techniques and tools that will affect the success of the significantly plagiarism detection.

CONCLUSION

In this study, the problem of plagiarism detection was considered one of the most mediatized forms of text reuse around us today. In particular, it has been demonstrated in this study how the problem of plagiarism can be manipulated using different techniques and tools. However, there are still some weaknesses and shortages in these techniques and tools that will affect the success of plagiarism detection significantly.

REFERENCES

Ashworth, P., Bannister, P., & Thorne, P. (1997). Guilty in whose eyes? University students' perceptions of cheating and plagiarism in academic work and assessment. *Studies in Higher Education, 22*(2), 187–203. doi:10.1080/03075079712331381034

Basile, C., Benedetto, D., Caglioti, E., Cristadoro, G., & Esposti, M. D. (2009, September). A plagiarism detection procedure in three steps: Selection, matches and "squares". In *Proc. SEPLN* (pp. 19-23). Academic Press.

Berry, M. W. (2004). Survey of text mining. *Computer Review, 45*(9), 548.

Clough, P. (2003). *Old and new challenges in automatic plagiarism detection.* National Plagiarism Advisory Service. Retrieved from http://ir. shef. ac. uk/cloughie/ index. html

Currie, P. (1998). Staying out of trouble: Apparent plagiarism and academic survival. *Journal of Second Language Writing, 7*(1), 1–18. doi:10.1016/S1060-3743(98)90003-0

Kasprzak, J., Brandejs, M., & Kripac, M. (2009, September). Finding plagiarism by evaluating document similarities. In *Proc. SEPLN* (*Vol. 9*, No. 4, pp. 24-28). Academic Press.

Liu, C., Chen, C., Han, J., & Yu, P. S. (2006, August). GPLAG: detection of software plagiarism by program dependence graph analysis. In *Proceedings of the 12th ACM SIGKDD international conference on Knowledge discovery and data mining* (pp. 872-881). ACM. 10.1145/1150402.1150522

Lukashenko, R., Graudina, V., & Grundspenkis, J. (2007, June). Computer-based plagiarism detection methods and tools: an overview. In *Proceedings of the 2007 international conference on Computer systems and technologies* (p. 40). ACM. 10.1145/1330598.1330642

Matallah, H. (2011). *Classification Automatique de Textes Approche Orientée Agent* (Doctoral dissertation).

McGregor, S., & Harvey, I. (2005). Embracing plagiarism: Theoretical, biological and empirical justification for copy operators in genetic optimisation. *Genetic Programming and Evolvable Machines, 6*(4), 407–420. doi:10.100710710-005-4804-9

Potthast, M., Barrón-Cedeño, A., Eiselt, A., Stein, B., & Rosso, P. (2010). Overview of the 2nd international competition on plagiarism detection. *Proceedings of the 4th Workshop on Uncovering Plagiarism, Authorship, and Social Software Misuse*, 1-14.

Potthast, M., Eiselt, A., Barrón Cedeño, L. A., Stein, B., & Rosso, P. (2011). Overview of the 3rd international competition on plagiarism detection. *CEUR Workshop Proceedings*.

Si, A., Leong, H. V., & Lau, R. W. (1997, April). Check: a document plagiarism detection system. In *Proceedings of the 1997 ACM symposium on Applied computing* (pp. 70-77). ACM. 10.1145/331697.335176

Uzuner, Ö., Katz, B., & Nahnsen, T. (2005, June). Using syntactic information to identify plagiarism. In *Proceedings of the second workshop on Building Educational Applications Using NLP* (pp. 37-44). Association for Computational Linguistics. 10.3115/1609829.1609836

Werner, H. (1993). *Integration ausländischer Arbeitnehmer in den Arbeitsmarkt-Deutschland, Frankreich, Niederlande, Schweden (No. 992967913402676)*. International Labour Organization.

Zu Eissen, S. M., & Stein, B. (2006, April). Intrinsic plagiarism detection. In *European Conference on Information Retrieval* (pp. 565-569). Springer.

ENDNOTES

[1] Hash function is a particular feature that, from a given inputted, calculates a fingerprint for identifying rapidly, although incompletely, the initial data.

[2] The tool stanford analyzer is available in the website: http://nlp.stanford.edu/software/tagger.shtml#Download.

[3] The Levenshtein distance is a mathematical distance giving a measure of the similarity between two strings.

Chapter 5
Enrichment Ontology via Linked Data

Salvia Praga
Poland University of Worcester, Poland

ABSTRACT

The automatic construction of ontologies from texts is usually based on the text itself, and the domain described is limited to the content of the text. In order to design semantically richer ontologies, the authors propose to extend the classical methods of ontology construction (1) by taking into account the text from the point of view of its structure and its content to build a first nucleus ontology and (2) enriching the ontology obtained by exploiting external resources (general texts and controlled vocabularies of the same domain). This chapter describes how these different resources are analyzed and exploited using linked data properties.

INTRODUCTION

In the last years, the Linked Data paradigm has found a huge application when combined with the publication of data with liberal licenses. The Open Data Movement, which aims to release huge data sets often from local government authorities, embraced the Linked Data technologies and best practices to publish a plethora of different interlinked data sets.

Roughly speaking, a bunch of data published with an open license is intended to be freely available to everyone to use and republished without restriction from copyright, patents or other restrictions. Where Open Data meets Linked Data, we have Linked Open Data1. The Linked Open Data movement has experienced exponential

DOI: 10.4018/978-1-5225-7338-8.ch005

growth in term of published data sets. Within four years, the number of published data sets has grown from 12 to 295 (Jentzsch, 2011). With all this development of linked data and semantic web, ontologies still later, we've come out with this idea "using these data to enrich an ontology "first, we must know the process of ontology enrichment which include ontology learning.

Ontology Learning

- Ontology learning is the process of acquiring (constructing or integrating) an ontology.
- (Semi-) automatically. The acquisition of ontologies can be performed through three.
- Major approaches: (Petasis, Karkaletsis, Paliouras, Krithara, & Zavitsanos, 2011).
- By integrating existing ontologies. The integration process tries to capture commonalities among ontologies that convey the same or similar domains, in order to derive a new ontology.
- By constructing an ontology from scratch or by extending (enriching) an existing.
- Ontology, usually based on information extracted from domain-specific content.
- By specializing a generic ontology, in order to adapt it to a specific domain. Ontology learning is not simply a replication of existing work under a different name.
- It adds novel aspects to the problem of knowledge acquisition:
- Ontology learning combines research from knowledge representation, logic, philosophy, databases, machine learning, natural language processing, image/audio/video analysis, etc.
- Ontology learning in the context of the Semantic Web must deal with the massive and heterogeneous data of the World Wide Web and thus improve existing approaches for knowledge acquisition, which target mostly small and homogeneous data collections. (Petasis, Karkaletsis, Paliouras, Krithara, & Zavitsanos, 2011)
- Substantial effort is being put into the development of extensive and rigorous evaluation methods in order to evaluate ontology learning approaches on welldefined tasks with well-defined evaluation criteria.

Ontology Enrichment

Ontology enrichment is the process of extending an ontology, through the addition of new concepts, relations and rules. It is performed every time that the existing domain knowledge is not sufficient to explain the information extracted from the corpus or linked data in our case.

RELATED WORKS

The purpose of this section is to discuss state-of-the-art

ASIUM

One of the first system on this field2, the main idea is Learns terms, synonyms, concepts and hierarchical relations from unrestricted text corpora, based on syntactic analysis. It employs machine learning (hierarchical clustering) in order to learn concept hierarchies, with manual supervision by the domain expert. (D & C, 1999).

Text-To-Onto (Maedche, 2000)

Text-to-Onto3 is an ontology learning environment for learning non-taxonomic conceptual relations from text embedded in a general architecture for semi-automatic acquisition of ontologies. It supports as well the acquisition of conceptual structures such as mapping linguistic resources to the acquired structures. The proposed approach uses shallow text processing methods to identify linguistically related pairs of words. In addition, an algorithm for discovering generalized association rules analyses statistical information about the linguistic output. The purpose of this step is to derive correlations at the conceptual level between the newly obtained concept and the concepts that are already defined in the taxonomy. On the other hand, the discovery algorithm determines support and confidence measures for the relationships between these pairs, as well as for relationships at higher levels of abstraction. It also uses the background knowledge from the taxonomy in order to propose relations at the appropriate level of abstraction.

According to the authors, the evaluation showed that though their approach is too weak for fully automatic discovery of non-taxonomic conceptual relations, it is highly adequate to help the ontology engineer with modelling the ontology through proposing conceptual relations. Therefore, much work remains to be done in terms of i) How to approach the naming and the categorization of relations into a relation hierarchy and ii) How to deal with ontological axioms.

DODDLE II (Yamaguchi, 2001)

DODDLE II, the extended version of DODDLE, acquires both taxonomic and nontaxonomic conceptual relationships, exploiting WordNet and domain-specific texts with the automatic analysis of lexical co-occurrence statistics, based on the idea that a pair of terms with high frequency on co-occurrence statistics can have non-taxonomic conceptual relationships. The taxonomic relationship acquisition module does spell match between the input domain terms and WordNet4. The spell match links these terms to WordNet resulting in a hierarchically structured set of all the nodes on the path from these terms to the root of WordNet. The non-taxonomic relationship learning module extracts the pairs of terms that should be related by some relationship from domain-specific texts, analyzing lexical co-occurrence statistics, based on Word Space that is a multidimensional, real-valued vector space where the cosine of the angle between two vectors is a continuous measure of their semantic relatedness. To evaluate the system, some case studies have been done in the field of law. A major issue with this approach is that it relies

on WordNet to obtain the taxonomic relations. This is because of the limited domain coverage of WordNet and lack of semantic knowledge represented in it. Therefore, many of the obtained relations can be missed because they are not defined in WordNet.

OntoLearn (Velardi, 2001)

This system has been developed with the purpose of improving human productivity in the process that a group of domain experts accomplishes in order to find an agreement on i)the identification of the key concepts and relationships in the domain of interest and ii) Providing an explicit representation of the conceptualization captured in the previous stage. OntoLearn employs a set of text-mining techniques to extract relevant concepts and concept instances from existing documents in the Tourism domain, arrange them in subhierarchies, and detect relations among such concepts. The produced sub-hierarchies are placed under the appropriate nodes in WordNet manually by the ontology engineer.However, as stated by the authors, structuring terms in sub-trees significantly reducesmanual work, because only term.

RelExt (Schutz, 2005)

RelExt is a system capable of automatically identifying relevant triples (pairs of concepts connected by a relation) over concepts from an existing ontology (from the football domain). It works by extracting relevant verbs and their grammatical arguments (terms) from a domain-specific text collection and computing corresponding relations through a combination of linguistic and statistical processing. For the linguistic annotation, the authors used the SCHUG-system (Buitelaar, 2003), which provides a multi-layered XML format for a given text, specifying dependency structure along with grammatical function assignment, phrase structure, part-of-speech and lemmatization (including decomposition, which is useful in particular for German where compound nouns are often used). For the statistical processing, the authors performed several computations on the extracted data, starting from relevance ranking, and cross-referencing relevant nouns and verbs with the predicate-argument-pairs, to computing co-occurrence-scores in order to construct triples that are specifically used in the football domain. To evaluate the system, the authors measured its performance against a gold standard that they constructed to benchmark different parameters. Specifically, they divided up the corpus into 4equally sized sub-corpora of 300 documents, from which they used one sample for benchmark construction.

Enrichment of WordNet by Extracting Semantic Relationships From Wikipedia

The presented approach is used to identify lexical patterns that represent semantic relationships between concepts in an on-line encyclopedia (Wikipedia5). These patterns are then applied to extend an existing ontology (WordNet 1.7) with hyperonymy, hyponymy, holonymy and meronymy relations. The followed procedure consisted of the next steps: Entry sense disambiguation: this step consists in pre-processing the Wikipedia definitions and associating each Wikipedia entry to its corresponding WordNet synset, so the sense of the entry is explicitly determined.

Pattern extraction: for each entry, the definition is processed looking for words that are connected with the entry in Wikipedia by means of a hyperlink. If there is a relation in WordNet between the entry and any of those words, the context is analyzed and a pattern is extracted for that relation.

Pattern generalization: the patterns extracted in the previous step are compared with each other, and those that are found to be similar are automatically generalized. Identification of new relations: the patterns are applied to discover new relations other than those already present in WordNet. Experimentally, the precision of relationships depends on the degree of generality chosen for the patterns and the type of relation. Generally, it was around 60–70%for the best combinations proposed. (Ruiz-Casado, M. Alfonseca, & Castells, 2007).

Figure 1. The BOEMIE bootstrapping process

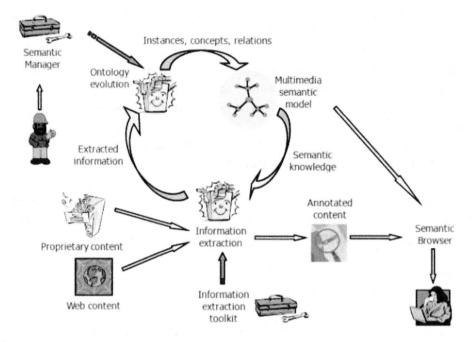

BOEMIE

BOEMIE Combines an ontology-based information extraction (OBIE) engine based on machine learning, with an inference engine, in order to extract "primitive" concept instances from multiple modalities, which are then fused and interpreted (through abdicative reasoning) to form instances of "composite" and more abstract concepts. (Paliouras, Spyropoulos, & Tsatsaronis)

Enriching an Ontology with Multilingual Information

It is a system that automatically localize ontologies, providing translations across different natural languages. The main features of this tool are the following:

1. It uses a translation mining service to obtain from different linguistic resources
2. the possible translations of each ontological label. A compound label is translated using
3. a compositional method that searches candidate translations of each lexical component
4. and then builds a translation using lexical templates. (Mauricio Espinoza).

5.   It uses a disambiguation method that ranks the possible translations of each
6.   ontology label. A gloss overlap scoring mechanism is used to calculate the similarity
7.   between two senses.

Ontology Enrichment and Automatic Population from XML Data

The method is to enrich and populate an OWL ontology for the integration of XML data. Basic mapping rules and advanced mapping rules are defined by users and can be reused for other conversions and populations of ontologies. The RDF rules can be used to automatically extract from XML schemas some elements that can be converted in order to help users during the mapping. (Christophe CRUZ, 2008) The principle of this solution consists in annotating and linking various levels which are the semantic level (OWL schema) and the schematic level (XML schema). This method is articulated in two steps.

The first step relates to the formalization of "mapping" rules between an XML schema and an OWL XML schema. The "Mapping" rules make it possible to enrich an existing ontology of domain from concepts and relationships conceptually present in XML schemas. This can be realized by a machine. Semantically it will not be richer than the XML schema. Actually, a rich semantic mapping cannot be done by a machine for the moment.

In addition, an ontology makes it possible to link the concepts and the relations from several schemas by amalgamating the attributes of common entities with the help of an identical semantic.

Using Social Media for Ontology Enrichment

The proposed approach exploits social media7 tags, which are crawled from existing social media applications, similarity measures, the DBpedia8 knowledge base, disambiguation algorithm and other heuristics to enrich existing ontologies with new semantic information. It considers the LT4eL domain ontology on computing that was developed in the Language Technology for eLearning project.9

It contains 1002 domain concepts, 169 concepts from OntoWordNet and 105 concepts from DOLCE Ultra lite. The connection between tags and concepts is established by means of language-specific lexicons, where each lexicon specifies one or more lexicalizations for each concept. A crawler that uses APIs provided by the social networking applications is used to get information about users, resources and tags. The crawler extracts links to resources from social media applications such as Delicious, YouTube and Slide share together with the tags used to classify the resources and information about the social connections developed inside these

Web sites. On the other hand, during the enrichment process, similarity measures such as term cooccurrence and cosine similarity are employed to identify tags that are related to the lexicalization of concepts already existing in the LT4eLdomain ontology. To identify relations among the existing LT4eL concepts and new concepts derived from the tags, a background ontology (DBpedia) is used. Several heuristics are employed to discover taxonomic relations, synonyms and new relations explicitly coded in DBpedia. To evaluate the proposed methodology, three different ontologies (i.e. the LT4eL computing ontology, a manually enriched ontology which takes the LT4eL one as basis, and an automatically enriched ontology) were used and compared (Monachesi & Markus, 2010)

Ontology Concept Enrichment via Text Mining (Wang, 2010)

The proposed approach by Wang et al., focuses on enriching the vocabulary of the ontology from domain-relevant documents. For each candidate concept, they measure the similarity between its context and the contexts of the concepts that are defined in the ontology. Then, they use the k-nearest neighbor algorithm to rank the final results and get the top pairs of closest concepts. In order to test the proposed ontology enrichment solution, the authors used a set which contained 530 concept names and 191 test synonyms. Promising results have been obtained compared to existing WordNet-based similarity measures. However, as stated by the authors, additional experiments need to be carried out in order to validate the effectiveness of the proposed solution.

Ontology Enrichment Using Semantic Wikis and Design Patterns

This approach addresses the task of ontology enrichment by exploiting the large amount of structured information available in semantic wikis. The proposed solution makes use of ontological design patterns to guide the semiautomatic enrichment process and regular Expressions or predefined values in the automatic enrichment process. (MARIUS GEORGIU, 2011)

Enrichment Ontology via Linked Data

We've seen some approaches about enrichment ontology in previous section, with different methods from extraction text, semantic relation Wikipedia, semantic wikis, our approach is a little different because our sources knowledge is linked data, as we can see in figure 2 The 10th International Semantic Web Conference October 23-27 2011 in Bonn, Germany, ISWC turns 10 years old and they showed a tag cloud

Figure 2. 2 Enrichment Ontology via linked data (EOLD System architecture)

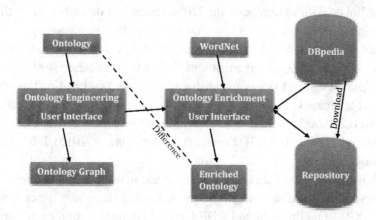

of the abstracts submitted in 2001 versus the tag cloud of the abstracts submitted 2011. Not surprising, the word "data" appears much larger, the word "ontology" has maintained its size, the word "web" has almost disappeared while the word "query" appears now and barely appeared 10 years ago.

Ontology not change, unlike data and query has increase, question is Can we really use "query "and "data" to enrich an ontology? The main idea about our approach is

Figure 3. From ISWC2011 the abstracts submitted in 2001 vs 2011

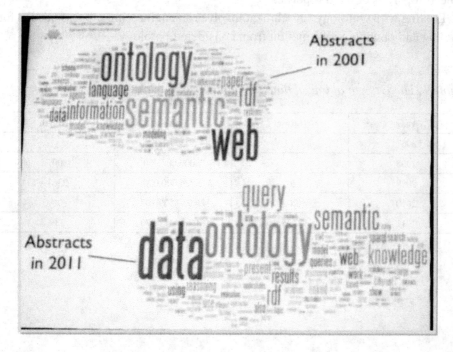

Enrichment ontology via linked data, as we can see in table 1 (Jentzsch, 2011) the growth of linked data in numbers, the DBpedia dataset describes more than 3.64 million things, out of which 1.83 million are classified in a consistent ontology, including 416,000 persons, 526,000 places, 106,000 music albums, 60,000 films, 17,500 video games, 169,000 organizations, 183,000 species and 5,400 diseases. The DBpedia data set features labels and abstracts for these 3.64 mil-lion things in up to 97 different languages; 2,724,000 links to images and 6,300,000 links to external web pages; 6,200,000 external links into other RDF datasets, 740,000 Wikipedia categories, and 2,900,000 YAGO2 categories. (dbpedia.org, 2013), DBpedia is king of knowledge sources.

The EOLD uses these data and wordNet to add new Concepts and relationships to ontology. These data stores can be queried using their own query language - SPARQL (SPARQL Protocol and RDF Query Language, pronounced "sparkle"). SPARQL is a W3C12 standard, e.g. if we want to add new superclass to class (person), DBpedia returns three term (Human, People, Self) All of these words can be superclass to class person.

To solve this problem, we're using WordNet. Our research is about adding annotation comment (rdfs:comment) with three different languages(English, French, German), these comment can help us with (WordNet hyponyms, synonym) to choose only one superclass. Adding new relations or properties is based on query. Our research work allows to find properties in DBpedia, in table 2 we will show you all the existing properties of class person in DBpedia. These properties can be objectProperties or dataProperties.

Dealing with Ontology Enrichment involves an engineering process needed for reading and obtaining information from considered ontology.

Table 1. The Growth of linked data in Numbers

Year	Dataset	Triples	Growth
2007	12	500000000	
2008	45	2.000.000.000	300%
2009	95	6.726.000.000	236%
2010	203	26.930.509.707	300%
2011	295	31.634.213.770	33%

Table 2. All properties of class person

Properties
deathPlace
deathDate
birthPlace
birthDate
individualisedPnd
influencedBy
party
child
award
restingPlace
board
philosophicalSchool
notableIdea
nationality
restingPlacePosition
stateOfOrigin
militaryBranch
birthYear
deathYear
influenced
almaMater
occupation
birthName
ethnicity
residence
deathCause
education
Pseudonym
birthYear
deathYear
Influenced
almaMater
electionDate

CONCLUSION

In this chapter we have surveyed state-of-the-art approaches/systems that have attempted to address this issue, we explained how we can use linked data as source of knowledge, we start by introducing ontology enrichment and ontology learning, in second section we present relevant work, the last section represents our research and also the architecture of EOLD our research is based on linked data specifically DBpedia.

REFERENCES

Faure, D., & Nedellec, C. (1999, May). Knowledge acquisition of predicate argument structures from technical texts using machine learning: The system ASIUM. In *International Conference on Knowledge Engineering and Knowledge Management* (pp. 329-334). Springer. 10.1007/3-540-48775-1_22

Heath, T., & Bizer, C. (2011). Linked data: Evolving the web into a global data space. *Synthesis Lectures on the Semantic Web: Theory and Technology, 1*(1), 1-136.

Maedche, A., & Staab, S. (2000, August). Discovering conceptual relations from text. *ECAI, 321*(325), 27.

Georgiu, M., & Groza, A. (2011). Ontology enrichment using semantic wikis and design patterns. *Studia Universitatis Babes-Bolyai, Informatica, 56*(2).

Espinoza, M., Gómez-Pérez, A., & Mena, E. (2008, June). Enriching an ontology with multilingual information. In *European Semantic Web Conference* (pp. 333-347). Springer.

Monachesi, P., & Markus, T. (2010, May). Using social media for ontology enrichment. In *Extended Semantic Web Conference* (pp. 166-180). Springer.

Paliouras, G., Spyropoulos, C. D., & Tsatsaronis, G. (2011). Bootstrapping ontology evolution with multimedia information extraction. In *Knowledge-driven multimedia information extraction and ontology evolution* (pp. 1–17). Springer Berlin Heidelberg. doi:10.1007/978-3-642-20795-2_1

Petasis, G., Karkaletsis, V., Paliouras, G., Krithara, A., & Zavitsanos, E. (2011). Ontology population and enrichment: State of the art. In *Knowledge-driven multimedia information extraction and ontology evolution* (pp. 134–166). Springer Berlin Heidelberg. doi:10.1007/978-3-642-20795-2_6

Ruiz-Casado, M., Alfonseca, E., & Castells, P. (2007). Automatising the learning of lexical patterns: An application to the enrichment of wordnet by extracting semantic relationships from wikipedia. *Data & Knowledge Engineering*, *61*(3), 484–499. doi:10.1016/j.datak.2006.06.011

Schutz, A., & Buitelaar, P. (2005, November). Relext: A tool for relation extraction from text in ontology extension. In *International semantic web conference* (pp. 593-606). Springer. 10.1007/11574620_43

Velardi, P., Fabriani, P., & Missikoff, M. (2001, October). Using text processing techniques to automatically enrich a domain ontology. In *Proceedings of the international conference on Formal Ontology in Information Systems-Volume 2001* (pp. 270-284). ACM. 10.1145/505168.505194

Wang, Q., Gauch, S., & Luong, H. (2010). Ontology concept enrichment via text mining. In IADIS international conference on internet technologies & society (pp. 147-154). Academic Press.

Yamaguchi, T. (2001). Acquiring conceptual relations from domain-specific texts. *Proceedings of the IJCAI 2001*.

Chapter 6

Big Data and Privacy State of the Art

Amine Rahmani
University of Algiers 1 Benyoucef Benkhadda, Algeria

ABSTRACT

The phenomenon of big data (massive data mining) refers to the exponential growth of the volume of data available on the web. This new concept has become widely used in recent years, enabling scalable, efficient, and fast access to data anytime, anywhere, helping the scientific community and companies identify the most subtle behaviors of users. However, big data has its share of the limits of ethical issues and risks that cannot be ignored. Indeed, new risks in terms of privacy are just beginning to be perceived. Sometimes simply annoying, these risks can be really harmful. In the medium term, the issue of privacy could become one of the biggest obstacles to the growth of big data solutions. It is in this context that a great deal of research is under way to enhance security and develop mechanisms for the protection of privacy of users. Although this area is still in its infancy, the list of possibilities continues to grow.

INTRODUCTION

The progress of new information technology and knowledge discovery allowing large scale pervasive surveillance over massive data sets had raised the need to such techniques permitting this technology to get more advanced without compromising privacy of users. Nowadays, privacy has been one of the most enduring issues associated with Big Data rising and digital electronic information spreading. There is a growing concern over information privacy. The world of privacy does

DOI: 10.4018/978-1-5225-7338-8.ch006

not rely only on avoiding observation or hiding personal matters and relationships, but it is more than that, it means the ability of sharing information selectively and not publicly. Every day, oceans of data are being collected over the planet using wireless sensors, and intelligent devices. These data are partly sensitive, some of the data are more sensitive than others. Other parts of the data can be considered as sensitive in some cases while not in other cases. People and researchers may have confused between anonymity and privacy. They may seem the same in context, but in reality they are quite different. One's shopping habits are private information but not anonym while authorship of a political tract are anonym data but not private. However, privacy preserving domain is not limited only on sharing information without revealing sensitive knowledge about it, but even more, it expands to the protection of users' rights, the ability to make intimate personal decisions without government interference is considered to be a privacy right, as is protection from discrimination on the basis of certain personal characteristics. This chapter offers a general overview about privacy preserving concepts and techniques focusing on ones used often in Big Data. The remainder of this chapter is addressed to the presentation and discussion of privacy in context, the debates of cybersecurity and privacy, and the presentation of general introduction of different techniques used to maintain privacy of users.

Context of Privacy

In the light of the advancement of Big Data, information technology had become a general threat to privacy. Privacy concerns had raised in the last few years opening new doors and challenges to scientific especially with the developing of such complex and advanced techniques of data mining. The promise of Big Data Analytics is, at first time, to offer information that can be used for good purposes for both individuals and societies. In fact, taking a closer look, we can realise that data mining had been developed in order to allow moving from information about individuals to generalizations that apply to broad classes. That means that data mining in practice should not pose any privacy risk. The real problem resides in the infrastructure used to support it. The more the data is complete and accurate the better are the results. Having complete, comprehensive and accurate data is what causes the raising of privacy issues. In other words, privacy issues rely on the misuse of existed data and not analytical algorithms. This section is addressed to the discussion of the context and outlines of the word "privacy".

A standard definition of privacy in dictionaries is often "freedom from unauthorized intrusion". However, according to the most of privacy laws, it is a concept that is only applied to "individually identifiable data". Regarding to these two definitions, we can define privacy in two extremities. One is that good data is the one gives us an accurate and complete knowledge without revealing any identifiable information about individuals. Meanwhile, in the other extreme, any improvement in our knowledge about individuals could be considered as an intrusion. Even though, data sets represent general information about group of individuals so there is no escape from the fact that analysing it can improve our knowledge about specific persons which requires to measure both knowledge gained and ability of relating these last to specific individuals.

Identifiability of Data

According to HIPAA, an individually non-identifiable data is a data "that does not identify an individual and with respect to which there is no reasonable basis to believe that the information can be used to identify an individual". That means for regular analytical process, the rate of risk of identification on disclosed data must be quite small in either cases alone or in combination with other information. A good example of that is the one given by Latanya Sweeny in (Sweeny, 2002) where she had presented an example of shared medical data without containing names and addresses in the U.S. These data, once it is combined with publicly available voter registrations that contain other information such as birthdays and genders could easily reveal specific information leading to identify persons and their medical records. As a result of that, a new phenomenon had seen the light that consists of preventing the identification of persons by combining multiple sources. It is often known as K-Anonymity. It is built on basic idea that a specific identifiable information could identify a group of k individuals and not specific one. That is to say that identifiable information had to be common on k individuals so that it does not reveal any information about one specific person among them. This idea have been used for long time. Census Bureaus have used it to publish aggregate data containing count of individuals under specific criteria rather than information about individuals. It is basically a statistical based approach. Apparently, this approach had shown some critical drawbacks in case of disclosure of data by combining multiple contingency tables resulted from aggregate data. The problem of combination of data mining techniques for cumulative disclosure of multiple tables rest the biggest problem that compromises privacy. For that, statistical disclosure limitation had attracted a lot of attentions among researchers. Consequently, a bunch of techniques have been developed allowing measurement of risk of identifying individuals within datasets. A set of these measurements interest by data value in which it consists of evaluating data utility without identifiers. The other part of techniques consist of providing metrics that measure the percentage of individuals that a particular well-equipped adversary could identify. These last assume that an adversary knows that some individuals are almost surely in the sample, and that this sample comes from a restricted dataset. Also, another assumption about the adversary is that he has a good estimation about sensitive and non-sensitive information. The second set of techniques consist of measuring the number of individuals an adversary can identify. However, there is many formal definitions of the concept anonymity that privacy tries to reach against different disclosure techniques. We mention from it two principal definitions quoted and cited in (Vaidya, 2006):

Definition 1: for two records I_1, and I_2 that belong to two different individuals. For a given data X. I_1 and I_2 are said to be p-indistinguishable if for every polynomial-time function $f:I \rightarrow \{0,1\}$

$$|Pr \{f(I_1)=1|X\} - Pr \{f(I_2)=1|X\}| \leq p \tag{1}$$

Where $0<p<1$

This definition does not prevent us from learning sensitive information. Instead, it only defines a measure that sensitive information X is tied more closely to a specific individual rather than another.

Definition 2 in this definition quoted from (Chawla, 2005), the data is presented as 'n' unlabelled points in high dimension space '$IR^{d'}$'.

Let 'y' be any real database (RDB) point and $\delta_y = ||q-y||_2$, we say the 'q' (c, t)-isolates 'y' if and only if B (q, c

δ_y) contains fewer than 't' points in the RDB, that is,

$$| B(q, c \delta y) \cap RDB| < t \tag{2}$$

In other words, if a data point 'y' has 't' close neighbours then the anonymity is ensured. The closeness of neighbours is defined according to a privacy threshold 'c' and how close the adversary's estimated point 'q' to 'y'. The function B denotes the ball of radius 'r' around 'y'. This idea still true independently of how strength is the adversary and his strategy – either by generating a region believing that 'y' will fall in or by estimating an exact point 'q'

Intrusiveness of Disclosure

Defining and measuring identifiability of information can be done offering broad definitions. Meanwhile, finding an exact definition of intrusiveness of information is much harder. Some information can lead explicitly to intrusive disclosure while others need conjunction with different kind of information. Releasing some data, such as date of birth, poses only a minor annoyance if it is released alone. But combining it with other information such as names or social numbers can identify individuals. Measuring intrusiveness of data is still an evolving new domain of research. For now, this measurement is evaluated independently for each domain. In each case, intrusiveness is measured by amount of sensitive data that is revealed to an adversary. Therefore, as it is a new open domain, there are several proposals in the literature measuring privacy according to intrusiveness of disclosed data. But it stay proposals rather than effective solutions.

Bounded Knowledge

This is one of the most known and used measures. It consists of introducing uncertainty in order to establish a good protection of privacy. It measures the ability of an adversary to estimate sensitive values starting from disclosed data. It uses a well-defined metric allowing measuring uncertainty of data using differential entropy h (A) of a random variable A. this metric is defined in equation 3 bellow

$$\prod (A) = 2^{- \int_{\Omega_A} f_A(a) \, log_2 \, (f_A(a)) \, da} \tag{3}$$

Where ΩA is the domain of A. is this case the privacy $\prod (A)$ is equal to 0 if the exact value of A is known. Otherwise, the adversary could know only that the data is in range of width α ($\prod (A) = \alpha$). This metric was proposed and applied in (Agrawal, 2001) to evaluate a noise addition scheme. However, this metric has a drawback. That is what if the adversary had already some knowledge about sensitive values. In that case, the real concern is how much this knowledge is improved. For that, equation 3 was extended to a conditional privacy that is shown in equation 4.

$$\prod (A|B) = 2^{- \int_{\Omega_{A,B}} f_{A,B}(a,b) \, log_2 \, (f_{A|B=b}(a)) \, dadb} \tag{4}$$

This metric had shown good usefulness not only in noisy disclosed data but in other kind of privacy schemes. In (Chiang, 2005), the authors had used conditional entropy to evaluate disclosure from distributed protocols. Their system consists of securing the data over secured distributed protocols consisting of set of linear equations that combine noise with real data.

Need to Know

This is not a real metric, rather than that, it is a rule. It consists simply to restrict which data should be disclosed for which purpose. A good example of that is the

European Union Privacy Guidelines who specifies that disclosure of data must be for governments' uses or a transaction from owner himself:

Member States shall provide that personal data may be processed only if:

1. *The data subject has unambiguously given his consent; or*
2. *Processing is necessary for the performance of a contract to which the data subject is party or in order to take steps at the request of the data subject prior to entering into a contract; or*
3. *Processing is necessary for compliance with a legal obligation to which the controller is subject; or*
4. *Processing is necessary in order to protect the vital interests of the data subject; or*
5. *Processing is necessary for the performance of a task carried out in the public interest or in the exercise of official authority vested in the controller or in a third party to whom the data are disclosed ; or*
6. *Processing is necessary for the purposes of the legitimate interests pursued by the controller or by the third party or parties to whom the data are disclosed, except where such interests are overridden by the interests for fundamental rights and freedoms of the data subject which require protection under Article 1 (1).[1]*

This is often applied in privacy preserving domain by developing approaches allowing disclosure only needed data. Such approaches use data mining classifiers, some of them release only classification model while others offer the ability of classify without revealing any information.

Protection From Disclosure

This is related more to a specific field in privacy preserving, it is privacy preserving data mining that we will discuss later on in this chapter. Sometimes, certain data are strictly proscribed to be revealed so that any knowledge about it is considered as too sensitive. In privacy preserving data mining, it is possible to develop such techniques allowing limitation of what data is inferred from results. Even though, with controlling of what results are released, data mining still a domain that consists of inherently resulting knowledge. Combining that knowledge with some other information available to the adversary can easily compromise confidentiality of sensitive information. Measuring privacy disclosure can be simply done through probability distribution of private values of confidence individuals meeting certain rules. Combining this with estimated values of prior knowledge of an adversary about attributes of antecedents of the rules, we can estimate privacy risk of disclosure.

What is difficult in this case is how to decide either the risk value is acceptable or not. Is that if the risk estimation outweighs the reward, this will decrease efficiency of mining process? Many approaches have been proposed in this part. It has the purpose of removing confident rules from the output rather than protecting it. In (Atallah, 1999), the authors had proved that the problem of minimizing changes on data while maintaining confidentiality of rules to be NP-hard. They had also presented a heuristic algorithm and demonstrated limits of amount of modification needed. This work was lately extended adding unknown values to the data in (Saygin, 2001).

Indirect Disclosure

Such techniques of determining privacy risks inside data mining define data as three classes: public, sensitive, and unknown to the adversary. These techniques are developed on principle that disclosure is a black-box classifier (an adversary consists of classifying instances and not look inside the classifier itself). This idea can be clearly observed in (Kantarğlu, 2004) using Bayes classification error rate. Assume we have a data set $(x_1, x_2 \ldots x_n)$ that we want to classify it into m classes. For any classifier C:

$$x_i \to C(x_i) \in \{0,1 \ldots m-1\}, i=1,2 \ldots n \tag{5}$$

The accuracy of C is defined as follows:

$$\sum_{i=0}^{m-1} \Pr\left\{C\left(x\right) \neq i | z = i\right\} * \Pr\left\{z = i\right\} \tag{6}$$

Where z defines a sensitive data. A good example of that let's consider n samples $X = (x_1, x_2 \ldots x_n)$ from a 2-point Gaussian mixture. $(1-\varepsilon) N(0,1) + \varepsilon N(\mu,1)$. The technique consists of generating sensitive data $Z = (z_1, z_2 \ldots z_n)$ where $z_i = 0$ if x_i is sampled from $N(0,1)$ and $z_i = 1$ if x_i is sampled from $N(\mu,1)$. In this problem, there are roughly ε n samples generated from $N(\mu,1)$ and $(1-\varepsilon)$ samples from $N(0,1)$ for n samples. Consequently, the total number of misclassified samples can be approximately equal to:

$$n (1 - \varepsilon) \Pr \{C(x) = 1 \mid z = 0\} + n\varepsilon \Pr \{C(x) = 0 \mid z = 1\} \tag{7}$$

Dividing the last equation by n we get the fraction of misclassified samples:

$$(1 - \varepsilon) \Pr \{C(x) = 1 \mid z = 0\} + \varepsilon \Pr \{C(x) = 0 \mid z = 1\} \qquad (8)$$

This gives us an overall measure of possibly misclassified instances of X across C but not a measure for specific instances.

However Kantarğlu and his friends discuss several problems. Many cases had been presented and analysed. What if we define an input containing both public and unknown data? If the training set is compound on only known values (public and sensitive), this will give the adversary no additional knowledge about sensitive values. Which is the purpose. But in reality, this is much different. The training data will be unknown, or at least partially unknown, for the adversary. This will in a way or another reveal sensitive data, *"even though the adversary does not have complete information as input to the classifier"*, (Kantarğlu, 2004). In another issue, the same authors at the same paper had presented an experimental approach that proves that such classifier which takes public data as input and discloses only non-sensitive knowledge can indirectly help the adversary to deduce sensitive information starting form analysis of disclosed one.

A final question that poses a considerable challenge is that the publicly available data contains already valuable information that many users consider it private. So if these information are revealed through a data mining process, can that be considered as privacy violation? Vaidya and his colleagues continue answering that in (Vaidya, 2006). If the disclosed data made the access to it easier, the answer is yes. Although, if the access to disclosed data is hard as the public records, the answer is not clear.

Privacy vs. Cyber-Security

Recently, there is a growing interest of privacy issues and its relation with security aspects. Lot of people may have a conflicts between these two fields because of the common concepts they hold inside. Cyber-security is a discipline that seeks to improve policies of using computers and data. It counts often on six major techniques classes that are: identification and authentication, authorization, availability, confidentiality, integrity, and non-repudiation. In other words, cyber-security refers to all the practices that consist of ensuring that the data will not be accessed and processed by unauthorized users. Its main aim is to enforce what we call "provably secure". Nowadays, reaching practically provable security is limited in few specific fields. The goal of cyber-security is to permit reaching it in larger domains.

While data security consists of ensuring a reliable and available data to only authorized users using basic facets including collecting only needed information, keeping it safe, and destroying any useless one. Privacy relies often on different definition. It is suitably defined as the appropriate use of data. That is to say that even with good security systems without failure, privacy might always be in risk. Violation of privacy does not remain on security breaks only, indeed, it can be caused from misuse of trusted parties. Many cases in real world have been conducted. Such company uses data of their customers for business improvements, but is this use appropriate? At such level, this company can sold, disclose or rent volumes of personal data of its customers without getting any approvals. A clear and simple example, lately, we all heard about Facebook had bought WhatsApp or even Microsoft had bought Nokia. In these cases, bought companies must reveal all their data to the buyers including clients' database containing personal information. The questions that should be asked here, are all clients of the old company trust the new one? Otherwise, are all users of WhatsApp uses trustfully Facebook? Users of Nokia phones, do they prefer Android based smartphones or Windows phone? If not, is this considered as privacy violation?

As discussed in previous section of this chapter, another point of difference can be touched as privacy can be compromised using data fusion and integration of external publicly information. So that even when developing highly provably secure systems. Publicly available data of other fields still out of control. Data mining is getting powerful each day which make full privacy much harder to be reached. Therefore, security policies can be expressed mathematically programmable language while privacy policies are difficult to be modelled because of the presuppositions and preferences of human beings that have greater diversity than the useful scope of assertions about computer security.

However, privacy and security may share same concept of confidentiality, but in reality there is a slightly difference between the two fields. Confidentiality of privacy is often applied on users' right to safeguard their personal data from being collected, monitored, inappropriately processed, and freely disseminated and sold to third parties. Meanwhile, confidentiality in security is offered as service to secure communications and companies' data from outside accesses but this means that companies' employees are still able to view and process personal data of clients. When security companies talk about security assurances of such systems they are asserting that today technological design features of that system will prevent attacks from violating pertinent security policies in it even tomorrow. Privacy assurances are much more precarious. Giving privacy assurances means to give promises that not-yet-invented applications that will be accessed to not-yet-invented sources of data using not-yet-invented powerful algorithms will be enable to violate privacy of tomorrow. That is to say, security deals with tomorrow's threats against today's platforms while privacy must deal with tomorrow's threats against tomorrow's platforms that include not just hardware and software but more complex sources of data and powerful algorithms.

Security engineers and computer scientists work from the basis of a formal policy for security, in order to describe explicitly their aims they had developed and design new ways to formalise this policy in purely technical means. However, as privacy concerns is attract more attentions. There is a growing attention of researches for articulation of privacy policy. Researches are tackling major challenges of aligning privacy regulations and policies with software specifications including formal languages for better expression of policies; tools to reason about conflicts, inconsistencies, and ambiguities; methods allowing the analysis and refine policies into measurable system specifications in order to permit control and monitor over the time; formalisation of privacy restrictions using audit and accountability systems; and privacy compliance in Big Data.

TECHNIQUES AND ALGORITHMS

Today, privacy preserving is a highly active domain of research. Many works have been done, others are still in progress in order to ensure an efficient protection of users' privacy, especially in the fact of losing the control of data by its owners once it accesses to big data services. These techniques can be classified in three major classes: cryptography protocols, anonymization and de-identification, and access control. This section is addressed to the discussion of some existed works within the domain.

Homomorphic Cryptography

Cryptography is a science that consists of transforming any kind of data, termed plaintext, into incomprehensible sets of provably random bits. These sets do not need for protection. It can be stored in Big Data services, sent promiscuously to both confident and non-confident parties. If it is generated using precise mathematical equations, it is useless for them. Before the coming of Big Data, cryptography algorithms were developed in purpose of protecting confidentiality of data in communications and storage processes. Recently, it has been expended to reach other features and needs. Recent cryptographic protocols developed for Big Data have been designed for complex goals reside principally in the ability of delegating computations to untrusted computers. This kind of cryptography is often known as *"Homomorphic cryptography"*.

Probabilistic Encryption

this kind of cryptography had been entered for first time by Goldwasser in 1984 in order to cover the major drawbacks that classical approaches had shown as they present deterministic algorithms. In their paper, Goldwasser et al. had presented a scheme that is based on computational complexity theory and therefore the intractability of some problems in number theory, such as factoring or deciding quadratic residuosity with respect to composite modulo. Deterministic algorithms have several drawbacks that comes from the fact that such plaintext m is always encrypted to one and only one ciphered text c. instead, probabilistic encryption uses randomness within encryption process which offers for single plaintext m multiple ciphered texts c1...cn. Indeed, the right key can decipher all the ciphered texts to the original text m.

Therefore, deterministic algorithms can be transformed into random algorithms introducing the notion of randomness by extending each plaintext using random strings of bits of length l that should be chosen largely sufficient. Even though, probabilistic algorithms still be more secured comparing to deterministic ones.

Public-Key Cryptography

A public-key scheme φ is a tuple (KeyGen, Enc, Dec) of probabilistic polynomial time algorithms.

1. **KeyGen:** Is a key generation algorithm that takes a security parameter k and generates pair of keys (*Pk, Sk*) where *Pk* refers to public keys and *Sk* refers to the secrete key. Both keys are of length at least equals to k and this last can be determined by *Pk*, and *Sk*.
2. **Enc:** Refers to the encryption algorithm that takes as input public key *Pk* and a message *m* from the message space (M) then it outputs a ciphered text *c* from ciphered texts space (C). In some references, they denote $c \leftarrow Enc_{Pk}(m)$ to describe an encryption algorithm when the used public key is known while in others they denote Enc (*m*) if the used public keys are unknown.

Figure 1. Schematic representation of deterministic cryptography vs. probabilistic cryptography

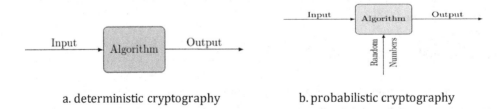

a. deterministic cryptography   b. probabilistic cryptography

3. **Dec:** Refers to the decryption process which is, without loss of generality, a deterministic algorithm that takes the secret key *Sk* and ciphered text *c* to produce the original corresponding text *m*. we denote $m := \text{Dec}_{Sk}(c)$

However, we may, the definition above, describe public-key schemes as probabilistic algorithms. We can find some classic schemes that are deterministic schemes such as RSA.

Homomorphic Encryption

A public-key encryption scheme is said to be *Homomorphic* if for all *k* and (*Pk*, *Sk*) from output of KeyGen (*k*); it is possible to define groups M, C so that:

- The plaintext M space and all ciphered texts results of Enc are elements of C.
- For each *m1*, *m2* ∈ M, and *c1*, *c2* ∈ C, if *m1*= Dec (*c1*) and *m2*=Dec (*c2*) then this holds that Dec (*c1*c2*) = *m1*m2*.

Where the group operations * is carried out by M and C.

In other words, homomorphic encryption is a scheme that allows execution of operations on encrypted texts without need to decrypt it. It is a typical public-key scheme with additional efficient algorithm (Eval) allowing computation of sum or/and product of two messages given public keys and encryption of the messages without leaking any information about original plaintexts.

The message space (M, *) is a finite (semi-) group. If this group is additive group, the cryptographic scheme is called *Additive Homomorphic Cryptosystem*. Else, the scheme is called *Multiplicative Homomorphic Cryptosystem*. Some references call the massage space and the ciphered texts *rings*[2]. So that such encryption and decryption processes within cryptosystem must be a ring homomorphism.

Problem of 0

Regarding to the definition 3.1.3 above, we can clearly notice that this definition is incompatible with some security properties. Let's suppose a scenario where an attacker would decide whether an encrypted text *c* is corresponding to 0 or not (Enc(0) = c). The simplest scenario we can suppose that the attacker has already prior information that Enc (1) = 1. According to Kirchhoff principle, the encryption algorithm must not be secret. Consequently, the attacker can deduct that Enc (2) = Enc (1+1) which is equivalent to Enc (2) = Enc (1) + Enc (1), indeed, Enc (2) = 2. And the same for any number n. starting from that, the quantity Enc (x) – Enc (n) =

Enc (x − n) can be computed for any n to find a match of x = n. as an encryption of 0 can be deducted, the attacker can easily do the same to decrypt any encrypted text.

Consequently, it is required for any homomorphic cryptosystem to be efficient:

- The size of ciphered texts must be polynomially bounded in the security parameter k for any repeated computations.
- Given an arbitrary long sequence of encryptions of 0 and an encryption of such x, it is crucial that answering the question "does x = 0" with a greater probability than a random chance remains impractical for any x.

Some Known Homomorphic Algorithms

Concerning the homomorphic encryption, many works are executed in this area. The majority of homomorphic propositions go to the fact of using the identity or specific attributes related to the user in order to ensure the aim of this topic such as in [02] where the authors give the general presentation of identity based encryption (IBE), then they pro-posed two approaches of IBE scheme based on fuzzy identity and study his security point in terms of keys sizes and security proofs. The homomorphic encryption was applied in several axis of privacy preserving domain. In access control such as in [25] the authors proposed a new attribute based encryption (ABE) scheme for fine-grained access control, and in [27], where we saw a proposition of a hierarchical key assignment (HKA) based encryption scheme for access control in which the. Another kind of researches interested by studying the homomorphic schemes like the papers in [13] and [07] where the authors present their surveys about some homomorphic encryption by evaluating it in term of their complexity and security levels. Since the invention of famous RSA scheme, mathematical properties of homomorphism had been largely studied for cryptographic ends. In (Rivest, 1978), Rivest, Adleman, and Dertouzos had presented the first homomorphic cryptosystem as an extension of RSA scheme. However, first schemes had been homomorphic with respect to one operation, RSA and El Gamal are multiplicative homomorphic schemes that means they are homomorphic with respect to multiplication

$$Dec (Enc (m) \cdot Enc (m')) = m \cdot m' \tag{9}$$

In the other hand, Goldwasser-Micali and Paillier schemes are additive schemes (homomorphic with respect to addition)

$$Dec (Enc (m) \cdot Enc (m')) = m + m' \tag{10}$$

RSA Scheme

The RSA scheme is an example of deterministic multiplicative homomorphic encryption scheme on message space $M = (\mathbb{Z}/N\,\mathbb{Z},\cdot)$ where N is the multiplication of two large primes (p and q). it often products a ciphered texts' space $C = (\mathbb{Z}/N\,\mathbb{Z},\cdot)$ using key space

$$K = \{(K_e, K_d) = ((N, e), d)|\ N=pq, ed \equiv 1 \bmod \varphi(N)\} \tag{11}$$

Regarding to encryption and decryption processes of this algorithm (Enc_{Ke} (m) = $m^e \bmod N$ and Dec_{kd} (c) = $c^d \bmod N$) we can clearly notice that the encryption of a product of two plaintexts m and m' gives the same result as computing two encryptions of the same messages

$$Enc_{ke} (m \cdot m') = (m \cdot m')^e \bmod N = (m^e \bmod N) \cdot (m'^e \bmod N) = Enc_{ke} (m) \cdot Enc_{ke} (m') \tag{12}$$

The security of RSA cryptosystem resides in the difficulty of factoring security parameter *k* that represents the bits size of N. *k* = 1024 bits is the most used one.

Goldwasser-Micali Scheme

Introduced for first time in (Goldwasser, 1984). This scheme is an example of probabilistic additively homomorphic cryptosystem over message space $M = (\mathbb{Z}/N\,\mathbb{Z}, +)$ and ciphered text space $C = (\mathbb{Z}/N\,\mathbb{Z})^*$ where N is the product of two large primes. The key space of this scheme is defined as follows:

$$K = \{(K_e, K_d) = ((N, a), (p, q))|\ N=pq, a \in (\mathbb{Z}/N\,\mathbb{Z})^*: (\frac{a}{p}) = (\frac{a}{p}) = -1\} \tag{13}$$

The probabilistic property of the scheme consists of adding random $r \in \mathbb{Z}$ within encryption algorithm as it is defined in the equation 14 bellow

$$Enc_{ke} (m, r) = a^m r^2 \bmod N \tag{14}$$

The decryption algorithm is defined as follows:

$$Dec_{kd} (c) = \begin{cases} 0\ if\ c\ is\ quadratic\ residue \\ 1\ otherwise \end{cases} \tag{15}$$

The homomorphic additivity property is verified in this scheme as the following equation shows:

$$\text{Eval}(\text{Enc}_{ke}(m, r), \text{Enc}_{ke}(m',r'), r'') = \text{Enc}_{ke}(m, r) * \text{Enc}_{ke}(m',r') * r'' \bmod N = \text{Enc}_{ke}(m+m', rr'r'') \qquad (16)$$

Where r'' is considered as equivalent to $\text{Enc}_{ke}(0, r'')$.

The complexity of decryption process of Goldwasser-Micali scheme, as it requires exponentiation, is $O(k * l(p)^2)$ where $l(p)$ represents the number of bits in p. therefore, this scheme still having limitations since its input consists of a single bit which gives us a complexity of encryption of k bits $O(k * l(p)^2)$ which is not efficient even if it is practical. In the other hand, the issue of expansion presents another concern for this cryptosystem (a single bit is encrypted in an integer modulo n that gives $l(n)$ bits). This fact lead us to a huge blowing up of the ciphered text causing serious problems of storage and treatment especially when talking about Big Data and its petabytes.

The next algorithms denotes the general framework of Goldwasser-Micali scheme:

Algorithm 1: Goldwasser-Micali

```
Step 1: KeyGen
    Choose 2 large primes p and q
Set n ← p *q
Choose a random y ∈ Z_n (y must be non-residue and (y/n) = 1)
    Public key Pk = (n, y) and secrete key Sk = (p, q)
    Step 2: Encrypt
m ∈ M={0,1}ⁿ
        for each x_i in m do
            choose random r < n
            c_i = r² * y^(x_i) mod n
    Step 3: decrypt
    For each c_i from c do:
```

$$x_i = \begin{cases} 0 \; if \; c_i \; is \; quadratic \; residue \\ 1 \; otherwise \end{cases}$$

Remark: the quadratic residuosity of c_i is defined according to p and q. and it is computed as follows: let's consider $X_p = c_i \bmod p$ and $X_q = c_i \bmod q$. if $X_p^{(p-1)/2} = 1 \bmod p$ and $X_q^{(q-1)/2} = 1 \bmod q$ then c_i is called quadratic residue.

Benaloh's Scheme

This scheme introduced in 1988 can be seen as a generalization of Goldwasser-Micali scheme allowing the control of inputs of l(k) bits where k is a prime satisfying some properties. It encrypts texts in the same way as the previous one (Enc_{ke} (m $\in$ {0, ..., k-1}) = $a^m r^k$ mod N). The decryption process is more complex and gives that if the input and output are respectively of sizes l(k) and l(n) then the expansion is equal to l(n)/l(k) which is quite smaller than the one in Goldwasser-Micali scheme. The complexity of encryption is not too expensive as it remains the same as the previous cryptosystem. However, the decryption complexity is estimated to be O($\sqrt{k}$ * l(k)) for pre-computation which is constant for each dynamic decryption step and implies such k to as small as possible which limits the expansion rate.

The homomorphism of this scheme is verified in the following equation:

$$Enc_{ke} (m) \cdot Enc_{ke} (m') \bmod n = (y^m u^r) (y^{m'} u'^r) \bmod n = (y^{m+m'}) (uu')^r \bmod n = Enc_{ke} (m+m') \bmod n \qquad (17)$$

The following algorithm shows a revisited version of this scheme, (Fousse, 2011):

Algorithm 2: Benaloh's revisited cryptosystem

```
        Step 1: KeyGen
        Choose 2 large primes p and q
Set n ← p *q
Choose a random bloc size r such that:
                - r divides (p-1)
                - r and (p-1)/r are relatively prime
                - r and (q-1) are relatively prime
Choose random set y ∈ (Z_n)* = { x ∈ Z_n: gcd(x, n) = 1} such
that:
                y^(φ/r) ≠ 1 mod n where φ = (p-1) (q-1)
                Public key Pk = (n, r, y) and secrete key Sk = (p, q)
        Step 2: Encrypt
m ∈ Z_r and u a random number in (Z_n)*
                c = {y^m u^r mod n: u ∈ (Z_n)*}
        Step 3: decrypt
```

We notice that for any m, u we have:

$$(y^m u^r)^{(p-1)(q-1)/r} = y^{m (p-1) (q-1)/r} u^{(p-1) (q-1)} = y^{m (p-1) (q-1)/r} \bmod n \qquad (18)$$

Since $m < r$ and $y^{m\,(p-1)\,(q-1)/r} \neq 1 \bmod n$ then $m = 0 \bmod n$ if and only if $(y^m\,u^r)$ $^{(p-1)(q-1)/r} = 1 \bmod n$. in other words, if $z = y^m\,u^r \bmod n$ is an encryption of m then using p and q, it is easy to determine whether $m = 0 \bmod n$ or not. Taking r much smaller, the decryption of z can be done using exhaustive search for the smallest non-negative integer m such that $(y^{-m}\,z \bmod n) \in \mathrm{Enc}_r\,(0)$.

Remark: as we mentioned before, Benaloh's scheme had shown more complex decryption step. Many optimisation works had been done in this purpose such as using baby-step giant-step algorithm [3] and precomputing values that allows the decryption in time $O(\sqrt{r})$.

Naccache-Stern Scheme

This scheme had been introduced in (Naccache, 1998). It represents an enhanced version of Benaloh's scheme as it uses a greater parameter k than the old one. With the same encryption step and different decryption process, this scheme achieves smaller expansion and higher efficiency. Its decryption process has smaller complexity that is $O(l(n)^5 \log(l(n)))$. The authors of (Naccache, 1998) had mentioned that with the right choosing of parameters in their system, we can achieve an expansion value equal to 4. The homomorphic property of this scheme is the same as Benaloh scheme (see the equation 17). The next algorithm shows the general work of this cryptosystem

Algorithm 3: Naccache-Stern cryptosystem

```
Step 1: KeyGen
        choose randomly k small distinct primes x1….xk
```

$$\text{set } u = \prod_{i=1}^{k/2} xi \text{ and } v = \prod_{i=\left(\frac{k}{2}\right)+1}^{k} xi$$

$$\text{set } \sigma = uv = = \prod_{i=1}^{k} xi$$

```
        choose two large primes a and b such that p = 2au+1
and q = 2av+1 are primes
set n=pq
choose randomly g mod n such that g has order of φ(n)/4
        public key Pk is (σ, n, g) and private key Sk is (p,
q)
        Step 2: encrypt
        for a message m in the group Z/σZ
        pick a random x from the group Z/nZ
```

```
c = x° g^m mod n
Step 3: decrypt
```

$ci \equiv c^{\varphi(n)/pi} \bmod n$

$c^{\varphi(n)/pi} \equiv x^{\sigma\varphi(n)/pi} g^{m\varphi(n)/pi} \bmod n$

$\equiv g^{(mi + yipi)\varphi(n)/pi} \bmod n$

$\equiv g^{mi\varphi(n)/pi} \bmod n$

Where mi $\equiv$ m mod n

Since pi is defined to be small, mi can be recovered using exhaustive search. After that, m can be easily recovered applying Chinese Remainder theorem.

Remark: if k is chosen to be 1 then this algorithm is simply the Benaloh's scheme.

Okamoto-Uchiyama Cryptosystem

In order to improve the efficiency of older homomorphic schemes, Okamoto and Uchiyama had come with the idea of changing the group of message space by taking $n=p^2q$ and the message space will be the group $(\mathbb{Z}_p^2)^*$, (Okamoto, 1998). The authors had reclaimed that their scheme achieves $k= p$ which gave them an expansion value equal to 3. The security of this scheme resides in the factorisation of n. therefore, this fact had been studied by proposing a Chosen-Ciphered Text attack known for its efficiency against factorisation problems. Okamoto-Uchiyama's scheme is an additive homomorphic scheme that verifies the following property:

Enc_{ke} (m) Enc_{ke} (m') mod n = $(g^m h^r)$ $(g^{m'} h'^r)$ mod n = $(g^{m+m'})$ $(hh')^r$ mod n = Enc_{ke} (m+m') mod n   (19)

The following algorithm shows the general framework of this cryptosystem:
Algorithm 4: Okamoto-Uchiyama cryptosystem

```
Step 1: KeyGen
Choose two random large primes p and q
Set n=p²q
Choose random g from (Z/n Z)* such that g^p ≠ 1 mod p²
Set h= g^n mod n
```

The public key is (n, g, h) and secrete key is (p, q)

Step 2: encrypt

Choose random r from (Z/n Z)

C = g^m h^r mod n

Step 3: decrypt

Supposing that L(x) = $\dfrac{x-1}{p}$

The decryption of texts is m = $\dfrac{L\left(c^{p-1}\,mod\,p^2\right)}{L\left(g^{p-1}\,mod\,p^2\right)}$ mod p

Paillier Cryptosystem

Paillier is one of most famous schemes, (Paillier, 1999). It had introduced major improvements on earlier schemes allowing the decrease of expansion value to be 2. The scheme uses n = p q and gcd (n, φ(n)) = 1. It consider the base group G = $(\mathbb{Z}_n^2)$*. With proper choice of parameters, this scheme can give $k= 1$ (n). However, this scheme needs, along the lines of older schemes, a heavier decryption step as it requires one exponentiation modulo n^2 to the power of λ(n) and a multiplication modulo n. Yet, Paillier had shown that the decryption step can be managed using Chinese Remainder Theorem. This scheme had known more acceptance at applicative level for its low computational cost and smallest expansion value. Although, it had been studied in the next few years trying improving it. Cramer and Shoup had proposed in their paper, (Cramer, 2002), an approach for protection against adaptive chosen-ciphertext attacks and applied on the original Paillier's scheme in order to provide more powerful variant of homomorphic encryption. The homomorphic property of this scheme is verified within the following equation:

Enc_{ke} (m) · Enc_{ke} (m') = (g^m r^n) (g^{m'} r'^n) mod n^2 = (g^{m+m'}) (rr')^n mod n^2 = Enc_{ke}(m+m') mod n^2 (20)

The following algorithms describes the working steps of Paillier cryptosystem:
Algorithm 5: Paillier cryptosystem

Step 1: KeyGen

Choose randomly two large primes p and q

Set n=pq and φ(n) = (p-1)(q-1)

Choose random g ∈ (Z_n^2) *

Ensure that n divides the order of g using modular

```
multiplicative inverse as follows:
                    μ = (L(gᴸ mod n²))⁻¹ mod n
(20)
```

where $L(x) = \dfrac{x-1}{n}$ and λ denotes the Carmichael function[4] λ(p ·

q) = lcm(p-1; q-1)

```
            The public key is (n, g) and the secrete key is (λ,
μ)
            Step 2: encrypt
Let m be the message to encrypt m∈ Zₙ
Choose a random r ∈ (Zₙ)*
            C = gᵐ rⁿ mod n²
            Step 3: decrypt
m = L(cᴸ mod n²) · μ mod n.
```

Applications of Cryptography in Privacy Preserving

Rather than that cryptography deals only with the ability of elaborating computation sharing of sensitive information. Instead, it aims to ensure a secure sharing of information without revealing sensitive information in term of visible data and hidden knowledge. In other words, such cryptographic protocol must allow computation on encrypted data ensuring that the encrypted result must not reveal any information about plaintexts. Homomorphic cryptography is used often for a specific problem known as Secure Multiparty Computation (SMC). It is a known problem that consists of a distributed computing system in which many parties share a confident computation in such way each party is unwilling to disclose any information about its input and output. Hence, homomorphic encryption had shown a lot of useful concepts in many fields we mentioned from:

Mobile Agent Protection

Mobile agents are systems that, as well as conventional computer architectures, are based on computations on binary strings using basic addition and multiplication operations. This fact allows homomorphic encryption to be used efficiently to protect these agents by encrypting whole programs without, or at least with minimum, loss of ability of being executed. Therefore, protecting mobile agents using homomorphic cryptography can be used in two ways: computing with encrypted programs; or computing with encrypted data.

Zero-Knowledge Proofs

This s one of the main primitive of homomorphic cryptography that acts on the theoretical level. It is used to prove that an attacker have no chance to improve intended knowledges by analysing encrypted private data. A simple example of that, we consider a remote access system that requires user name and password to enter. Users of the system are generally unwilling that their private information (i. e. passwords) to be leaked during the communications. That's to say that the protocol must ensure that only the intended knowledge are leaked and no (zero) other information. In this case, homomorphic cryptography presents a good solution to prove this kind of applications. A good example of that the work presented in (Cramer, 1998).

Watermarking and Fingerprinting Schemes

One useful trick that homomorphic encryption can ensure is digital watermarking. This last is a security issue that consists of embedding additional data to encrypted one in order to ensure right identification of owner of data providing high protection of copyrights. Hence, besides watermarking, digital fingerprinting presents another issue that homomorphic encryption can be used within. The aim of that is that a buyer of data must be identified in order to avoid illegal redistribution of data. More details about such schemes can be found in (Pfitzmann, 1997) and (Adelsbach, 2002).

Data Aggregation in Wireless Sensor Networks

Wireless sensor networks had posed many privacy problems because of its architecture based on ad-hoc networks and dynamic attribution of routes. This problems are generally related to trustfulness of intermediate nodes transmitting the data after combining partial results. At this stage, homomorphic cryptography represents an accepted issue that can be used. As data aggregation is, at some point, the process that causes data increasing; for that, the multiplicative homomorphic cryptosystems are definitely inadvisable to avoid communication problems and bandwidth occupation that can lead to serious problems. Many additive schemes are used in this field such as (Sen, 2009, 2010, 2011, 2012a, and 2012b), (He, 2007).

Privacy Preserving Data Mining

As the Data mining getting developed and advanced, many problems and fields had been emerged to be resolved using data mining techniques. Therefore, this advancement had raised new concerns about the ability of violating users' privacy using knowledge extraction and discovery. In addition, the expansion of huge volumes of data in Big Data services especially, the emergence of sensor networks technology, had led the research axis to avoid encryption solutions because of the complex computations that it needs which raise the problem of energy consummation. As a result, a novel domain of research had seen the light under the name of Privacy Preserving Data Mining (PPDM), (Agrawal, 2001). This domain had been recognised as a specific direction within data mining and statistical databases, (Verykios, 2004). PPDM aims to tackle two major axis of privacy: first, detect and remove the sensitive data over a row such as names, addresses, mails and many others. Second, ensure that the process of removing any sensitive information must provide an efficient security against knowledge discovery so that analysing non-sensitive information should not, in any way, reveal any information about sensitive one.

Classification of Privacy Preserving Techniques

The bunch of works within privacy preserving data mining is getting increased each day with new works and approaches published in different reviews and conferences over the planet. PPDM had, and still attract a lot of attentions. These approaches can be viewed, according to (Verykios, 2004), in five dimensions:

Data Distribution

That refers to the distribution of the data either it is centralized or distributed. Even more, either distributed data is vertically or horizontally distributed. Horizontal distributed data (known also as homogenous distribution) refers to the fact that different data records are managed in different places. Meanwhile, vertical data distribution (known also as heterogeneous distribution) refers to the fact the different attributes of the data are managed in different places. Formally speaking, let's assume k different sites collecting datasets $D1 \equiv (E1, I1)$, ... $Dk \equiv (Ek, Ik)$. Horizontal distribution means that different sites collect data in the same form (i.e. banks collect almost the same information about clients) that's to say, $E = \bigcup_i E_i = E_1 \cup E_2 ..... \cup E_k$ and $I = \bigcap_i I_i = I_1 \cap I_2 ..... \cap I_k$. Meanwhile, vertical distribution means that different sites collect different features of the same data (i.e. hospitals collect general information about patients such as morphological features, governments collect other information about the same people) that's to say $E = \bigcap_i \bigcup_i E_i = E_1 \cap E_2 ..... \cap E_k$ and $I = \bigcup_i I_i = I_1 \cup I_2 ..... \cup I_k$.

Data Modification

This class refers to the set of works that consist of modifying the data values in such way that ensures high privacy protection and maintain data utility with respect to the privacy policy adopted in such case. Approaches in this class can be classified in five major techniques:

- Data perturbation that consists of modifying an attribute value by a new value.
- Blocking that consists of modifying an attribute value by an "?" or "*".
- Aggregation that consists of merging and combining several values of the same attribute to replace them with a coarser value.
- Swapping that consists of interchanging values of individual records.
- Sampling that consists of limiting the number of authorised persons who can access to data. In other words, releasing data to limited range of population.

Data Mining Algorithms

This dimension refers often to a set of works that consists of elaborating such approaches for data modification. Works in this field consist of using data mining and classification algorithms in order to hide sensitive data either by altering it meaningfully or by limiting the cases of data releasing. Many works had been done using several algorithms such as decision tree, association rules, clustering, rough sets and Bayesian networks.

Data or Rule Hiding

This dimension defines the way the data is released. It refers to whether raw data or aggregated one is hidden. Hiding data in form of rules is a process require highly complex computations. For that, many heuristics have been developed for this purpose. It requires the definition of such approaches allowing the production of weaker inference rules in order to avoid inference of confidential values.

Privacy Preserving

This is the most important dimension that refers to the techniques allowing selective modification of data. It aims to reduce the gap between data modification the data utility maintain so that the privacy is not jeopardized. These techniques can be covered on three essential groups:

Figure 2. Privacy preserving data mining techniques

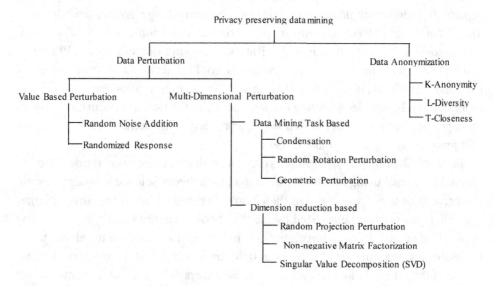

- Heuristic based approaches in which a set of works are done using data mining algorithms in the form of adaptive modification of selected data. This is based on the fact that the selective data modification is an NP-hard problem so that this group of methods is addressed to the complex problems.
- Cryptography based approaches that are represented by a secure multiparty computation where the privacy is guaranteed basing on a probabilistic function in order to ensure that at the end for multiparty computations neither party can knows except its own input and the final results of computation.
- Perturbation and re-construction of data in which the proposed approaches consist of ensuring data by re-constructing randomly the distribution of data on such aggregated level.

As Big Data being expanded and data management techniques are mainly directed towards distribution of data, the major recent works are designed to deal with distributed data. The figure 2 shows the general classification of privacy preserving data mining techniques

De-Identification or Data Anonymization

Data in its different forms contains pieces of information that can be used, alone or in aggregated form, to identify individuals. That's to say, some of information can identify explicitly persons while others must be collected and combined with other terms. For instance, birth days, names, and addresses cannot, if treated separately, identify single person while if it is combined together this leads to exact identification of individuals. At this point, de-identification comes as a solution. Automatic De-identification is a specific ever growing domain within PPDM, it consists of developing such approaches that could detect and obscure pieces of personal identifiable information (PII) in such data without influencing the context of the data itself. Besides detecting PII, such de-identification algorithm must respect main privacy goals such as zero-knowledge property. This domain had attracted lot of attentions as it get larger and larger every day.

In (Kerschbaum, 2011), the authors present an idea that consists of the detection of anomalous events using immune system and graph theory science in order to secure the privacy of users according to their compartments. Other works that interpret the bulk of works were interested by medical books because of its sensitivity. The application of de-identification algorithms in this field was on structured data using terms that are recognized in the medical field. In (Uzuner, 2007) the authors present a state of the art on de-identification of medical records by evaluating some known systems in this topic such as HIPAA as part of the i2b2 (Informatics for Integrating Biology to the Bedside) projects. In (El Emam, 2009), the authors propose a new de-identification algorithm named OLA (Optimal Lattice Anonymization) and evaluate it by comparing its efficiency on medical data with three other algorithms: datafly, Samarati, and Incognito. In (Fernandes, 2013), the authors propose and discuss their new de-identification procedure on mental health records by evaluating the obtained results from applying this procedure on two different datasets: CRIS and MIST.

Other works were interested by domain of image treatment such as the written document represented in (Newton, 2003) and (Goss, 2008) where the authors propose their models for privacy protection of facial images in shared data sets. The primary end of these works is how to de-identify pictures while conserving their utility. In (Du, 2011) the authors demonstrate their mind for protecting privacy of license plate images named IPCB (Inhomogeneous Principal Component Blur) so that they discuss the efficiency of this idea by comparing it with several previous works and also by variating some parameters. In (Gedik, 2008) the writers describe in their paper, a new customizable k-anonymity model for shelter of privacy of users' location through location based services. Their model is grounded on two major features: a customizable framework for k-anonymity and spatio-temporal cloaking algorithm.

In addition, some other works were done within big data, such as in (Gardner, 2009), where the inventors propose a prototype for de-identification of data. Their model allows the treatment of the main problem of big data and shared data generally, the heterogeneity of data so that this model permits to de-identify both structured and unstructured data forms.

K-Anonymity

According to (Sweeny, 2002), the problem of privacy through personal records is an old problem. Therefore, Sweeny had discussed a problem of releasing privately held data where she proved through a simple example of publicly available database of the Group Insurance Commission (GIC) in Massachusetts in U.S. this organization had collected information from hospitals, physicians offices and clinics. However, the collected data was limited on what collectors had though that it is non-identifiable information such as ZIP codes, birth days, and genders. The left circle in Figure 3 shows a subset of collected attributes. What Sweeny did in here experience had led to a shocking result. She had combined the database with publicly available database of voters of Massachusetts which allowed her to identify single person even without knowing his name.

For example, William Weld was governor of Massachusetts at that time and his medical records were in the GIC data. Governor Weld lived in Cambridge Massachusetts. According to the Cambridge Voter list, six people had his particular birth date; only three of them were men; and, he was the only one in his 5-digit ZIP code. (Sweeny, 2002)

As a result, Sweeny had continued her research proposing a new concept within PPDM known as k-anonymity. K-anonymity is proposed to answer a set of problems that conventional solutions had suffered from. Problems that we resume in:

- **Statistical Databases Based Solutions:** Some earlier works had proposed to release statistical analysis of databases instead of data itself. The solutions consist of involving ways of adding small random noise while maintaining

Figure 3. Re-identification of persons by linkage

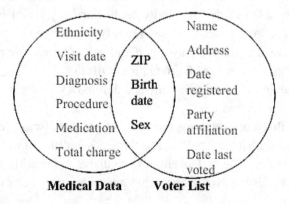

some statistical invariants (Kim, 1986), (Palley, 1986), and (Duncan, 1991). Even though, this solutions had shown many drawbacks resides principally in destroying data integrity.

- **Multi-Level Databases:** Some specific solutions had proposed using aggregation and inference in multi-level databases. These solutions consist mainly of releasing lower classified data in such way that prevent derivation of higher classified one. In (Denning, 1987), the authors propose a solution using multi-level relational database system in which data is stored in different security classifications implying different security clearances to users. However, Sweeny had reclaimed that this kind of solutions still be impractical regarding to the rich setting of today's data. Hence, the works over this field have a common property that is releasing data using suppression which, according to Sweeny, reduces quality of data and returns it at some point, especially in case of statistical analytics, practically useless.

- **Computer Security Solutions Don't Ensure Privacy:** This is something different. Looking closely to conventional security solutions based mainly on access control and authentication, we can notice clearly that these last can be very useful only against direct disclosure while it cannot avoid privacy compromise using inference based attacks and knowledge discovery algorithms.

K-anonymity is a way of evaluating systems and algorithms releasing data so that the released information limits what can be revealed about properties of entities. It uses often the concept of quasi-identifier. A quasi-identifier is a set of attributes that appear in both private and public data used for linkage. Let's take an example of private hospital patient data and public voters' registration data in U.S. tables 1.a and 1.b shows some information from them.

Linking these two tables we can easily identify that Beth has diabetes which is considered highly sensitive. In this case the set QIT= {DOB, sex, ZIP} is called quasi-identifier. For that, k-anonymity consist of ensuring that for such specific value data must identify at least k different individuals. Formally, let RT be a table with n attributes (A1... An) And QIRT the quasi-identifier (Sweeny, 02) corresponding to RT. Such system verifies the k-anonymity if and only if for each sequence of values in RT [QIRT], it appears at least k time in RT [QIRT].

Taking the previous example, Sweeny had defined a k-anonym version of it that is presented in table 2.a and 2.b

As noticed in this table, releasing the table 2.a prevent disclosure of information even using linkage with table 2.b. Beth had three possibilities, if we consider that he is already in the table, so he suffers either from diabetes, hepatitis, or FLU. Hence, from the table 2 we distinct two major techniques allowing to achieve k-anonymity:

Table 1. Examples of disclosure of identity using linkage of private and public data

DOB*	SEX	ZIP	Disease
10/21/74	M	528705	DIABETES
1/22/86	F	528718	BROKEN
8/12/74	M	528745	HEPATITIS
5/7/74	M	528760	FLU
4/13/86	F	528652	FLU
9/5/74	F	528258	BRONCHITIS
a) Hospital Patient Data			
Name	DOB*	Sex	ZIP
Beth	10/21/74	M	528705
BOB	4/5/85	M	528975
Keele	8/7/74	F	528741
Mike	6/6/65	M	528985
Lola	9/6/76	F	528356
Bill	8/7/69	M	528459
b) Voter registration Data			

DOB*: Date of birth

Table 2. Examples of disclosure of identity using linkage of private and public data

YOB*	SEX	ZIP	Disease
1974	M	5287**	DIABETES
1986	F	5287**	BROKEN
1974	M	5287**	HEPATITIS
1974	M	5287**	FLU
1986	F	5286**	FLU
1974	F	5282**	BRONCHITIS
a) Hospital Patient Data			
Name	DOB*	Sex	ZIP
Beth	10/21/74	M	528705
BOB	4/5/85	M	528975
Keele	8/7/74	F	528741
Mike	6/6/65	M	528985
Lola	9/6/76	F	528356
Bill	8/7/69	M	528459
b) Voter registration Data			

DOB*: Date of birth, YOB*: Year of birth

- **Suppression:** The attributes value are replaced by an asterisk '*'. In this method some or all the values of a sensitive attributes are replaced.
- **Generalization:** In this method the values are replaced by a broader category. For instance, the age attribute can be replaced by intervals. 19 replaced by <20, 25 replaced by 20<<30...etc.

Unfortunately, k-anonymity, even after it gains popularity, some recent works had shown major limitations of it. (Machanavajjhala, 2007) had presented two attacks against it known often as homogeneity attack and background knowledge attack.

Homogeneity Attack

It is proven that k-anonymity can create such groups that can reveal information due to the diversity of sensitive information. Let's look the next example that Machanavajjhala had presented:

"Alice and Bob are antagonistic neighbours. One day Bob falls ill and is taken by ambulance to the hospital. Having seen the ambulance, Alice sets out to discover what disease Bob is suffering from. Alice discovers the 4-anonymous table of current inpatient records published by the hospital (table 3), and so she knows that one of the records in this table contains Bob's data. Since Alice is Bob's neighbour, she knows that Bob is a 31-year old American male who lives in the zip code 13053 (the quiet town of Dryden). Therefore, Alice knows that Bob's record number is 9, 10, 11, or 12. All of those patients have the same medical condition (cancer), and so Alice concludes that Bob has cancer" (Machanavajjhala, 2007).

The authors of that paper had reclaimed that an experiment on real data set containing 60000 distinct tuples where sensitive attribute can take three different values and it is uncorrelated with the non-sensitive one, had 12000 groups using

Table 3. Example of private and released patient data set (Machanavajjhala, 2007)

	Non-Sensitive			Sensitive
	Zip Code	Age	Nationality	Condition
1	13053	28	Russian	Heart Disease
2	13068	29	American	Heart Disease
3	13068	21	Japanese	Viral Infection
4	13053	23	American	Viral Infection
5	14853	50	Indian	Cancer
6	14853	55	Russian	Heart Disease
7	14850	47	American	Viral Infection
8	14850	49	American	Viral Infection
9	13053	31	American	Cancer
10	13053	37	Indian	Cancer
11	13068	36	Japanese	Cancer
12	13068	35	American	Cancer

a) Patient private dataset

	Non-Sensitive			Sensitive
	Zip Code	Age	Nationality	Condition
1	130**	< 30	*	Heart Disease
2	130**	< 30	*	Heart Disease
3	130**	< 30	*	Viral Infection
4	130**	< 30	*	Viral Infection
5	1485*	≥ 40	*	Cancer
6	1485*	≥ 40	*	Heart Disease
7	1485*	≥ 40	*	Viral Infection
8	1485*	≥ 40	*	Viral Infection
9	130**	3*	*	Cancer
10	130**	3*	*	Cancer
11	130**	3*	*	Cancer
12	130**	3*	*	Cancer

b) Patient released dataset

5-anonymity algorithm. These groups had revealed that 1 out of each 81 group will have no diversity of values. Consequently, the anonymization will allow disclosure about 740 person using homogeneity attack.

Background Knowledge Attack

This is, at some point, similar to homogeneity attack except it supposes that the attacker has already prior information, yet, Machanavajjhala had proposed another scenario verifying this. "Alice has a pen-friend named Umeko who is admitted to the same hospital as Bob and whose patient records also appear in the table shown in Figure 3. Alice knows that Umeko is a 21-year old Japanese female who currently lives in zip code 13068. Based on this information, Alice learns that Umeko's information is contained in record number 1, 2, 3, or 4. Without additional information, Alice is not sure whether Umeko caught a virus or has heart disease. However, it is well known that Japanese have an extremely low incidence of heart disease. Therefore Alice concludes with near certainty that Umeko has a viral infection." (Machanavajjhala, 2007).

These two attacks had led the researchers to search for new solutions implying the integration of diversity of anonymous data within a group. This property is often known as l-diversity.

L-Diversity

L-diversity can be defined as an extension of k-anonymity in which the aim is to cover weaknesses previously discussed. It consists of reducing the granularity of data representation even if that came at a cost of effectiveness and data utility. Formally, to have an l-diversity model is that if there are at least l "well presented" data of a sensitive attribute. For a given table that holds q-block sets of sensitive values, we say that the table is l-diverse if every block in it is l-diverse. Nevertheless, (Machanavajjhala, 2007) defines the expression "well presented" in three ways:

- **Distinct l-Diversity:** At least there are l distinct values for the sensitive attributes in each equivalent class. However, distinct l-diversity does not prevent probabilistic inference attacks. For such sensitive attribute, a specific value can appear more frequently than other values. Which in term of probability, an attacker can derive that for a specific entity there is a high probability to have that value. Consequently, researchers had been motivated to develop more complex extensions of l-diversity known as entropy l-diversity and recursive l-diversity.

- **Entropy l-Diversity:** Entropy l-diversity was proposed for first time in order to prevent the homogeneity problem. It relies often of the idea of *"well presented groups"* regarding to the fact that the entropy of such group increases as content become more uniform. Given E an equivalence class. The entropy of E equals to the negation of summation of fraction of records p (E, s) containing sensitive value s across the domain of the sensitive attribute S.

$$\text{Entropy (E)} = -\sum_{s \in S} p(E, \ s) \log p(E, s) \qquad (21)$$

For such table T, we said it has entropy l-diversity if for each equivalence class E

$$\text{Entropy (E)} \geq \log (l) \qquad (22)$$

However, it is obviously that entropy l-diversity provides more efficient environment for privacy preserving measurement rather than distinct l-diversity.

- **Recursive (c, l)-Diversity:** The most common value does not appear too often while the less common ones appear more frequently. Given E an equivalence class. Consider m the number of values in E, r_i is the number of occurrences of the ith element in E ($1 \leq i \leq m$). E is said to satisfy recursive (c, l)-diversity if, for a given constant c, $r_1 < c (r_1 + r_{l+1} + \dots + r_m)$. A table is said to be recursive (c, l)-diversity if every equivalence class has recursive (c, l)-diversity. In other words, a table is said to have recursive (c, l)-diversity if we can eliminate one possible sensitive s value among the l values of S and still have (c, l-1)-diversity.

Entropy and recursive l-diversity have both some drawbacks resides on their mathematical definitions. Both of them are restrictive and cannot be used for all the cases. Looking closely to entropy l-diversity, mathematically, it is known that −x log(x) is a concave function. So that if we split an equivalence class E into two parts 'a' and 'b' then entropy (E) $\geq$ min (entropy (a), entropy (b)). That's to say the entropy of an entire table must be at least log (l) which is not the case in some tables where it contains fewer common values or one specific sensitive value is more common than others. This restrictive fact had been shown as major drawback of entropy l-diversity. In case of recursive l-diversity, the problem of such sensitive value that is more frequent than others will prevent for some chosen c values the satisfaction of generalisations for recursive l-diversity. In addition, l-diversity principle had been developed in purpose of protection against attribute disclosure beyond k-anonymity. Meanwhile, it shows-up several shortcomings resides in two major attacks: skewed attack, and similarity attack.

Skewed Attack

The l-diversity principle is based principally in the fact that sensitive values are well distributed in their domain. So that if the overall distribution is skewed, the l-diversity could not prevent attribute disclosure. For instance, suppose an example of a data set for analysis of specific virus that can have one of two values (positive or negative). Suppose that it has 10000 records in which 99% of it has negative value while only 1% has positive value. Now, for a equivalence class within this set has equal number of negative and positive individuals, in this case the equivalence class satisfies the distinct 2-diversity, entropy 2-diversity, and recursive (c, 2)-diversity. Despite that, the class still shows a high risk of privacy as each individual has possibility of 50% to be positive among the 1% already exist in the dataset. In another example, let's consider an equivalence class that has 1 negative record and 49 positive records. In this case, the class satisfies distinct 2-diversity and entropy 2-diversity as it has higher entropy than the overall table. Even tough, this class shows serious privacy risk as each individual of it has 98% possibility of being positive rather than the 1% of the overall population.

Similarity Attack

This is a serious drawback of l-diversity. This last is not efficient if the sensitive values of such equivalence class are distinct but semantically similar. (Li, 2007) had presented a good example of that. Consider a dataset that has two sensitive values (Tables 5 a and b shows the original and released samples of the dataset).

Looking to this figure we can clearly notice that the released version of the dataset satisfies both distinct and entropy 3-diversity. Similarity attack can be seen as knowledge based attack. Suppose an attacker knows that Bob's records situated

Table 4. Example of dataset containing two sensitive values

	ZIP Code	Age	Salary	Disease
1	47677	29	3K	gastric ulcer
2	47602	22	4K	gastritis
3	47678	27	5K	stomach cancer
4	47905	43	6K	gastritis
5	47909	52	11K	flu
6	47906	47	8K	bronchitis
7	47605	30	7K	bronchitis
8	47673	36	9K	pneumonia
9	47607	32	10K	stomach cancer

a) Original dataset

	ZIP Code	Age	Salary	Disease
1	476**	2*	3K	gastric ulcer
2	476**	2*	4K	gastritis
3	476**	2*	5K	stomach cancer
4	4790*	≥ 40	6K	gastritis
5	4790*	≥ 40	11K	flu
6	4790*	≥ 40	8K	bronchitis
7	476**	3*	7K	bronchitis
8	476**	3*	9K	pneumonia
9	476**	3*	10K	stomach cancer

b) released dataset

on one of the three first records, as a result, the attacker knows that his salary is in the range [3k – 5k]. Also, knowing this information can reveal that Bob has problems in his stomach because all the three records had problems related to that. So even if we analyse only three records we can see that they satisfy 3-diversity but the problem is that sensitive values (in spite that they are distinct) but the three of them are semantically related.

As a result of that, a new solution had been proposed by Li known as *t-closeness*

T-Closeness

T-closeness had been developed on the fact that measuring privacy relies often on the information gain the attacker would have. This gain is measured by the difference between prior believes of the attacker (ideas he already has before seeing generalized dataset) and posterior believes (ideas he will get after analysing generalized dataset). So, an equivalence class is said to have t-closeness if the distance between the distribution of sensitive values in this class and the distribution of these values in the whole table in is at most equal to a threshold t. for more details, Li and his friends had discussed a motivating example: first of all an adversary has prior information B0 about sensitive attribute. At the beginning, the adversary had to observe a completely generalized version of the table where all the attributes composing quasi-identifier are removed. The adversary knowledge is changed to B1 according to a distribution Q. then, giving the adversary the final released table. Knowing the quasi-identifier values of such individual, the adversary will be able to identify the equivalence class this last belongs to. Consequently, he can learn the distribution P of sensitive attribute values if that class. This gives the adversary a knowledge B2. As l-diversity consist to limit the difference between B0 and B2. T-closeness supposes that the distribution Q is a public information so that it consists to limit the difference between B1 and B2 preventing attackers from learning additional information about specific individuals. Limiting the gain between B1 and B2 is done, according to Li, by limiting the distance between P and Q. the closest are P and Q the least the gain is. To measure the distance between P and Q, as they are probabilistic distributions, there is several distance measures that we mention two of them: the variational distance (23), and Kullback-Leibler distance (24)

$$D\ [P, Q] = \sum_{i=1}^{m} \frac{1}{2} \left| p_i - q_i \right| \tag{23}$$

$$D\ [P, Q] = \sum_{i=1}^{m} p_i \log \frac{p_i}{q_i} = H\ (P) - H\ (P, Q) \tag{24}$$

Where H (P) is the entropy of P and H (P, Q) is the cross-entropy of P and Q.

Therefore, these measures do not handle the semantic distance between values. For that, Li and his friend had proceeded to the use of Earth Mover's Distance (EMD)[5]. This last aims to minimize the amount of work needed to transform on distribution to another moving distribution mass between them. Formally speaking, let's consider two distributions P= (p1, p2…. Pm) and Q = (q1, q2….qm) and consider d_{ij} the ground distance between i^{th} element of P and j^{th} element of Q. the goal is to find the right flow F=[f_{ij}], where f_{ij} represents the flow of mass between i^{th} element of P and j^{th} element of Q, in which the overall work shown in equation 25 is minimized:

$$\text{WORK (P, Q, F)} = \sum_{i=1}^{m}\sum_{j=1}^{m} d_{ij} f_{ij} \tag{25}$$

(Li, 2007) had presented the way of how to compute this distance in more details.

Data Perturbation

According to (Chen, 2007) which had presented and discussed the major drawbacks of data anonymization, this last may remove sensitive information but it keeps other data such as race, birth date, sex and ZIP codes. These last may not identify uniquely and directly one individual but it can be combined with publicly available information from other sources. In fact, as we had already discussed in anonymization techniques, in spite of development and efficiency of these last, it still suffers from drawbacks reside mainly on the use of information from other sources or even attacks based on prior knowledge for the adversary. As result, the research area of privacy preserving had been recently enriched with new bunch of techniques that consist of, instead of removing only sensitive information, modifying the whole dataset in such way that ensures both data and knowledge hiding and good utility of data. This new domain is known as data perturbation. It is widely known research area in privacy preserving data mining. Privacy protection and data quality are two known pairs of contradictive factors. This wide gap between them presents the major challenge that data perturbation tries to tackle

Data perturbation methods can be classified in two major categories: probability distribution, and fixed data perturbation.

Probability distribution based techniques that consider the data set as a sample of given population that has specific probability distribution. In this case, sensitive values is replaced by another values from the same distribution or by the distribution itself. We mention two class of techniques in this category:

- The first is called "data swap-ping" or "multidimensional transformation" and consists of generating randomly a new set of values that has almost the same probability distribution of the original one. In this case, such system must take in consideration the relationship of an added or deleted entity with the rest of the data when perturbing. For that, a one-to-one mapping between original and generated dataset is an indispensable step. Therefore, resulted precision of this method may seem unacceptable since it can reach an error up to 50%.
- The second one is called probability distribution, this is also consists of replacing dataset with another one maintaining probability distribution of the original one. First, the method identifies density function of the sensitive attribute and estimates the parameters of this function. Then, it generates a sample from that function that should have the same size of the original data. At the end, the method consists of substituting the generated sample in the original dataset replacing sensitive values of the same rank.

Concerning fixed data perturbation, it represents set of techniques that consist of perturbing data values once for all. It is often known as "value distortion based data perturbation". It uses different techniques such as additive or multiplicative noise, or simply randomization procedures.

Here are some known techniques of privacy preserving data mining (figure 2)

Noise Additive Perturbation Techniques

Noise addition techniques are the most used ones in research area. This kind of techniques represents a set of techniques that consist of adding or multiplying several stochastic or randomized numbers to a quantitative confidential data in order to protect the confidentiality of these last. Many approaches have been developed for noise addition based perturbation that can be classified in three classes:

Additive Noise

This class of methods was first introduced in (Kim, 1986) in which the authors described it in general expression presented in equation 1:

$$Z = X + \varepsilon \tag{26}$$

Where Z represents the perturbed data, X is the original data, and ε is a random variable with distribution of e $\sim N$ $(0,\sigma^2)$. Another work had been presented in (Domingo-Ferrer, 2004), the authors presented an approach of stochastic noise addition, and they called it also white noise. They proved that the dissimulation of data using additive noise can foresee that the variable of measurement xj of the original data Xj is continuously replaced by the variable

$$Z_j = x_j + j \tag{27}$$

Where j is the additive noise. Ciriani et al; noticed in (Ciriani, 2007) that classical additive noise techniques preserve the mean and covariance of the original data but not the correlation coefficient and variance. For that, they proposed another variation known as correlated additive noise in which the aim is to maintain both the mean of data and correlation coefficient.

Multiplicative Noise

This kind of noise is not much different from the additive one. It was introduced by Kim and Winkler in (Kim, 2003). The only difference is that the noise here is generated from a normal distribution of a small variance and a mean $= 1$, then this noise will be multiplied by the original data instead of adding it.

$$Z = X * \varepsilon \tag{28}$$

Logarithmic Multiplicative Noise

Another variance of multiplicative noise was introduced in (Kim, 2003) in which the original data passes first by an alteration of logarithmic process:

$$Y = \ln(X) \tag{29}$$

After that, a stochastic noise is generated and added to the altered data Y

$$Z = Y + \varepsilon \tag{30}$$

Randomized Response Technique

Is a technique that consists of dealing with structured survey interview in which the purpose is to respond a sensitive issues while maintaining the confidentiality? This technique was introduced by S.L Warner in 1965 and modified later by Greenberg in 1969. Formally, for a respondent who has an attribute A, let P be the probability of A being sensitive so that the other side will have probability of 1-P. in order to avoid any revealing of information about the selected statement to the interviewer, an elementary probability is used to get an estimation of proportion named λ of A in the population as follows:

$$\lambda = P \lambda + (1\text{-}P) (1\text{-} \lambda) \tag{31}$$

Condensation Based Perturbation

This technique belongs to the set of multi-dimensional perturbation techniques. It consists of preserving covariance matrix for multiple columns and some other properties such as the shape of decision boundary. Unlike randomization approach that treats each column independently, condensation based approach perturbs multiple columns at once which allows many data mining algorithms to be applied directly on perturbed data without revealing sensitive knowledge. This technique preserves mainly eigenvectors and eigenvalues of a database. To do that, the approach first consists of dividing the set into groups of size k. Each group is formed in two steps:

1. Choose randomly a record to consider it as centre of the group
2. Search for k-1 nearest neighbours of that record to construct the group and remove them then pass to the next group

This technique facilitate the regeneration of k records that have approximately the same distribution and covariance as the original one since it removes k records of small locality.

Random Rotation Perturbation

This technique consists of choosing randomly a set of records and so applying the perturbation by randomly rotate or transform the data. To do that, the data are represented by a matrix Xn*m then a random orthonormal rotation matrix R is generated. Finally, the perturbed data equals to the product of R with X. Many approaches are published in this kind of techniques using classification and transformation techniques such as SVM, KNN, K-means, Inner product and kernel methods.

Geometric Perturbation

The geometric based models are a combination between rotation, transformation and noise addition techniques. Formally, let's consider Xn*m a dataset matrix with n columns and m records, Rd*d a random rotation orthonormal matrix, T a translation random matrix and Nn*m a random noise matrix. The geometric perturbation then is the results of the following formula (Patel'13) and (Chen'07):

$$G(X) = RX + T + N \tag{32}$$

In addition, the geometric perturbation is known by her invariance against geometric modification. Nevertheless, this kind of techniques guarantees more privacy rather than random rotation and condensation based techniques.

Random Projection Perturbation

Introduce by Johnson-Lindenstrauss, this technique based on the use of random matrix to project the original dataset in low dimensional subspace. Formally, consider ϵ > 0 and 0 < δ < ½, let k be a positive integer in which k ≥ k0 = O (ϵ-2 log (1/δ)). For each dataset P in Rd there is a function φ: Rd → Rk such that for all x, y ϵ P:

$$(1 - \epsilon) \|x-y\|\_2^2 \leq \|\varphi(x)- \varphi(y)\|\_2^2 \leq [(1+\epsilon)\|x-y\|] \_2^2 \tag{33}$$

So that this lemma is conducted on the fact that n points could be projected from Rd to Rk while preserving the Euclidean distance between points within an arbitrarily small factor.

Non-Negative Matrix Factorization (NMF)

The NMF technique refers to the use of non-negative matrices and formulated as follows: given a matrix V of size n x r. NMF consists to find an approximate factorization V≈ WH where W and H are non-negative matrices of size n x m and m x r respectively. The product WH can be seen as the compressed form of V. however, the optimality of the algorithm resides in the choosing of W and H matrices in such way that reduces the error rate between V and WH. Several error functions had been proposed in this area, but the most known and used ones are two major functions that are the squared error (Euclidean distance) presented by function (34) and K-L Divergence presented by the function (35)

$$E(W, H) = \sum\nolimits [(V\_{ij} [(WH)] \_{ij})] ^2 \tag{34}$$

$$D(A\|B) = \sum\nolimits\_{ij} [(A\_{ij} \log_{fo} [A\_{ij}/B\_{ij}] - A\_{ij} + B\_{ij})] \tag{35}$$

Where A is the matrix V and B is considered as WH. Thus the NMF requires that all the components of W and H must be non-negative.

Singular Value Decomposition (SVD)

This technique is one of the most known techniques of privacy preserving data mining. It offers a perturbed data so that the user will be charged of extracting original data patterns. Formally, given a matrix A of size n x m where n is the number of data objects and m is the number of attributes. The SVD of matrix A is defined by the following function:

$$A = USVT \tag{36}$$

Where U is an orthonormal matrix of size n x n, S is an n x m diagonal matrix in which the diagonal entries are nonzero and equal to Rank (A) in a descending order. Rank (A) id the rank of the matrix A. and VT an m x m orthonormal matrix. However, the perturbed data of this technique is computed as follows:

$$Ak = Uk\ Sk\ Vk\ T \tag{37}$$

Where Uk is an n x k matrix that contains the first k columns of U, Sk is an k x k diagonal matrix that holds the k largest nonzero diagonal entries of S, and VkT is an k x m matrix that contains the k first rows of VT. The privacy of this technique resides in the number k. The more k is increased, the more amount of original data is retained. The increasing rate of k improves utility of data at a cost to privacy.

Access Control

The access control presents a sensitive domain in informatics security where it consists of defining such policy that allows or not for such user to get the access to such object; with the coming of concepts of big data and data sharing, this domain became a real challenge in research area. Many works and propositions are passed by many researches such as in (Miklau, 2003) and (Crampton, 2009) using cryptography concepts and also in some of the works basing on users' identities. Many works are done within this highly active topic where the most of these works use a promising technique called Attribute Based Encryption such as in (Yang, 2011) (Tu, 2012) (Yu, 2010) and (Li, 2013); in (Crampton, 2009) the author presented his approach of controlling hierarchical access using multiple key assignment in cryptography where he proposed four schemes, in other words four extensions of his work: bounded, unbounded, synchronous and asynchronous in order to give the general idea under temporal access control; in (Astorga, 2012) the authors show their new approach of controlling access on resource-deprived environment in sensor data by integrating the Ladon Security Protocol that offers a secure access using end-to-end authentication, authorisation and key establishment mechanisms in PrivaKERB user privacy framework of KERBEROS environment; in (Wang, 2006) the authors introduced a purpose of using Elliptic Curve Cryptography (ECC) to control the access to data over sensor networks so that they presented their implementation of ECC in TelosB sensor network platform and evaluated their results by comparing it with the results of (Liu, 2008) and (Malan, 2004); in (Thilakanathan, 2013) the paper is addressed to introduce the idea of SafeShare that consists of controlling the access by encapsulation of shared data so that their point of view consists of using the ABE to encrypt, encapsulate, audit and log the data in order to define a perform access control policy; other works go to the fact of using data content to control the access such as it is pointed out in (Zeng, 2013) and (Nabeel, 2011).

According to (Majumder, 2014), in which the authors had provided an overview about access control models in Cloud Computing, these models can be classified in two ways: either by use or not of identity of users; or by centralized or collaborative approaches. Figure 4 shows the two classifications.

The rest of this subsection will be addressed to a brief presentation of the models:

Mandatory Access Control (MAC)

MAC model is a classic model that consists of defining a centralized access policy that is controlled and attributed by an administrator or a major entity (Ausanka-Crues, 2006). This model is also known as Bell-Lapadula model where entities are

Figure 4. Classification of access control models in Big Data (Majumder, 2014)

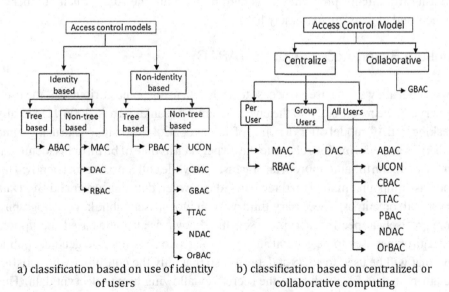

a) classification based on use of identity of users

b) classification based on centralized or collaborative computing

classified into confidentiality levels and the control is based on two major rules: no-write-up, and no-read-down. This means that only the administrator can add, delete or change access rights.

Therefore, MAC model has a good advantage resides on its simplicity and high security since only the administrator can alter controls which represents a good solution in case of applications in hostile environments. But, in the other side, having one only entity that controls everything poses many problems resides mainly in high complexity of computations and absence of dynamic separation of duty which does not ensure fine-grained least privileges.

Discretionary Access Control Model (DAC)

Unlike MAC model, DAC model consist of restricting access rights within group of users to which they belong. In this case, an entity that owns such object can pass its own rights to another entity, (Ausanka-Crues, 2006). As classical model, DAC is the most used model in almost all operating systems for its flexibility. It uses often a tabular representation of access rights known as Access Control Matrix (ACM). However, in this model, the major entity knows only for such process who is the user that uses it but not the access rights on the objects of the system which leads to a difficulty of maintaining ACM. At this stage, the system or major entity harbours to such techniques such as performing right lookup on each object access or maintaining only active rights of the subject.

The major advantage of DAC model is that it ensures fine-grained access control through the ACM and object level permission modes. Therefore, this model is still suffering from major problem that is hard to maintain the ACM when number of subjects and objects are extremely high.

Attribute Based Access Control (ABAC)

This model allows such user to access to such data using some attributes of the user, the service, the resources, and the environment, (Ausanka-Crues, 2006). Generally speaking, ABAC model offers a policy of access control to sensitive data using some properties and information related to the owner such as date of birth, or his identity. It aims to maintain the autonomy of an organisation while collaborating efficiently. This model is compound mainly on three parts: data owner, data consumer and Big Data server, and sometimes, if necessary, third party auditor. It uses public key cryptography, more precisely a specific encryption schemes known as attribute based encryption. The data owner uses some general attributes related to consumers to generate public keys that will be used to encrypt data files so that only the consumer who satisfies the attribute data files will have the secret key allowing him to decrypt data. This strategy ensures good fine graininess of access control policy. (Majumder, 2014) shows an example of healthcare centre which provides a cloud computing storage service. However, ABAC model shows some major drawbacks resides mainly in the heaviness of computations especially in some cases that requires users to revoke; in this case data owners must re-encrypt all the data files that revoked users could access. As a solution of that, a combination process of proxy based re-encryption and attribute based encryption is required allowing data owner to delegate heavy computations into Big Data servers without disclosing content of sensitive data.

Role-Based Access Control (RBAC)

RBAC model is, at some point, a solution that handles the problem of maintaining the large number of access rights that a huge access control matrix can have in DAC or MAC models, (Ferraiolo, 1992). It consists often to group access rights in groups named roles so that these last can be treated both as subjects when assigning new rights to them and objects when assigning it to users. The main objective of RBAC model is to avoid the assignment of same group of access rights to set of subjects. For example, in healthcare research projects, all the employees of the same degree of all participant hospitals and centres must have the same access rights on the database, in this case it is preferable to define these rights in a single role that will be assigned to that employees rather than repeat it all for them. Figure 5 shows general principal of RBAC model

Figure 5. General principle of RBAC model

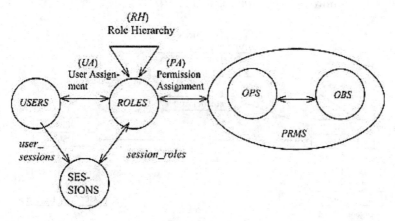

Gateway-Based Access Control (GBAC)

As its name indicates, GBAC model consists of allowing access to data using gateway, (Suhendra, 2012). This model ensures dynamic and anonymous access to data of several enterprises in collaborative services by transforming users' original data into Security Assertion Mark-up Language (SAML). This last ensures secure connection between users which form a virtual team. The connection uses often third party to manage communication in order to avoid problems related of connection platform. Figure 6 shows an example of implementation of GBAC model in collaborate virtual private cloud (VPC) presented in (Sasaki, 2010)

Such gateway is compound on six components:

- Traffic collection unit which consists of collecting the flows of traffic
- Traffic processing unit that consists of classifying the collected traffic while recording general information such as IP addresses and timestamps in a database
- Network Security Unit (NSU) that consists of a set of security tools such as firewalls and virus scanners. This is one of two main units. It aims to handle security functions as local legacy gateway and informs response unit if any suspect threats are detected.
- Data Security Unit (DSU) which the second important unit. This unit consists of using a set of rules defined by policy management unit to analyse traffic and informs the response unit.
- Policy management unit which contains predefined rules related to behaviour of analysis unit

Figure 6. VPC gateway connection (Sasaki, 2010)

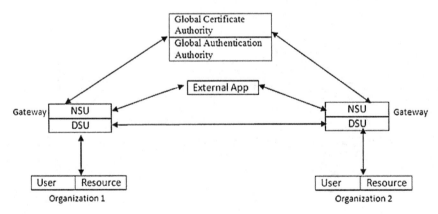

- Response unit consists of managing active and passive responses and log processes if any threats are detected.

The fact that, in GBAC model, resources are converted into SAML format presents a good advantage of ensuring that only authorized users can access to it. Hence, GBAC is one way access control model. This means in collaborative tasks, the access of entities to other entities' resources is unidirectional.

Novel Data Access Control Model (NDAC)

NDAC model, (Gao, 2012) aims to ensure confidentiality of access to data between user and Big Data server. It is built on three actors' scenario: Data owner (DO), Big Data Server (BDS), and a user. This model is compound on three major processes: File storage, user authentication, and file access.

- File storage consists of managing the access between DO and BDS. First of all the DO computes a hash code of the file to stored then encrypts the file and the code with secret key K0. After that, DO computes a capability list that contains user ID (UID), file ID (FID) and access right (AR). At the end, DO uses a public key of BDS to encrypt the pair UID and an encrypted version of the encryption of the file with its hash code and capability list using his own private key to BDS that decrypts and stores them.
- User authentication that consists of defining an authorisation to the user in order to allow him to access a file. For that, the user sends first a registration request that is encrypted using DO's public key. After that, DO decrypts the request and check it then, if it is valid, adds the user into the capability list and sends the updated version into BDS after encrypting it using public key of this last. BDS in his turn decrypts the message of DO and check the validity of the timestamp then updates his own capability list. Then DO uses public key of the user to encrypt the quadruplet (N+1, timestamp, k0, MD5) where N+1 is a random generated number, k0 is the symmetric secret key of DO, and MD5 is a hash algorithm. At the end, the user checks N+1 and timestamp then, if they are correct, stores k0 and MD5.
- File access which the final process that consists of exchanging basically the data between BDS and the user. First, the user encrypts a data request using BDS' public key and sends it to him. The BDS then decrypts the message using his own secret key and checks timestamp. In case of validity, the BDS authenticates the user through a comparison of UID got from DO, UID got from the user, the file ID and access right AR. After that, BDS computes a private value Y_A and generates a new Diffie-Hellman key exchange algorithm

parameters and encrypts them using public key of the user. The user, after receiving the encrypted message, decrypts it using his own secret key and computes a private value Y_B. The user encrypts this last using BDS' public key and sends it to him. The BDS, after decrypting it, checks a new random generated value N'+1 then calculates the shared session key K. at the end, BDS encrypts the data using K and sends it to the user.

The main problem of NDAC model is that the DO must be all the time available in case of a user wants to access data. However, this model shows high efficiency in protecting confidentiality of data against several attacks especially replay attack, and man-in-the-middle attack. For more information about that, (Majumder, 2014) provides detailed discussion of these attacks.

Usage Control-Based Access Model (UCON)

UCON model presents an inheritance of all the classical access control models (mainly MAC, DAC, and RBAC). It is based on authorizations, obligations and conditions (Danwei, 2009). According to Majumder and his friends, this model provides a superior decision making ability which makes it a better choice for Big Data services especially cloud computing. Even though, it is still a conceptual model without any given exact specification. UCON model is built on six parts: subject, rights, objects, authorizations, obligation, and conditions. Figure 7 shows the main construction of this model.

- Subjects are users which have some rights and noted by S. each subject is identified by a set of features such as identity, role, capacity list…etc. these features are specified within subject attributes
- Objects represent the entity in which a subject can access. It represents mainly the data and it is also identified through object attributes that contains main features such as security level, relations, type…etc.
- Rights are the actions that a subject can perform on an object. The decisions within rights are defined according to a set of conditions, authorizations, and restrictions.
- Authorization represents a decision-making factor which allows or not certain action of a subject on an object according to three major variables: subject's attributes, object's attributes, and the rights. However, authorization can modify some values in that variables depending on the use case.
- Obligation is also a decision-making factor that is defined before or during the existence of a subject at real time. It depends on variable attributes as well as authorization. The main difference between these two is that obligations are

Figure 7. UCON model

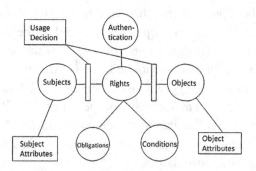

defined dynamically and system's administrator could not set it in advance. Obligations can also in their turn update variables' attributes if needed.

- Condition is the last part. It is also a decision-making factor which reacts with current hardware environment and system limitations to decide whether a subject request will be treated or not. Therefore, condition has no interference on variables' attributes since it only manages requests scheduling.

The change of variables' attributes is done within a negotiation process. This process aims, in case of a subject's request that does not satisfy condition, instead of rejecting directly the request, it calls the authorization part which starts a process changing subject and/or object's attributes in order to give the subject another chance to access the object in other access choice. This process is presented in details in (Majumder, 2014). The main problem of UCON model is that negotiation process must pass through several conditions that subject request must satisfy one by one and if any condition is not satisfied, the request will be rejected automatically.

Purpose-Based Usage Access Control Model (PBAC)

This model proposed in (Bertino, 2005) is built in aim to control the access depending on use purpose. It allows the checking of access purpose against intended purpose. Purposes are attributes that defines reasons why such data should be accessed for. They are grouped in groups of purposes P in which each group is represented in tree structure called purpose tree (PT) where each node represents a purpose, and each edge represents the hierarchical relation between them. Intended purposes are attributes related to object items. They are composed on two parts, (Sun, 2010): allowed intended purposes (AIP) and prohibited intended purposes (PIP). To access such data, a subject must state access purpose within the request so that this last must match a purpose in AIP and not in PIP. Consider the example presented by Majumder. Let PT be a purpose tree that defines P as set of purposes. Let PU = (AIP, PIP) be the set of intended purposes associated to the data. Let AP be the access purpose defined in PT. such request stating AP is said to be compliant with PU if and only if two conditions are satisfied: AP $\in$ AIP, and AP $\notin$ PIP.

However, PBAC model is very suitable for hierarchical data as it can be easily used in dynamically access environment. In the other side, PBAC has a major drawback resides in the fact that this model describes only authorizations without ensuring the rest of steps necessary for secured access to data which requires it to be combined with other security issues.

Capability-Based Access Control Model (CBAC)

This model was proposed in 2011 by Hota and his friends, (Hota, 2011). As well as NDAC model, CBAC is compound on three types of actors: data owner, users, and Big Data server. It gives the DO the ability to create, modify, or delete the capability list of a user. Figure 8 shows the general view of the model

The DO starts by encrypting his data using his private key then sends it to the server in order to be stored. Once a new user or new request comes, the DO comes online and accept the request by sending the certificate and key to the user. At the end the user presents the certificate to the server, gets encrypted data, and decrypts it using the received key. Communications between entities are managed using cryptography primitives like secure socket layer (SSL) and transport layer security (TLS). In purpose of minimizing computational cost of cryptography protocols,

Figure 8. General view of CBAC model

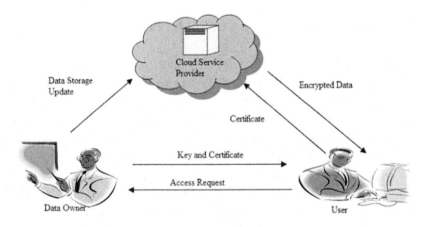

symmetric cryptosystems are often used to encrypt and decrypt stored data while the communication between user and server is secured using symmetric key generated by modified Diffie-Hellman key exchange protocol. Also, the construction of the model relieves the DO from annoying about every access request.

In more detailed process, when DO receives a request form a user, he adds an entry into the capability list in case of valid request. After that, he sends this list and an encrypted message for the user with key parameters needed for decryption of data files to the server. The server in his turn stores the information and sends a registration replay to the user with an over-encryption, this last avoid the server from knowing any information about original data files. At the end, the user sends data request to the server which sends the encrypted data and then the user decrypts it. This mechanism is presented in more details by Majumder.

CBAC model is a flexible access control model that allows adding, updating, and deleting capabilities when required. Also it ensures an efficient protection of data confidentiality, authentication and integrity.

Towards Temporal Access Control Model (TTAC)

Proposed in 2012 by Zhu and his friends in (Zhu, 2012), TTAC model had attracted a lot of interest for his emphasis of security issues. It aims principally to control the access to data using temporal attributes. Each subject is assigned with a licence including privileges based on comparative attributes using the algorithm presented in (Bertino, 2001). For more security and valid matches, a proxy-based re-encryption algorithm presented in (Ateniese, 2006) is used with respect to current time. To access the data, the data owner (DO) first encrypt data using temporal access policy P and stores it in the server. After receiving an access request from the user, the server checks whether the temporal constraints satisfy P with respect to the current time. If it does, the server converts the encrypted data into another encrypted data using re-encryption method and sends the result to the user. At the end, the user uses his own private key and access privilege to decrypt the data and gets original one. In order to avoid problems of temporisation of access is ensured using a clock server that is set-up in order to provide exact same time communicating the user with the server. TTAC model ensures three main advantages:

- Flexibility of controlling the access based on temporal constraints such as day control or periodic control, and even more, every digital comparison possible.
- Supervisory as it uses proxy-based re-encryption algorithm which offers the possibility of re-construction of encrypted data according to current time and allows the determination of legitimacy of user's behaviours.

- Privacy protection because this model ensures an access that depends entirely on temporal attribute matches of ciphered texts and private keys in client side. In server side, the re-encryption mechanism does not require any information about users.

Organization-Based Access Control Model (OrBAC)

This scheme was proposed in 2003 by El Kalam in (El Kalam, 2003). Its purpose is to define access control policy for abstract entities by assigning permissions, prohibitions, recommendations, and obligations. It is built on eight major entities:

- Subjects which aims to access to data and represents active users.
- Objects which represents the data to be accessed.
- Organization that represents a set of active users in which each one has specific roles.
- Role that is used often to structure the relationship between a subject and an organization when that subject wants to access an object in server.
- Action that is an operation to be performed by accessing the data such as open files()...etc.
- View that contains a set of objects that have certain common property such as administrative view that contains all administrative records of users.
- Activity that defines the action that has a common goal such as consult, edit...etc.
- Context which represents the current situation of the action whether it is normal or emergency. It can be seen also as temporal access history.

The figure 9 shows the general construction of OrBAC model.

Figure 9. OrBAC model

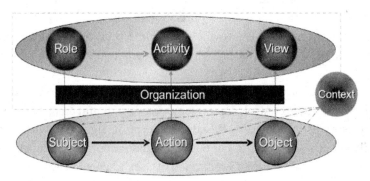

In this model, the access is defined as permissions, obligations, and prohibitions

- *Permissions (org, rol, act, vie, cont)* means that for an organization *org*, a role *rol* is allowed to perform an activity *act* on a view *vie* if a context *cont* is satisfied.
- *Obligation* means that some role *must* perform certain activity on some view when a context is satisfied.
- *Prohibition* means that a role *is not* allowed to perform an activity on some view when a context is verified.

OrBAC model does not provide any information about relationship between trust and reputation for service quality. Instead, it considers that trust is already managed using trusted third party and parameter confidence indicators.

CONCLUSION

As Big Data is getting more attentions nowadays, privacy concerns are getting expanded from day to another. Privacy techniques in Big Data can be seen as a double-edged sword. From cryptography to access control passing by de-identification and data perturbation, many works have been done in order to ensure high performance and protection of users' privacy with respect to data quality. However, till today there is still a big problem on how to measure exactly the efficiency of different privacy preserving techniques given the lack of exact specifications of models and the large variance of their constructions and concepts. This chapter was addressed to the presentation of a state-of-the-art about privacy preserving techniques and measures applied on Big Data. Yet, this domain is still young, many research projects had been made and others still in progress promising for opening new era in order to ensure the maximum of privacy of users allowing the benefit of this technology.

REFRENCES

Adelsbach, A., Katzenbeisser, S., & Sadeghi, A. R. (2002, September). Cryptography meets watermarking: Detecting watermarks with minimal or zero knowledge disclosure. In *Signal Processing Conference, 2002 11th European* (pp. 1-4). IEEE.

Agrawal, D., & Aggarwal, C. C. (2001, May). On the design and quantification of privacy preserving data mining algorithms. In *Proceedings of the twentieth ACM SIGMOD-SIGACT-SIGART symposium on Principles of database systems* (pp. 247-255). ACM. 10.1145/375551.375602

Astorga, J., Jacob, E., Huarte, M., & Higuero, M. (2012). Ladon 1: End-to-end authorisation support for resource-deprived environments. *Information Security, IET, 6*(2), 93–101. doi:10.1049/iet-ifs.2010.0259

Atallah, M., Bertino, E., Elmagarmid, A., Ibrahim, M., & Verykios, V. (1999). Disclosure limitation of sensitive rules. In *Knowledge and Data Engineering Exchange, 1999.(KDEX'99) Proceedings. 1999 Workshop on* (pp. 45-52). IEEE.

Bandara, K. K., Wikramanayake, G. N., & Goonethillake, J. S. (2007, August). Optimal selection of failure data for reliability estimation based on a standard deviation method. In *2007 International Conference on Industrial and Information Systems* (pp. 245-248). IEEE. 10.1109/ICIINFS.2007.4579182

Bellare, M., Namprempre, C., & Neven, G. (2009). Security proofs for identity-based identification and signature schemes. *Journal of Cryptology, 22*(1), 1–61. doi:10.100700145-008-9028-8

Boyd, D., & Crawford, K. (2012). Critical questions for big data: Provocations for a cultural, technological, and scholarly phenomenon. *Information Communication and Society, 15*(5), 662–679. doi:10.1080/1369118X.2012.678878

Capkun, S., Hubaux, J. P., & Jakobsson, M. (2004). *Secure and privacy-preserving communication in hybrid ad hoc networks* (No. LCA-REPORT-2004-015).

Chawla, S., Dwork, C., McSherry, F., Smith, A., & Wee, H. (2005, February). Toward privacy in public databases. In *Theory of Cryptography Conference* (pp. 363-385). Springer Berlin Heidelberg.

Chiang, Y. T., Wang, D. W., Liau, C. J., & Hsu, T. S. (2005, August). Secrecy of two-party secure computation. In *IFIP Annual Conference on Data and Applications Security and Privacy* (pp. 114-123). Springer Berlin Heidelberg.

Ciriani, V., Di Vimercati, S. D. C., Foresti, S., & Samarati, P. (2007). Microdata protection. In Secure data management in decentralized systems (pp. 291-321). Springer US. doi:10.1007/978-0-387-27696-0_9

Craig, T., & Ludloff, M. E. (2011). *Privacy and big data*. O'Reilly Media, Inc.

Crampton, J. (2009). Cryptographically-enforced hierarchical access control with multiple keys. *Journal of Logic and Algebraic Programming, 78*(8), 690–700. doi:10.1016/j.jlap.2009.04.001

Domingo-Ferrer, J., Sebé, F., & Castella-Roca, J. (2004, January). On the security of noise addition for privacy in statistical databases. In *Privacy in statistical databases* (pp. 149–161). Springer Berlin Heidelberg. doi:10.1007/978-3-540-25955-8_12

Dwork, C., Kenthapadi, K., McSherry, F., Mironov, I., & Naor, M. (2006, May). Our data, ourselves: Privacy via distributed noise generation. In *Annual International Conference on the Theory and Applications of Cryptographic Techniques* (pp. 486-503). Springer Berlin Heidelberg. 10.1007/11761679_29

Fernandes, A. C., Cloete, D., Broadbent, M. T., Hayes, R. D., Chang, C. K., Jackson, R. G., ... Callard, F. (2013). Development and evaluation of a de-identification procedure for a case register sourced from mental health electronic records. *BMC Medical Informatics and Decision Making, 13*(1), 71. doi:10.1186/1472-6947-13-71 PMID:23842533

Fousse, L., Lafourcade, P., & Alnuaimi, M. (2011, July). Benaloh's dense probabilistic encryption revisited. In *International Conference on Cryptology in Africa* (pp. 348-362). Springer Berlin Heidelberg.

Fuchsbauer, G. J. (2006). An Introduction to Probabilistic Encryption. *Osječki matematički list, 6*(1), 37-44.

Gedik, B., & Liu, L. (2008). Protecting location privacy with personalized k-anonymity: Architecture and algorithms. *IEEE Transactions on Mobile Computing, 7*(1), 1–18. doi:10.1109/TMC.2007.1062

Goluch, S. (2011). *The development of homomorphic cryptography: from RSA to Gentry's privacy homomorphism.* Academic Press.

Guellier, A., Bidan, C., & Prigent, N. (2014, November). Homomorphic cryptography-based privacy-preserving network communications. In *International Conference on Applications and Techniques in Information Security* (pp. 159-170). Springer Berlin Heidelberg.

Gunasekaran, M., & Premalatha, K. (2013). SPAWN: A secure privacy-preserving architecture in wireless mobile ad hoc networks. *EURASIP Journal on Wireless Communications and Networking,* (1): 1–12.

Holmes, M. H. (2012). *Introduction to perturbation methods* (Vol. 20). Springer Science & Business Media.

House, W. (2014). *Big Data and Privacy: a technological perspective.* Washington, DC: Executive Office of the President, President's Council of Advisors on Science and Technology.

Index–Forecast, C. V. N. (2008). *Methodology 2007–2012.* Cisco System.

Kargupta, H., Datta, S., Wang, Q., & Sivakumar, K. (2003, November). On the privacy preserving properties of random data perturbation techniques. In *Data Mining, 2003. ICDM 2003. Third IEEE International Conference on* (pp. 99-106). IEEE. 10.1109/ICDM.2003.1250908

Kerschbaum, F., & Oertel, N. (2011). *U. S. Patent No. 8,015,080*. Washington, DC: U. S. Patent and Trademark Office.

Klosek, J. (2007). *The war on privacy*. Greenwood Publishing Group.

Layouni, M. A. (2009). *Privacy-preserving Personal Information Management* (Doctoral dissertation). McGill University.

Liu, A., & Ning, P. (2008, April). TinyECC: A configurable library for elliptic curve cryptography in wireless sensor networks. In *Information Processing in Sensor Networks, 2008. IPSN'08. International Conference on* (pp. 245-256). IEEE. 10.1109/IPSN.2008.47

Machanavajjhala, A., Kifer, D., Gehrke, J., & Venkitasubramaniam, M. (2007). l-diversity: Privacy beyond k-anonymity. *ACM Transactions on Knowledge Discovery from Data, 1*(1), 3, es. doi:10.1145/1217299.1217302

Maimut, D. S., Patrascu, A., & Simion, E. (2012). Homomorphic Encryption Schemes and Applications for a Secure Digital World. Journal of Mobile. *Embedded and Distributed Systems, 4*(4), 224–232.

Majumder, A., Namasudra, S., & Nath, S. (2014). Taxonomy and classification of access control models for cloud environments. In *Continued Rise of the Cloud* (pp. 23–53). Springer London. doi:10.1007/978-1-4471-6452-4_2

Malan, D. J., Welsh, M., & Smith, M. D. (2004, October). A public-key infrastructure for key distribution in TinyOS based on elliptic curve cryptography. In *Sensor and Ad Hoc Communications and Networks, 2004. IEEE SECON 2004. 2004 First Annual IEEE Communications Society Conference on* (pp. 71-80). IEEE. 10.1109/SAHCN.2004.1381904

Mashey, J. R. (1997, October). Big Data and the next wave of infraS-tress. In *Computer Science Division Seminar*. University of California.

Meyer, F. G., & Shen, X. (2014). Perturbation of the eigenvectors of the graph laplacian: Application to image denoising. *Applied and Computational Harmonic Analysis, 36*(2), 326–334. doi:10.1016/j.acha.2013.06.004

Patel, A., & Patel, H. S. (2014). *A Study of Data Perturbation Techniques For Privacy Preserving Data Mining*. Academic Press.

Sen, J. (2013). *Homomorphic Encryption: Theory & Applications*. arXiv preprint arXiv:1305.5886

Sweeney, L. (2002). Achieving k-anonymity privacy protection using generalization and suppression. *International Journal of Uncertainty, Fuzziness and Knowledge-based Systems*, *10*(05), 571–588. doi:10.1142/S021848850200165X

Sweeney, L. (2002). k-anonymity: A model for protecting privacy. *International Journal of Uncertainty, Fuzziness and Knowledge-based Systems*, *10*(05), 557–570. doi:10.1142/S0218488502001648

Szarvas, G., Farkas, R., Iván, S., Kocsor, A., & Busa-Fekete, R. (2006). *An iterative method for the de-identification of structured medical text. Workshop on Challenges in Natural Language Processing for Clinical Data*.

Townsend, A. M. (2013). *Smart cities: Big data, civic hackers, and the quest for a new utopia*. WW Norton & Company.

Vaidya, J., Clifton, C. W., & Zhu, Y. M. (2006). *Privacy preserving data mining* (Vol. 19). Springer Science & Business Media.

Verykios, V. S., Bertino, E., Fovino, I. N., Provenza, L. P., Saygin, Y., & Theodoridis, Y. (2004). State-of-the-art in privacy preserving data mining. *SIGMOD Record*, *33*(1), 50–57. doi:10.1145/974121.974131

Zeng, W., Yang, Y., & Luo, B. (2013, October). Access control for big data using data content. In *Big Data, 2013 IEEE International Conference on* (pp. 45-47). IEEE. 10.1109/BigData.2013.6691798

ENDNOTES

[1]   Directive 95/46/EC of the European Parliament and of the Council of 24 October 1995 on the protection of individuals with regard to the processing of Personal data and on the free movement of such data. Official Journal of the European Communities, No I. (281):31-50, Oct.24 1995.

[2]   http://www.saylor.org/site/wp-content/uploads/2011/04/Ring-mathematics.pdf

[3]   https://math.berkeley.edu/~sagrawal/su14_math55/notes_shank.pdf

4   http://yimin-ge.com/doc/carmichael.pdf

5   The Earth Mover's Distance (EMD) is a method to evaluate dissimilarity between two multi-dimensional distributions in some feature space where a distance measure between single features, which we call the ground distance is given.

Chapter 7
Cardiovascular Disease Prediction Using Data Mining Techniques:
A Proposed Framework Using Big Data Approach

Kalyani Kadam
Symbiosis International University (Deemed), India

Pooja Vinayak Kamat
Symbiosis International University (Deemed), India

Amita P. Malav
Symbiosis International University (Deemed), India

ABSTRACT

Cardiovascular diseases (CVDs) have turned out to be one of the life-threatening diseases in recent times. The key to effectively managing this is to analyze a huge amount of datasets and effectively mine it to predict and further prevent heart-related diseases. The primary objective of this chapter is to understand and survey various information mining strategies to efficiently determine occurrence of CVDs and also propose a big data architecture for the same. The authors make use of Apache Spark for the implementation.

DOI: 10.4018/978-1-5225-7338-8.ch007

INTRODUCTION

Heart is an important organ in human body which draws blood through blood veins of circulatory system. Factors responsible for the risk of CVDs are smoking, alcohol, obesity, high BP (blood Pressure).

As per WHO (World Health Organization, around 20 million people die around the world due to cardiovascular disease. If proper medical care is given, many lives can be saved. Heart disease prediction is one of the difficult tasks in field of health sciences.

In 2015, an expected 17.7 million humans died from cardiovascular disease which is 31% of total worldwide deaths. An estimated 7.4 million people's deaths out of total deaths were due to coronary heart sickness and estimated 6.9 million deaths have been due to heart stroke. We know that heart disease is topmost reason for deaths of humans all across the globe. Every one of the five deaths is due to heart disease. Almost 1/2 folks residents of US have minimum one risk component for heart sickness along with high blood strain, obesity, sedentary lifestyle, high blood sugar etc.

Coronary illness is a common sickness these days. Presently due to expanding costs of coronary illness, there was a need to build up another framework which can foresee heart sicknesses in a simple and less expensive way. Information mining systems and learning disclosure assumes a significant part in such discoveries. We know that experts who treat heart disease keep data records of patient. To extract the useful information these datasets are analyzed. Therefore data mining turns out to be a productive and fruitful tool.

Figure 1. Causes of Heart Disease

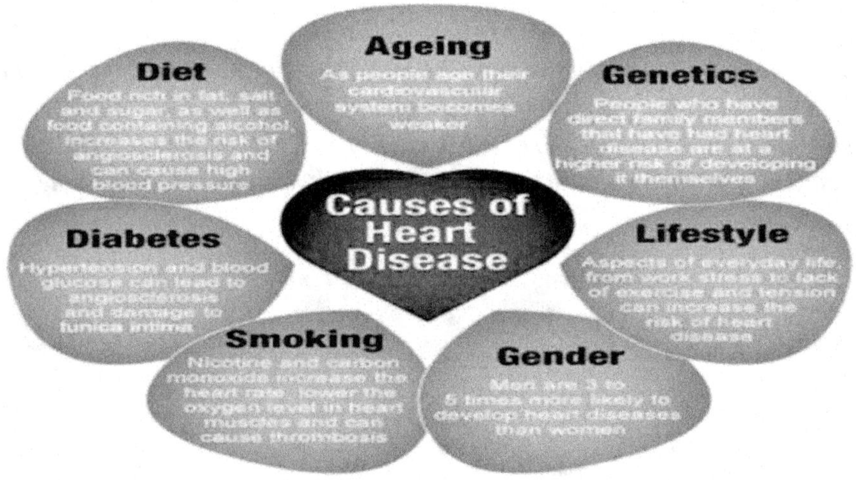

Data mining is clearly defined as "The repetitive and interactive manner of coming across logical, novel, beneficial, and understandable knowledge (patterns, models, guidelines etc.) in huge databases"

(Fayyad et al, 1996; Kurgan et al, 2006; Gobel et al, 1999). The discovery of knowledge in databases is simply well-described step comprising numerous distinct movements. Information mining is the important stage that comes within the uncovering of hidden however beneficial information from significant databases.

Health Science information mining is a field which connects with parcel of imprecision and vulnerability. Providing value facilities at reasonable price is the main concern of the healthcare framework. Inappropriate medical outcome may prompt terrible results. Medical science is very large and medical conclusions are made depend on medical doctor's knowledge not on the data covered up in the database which in some cases will result in improper results and also changes the nature of service to the patients (Wasan et al, 2006). Health checkup past data consists of a number of investigations needed to make a diagnosis of a specific illness .It is conceivable to accomplish the benefit of information mining in medicinal services via utilizing it as a shrewd investigative instrument. The specialists in the healthcare system recognize and anticipate the disease by making use of Information mining systems (Setiawan, 2009).

Researchers have suggested that the use of statistical mining in figuring out powerful remedies for patients can enhance practitioner overall performance. Experts investigated and came to result that by applying specific information mining strategies for the examination of cardiovascular sickness to find out which information mining method can offer prominent exactness. Many distinct data mining strategies were already used to help medical care departments to detect coronary heart ailment (Dewan et al, 2015; Chandna, 2014).

Data mining examines vast datasets to find out unrevealed and unknown designs, connection between them which are not easy to find with statistical methods. Also statistical mining is increasing speedily and getting successful in various applications like organic compounds analysis, business forecasting, medical care and meteorology prediction (Das et al, 2009).Various applications of data mining in medical care include hospitals analysis for making finer medical policies and avoiding health facility mistakes, early detection, prevention of illnesses and deaths of patient and financial savings.

A number of various warning signs are associated with cardiovascular disease that makes it difficult to identify it early and better. Focusing on cardiovascular illness patients record could be check with real-life program. Doctor understands to allocate the excess weight to each parameter. High weightage is given to the parameter having high impact on illness forecasting. So that it become acceptable to make use of information in order to have connection with various experts which are gathered to assist the process of medical detection. When hybrid and single data mining procedures were compared for the recognition of cardiovascular illness they showed accuracies, where the hybrid one proved that it provides better accuracy as compared to single techniques (Das et al, 2009).

BACKGROUND

See Table 1.

Table 1. Papers who have done work on Heart Disease Prediction

Sr. No	Title	Author	Year	Methodology
1	Comparative Analysis of Accuracy on Heart Disease Prediction using Classification Methods.	Dbritto, Rovina, AnuradhaSrinivasaraghavan, and Vincy Joseph	2016	Naïve Bayes, K-nearest Neighbor, SVM i.e. Support Vector Machine and Logistic regression
2	Heart Disease Prediction using K Nearest Neighbor and K Means Clustering	Dr.Mohanraj,SubhaSuryaa, Sudha, Sarath Kumar,	2016	KNN and K-means
3	Prediction of heart disease using a hybrid technique in data mining classification	Ankita Dhewan and Meghana Sharma	2015	Artificial Neural Network and Genetic Algorithm (GA)
4	Improved K-means and Naive bayes for Prediction of Heart Disease	SAIRABI MUJAWAR P.R.DEVALE	2015	K-means and modified K-means.
5	Performance comparison of data mining techniques for predicting of heart disease survivability.	Lakshmi, K. R., Krishna, M. V., & Kumar, S. P.	2013	KNN, K-means, Apriori, PLS-DA
6	Classification of heart disease using k-nearest neighbor and genetic algorithm.	Deekshatulu, B. L., & Chandra, P.	2013	k-nearestneighbor,genetic algorithm.
7	Improved Study of Heart Disease Prediction System using Data Mining Classification Techniques	Chaltrali S. Dangare and Sulabha	2012	decision trees, Naïve bayes, and Artificial Neural Network
8	A Data Mining Technique for Prediction of Coronary Heart Disease Using Neuro-Fuzzy Integrated Approach Two Level	A. K. Sen, Shamsher B Patel, Dr. D. P. Shukla	2013	Neuro-fuzzy
9	Using data mining techniques in heart disease diagnosis and treatment.	Shouman, M., Turner, T., & Stocker, R.	2012	Neural Network ensemble
10	Improving the performance of Data Mining Algorithm in Health Care data	Santhi. P	2011	Bayes, functions, Lazy,Metamulti Boost AB, Rules, Trees,
11	Effective Diagnosis of Heart Disease through Bagging Approach	Chau Tu, D. Shin, Dong Shin	2011	Bagging Approach (single)Acc=81.41, Decision tree (single). Accuracy:81.48%
12	Effective Diagnosis of heart disease through neural network ensembles	R. Das, T. Ibrahim, A. Sengur.	2009	Neural Network and ensemble based methods Accuracy: 89.01%
13	Design of a hybrid system for the diabetes and heart diseases	Kahramanli H., Allahverdi, N.,	2008	ANN and fuzzy neural network. Accuracy:87.4%
14	A hybrid approach to medical decision support systems: Combining feature selection, fuzzy weighted pre-processing and AIRS	Kemal Polat, Salih Gunes	2007	Feature selection, fuzzy weighted pre-processing and artificial immune recognition system (AIRS).

SYSTEM ARCHITECTURE

Knowledge Discovery Process

Data Mining provides a procedure to search for unseen information of data and their patterns.

The flow of Data mining's KDD (Knowledge Discovery of Databases) is given below.

It consists of following steps

1. **Data Cleaning:** Dispose of clamor and conflicting information.
2. **Data Integration:** In this various information resources might be joined.
3. **Data Selection:** Where information material to the examination errand are gathered from the recordset.
4. **Data Transformation:** In this method information are altered and consolidated into frames reasonable for mining via executing rundown or total activities.
5. **Data Mining:** Which is an essential procedure where savvy techniques are helpful to recover information designs.
6. **Pattern Evaluation:** To recognize the truly attractive patterns appealing information depend on interesting measures.
7. **Knowledge Presentation:** Where perception and data portrayal procedures are utilized to display mined data to the clients.

The whole procedure is nothing but extraction of probably useful information from huge databases. It gives the choice for selection, cleansing and enhancing the data. Also data mining helps in understanding the procedure of knowledge where we are keen to discover desired information from relevant databases (Sumathi et al, 2006; Zhang et al, 2009).

Figure 2. Knowledge Discovery of Databases in Data Mining

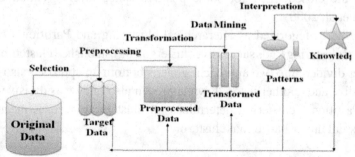

ANN Algorithm

Neural networks resembles biological network of brain neurons. Similar to central nervous systems, an interconnected group of neurons forms neural network. Each node gets input from other nodes and weights between nodes adjust so that the whole network learns to compute the output. There are various types of neural networks structures with each having its own learning algorithm. The neural network is a novel computer architecture compared to traditional computers. An artificial network of neurons connected with each other to give a specified output on applying input is called neural network (Acharya et al, 2003; Manikantan et al, 2013).

Different Types of ANNs are as follows:

- Single Layer Perceptron
- Multilayer Perceptron (MLPs)
- Radial-Basis Function Networks (RBFs)
- Hopfield Network
- Boltzmann Machine
- Self-Organization Map (SOM)
- Modular Networks (Committee Machines)

In our approach we used Multilayer Perceptron. It is used to map input into outputs with the help of input layer, various hidden layers and output layer. To achieve optimal solution, it makes use of trial and error method. The design of artificial neural network is shown below in Figure 2 (Kurgan et al, 2006; Gobel et al, 1999; Rajkumar et la, 2010).

K-MEANS ALGORITHM

When objects are classified into several groups or isolating of dataset into different categories so the information in each of the subcategory share a typical property, frequently the closeness as for some positive space level is called Clustering (Steinbach et al, 2000).

It is further categorized as Hierarchical clustering and Partitional clustering. Hierarchical clustering finds successive clusters using established clusters previously. It is further divided into two approaches one is bottom up approach also known as agglomerative and another is top down approach also known as divisive approach whereas Partitional clustering determines all clusters at once. K-means and its derivatives fall under Partitional clustering.

Figure 3. Layers of ANN

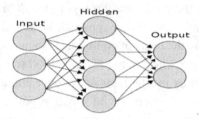

K-means clustering is clustering technique based on partition launched in 1967 by Macqueen. To resolve cluster based problem, it is easiest form of unsupervised learning algorithm (Ahmed et al, 2008; Hartigan et al, 1979). It is one of the cluster analysis algorithm where 'k' clusters are formed by partitioning 'n' observations. Also the addition of square of distance within the data is minimized using Euclidean Distance Formula. The primary goal of using K-means clustering technique is that the data are organized by it into classes such as

- High intra-class similarity
- Low inter-class similarity

Algorithm for K-Means

1. Groups information into k parts where k is predefined.
2. Pick k points arbitrarily as cluster centers.
3. Euclidean distance function used to assign objects with their closest cluster
4. Compute the centroid or indicate of most objects in every group.
5. Do again step number 2, 3 and 4 before similar factors are allocated to each group in successive rounds.
   Input: The given participation is a d-dimensional dataset of length n, and a k value, which shows amount of clusters mean to be produced.
   Output: data set points assigned to centroid
   Complexity: It is relatively efficient and fast. Complexity for K-means is calculated as O.

Where,

n: number of points or objects,
k: number of clusters and
i: number of iterations

Classifier:

Classification means the process of arranging the data into various groups or classes based on their similarities. In our approach we use ANN classifier on various heart diseases attribute on the basis of common characteristics which can either be descriptive such as age, sex, cholesterol, fasting blood sugar etc.

Whenever using statistics and the areas where huge amounts of data are collected and analysed, it's important to sort the information points into sub-groups often. This can be a very hard task for human beings, who often aren't able to recognize which class a data point belongs to due to large amounts of data present in each data point. Instead, a digital classier is used.

Hybrid Approach Architecture Using K-Means and ANN

The basic idea behind hybrid approach is to increase the accuracy of prediction so that heart disease can be diagnosed more precisely.

1. **Understanding Domain Dataset:** Dataset is provided as input to system. We also provided feature of loading excel dataset or manual entries into the system.
2. **Data Preparation:** is method of recognizing and redressing (or removing) damage or erroneous records from a record set, database or table and alludes to distinguish deficient, incorrect, mistaken or immaterial parts of the data and replacing, substituting or erasing the dirty (Purao et al, 2011; Rahadi et al, 2016).
3. **Processing Module:** This specifies the algorithm over the system in order to achieve high accuracy result. As an algorithmic approach we use ANN classifier and K-means clustering data mining techniques.
4. **Evaluation and Deployment:** In this it gives the information related to generated output. We obtain a confusion matrix, our system perform comparison and conclude about measurable resultant artefacts like sensitivity, accuracy etc.

A detailed flow of cardiovascular disease prediction System Architecture by making use of information mining method is shown below in Figure 4

Pseudo Codee

Allocate all network inputs and outputs
Assign all weights with small random numbers in the range from -1 to 1
Perform following operations repetitively
for each pattern in the training set

Figure 4. K-Means Clustering

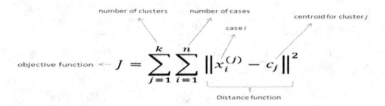

Show the pattern to the system
// Spread the input forward through the system:
for each layer in the network

Each hub in the layer

1. Compute the weight total of the inputs to the hub
2. Sum up the threshold to the sum
3. Compute the activation for the node

    end of each hub in the layer

Figure 5. Heart Disease Prediction System Architecture

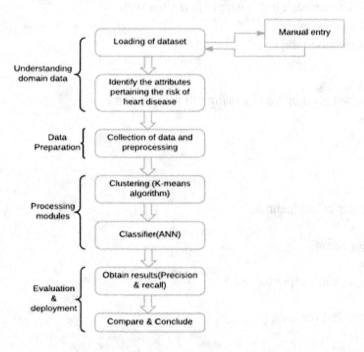

Figure 6. Heart Disease Prediction System Detailed Architecture

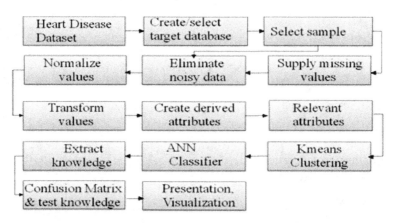

end for each layer in the network
// Spread the errors backward through the system
Each hub in the output layer
Compute the error signal
end of each hub in the output layer
for all concealed layers
for every hub in the layer
    1.   Compute the node's signal error
    2.   Update each hub's weight in the network
end of all hidden layers
end of every hub in the layer

Where,
The output is computed by using following formula.

$$y_j = \sum w_{ij} x_i$$

f=1

Yj - indicates output neuron.

Xi - input neuron

Wij - weight connecting Xi and Yj

$\sum$ - is sigmoidal function

Figure 7. Graphical Representation of Neuron in ANN

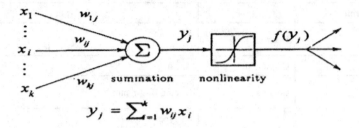

Input: A vector of real values (attribute, value) / obtained clusters from K-means.
Output: Classified classed with associated weight
Activation function: sigmoidal function
Complexity: depends on the structure and number of layers in a neural network.

In our case to obtain optimal solution: O (2^n) to converge to optimal solution whereas below equations give a complexity solution to calculate approximate solution.

O (#epochs * # examples * #features * #neurons) => approximate solution.

Implementation and Results

Keeping in view the recent literature, we given a methodology for our workflow in order to achieve our objectives. The way to discover the patterns important to cardiovascular disease expectation are decided depend on calculated assigned weightage. Weightages are offered rely upon the range decided for the chosen parameter from the dataset.

Total 718 records were given as input to the framework. Dataset of heart disease is given as input to the system on which basically pre-processing task is performed. In preprocessing we have taken care of missing values, Noisy data, and inaccurate data. In data preparation a major factor causing CVDS are considered for analysis purpose. Description about this attributes are mention in Dataset detail section.

Pre-processed data is input to K-means Clustering (dataset, k) where k in K-means indicates total number of centers.

All data points/seeds (records) and iteratively converging to centroid still the optimal solution is obtained. Local optima and outlier problem is properly analyzed, So that an optimal solution can be obtained. Clustered output is given as input to feed forward layer of ANN classifier where recursive classification iteration converges the data point to respective class. In theory, ANN led to longer training times, but faster classifications. This is because an ANN requires a lot of computer power to

Table 2. Input Attributes

Name	Type	Description
Sex	Discrete	1 = male 0 = female
Age	Continuous	Age in years
Trestbps (resting BP)	Continuous	Resting BP (in mm Hg)
Cp(chest pain)	Discrete	CP type: 0= typical angina 1 = atypical angina 2 = non-anginal pain 3 =asymptomatic
Fbs (fasting blood sugar)	Discrete	FBS > 120 mg/dl: 1 = true 0 = false
Chol (cholesterol)	Continuous	Serum cholesterol in mg/dl
Thalach	Continuous	Maximum heart rate achieved
Restecg (resting ECG)	Discrete	Resting ECG results: 0= normal 1= having ST-T wave abnormality 2=showing probable 3=define left ventricular hypertrophy
Slope	Discrete	The slope of the peak exercise segment: 0= up sloping 1= flat 2= down sloping
Thal	Discrete	0 = normal 1= fixed defect 2= reversible defect
Exang	Discrete	Exercise induced angina: 1 = yes 0 = no

converge, but once it has, the computations are fairly simple. This limitation was successfully managed by K-means output. K-means Converges faster than any other method. So a new combination of ANN and K-means leads to provide faster and optimal solution. Using this method we already achieved a precision of 97.02% and sensitivity of 93.45%.

Data Set Details

The Cleveland dataset from UCI repository is used for heart disease prediction using ANN and K-means. The dataset has 76 attributes. Cleveland dataset from UCI repository is a real time datasets generated from patient records and they have around 76 attributes including a prediction attribute, which suggests regarding the severity of disease on scale of 1 to 4 or no presence at all. In this experiment 11 attributes are used for this research & testing as given in Table 1.

Dataset repository: UCI repository

True Positives (TP): The experiments which are anticipated yes i.e those individuals have the cardiovascular infection and they really have them.

True Negatives (TN): The experiments which are anticipated no, and furthermore they those people don't have the illness.

False Positives (FP): It is called as Type I error. The cases that are predicted yes while those people actually don't have the disease.

False Negatives (FN): It is also called as Type II error. The cases which are predicted no, while those people they do have the disease.

Confusion matrix is drawn which shows the rate of occurrence of correct and incorrect predictions of heart disease in the trained model where actual values are compared predicted values

Experimental Results:

Sensitivity and Precision are standard measures to check efficiency of implemented algorithm.

Precision= | (Relevant documents intersect Retrieved documents) |
| (Retrieved documents)|

Accuracy= | (Relevant document intersect Retrieved document) |
|(Relevant documents)|

An experimental setup for evaluating the performance of proposed algorithm consists of Intel core i3 processor CPU @2.60GHz system with 4GB RAM. A dataset file is given as an input to find the accuracy. Figure 8 shows loading of datasets for purpose of training.

Figure 8 shows that dataset is loaded for training purpose.

In Figure 9 The dataset can be viewed which is loaded from UCI repository dataset. One can also add or remove the record from these dataset.

Table 3. Confusion Matrix

	True Positive	True Negative
Predicted Positive	464	192
Predicted Negative	7	53

Table 4. Standard Measures

Measure	Value	Derivations
Precision	97.02	PPV = TP / (TP + FP)
Recall	93.45	TPR = TP / (TP + FN)

Figure 8. Load CSV File

Figure 9. Manage Dataset

Figure 10. Single Data Entry

Heart Disease Prediction System

Add New Entry

AGE	YOUTH
SEX	FEMALE
CHEST PAIN	TYPICAL ANGINA
RESTING BLOOD PRESSURE	NORMAL
CHOLESTROL	NORMAL
FASTING BLOOD SUGAR	FALSE
RESTING ECG	NORMAL
EXERCISE INDUCED ANGINA	NO
SLOPE	NORMAL
THAL	UP

CANCEL   OK

Here, making use of parameters such as age, CP, fasting BP, cholesterol, resting ECG, slope,sex, Thal, etc. single data entry can be done.

In figure 11.Single and multiple data entry can be calculated and then analyzed to calculate accuracy. Hybrid methodology showed that true positive rates are 457 and True negative rates are 213 while false positive rates are 14 and false negative rates are 32.The accuracy calculated are 97.02 and recall is 93.45.

Figure 11. Prediction Results

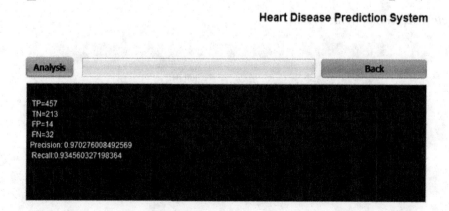

Heart Disease Prediction System

Analysis   Back

TP=457
TN=213
FP=14
FN=32
Precision: 0.970276008492569
Recall:0.934560327198364

Proposed Bigdata Architecture

Accurate analysis in big data can lead to more certain decision-making. Apache Spark is used for this, which a cluster is computing innovation produced for quick calculation. It depends on Hadoop MapReduce and which broadens the MapReduceidea.The center thought behind Spark is its in-memory group processing which speedups the getting ready rate of an application. It is produced for dealing a tremendous scope of application such as iterative calculations, interactive queries, batch applications and streaming. It gives a quicker and broader information managing out stage. Spark allows you to run programs up to 100 times speeder in memory, or 10 times quicker on disk, than Hadoop.

Components of Spark

Figure 12 gives us the components of Spark.

Apache Spark Core

Spark Core is the core part for extensive parallel and distributed information preparing and is accountable for following tasks:

- Fault recuperation and memory management.
- Allocating and observing jobs on a cluster and scheduling.
- Interaction with storage organizations.

It presents the idea of a Resilient Distributed Dataset. RDD is unchanging fault-tolerant, distributed collection of objects which can be functioned in parallel and provides below mention types of activities:

Figure 12. Components of Spark

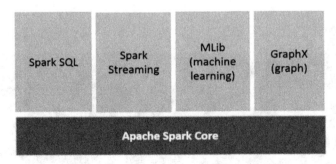

- Transformations operations are which includes map, filter, join, union, etc which are carry out on Resilient Distributed Dataset(RDD) and produces another Resilient Distributed Dataset holding the outcome.
- Actions are operations include reduce, count, first etc which generates a value after performing computation on Resilient Distributed Dataset.

Transformations operation in Spark don't creates their outcomes however simply "recollect" the task to be performed and the recordset (e.g., document) on which the activity is to be completed. The transformations are figured when an action operation is called and the outcome is again come back to the driver program. It offers in-memory computing and referencing datasets in exterior storing organizations.

2. Spark SQL

It provides querying data either using HQL (Hive Query Language) or SQL. It created as the Apache Hive port to run on top of Spark (in place of MapReduce) and is presently combined with the Spark stack.

3. Spark Streaming

Deals real time processing of streaming information such as web-based social networking like Twitter, creation web server's log records (e.g. HDFS/S3 and Apache Flume) and numerous informing lines like Kafka.. It accepts input data and splits into groups. Next, they get worked by the Spark engine and produce final stream of outcomes in groups.

4. MLlib

Is a machine learning library which bolsters various algorithms for regression, clustering, classification and collaborative filtering which is nine times faster than ApachMahut (machine learning library for Hadoop) .

5. GraphX

This library is utilized for graphs and performs graph-parallel tasks.
In order to make use of Apache spark following steps have to be taken:

1. Data collection and exploration.
2. Load all required packages and APIs.
3. Create Spark session.

4.   Data parsing and RDD of Label point creation.
5.   Splitting the RDD of label point into training and test set.
6.   Training the model and predict the heart diseases possibility.
7.   Predictive analysis using the test set.
8.   Predictive analytics using the new dataset and check the accuracy by using the same classifier algorithm on different data set.

CONCLUSION

Data which is related to Health care are massive in nature and arrive from different places and which are in dissimilar form. Nowadays, the use of information and experience of experts and restorative screening information of patients are created in a database amid the analysis procedure. Care managers, mainly skilled nurses who are developing healthcare by allowing patients directly to change their routine and habits based on study and data are required to help patients in this new data-driven healthcare scene. Apache spark is used as the processing framework for doing big data analysis.

FUTURE SCOPE

Information produced through this research can be used

1.   To develop a tool for healthcare manufactures which are running their business on outcome based method.
2.   Implementation of correct machine learning algorithms are used to decide the heart disease possibility and comparison of different algorithms are done to assess the accuracy using graphs which are easier to understand and the user can also control their risk level and get the similar report.
3.   It is a major concern, needs to provide privacy against hackers, identity theft, and the illegal uses of healthcare data is to be secured.
4.   Use of IOT - The IoT can also be used to predict heart disease prediction based on monitoring of the elderly, sensors, and data which can then be processed using Big Data analytics. Same for IoT
5.   Wireless detection of a heart attack - Smartphones, smartwatches and other human-based sensors can be used for predicting and preventing heart attacks prior to occurrence by reading the electrocardiogram which may show changes prior to heart attack and alert the person immediately.

REFERENCES

Acharya, U. R., Bhat, P. S., Iyengar, S. S., Rao, A., & Dua, S. (2003). Classification of heart rate data using artificial neural network and fuzzy equivalence relation. *Pattern Recognition*, *36*(1), 61–68. doi:10.1016/S0031-3203(02)00063-8

Ahmed, M. M., & Mohamad, D. B. (2008). Segmentation of brain MR images for tumor extraction by combining k-means clustering and perona-malik anisotropic diffusion model. *International Journal of Image Processing*, *2*(1), 27–34.

Begum, S., & Sulegaon, K. (2016). Analysis of various big data techniques for security. *International Journal of Computer Science and Mobile Computing*, *5*(3), 54-58.

Chandna, D. (2014). Diagnosis of heart disease using data mining algorithm. *International Journal of Computer Science and Information Technologies*, *5*(2), 1678–1680.

Dangare & Sulabha. (2012). Improved Study of Heart Disease Prediction System using Data Mining Classification Techniques. *IJCA*, *47*(10), 44-48.

Das, R., Turkoglu, I., & Sengur, A. (2009). Effective diagnosis of heart disease through neural networks ensembles. *Expert Systems with Applications*, *36*(4), 7675–7680. doi:10.1016/j.eswa.2008.09.013

Devi, S. K., Krishnapriya, S., & Kalita, D. (2016). Prediction of Heart Disease using Data Mining Techniques. *Indian Journal of Science and Technology*, *9*(39).

Dewan, A., & Sharma, M. (2015 March). Prediction of heart disease using a hybrid technique in data mining classification, In *Computing for Sustainable Global Development (INDIACom), 2015 2nd International Conference* (pp. 704-706). IEEE.

Dharma Rahadi, P. S. A., Shobirin, K. A., & Ariyani, S. (2016). Big Data Management. *International Journal of Engineering and Emerging Technology*, *1*(1).

Fayyad, U. M., Piatetsky-Shapiro, G., & Smyth, P. (1996, August). Knowledge Discovery and Data Mining. *Towards a Unifying Framework in KDD*, *96*, 82–88.

Goebel, M., & Gruenwald, L. (1999). A survey of data mining and knowledge discovery software tools. *ACM SIGKDD Explorations Newsletter*, *1*(1), 20-33.

Hartigan, J. A., & Wong, M. A. (1979). Algorithm AS 136: A k-means clustering algorithm. *Journal of the Royal Statistical Society. Series C, Applied Statistics*, *28*(1), 100–108.

Kadam, Paikrao, & Pawar. (2013). Survey on Cloud Computing Security. *International Journal of Emerging Technology and Advanced Engineering, 3*(12).

Kahramanli, H., & Allahverdi, N. (2008). Design of a hybrid system for the diabetes and heart diseases. *Expert Systems with Applications, 35*(1), 82–89. doi:10.1016/j.eswa.2007.06.004

Kahramanli, H., & Allahverdi, N. (2008). Design of a hybrid system for the diabetes and heart diseases. *Expert Systems with Applications, 35*(1), 82–89. doi:10.1016/j.eswa.2007.06.004

Kalyani, D., & Pooja, K. (2017). Prediction of heart disease using k-means and artificial neural network as hybrid approach to improve accuracy. *International Journal of Engineering and Technology, 9*(4), 3081–3085. doi:10.21817/ijet/2017/v9i4/170904101

Kurgan, L. A., & Musilek, P. (2006). A survey of Knowledge Discovery and Data Mining process model. *The Knowledge Engineering Review, 21*(1), 1–24. doi:10.1017/S0269888906000737

Manikantan, V., & Latha, S. (2013). Predicting the analysis of heart disease symptoms using medicinal data mining methods. *International Journal of Advanced Computer Theory and Engineering, 2*, 46–51.

Polat & Gunes. (2007). A hybrid approach to medical decision support systems: Combining feature selection, fuzzy weighted pre-processing and AIRS. *Computer Methods and Programs in Biomedicine, 88*, 164–174.

Purao, S., Storey, V., Sugumaran, V., Conesa, J., Minguillón, J., & Casas, J. (2011). Repurposing social tagging data for extraction of domain-level concepts. *Natural Language Processing and Information Systems,* 185-192.

Rajkumar, A., & Reena, G. S. (2010). Diagnosis of heart disease using data mining algorithm. *Global Journal of Computer Science and Technology, 10*(10), 38-43.

Ratnaparkhi, D., Mahajan, T., & Jadhav, V. (2015). Heart Disease Prediction System Using Data Mining Technique. *International Research Journal of Engineering and Technology, 2*(08), 2395–0056.

Santhi, P. (2011). Improving the performance of Data Mining Algorithm in Health Care data. *International Journal of Clothing Science and Technology, 2*(3).

Sen, A. K., Patel, S. B., & Shukla, D. P. (2013). A data mining technique for prediction of coronary heart disease using neuro-fuzzy integrated approach two level. *International Journal of Engineering and Computer Science, 2*(9), 1663–1671.

Setiawan, N. A. (2009, December). Rule Selection for Coronary Artery Disease Diagnosis Based on Rough Set. *International Journal of Recent Trends in Engineering, 2*(5), 198–202.

Shukla, D. P., Patel, S. B., Sen, A. K., & Yadav, P. K. (2013). *Analysis of Attribute Association Rule from Large Medical Datasets towards Heart Disease Prediction.* Academic Press.

Soni, J., Ansari, U., Sharma, D., & Soni, S. (2011). Predictive data mining for medical diagnosis: An overview of heart disease prediction. *International Journal of Computers and Applications, 17*(8), 43–48. doi:10.5120/2237-2860

Steinbach, M., Karypis, G., & Kumar, V. (2000 August). A comparison of document clustering technique. KDD Workshop on Text Mining, 400(1), 525-526.

Sumathi, S., & Sivanandam, S. N. (2006). *Introduction to data mining and its applications* (Vol. 29). Springer. doi:10.1007/978-3-540-34351-6

Taneja, A. (2013). Heart disease prediction system using data mining techniques. Oriental. *Journal of Computer Science and Technology, 6*(4), 457–466.

Tu, Shin, & Shin. (2009). Effective Diagnosis of Heart Disease through Bagging Approach, study report, 2009. *2009 2nd International Conference on Biomedical Engineering and Informatics.*

Vijayarani, S., & Sudha, S. (2013). An efficient classification tree technique for heart disease prediction. *International Journal of Computer Applications, 201.*

Wasan, Bhatnagar, & Kaur. (2006, October). The Impact of Data Mining techniques on medical diagnostics. *Data Science Journal, 5*(19), 119–126.

Zhang, L., Li, J., Shi, Y., & Liu, X. (2009). Foundations of intelligent knowledge management. *Human Systems Management, 28*(4), 145–161.

Chapter 8
Classification and Machine Learning

Damian Alberto
Indian Institute of Technology Bombay, India

ABSTRACT

The manual classification of a large amount of textual materials are very costly in time and personnel. For this reason, a lot of research has been devoted to the problem of automatic classification and work on the subject dates from 1960. A lot of text classification software has appeared. For some tasks, automatic classifiers perform almost as well as humans, but for others, the gap is still large. These systems are directly related to machine learning. It aims to achieve tasks normally affordable only by humans. There are generally two types of learning: learning "by heart," which consists of storing information as is, and learning generalization, where we learn from examples. In this chapter, the authors address the classification concept in detail and how to solve different classification problems using different machine learning techniques.

INTRODUCTION

The manual classification of a large amount of textual materials are very costly in time and personnel for this reason a lot of research has been devoted to the problem of automatic classification and work on the subject dates from 1960.

These days a lot of text classification software have appeared For some tasks, automatic classifiers perform almost as well as humans, but for others, the gap is still large, these systems are directly related to machine learning (machine learning) it aims to achieve tasks normally affordable only by human there are generally two

DOI: 10.4018/978-1-5225-7338-8.ch008

Figure 1. Classification of texts (Sriram, 2010)

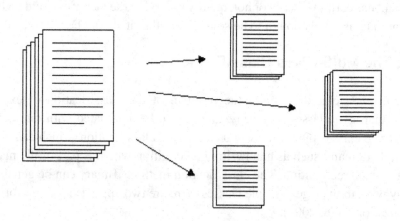

types of learning: learning "by heart" which consists of storing information as is, and learning generalization where we learn from examples a model we will recognize new examples (Ko, 2012).

In this chapter we will address the classification concept in detail how to solve different classification problems were appealed to different machine learning kind. The text classification is a generic task of assigning one or more categories from a predefined list or not a document by finding a functional link between a set of texts and a set of categories (tags, classes) according to criteria. They apply to many human activities and particularly suited to the problems of automated decision-making.

For example: we are faced with a set of target text and the goal is to make a computer application capable of autonomously determine in which category classified each text, based on statistical data. Habitually the categories refer to the text subjects, but for particular applications, they can take other forms (Nigam, 2000).

Classification can be found in several application domains as the language identification, recognition of writing, Categorization of multimedia document, spam detection, speech recognition, aid to medical diagnosis.

CLASSIFICATION DUAL CLASS AND MULTI CLASS

The Bi-Classes Classification

The bi-classes classification is a kind of problem examples for which the classification system answers the question: Does the text belongs to the category "C" or to its complementary class (Wu, 2004). some tasks Typical of binary classification are:

determining whether a document is it plagiarize or not, Medical tests to determine if a patient has certain disease or not, quality control in the factories decide whether a new product is good enough to be sold, or whether it should be eliminated.

III 3-2-The Multi-Class Classification

The multi-class classification is the problem of the classification of examples in more than two classes or given example can be associated with one or more classes or no class is the most general case of the classification, which can be used in multiple domain: such as handwriting recognition which is part of the marking speech, speech recognition. The classification methods Binary can be generalized in many ways to manage multiple classes there are two approaches to perform this generalization. (Wu, 2004).

- **Approach One-Against-All (OAA):** Allows the direct use of standard binary classifiers to encode and form the output label and assume that for each class, there is only one (single) separation between this class and all other classes that is to say each class is opposed to all other classes. The mth classifier separates the data from the M class all data remains latter takes one sign and another class -1.
- **One Against One (OAO):**Is a more expressive alternative that assumes the existence of a separator between each two classes this method is called a one against this is to say that each class is discriminated from another or one must calculate M (M-1) / 2 classifier (Polat, 2009).

WHY AUTOMATIC DOCUMENT CLASSIFICATION?

The major consequences that pose a manual processing (by a human) classification of textual documents are:

- The classification of textual material is difficult to be manually performed by a human being because it takes a long time for:
  - Read and reread each document line by line and memorize it.
  - Much time is used in reflection to the final decision (associate a text category).
  - The number of class play a very important role in the classification of costs.
- The playback speed changes from one person to another so it is on decision making also not going to be the same for each person.

- Check other texts that are in the same category as the text filed to validate the decision.
- The difference between the class of such classified document into two category "Medicine" and "right" is easier than classified document any of the following categories "Natural Language Processing" and "Artificial Intelligence"
- The classification shall be made in a way that the groups obtained are made of similar observations and that the groups are as different as possible between them.
- The generalization of a manual classification to other areas is almost impossible. (Lodhi, 2002)

The classification of texts is a problem that can be directly related to machine learning (artificial).

Machine Learning (Machine Learning)

Machine learning is at the crossroads of many other areas: artificial intelligence, statistics, cognitive science, probability theory, which refers to computer algorithms that allow a machine to evolve through a learning process, it is based on a kind of observation or data as examples or experiences to fulfill the tasks that it is difficult to fill by algorithmic means more classics such as make precise prediction or retrieve and operate automatically information presented in a dataset. (Liu, 2002)

In general: machine learning is to learn to do better in the future on the basis of what was known in the past or we can consider it as programming example.

"Learning denotes changes in a system that allows it to do the same task more efficiently the next time," Herbert Simon. Machine learning is surrounded by several disciplines as shown in the following figure (Kubat, 1998).

5-1-FROM LEARNING NATURAL TO THE ARTIFICIAL

Natural learning is done differs from the artificial it is achieved not by a machine but by a human For example:

We ask a human review to classify by theme how it will make no particular or prior knowledge?

If he is alone he reads the magazine and try to observe points of similarity or difference between them so he can find a way to combine the review theme.

If it is accompanied by an expert can help the problem but it No there's not much time for him so he just some example classified by the expert for the rest

Figure 2. Discipline around machine learning

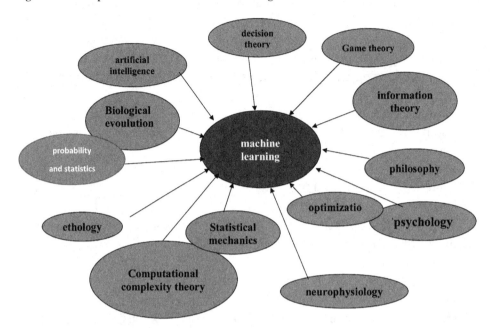

classified examples that did not had time them classified. all his shows the machine learning process. The machine can be faced with situation where she must learn only (not supervise learning) or on the contrary with the help of an expert (learning supervision). (Liu, 2002)

Learning Algorithm

Learning algorithm is an algorithm taking into entering a given set of "D" (set of training or learning) and returns a function F (model) model obtained was train on all "D".

Set "D" contains the form of vector information needed to solve a problem (e.g. classification) Learning .Algorithme enables automatic adaptation to the production of a stain or each algorithm is known to work on some type of spot and unsure else.

Choosing a learning algorithm usually depends on the type of text to be classified (form, article, quiz, etc.), purpose and scope of application. For example, applications designed for the medical field requires the most accurate algorithms learning possible that different learning algorithms used to design a search engine in a bookstore website and DEPOND also the task to solve (classification, estimation values, ect) and for each task there are a variety of algorithms (Nasrabadi, 2007).

Learning Models

The model will allow the learner to learn effectively as a means for achieving the desired task. The choice of model to use is therefore essential for success optimal learning. This bias is different in nature depending on the model chosen:

- **Functional:** He is then based on a decision function on the input attributes for establishing a separation. The most famous and easiest is probably the linear function (eg SVM Support Vector Machine).
- **Probabilistic:** It is then based on a probability distribution on the attributes of entries. Bayesian networks are probably typical of this kind of model.
- **Connexionnis:** The is then based on a neural network. This type of model is based on the basis of how the human brain We quote perceptrons and multilayer neural networks (MLP) as typical examples connectionist.
- **Time:** It will be based on a temporal coupling between the inputs. This type of model describes different temporal states in which one is likely to be the typical example is the Hidden Markov Model.

Why Machine Learning

- Certain tasks are well defined as via a set an example to clearly specify the relationship between the output entries.
- The amount of data can contain important relationships that the methods of machine learning allow to find out.
- The machine learning may better exploit the knowledge or the human brain can not explicit.
- The machine learning, machine to adapt to environmental changes without systematically re-design after changing the environment.

TYPES OF LEARNING

Supervised Learning

A supervisor (expert or oracle) is available to correctly labeled learning or training data in this case, D is a set of "n" pairs of inputs "xt" and associated label "yl" and the "F" going to be defined in an explicit way by the learning algorithm such learning consists of two Phase

- **Learning Phase (Training):** In this phase the learning algorithm receives input labeled learning example "D" and produced a most powerful predictive model possible, that is to say the model that produces the lowest prediction errors as presented in Figure 3.
- **Prediction:** This task is to predict one or more unknown characteristics from a set of characteristic known .For example: predicting the quality of a customer based on his back and his many children. (Liu, 2002)
- **The Test Phase:** This is the phase of prediction of the new instance depending on the model obtained during the learning phase that going associating each enter "X" any outlet (label) "Y" which typically will have been given by the supervisor (test the accuracy of the model).

These two phases can be Executed consecutively ways supervised learning offline or iterative supervised learning online.

PROBLEM SOLVED BY LEARNING OVERSEE

the application of learning oversee concerns medicine: given a patient's test results and the knowledge of the other patients state where the same analyzes were carried out it is possible to assess the risk sick of this new patient based on the similarity of its analyzes with those of another patient. in general, two major types of problems that the supervised learning is applied: the supervised classification (categorization), the regression.

Figure 3. Learning Phase

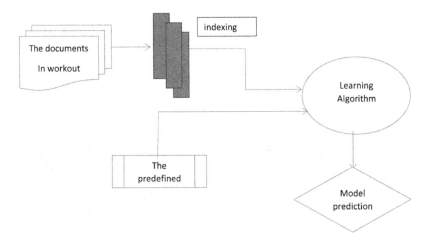

Figure 4. Test phase

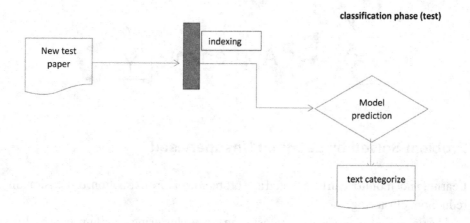

Text Categorization (Supervised Classification): She predicts whether a text is a member of a group or a predefined class .It classification of each text $x \in X$ from a class together existing (known in advance).

The general principle is to seek a prediction model estimated by supervised learning.This classification can be used to type in a number field, for example.

Spam Filtering: Identify emails as spam or non-spam.
Medical Diagnosis: Diagnose a patient as a sick or not sick from a disease.
Forecast Weather: Predicting, for example, whether it will rain tomorrow.

Unsupervised Machine Learning

No supervisor is available and D training data contains entries "X" label and not the prediction model produced by the learning algorithm will be implied. The algorithm must discover for himself the similarities and differences between data and aims to characterize the distribution of data, and relationships between variables, without discriminating between the observed variables and variables to predict. for this type of learning rather it is the user who has to specify the problem to solve .the figure **5** presents a learner who receives three input X1, X2, X3 and X1 and X2 are label output by Y1 and Y2 with X3.

Figure 5. Unsupervised learning operation

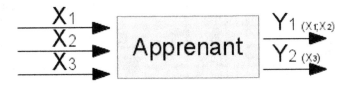

Problem Solved by Learning Unsupervised

Learning not monitor can be adapted as a problem: feature extraction, dimensionality reduction, clustering.

Unsupervised classification (clustering): the clustering problem is a problem Logical partitioning of the set of D data sub set (cluster) or each cluster has a certaindegree of internal coherence as shown in Figure 6 (Pedregosa, 2011).

The classification is not oversee the search for main classes of distribution through the process of learning not supervise because the class are not known in advance (data cache).

Similarly one can also consider that each instance can belong has one group (hard clustering) Consider that each example has a given probability of belonging to each of the groups (clustering software). [C03] [C01]

The problem here is more difficult because the available observations are not initially identified as belonging to a particular population: it will deduct this information at our classification (Arai, 2007).

Figure 6. Clustering (Arai, 2007)

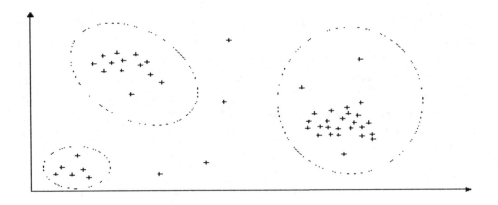

Application Example

Marketing: Market Segmentation by finding groups of separate customers from purchasing databases. city planning: identification of groups of dwellings according to the type of dwelling, value, geographical location ect ......

Insurance: identification of distinct groups of insured associated with a large number of claims.

NO-SUPERVISED LEARNING ALGORITHM

The Hierarchical Classification

Allows you to build a cluster tree, called dendrogram which shows how clusters are organized .or the number of cluster "K" is not required as data By cutting the dendrogram at the desired level, a classification of data into disjoint groups is obtained with the use of a distance matrix as clustering criterion. (de Hoon, 2004)

The hierarchical classification methods are divided into two types of approaches: ascending and descending that are presented in the following figure:

The Data-Partitioning Algorithm (Non-Hierarchical)

The algorithm shares data into several together and seeks to directly decompose the database in a cluster together disjointed More specifically, they try to determine a number of scores that optimize certain criteria (objective function). [C04] The objective function can enhance the local or global data structure and its optimization is an iterative process Among the non-hierarchical algorithms most used:

Kmeans (k-Average)

K-means with the intention of n objects into k classes where each object belongs to the cluster with the nearest average. This method produces exactly k different groups distinguish the greatest. The best number of clusters k leading to greater separation (distance) is not known as a priori and must be calculated from the data. The objective of K-means is to minimize total intra-cluster variance, or function of the squared error (Jain, 2010).

Figure 7. Upward and downward classification (Arai, 2007)

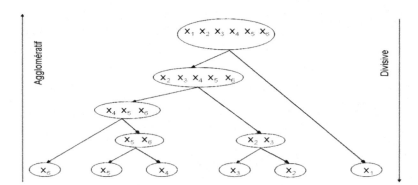

Algorithm

Input: x1 data sample, ..., xm

1. Select k random points as the classes.c1 centers ..., ck
2. Assign each of the m data in group i whose center is nearest. using the Euclidean distance function
3. If no element group changes then stop and get out groups
4. Calculate the new centers: for all i, is the average of the i group elements.
5. Go 2 and repeating steps until the same points are assigned to each group

Advantages

- Relatively extensible in the overall processing of large
- The results are relatively effective
- Generally produces a local optimum and global optimum can be obtained by using another technique: genetic algorithms ... .ECT
- The downside: Applicable only if the average of the objects is defined to specify the number of cluster K a priori unable to process noisy data, the point isolate poorly managed.

Method Based on the Density

the use of similarity measures (distance) is less efficient than using central idea neighborhood density is to group related items of all data in classes according to a density function for minimizing the distance inter -clusters is not always a good criterion to recognize the "form".

The Semi-Supervised Machine Learning Algorithm (Hybrid)

It's a mix between the basic principle of learning and not supervise supervise use when labeling example is expensive this type of learning that has been very important in recent years improves outcome.

A supervisor is partly available and some label data. The algorithm will then learn the classification task based on the supervisor put labels and discovering for himself the missing information (the unlabeled example).

Semi-supervised algorithms operate on the same two phases but accept more untagged data during the training phase as the figure or the training set (not labeled x1 and x2 labeled). [C05]

Ex: In medicine, it can be an aid to diagnosis.

Reinforcement Learning

The main objective is to lead an agent to act intelligently in a given environment. An agent interacts with the environment by choosing, at any given time to perform an action from a set of allowable actions. The intelligent behavior must learn this agent is given implicitly via enhanced signal after each officer's decision, says it has right or wrong and the officer enter as an indicator or set of characteristic describing the environment as shown in the following figure:

Ex: The algorithm Q-learning(The concept of time does not exist) or Td-Learning (dynamic: the concept of time exists). This type of learning is applied in many fields such as games (ladies), robotics .... ect.

Figure 8. Semi supervised learning operation

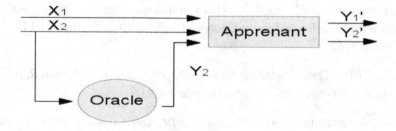

Figure 9. Learning operation by strengthening (Lin, 1992)

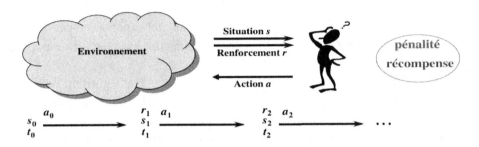

CONCLUSION

This chapter includes the text classification problem and how to solve this problem at Eid a machine learning as we view the type of learning defeated their limits and areas of application of each of them in detail some popular learning algorithm.

REFERENCES

Arai, K., & Barakbah, A. R. (2007). Hierarchical K-means: An algorithm for centroids initialization for K-means. *Reports of the Faculty of Science and Engineering, 36*(1), 25–31.

de Hoon, M. J., Imoto, S., Nolan, J., & Miyano, S. (2004). Open source clustering software. *Bioinformatics (Oxford, England), 20*(9), 1453–1454. doi:10.1093/bioinformatics/bth078 PMID:14871861

Guo, G., Wang, H., Bell, D., Bi, Y., & Greer, K. (2003, November). KNN model-based approach in classification. In *OTM Confederated International Conferences On the Move to Meaningful Internet Systems* (pp. 986-996). Springer. 10.1007/978-3-540-39964-3_62

Jain, A. K. (2010). Data clustering: 50 years beyond K-means. *Pattern Recognition Letters, 31*(8), 651–666. doi:10.1016/j.patrec.2009.09.011

Jambu, M., & Lebeaux, M. O. (1978). *Classification automatique pour l'analyse des données* (Vol. 1). Paris: Dunod.

Ko, Y. (2012, August). A study of term weighting schemes using class information for text classification. In *Proceedings of the 35th international ACM SIGIR conference on Research and development in information retrieval* (pp. 1029-1030). ACM. 10.1145/2348283.2348453

Kubat, M., Holte, R. C., & Matwin, S. (1998). Machine learning for the detection of oil spills in satellite radar images. *Machine Learning, 30*(2-3), 195–215. doi:10.1023/A:1007452223027

Lin, L. J. (1992). Self-improving reactive agents based on reinforcement learning, planning and teaching. *Machine Learning, 8*(3-4), 293–321. doi:10.1007/BF00992699

Liu, B., Lee, W. S., Yu, P. S., & Li, X. (2002, July). *Partially supervised classification of text documents* (Vol. 2). ICML.

Lodhi, H., Saunders, C., Shawe-Taylor, J., Cristianini, N., & Watkins, C. (2002). Text classification using string kernels. *Journal of Machine Learning Research, 2*(Feb), 419–444.

Nasrabadi, N. M. (2007). Pattern recognition and machine learning. *Journal of Electronic Imaging, 16*(4), 049901. doi:10.1117/1.2819119

Nigam, K., McCallum, A. K., Thrun, S., & Mitchell, T. (2000). Text classification from labeled and unlabeled documents using EM. *Machine Learning, 39*(2-3), 103–134. doi:10.1023/A:1007692713085

Pedregosa, F., Varoquaux, G., Gramfort, A., Michel, V., Thirion, B., Grisel, O., ... Vanderplas, J. (2011). Scikit-learn: Machine learning in Python. *Journal of Machine Learning Research, 12*(Oct), 2825–2830.

Polat, K., & Güneş, S. (2009). A novel hybrid intelligent method based on C4. 5 decision tree classifier and one-against-all approach for multi-class classification problems. *Expert Systems with Applications, 36*(2), 1587–1592. doi:10.1016/j.eswa.2007.11.051

Sriram, B., Fuhry, D., Demir, E., Ferhatosmanoglu, H., & Demirbas, M. (2010, July). Short text classification in twitter to improve information filtering. In *Proceedings of the 33rd international ACM SIGIR conference on Research and development in information retrieval* (pp. 841-842). ACM. 10.1145/1835449.1835643

Wu, T. F., Lin, C. J., & Weng, R. C. (2004). Probability estimates for multi-class classification by pairwise coupling. *Journal of Machine Learning Research, 5*(Aug), 975–1005.

Chapter 9
Clear and Private Ad Hoc Retrieval Models on Web Data

Souria Ortiga
Mente Argentina University, Argentina

ABSTRACT

During the 1980s, and despite its maturity, the search information (RI) was only intended for librarians and experts in the field of information. Such tendentious vision prevailed for many years. Since the mid-90s, the web has become an increasingly crucial source of information , which has a renewed interest in IR. In the last decade, the popularization of computers, the terrible explosion in the amount of unstructured data, internal documents, and corporate collections, and the huge and growing number of internet document sources have deeply shaken the relationship between man and information. Today, a great change has taken place, and the RI is often used by billions of people around the world. Simply, the need for automated methods for efficient access to this huge amount of digital information has become more important, and appears as a necessity.

INTRODUCTION

During the 1980s and despite its maturity, the search information (RI) was only intended for librarians and experts in the field of information. Such tendentious vision prevailed for many years. Since the mid 90s, the Web has become a source of information increasingly crucial, which has a renewed interest in IR. In the last decade, the popularization of computers, the terrible explosion in the amount of unstructured data, internal documents and corporate collections, and the huge and growing number of internet document sources, have deeply shaken the relationship

DOI: 10.4018/978-1-5225-7338-8.ch009

between man and information. Today, in modern life a great change has taken place and the RI is often used by billions of people around the world. However, we are awash in a rising tide of information that the social web has had a wider impact on all sectors of our life. Simply, the need for automated methods for efficient access to this huge amount of digital information has become more important, and appears as a necessity (Frakes, 1992).

IR is the discipline that deals with the search for unstructured data in response to a need for user, which can itself be unstructured, for example, a sentence, a profile or even another document, which can be as structured, for example, a Boolean expression.

In this chapter we highlight an overview of the state of the art on different spots and IR issues we discussed during this chapter are: The ad hoc research, clear and private; information filtering and especially spam filtering problems and plagiarism detection;

AD-HOC RESEARCH (AR)

The ad-hoc research (RA) is the standard task in classical IR, based on the interrogation of the information elements (documents in the collection) by the user to obtain the necessary documents after a specified query. The RA has recently conquered the world, fueling not only sought engines in the web, but also any type of unstructured research behind the great web ecommerce. . The objective of this task is to automate the document analysis process calculates the comparison between the representation of the need for the information (query) and representation of documents (Larson, 2010).

RA is a process quite familiar to most of us because we all probably use Google at least once a day on average. This task order is to maintain a collection of documents and when a new request comes, we seek in this collection to identify the appropriate documents (called relevant) for this request. The need for information is supposed to be on time rather than long term (as the case in the filtering task see section) and one request at a time is compared to a static document collection. This type of research provides an open field for the user to specify what he needs as a query without any restrictions. Finally,(Kowalski, 2006).

General Architecture of an Ad-Hoc Research Model (MRA)

A research model Ad-Hoc (MRA) is a process that stores and manages information on documents, often text documents but can also be multimedia (pictures or video). For example we have some query, q, which is an expression of user needs. An MRA compared with a corpus of documents, $C = \{d\ (1)...D\ (n)\}$. The goal is to select some documents C and classified according to a score of relevance to the needs of the user as expressed by q.

A perfect MRA should retrieve only relevant documents and any non-relevant documents. However, this is impossible, because search statements are incomplete and relevance depends on the subjective opinion of the user. In practice, two users can put the same request to a MRA and judge the relevance of documents retrieved differently: some users will appreciate the results, others not (Qin, 2010).

As shown in the figure above is an MRA up of three main components. The inputs of a MRA are: the query expression that represents the user's information needs and a set of documents in the collection (can be images, text, objects etc ...) which are a source of interest. These data elements will be the entrance of representation component.

Representation

Regardless of the format that can take the documents in the collection or query, they need representation before they can be compared. This representation component also called indexing, is a set of rules and notations for transforming the query or collection document into an index using different steps such as: the definition of the data source, cleaning, segmentation generating a set of terms representing a logical view of the documents and the query, coding to make the manipulatable terms by the machine. Finally a set of indexes are built to allow quick search of large amounts of data. The objective is that the semantics of documents and requirements of the

Of course, this can be regarded as a considerable simplification of the problem. The terms are to be extracted directly from the text of the document or specified by a subject (eg, labels and comments) human. Some MRA represents a document by all the words that constitute it; However, with very large collections, all representative terms should be reduced, this can be accomplished by eliminating empty words, the use of stemming, and identifying noun (eliminating adjectives, adverbs and verbs) .

RESEARCH

This is the heart of each MRA to calculate the correlation between the index of the query and the index of each document collection built in the previous step. It includes a decision function that is used to send the user a list of relevant documents ordered in a matching score. The performance of this component are closely related to representation component (Metzler).

Figure 1. Generic architecture of a research model Ad-Hoc (MRA) (Baeza-Yates, 1999)

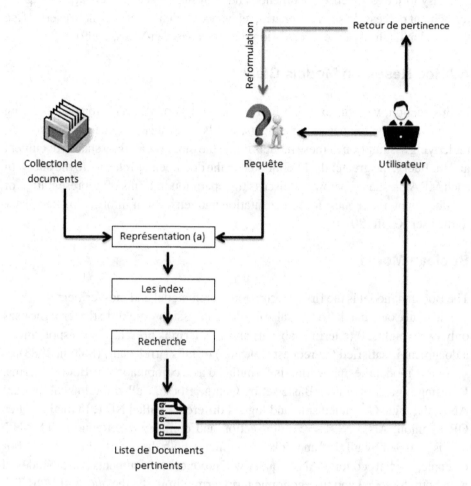

Relevance Feedback (RP)

The main purpose of a MRA is to satisfy the user's needs expressed by a query. The rear of the idea relevance feedback (RF) is to involve the user in the search process to improve the final result set. In particular, the user gives a judgment on the relevance of the documents for the first series of results by marking certain documents returned as relevant or irrelevant. From the user's judgment the model calculates a new representation need the information by restating the original query by adding new terms and a new search will be performed to improve the relevance of previous results. This PR component can pass through one or more iterations of this kind. The process exploits the idea that it can be difficult to formulate a good query when you do not know well the collection of intérogés documents, but it is easy to judge specific documents, and so it makes sense to engage in a query refinement process. In such a scenario, relevance feedback can also help users refine their understanding of the information they need (Baeza-Yates, 1999).

Ad Hoc Research Models Clear

In this section, we will examine four basic models of RA base for manipulating several variables: the needs, documents, words, relevance judgments, ...etc. The underlying assumption of these models is that the more vocabulary share a document and the query, the greater the likelihood that the document is relevant to the query. In each MRA presented below we discuss the operation in terms of: representation of the document, the request for representation and retrieval of information necessary to the user (Croft, 2010).

Boolean Model

The Boolean model is the first information search model and most criticized, which provides an exact match (true or false). It does not assign weights to the terms he uses only two weights, 0 (a term is absent) and 1 (a term is present). Correspondingly, a document is satisfied the request (relevant) or fails (irrelevant) (Salton, 1983).

In this model the application is formulated as a combination of Boolean terms. By using logical operators Basic set by George Boole, Called the logical product AND, the logic OR called sum and logical difference called NOT. In mathematics OR = union, AND NOT = = intersection and complement. Request "T1 AND T2" is satisfied by a D1 if and only if it contains both the terms "T1 and T2". For example, "social economy AND" query will produce all documents that are indexed with both the social and the economic term term. Similarly, the query "T1 OR T2" is satisfied by "D1" if and only if it contains the term "T1" and "T2" or both, such as "political social OR" query will match all documents are indexed with either the term social, or political term, or both. The query "AND NOT t1 t2" D1 satisfied if and only if it contains t1 and t2 does not contain. One advantage of the Boolean model is that it is quick and easy to implement, and gives users (experts) a sense of control as it is immediately clear why a document is found to be relevant to a query. It works well when you know exactly (or so) that the collection contains and what you want (Baeza-Yates, 1999). This model suffers from a number of serious drawbacks summarized below:

- No control over the size of the output: The number of documents satisfying a boolean query varies depending on the frequency of query terms and the number of conjunctions / disjunctions in the expression of motion. For example the union of common terms can cause many more documents that the user could possibly consider. For that a user must set the query by adding conjunctions to increase the size of all relevant documents or disjunctions to decrease. but this is very inaccurate due to lack of knowledge of the user on the frequency of words.

- The request is extremely sensitive to the choice of words and logical connectors used to connect them. The addition of a single term in the query can change the output significantly. In this case users must know exactly what they want.

- Does not provide a ranking of relevant documents: The model is retrieves a document or not, which could lead this model makes decisions rather frustrating. For example, the query "social AND AND union worker" does not match the indexed document with the terms "university AND cake" but not to the indexed document with the words AND social worker.

- The formulation and modification of complex queries is not always obvious to many users (Llopis, 2002).

An Example of Boolean Search

We have a request "(Bayern Bouarara AND AND ahmed) OR ((NOT Madrid) AND (OR Palestine Algeria))" and we are facing a collection of 8 documents. The index of each document is detailed in the following table show the presence (1) and absence (0) of each word in each document. The relevant documents returned by the Boolean model for this query are {document 1, Document 4, paper6, Document 8}

Vector Space Model (MEV)

The SRM recognizes that the use of binary weight is too restrictive, and provides a vector frame in which a partial match is possible. This is achieved by assigning non-binary weights to terms in queries and documents. This allows to consider the documents that match the query terms only partially (Silva, 2000). The main disadvantage of this model is that all relevant documents returned is inaccurate to compare all relevant documents retrieved by the Boolean model. The general process of the SRM comprises two following steps:

Table 1. Boolean indexing Example 8 randomly built documents.

	Saida	Ahmed	Bouarara	Bayern	Madrid	Algeria	Palestine	Arsenal	Match
Document 1	1	1	1	1	0	0	0	0	1
Document 2	0	0	0	0	1	1	0	0	0
Document 3	1	1	1	0	1	0	1	0	0
paper 4	0	0	0	0	0	1	1	1	1
Document 5	1	0	0	0	1	0	0	1	1
Document 6	1	0	1	1	0	1	0	1	0
Document 7	0	0	0	1	1	0	0	1	1
Document 8	1	1	1	1	0	1	0	1	1

Trace

Peter Luhn was the first to propose a statistical approach for RA. He suggested that, to search in a collection of documents, the user must first prepare a query that is similar to the necessary documents. The degree of similarity between the representation of the petition prepared and representations of documents in the collection is used to rank search results (Luhn, 1957). Following this principle Gerard salton and his colleagues have proposed a new matching model approached to represent queries and documents as vectors of weight terms. This model was first proposed for the SMART system (Salton, 1975). Each document element of the vector represents the importance of a specific term in this document, including:

$Qi = (qi1, \ldots\ldots .qin), Dj = (dj1 \ldots\ldots .djn)$ (II.1)

qik djk and give the value of the weight of term k in the Qi request and the document Dj respectively. The goal of this model is to extract the terms from the documents and the query in order to calculate their weight as components of each vector as shown in the following process:

Construction of the Document Space

A common approach to document representation for statistical purposes is to represent each document as a set of terms. The terms are automatically extracted from the documents themselves, they can be sentences, n-grams, word, or manually assigned descriptors. It depends on the technique of representation used as a bag of words, sentence bag, N-gram characters, … .etc (Liu, 2011).

This step aims to generate a set of terms representing each document. Then, when we take the union of sets of terms of all documents, we get all the terms representing the entire collection. This set of words is called a space Documents such that each distinct term represents a size in this space.

Calculate the Weight of the Words

In this step, we need to assign a numerical weight to each word in each document, which is a statistical estimate. It should be noted that a given term may receive a different weight in each document in which it appears; a term can be a better descriptor in a document against another. A term that does not appear in a document given a zero weight in the vector of this document. Weights for terms in D1 can then be interpreted as D1 coordinates in the document space. Finally, the collection of documents can be viewed as a matrix (documents * terms). Each line of this matrix is a document and each column is a term. The element in row i, column j, is the weight of term j in document i (Salton, 1988).

A query can be specified by the user as a set of terms with accompanying digital weight or using a natural language. In the latter case, the request can be treated exactly as a document; Indeed, the application must be added to the document space if it contains words that are not in the collection (the document area), these represent additional dimensions in the space documents. An important question is how the weights are assigned to terms either in documents or in queries. For this, a variety of weighting schemes has been proposed as the frequency-weighted terms, the binary weighting ...... ect. More details concerning some calculates weighting is in the section (Mihalcea, 2011).

The Calculation of Relevance

Once the vectors are formed in the previous step, a numeric similarity to be calculated between the query and each document in the collection. The goal is to classified documents in the form of an ordered list based on their degree of similarity to the query, ie, the first document in the ranking is the most similar to the query. The classification allows the user to limit his attention to a set of manageable size documents, for example, the first 20 records only.

When the terms are assumed to be independent, then the similarity usually used by the model between a query and a document is the inner product of their corresponding vectors. As shown in the following equation, the inner product between a query vector and the document vector is calculated by multiplying the component of the motion vector (e.g., weight) for each term k, by the weight of the term K in the document j, and summing these products on all terms k: $Q_i D_j q_{ik} d_{jk}$

$$sim\left(Q_i, D_j\right) = \sum_K q_{ik} * d_{jk} \text{ (II.2)}$$

Essentially, we can consider the score of domestic product to a heuristic estimate of the similarity between a query and a document. The vector space model does not suffer defects associated with Boolean model. The records are arranged on a continuous scale and is easy to control the size of the output. The model easily handles both short and long queries because any free text can be used as a query. Therefore, the user can enhance the query by incorporating some or all of the text from a relevant document known directly in the application. The ability to easily handle the query text gives the MEV considerable advantage over the Boolean model validated by a number of research experiments. In the literature we can distinguish different similarity measure as cosine, Euclidean, The Probabilistic Model

In the models, boolean and MEV matching between the query and the collection of documents is done in a formally defined calculation, but the computation of the index terms is semantically inaccurate and even understanding of the need for information (query) is uncertain. View the process of representation of documents and the query used, SRM has an accurate estimate of whether a document has content relevant to the need of the information. In 1977 Robertson to prove that the theory of probability provides a basic principle to quantify such uncertainty reasoning and appears to be adequate to account for this inaccuracy ranking. This section provides a response on how that frame was exploited to estimate what is the probability that (Robertson, 1977).

For Robertson and his colleagues found that if we have the relevant and irrelevant documents known, then we can begin to downright estimate the probability of a T term in a relevant document and that this could be the basis of a classifier decides whether the documents are relevant or not. The MPC attempt to estimate the probability of observing events related to the document and the query. The goal is to find documents that have the same time a high probability of being relevant P (Per / D, Q), and a low probability of being irrelevant P (NPer / D, Q).

The basic idea of MPC is that if the response to each request is a ranking of documents in the collection in descending order of probability of use for the user who made the request, where the probabilities are estimated as accurately as possible based on all the data are betting available for this purpose, the overall efficiency for users will be the best that can be achieved on the basis of such data (Robertson, 1977). For that a document D is declared as relevant to a query Q if P (Per / D, Q)> P (NPer / D, Q) and the relevance score of the document is equal to. To put this principle into practice, models have been proposed based on the Bayes rules defined in the following equation: $\dfrac{P\left(\text{Per / D, Q}\right)}{P\left(\text{NPer / D, Q}\right)}$

$$P(P/D, Q) = (II.3) \frac{p(D|P,Q)\, p(P|Q)}{p(D)}$$

$$P(NP/D, Q) = (II.4) \frac{p(D|NP,Q)\, p(NP|Q)}{p(D)}$$

- P (D) constant value for the two classes (relevant (Per) and irrelevant (NPer)) which represents the probability of choosing D.
- P (D | P, Q): the probability that the document D is relevant to the query Q.
- P (D | NP, Q): the probability that the document D is not relevant to the query Q.
- $p(P|Q)$ and: the probability of relevance and irrelevance of a document that are set. $p(NP|Q)$

Binary Independence Model (MIB)

The binary independence model (MIB), presents some simple assumption to make the estimate of the probability function P (Per / D) practice. Documents and the query are represented as binary vectors. In other words, a document D and a query Q are represented by the vectors VD = (x1, ..., xM) and VQ = (q1, ..., qm) xM where xt = 1 if the word is present in D and xM = 0 if xt is absent in D (the same for the query Q). With this performance, many possible documents have the same vector representation. Independence in this model means that the terms are modeled as occurring in documents independently (Yu, 1976).

The basic idea of the MIB is to estimate how many terms in documents contribute to relevance. This model calculates the value of the research status (VSR) for each document in the collection to a query Q to assess its degree of relevance. For this a contingency matrix must be constructed that provides information on every relevant document or irrelevant depending on the presence and absence of each term in the vector space as shown in the following table:

- S: number of relevant documents where the term xt is present.
- Ss: number of relevant documents where the term is absent xt.
- Dft-s: number of irrelevant documents where the term xt is present.
- (N Dft) - (Ss): number of irrelevant documents where the term is absent xt.

RSV of a document di to any query Q is calculated through the following equation:

Table 2. Contingency matrix for each term in the vector space based on their presence and absence in the relevant documents and irrelevant.

Documents Collection		Relevant	Non pertinent	Total
this term	Xt = 1	S	Dft-s	dft
missing term	Xt = 0	Ss	(N DFT) - (Ss)	N- Dft
Total		S	NS	NOT

$$VSR(d_i) = (II.5) \sum_{x_t=q_t=1} c_t$$

$$c_t = (II.6)\, log \, \frac{\dfrac{s+\dfrac{1}{2}}{S-s+\dfrac{1}{2}}}{\dfrac{df_t - s + \dfrac{1}{2}}{N - df_t - S + s + \dfrac{1}{2}}}$$

- $VSR(d_i)$: Research the value status for the relevant document number i.
- c_t : VSR coefficient for the term t.
- The value of ½ is added to avoid falling in the case of zero:

The binary independence model improved:

In this model some assumptions of the original MIB were amended as the assumption of independence of the terms because they exist cases where the terms are composed and highly dependent. This violates this assumption for example the word "text mining" or "data mining." For that a tree structure has been proposed to take into account the dependence between the terms.

The OKABI model:

The OKABI model was proposed to take into account the length of documents and frequency of terms in the calculation of probability of each document. For this a new equation to calculate the value of the research status was proposed to classify documents according to their VSRs compared to the query Q:

$$VSR(d_i) = \sum_{t \in Q} log \frac{N}{N_t d} ** (II.7) \frac{(k_1 + 1)ft_{td}}{k_1 \left((1-b) + b * \left(\dfrac{L_d}{L_{moy}} \right) \right) + ft_{td}} \frac{(K_3 + 1) ft_{tQ}}{K_3 + ft_{tQ}}$$

- ft_{td} : The frequency of the term t in the document.
- N : Number of documents in the collection.
- $N_t d$: number of documents containing the term t.
- L_d : The length of the document
- L_{moy} : The average length of all documents in the collection.
- k_1 : positive parameter which sets the importance of the frequency of the word in the document. A value of k1 = 0 corresponds to a bit pattern (no term frequency), and a high value corresponds to the use of the raw frequency weighting of the term.
- k_3 : positive parameter which sets the importance of the frequency of the term in the query.
- The values and must be between 0 and 1. $k_1 k_3$
- b: setting parameter ($0 \leq b \leq 1$), which determines how the document length.

Inference Model

In this model, the ad hoc research is modeled as a reasoning process as a network inference in which we estimate the probability that a user's information needs, expressed as a query is satisfied by a document. The techniques required to support this kind of inference are similar to those used in expert systems that have to reason with uncertain information. some inference developed for expert systems can be adapted to the ad hoc research task as Bayesian networks are a form of graphic probabilistic model to model the complex dependencies between a document and a query.

Private Ad Hoc Research (PAR)

PAR is a type of private research, defined as the search secure data. This principle uses a specific field of cryptography called homomorphic encryption. Homomorphic crypto-systems are algorithms for performing operations such as indexing and search on encrypted data without the need for the decrypted. The PCR protocols are to hide the user request and the stored documents searched to the server using the homomorphic cryptography. This concept is now widely used for data privacy in the cloud services. Figure 1 describes the general idea of the RAP:

As shown in the previous figure, PAR works as follows:

- First, the client sends its own information (att) used to generate the key (identity, attributes or predicate) to a specific server regarded as third parties.

Figure 2. General architecture of ad hoc private research

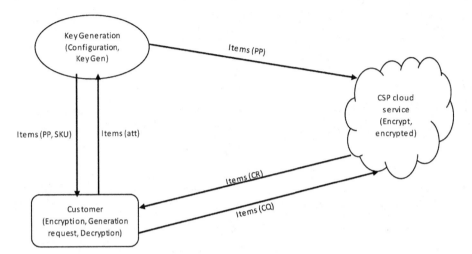

- This server known as the key generator name can:
- Run the configuration function to generate the public key that is in the case homomorphic a set of parameters known by the public parameters (PP).
- Run Key-Gen function to obtain a secret key corresponding to a user (Sku).
- PP Send the client and the cloud service provider (CSP) and Sku customer only.
- **Encryption:** The client and the cloud service performs the function of encrypting to encrypt their data (the request by the client and the data by the CSP).
- The customer, once he has finished his request encrypt (need information) using PP, it sends the request to CQ encrypted cloud service.
- The cloud service in turn applies CQ its encrypted data to select the encrypted CR relevant documents to be sent to the client.
- Finally, the client decrypts the CR and gets a clear result he wants.

In our work we used two homomorphic encryption algorithms the best known in the literature:

Algorithm Okamoto-Uchiyama

To improve the efficiency of older homomorphic systems, Okamoto and Uchiyama came with the idea of changing the group of the message space by taking $n = p^2q$ and the message space will be the group () * (Okamoto 1998). The authors had recovered their system performs $k = p$ that gave them an expansion value equal to

3. The security of this system is the factorization of n. therefore, this fact had been studied by proposing a ciphertext attack selected known for its effectiveness against the problems of factorization. The diagram of Okamoto-Uchiyama is a homomorphic additive system which satisfies the following property: $\mathbb{Z}_{q^2}$

Encke (m)· Encke (m) mod n = (gm hr) (gm 'h'r) mod n = (g m + m') (hh ') r mod n = Encke (m + m') mod n (II.8)

Procedure: The following pseudo-code shows the general framework of this system: Nickname II.1 code:algorithm Okamoto-Uchiyama

```
beginning
                    / * Key generation (Key Gen) * /
            Choose two large prime numbers p and q random
            Fix n = p²q
            Choose random g from (Z/not Z) * Such that gp 1 mod
p²≠
            Fix h = gn mod n
            The public key is (n, g, h) and the secret key is (p,
q)
                                / * Encrypting step * /
            For the message m from the message space M 2k-1
            Choose random r from (Z/not Z)
                                        C = hr gm mod n
                            / * Read step * /
          Assuming that L (x) =  (x − 1)/p
          Text Decryption is:
                                        m = mod p
```

$$\frac{L\left(c^{p-1}\ mod\ p^2\right)}{L\left(g^{p-1}\ mod\ p^2\right)}$$

```
End
```

II.2.3.2.TSZ Algorithm

As homomorphic system TSZ (Chabanne, 2005), is based on a bilinear map ê: G1 x G1 → G2 where G1 and G2 are two groups of prime order q, the main objective of this program is to allow a user identity of a 'u' to share data with users k. The steps of the algorithm are as follows:

Nickname II.2 code:Algorithm TSZ

```
                                    /*configuration*/
Entry: parameter secret 1α / Output: PK and MSK
beginning
    Generate a random integer n and two first prime BigInteger p
and q
    Put G1 and G2 of order two sets n such that G1 [0] ← p and
G1 [1] ← q
    Fill in the rest of the G G1 [i] ← G1 [i-1] + G1 [i-2] for i
= 2 ... n
    Put e: G1 x G1 → G2 wherein e (x, y) = x * y
    Fill G2 using e
    Select a random sequence a0, a1 ...... a2k-1
    E1 choose randomly from G and put g1 = e12
        E2 select another random from G and put g2 = 4 * e2 - 1
        Master secret key MSK = (g1, a0, a1 ...... a2k-1)
        public parameter PK = (gt, g2, g2 '= g2a0, FP) wherein
gt is a random generator in G2
end
                        / * Key-Gen * /
Entered: PCT user, MSK / output: the secret key of the user Sku
beginning
    F = a0 + a1 * ID + ....... + A2k-2 * + ID2k ID2k-2-one
    Sku = g11 / F
    gt = e (SKU, g2 (PCT + a0))
end
                    / * * Encrypt /
Admission: pre-encrypted text PCT PK
Release Date: ciphertext CT
beginning
    randomly choosing r   ∈ ℤ_q
    calculate CT = (PCT * GTR g2'r, G2R)
end
                    / * Read * /
 Input: text encrypt CT, Sku, PK, SK, IP / Output: plain text M
 beginning
     GTR = e (SKU, g2'r) * e (SKU ID, G2R)
     Put M = C [0] / gtr
```

```
Starting from M 'M deduct using IP initial population
End
```

GROUPING INFORMATION

The consolidation plays an important role in organizing the results of an ad hoc research to address the problem of information overload and providing the user with easy access to the information he is interested. This role can be summarized assuming that the documents in the same cluster behave similarly. This mean that if will have one document from a cluster that is relevant to a search request, then it is likely that other documents in the same cluster are also relevant because the consolidation process brings together documents that share many terms in the same cluster. The usefulness of information consolidation can be summarized in the following three features:

Organization of Search Results

The MRA return as a response to a request a list of documents. This list can be very high where the user will be difficult to browse all the results returned to find the information they want. For this grouping can be used to partition the search results into groups so that similar documents appear together since it is often easier to scan a cohesive group that many individual documents. For example the results of a query to a search engine can return thousands of pages. The clustering can be used to group the search results in a small number of clusters, each of which captures a particular aspect of the request.

Improve Search Results

The MRA used to initially select a set of documents that match the query. By partitioning a collection of documents into groups, it can improve search results by adding other documents from the same cluster that the documents initially select. For example if the query is "New York" and some documents that speak of New York were selected from the cluster USA, then we added documents from the cluster that contain other terms as "New York" (eg USA, Washington... ect).

Heuristic Search

The combination of clustering collection can improve search speed and eliminate unnecessary comparisons. Instead of calculating the similarity between each document and the query, we seek only the nearest cluster to the motion to calculate the similarity between the query and the centroid of each cluster and then we calculate the similarity between the query and documents belonging to this cluster (documents might be relevant) to classify and presented to users.

This task is performed by clustering techniques that will be the subject of the next section:

CONCLUSION

In conclusion we can say that information is the oil of the 21st century, and the mystique of information retrieval (IR) is the combustion engine that guarantees access to relevant information. The study presented in this chapter is brought into context to detail the new trends and challenges to separate the wheat (relevant information) from the chaff (irrelevant information) and meet the needs of modern users.

REFERENCES

Baeza-Yates, R., & Ribeiro-Neto, B. (1999). *Modern information retrieval* (Vol. 463). New York: ACM press.

Croft, W. B., Metzler, D., & Strohman, T. (2010). *Search engines: Information retrieval in practice* (Vol. 283). Reading, MA: Addison-Wesley.

Frakes, W. B., & Baeza-Yates, R. (Eds.). (1992). Information retrieval: Data structures & algorithms (Vol. 331). Englewood Cliffs, NJ: Prentice Hall.

Hervé Chabanne, D. H. (2005). *Public Traceability in Traitor Tracing Schemes. Eurocrypt'05*. Aarhus, Denmark: Springer.

Kowalski, G. J., & Maybury, M. T. (2006). *Information storage and retrieval systems: theory and implementation* (Vol. 8). Springer Science & Business Media.

Larson, R. R. (2010). Introduction to information retrieval. *Journal of the American Society for Information Science and Technology, 61*(4), 852–853.

Liu, T. Y. (2011). *Learning to rank for information retrieval*. Springer Science & Business Media. doi:10.1007/978-3-642-14267-3

Llopis, F., Ferrández, A., & Vicedo, J. L. (2002, February). Text segmentation for efficient information retrieval. In *International Conference on Intelligent Text Processing and Computational Linguistics* (pp. 373-380). Springer.

Metzler, D., & Croft, W. B. (2007). Linear feature-based models for information retrieval. *Information Retrieval, 10*(3), 257–274. doi:10.100710791-006-9019-z

Mihalcea, R., & Radev, D. (2011). *Graph-based natural language processing and information retrieval*. Cambridge university press. doi:10.1017/CBO9780511976247

Okamoto, T., & Uchiyama, S. (1998, May). A new public-key cryptosystem as secure as factoring. In *International Conference on the Theory and Applications of Cryptographic Techniques* (pp. 308-318). Springer Berlin Heidelberg. 10.1007/BFb0054135

Qin, T., Liu, T. Y., Xu, J., & Li, H. (2010). LETOR: A benchmark collection for research on learning to rank for information retrieval. *Information Retrieval, 13*(4), 346–374. doi:10.100710791-009-9123-y

Robertson, S. E. (1977). The probability ranking principle in IR. *The Journal of Documentation, 33*(4), 294–304. doi:10.1108/eb026647

Salton, G., & Buckley, C. (1988). Term-weighting approaches in automatic text retrieval. *Information Processing & Management, 24*(5), 513–523. doi:10.1016/0306-4573(88)90021-0

Salton, G., Fox, E. A., & Wu, H. (1983). Extended Boolean information retrieval. *Communications of the ACM, 26*(11), 1022–1036. doi:10.1145/182.358466

Silva, I., Ribeiro-Neto, B., Calado, P., Moura, E., & Ziviani, N. (2000, July). Link-based and content-based evidential information in a belief network model. In *Proceedings of the 23rd annual international ACM SIGIR conference on Research and development in information retrieval* (pp. 96-103). ACM. 10.1145/345508.345554

Yu, J., & Branton, D. (1976). Reconstitution of intramembrane particles in recombinants of erythrocyte protein band 3 and lipid: Effects of spectrin-actin association. *Proceedings of the National Academy of Sciences of the United States of America, 73*(11), 3891–3895. doi:10.1073/pnas.73.11.3891 PMID:1069273

Chapter 10
Spam Filtering and Detection:
State of the Art and Overview

Yasmin Bouarara
Dr. Tahar Molay University of Saida, Algeria

ABSTRACT

In today's world of globalization and technology without borders, the emergence of the internet and the rapid development of telecommunications have made the world a global village. Recently, the email service has become immensely used, and the main means of communication because it is cheap, reliable, fast, and easy to access. In addition, it allows users with a mailbox (BAL) and email address to exchange messages (images, files, and text documents) from anywhere in the world via the internet. Unfortunately, this technology has become undeniably the original source of malicious activity, in particular the problem of unwanted emails (spam), which has increased dramatically over the past decade. According to the latest report from Radicati Group, which provides quantitative and qualitative research with details of the e-mail, security, and social networks, published in 2012, 70-80% of email traffic consists of spam. The goal of the chapter is to give a state of the art on spam and spam techniques and the disadvantages of this phenomenon.

INTRODUCTION

After the mailbox of our home, it is now our electronic mailbox with the explosion of Internet use. Nowadays, social networking sites such as Facebook, Myspace, and Twitter have become one of the main vectors for users to keep track and communicate with their friends online. Merely, the number of electronic mail box is increasing. Each user has at least an email address; the minimum number of BALE (Box for

DOI: 10.4018/978-1-5225-7338-8.ch010

Electronic Arts) is 800 million worldwide. Such mass approachable person is of course a boon to advertisers, but also a favored means of communication for the spammers, scammers, hackers, political, publicity…. etc.

In this chapter we will see an overview concerning the preliminary concepts of spam detection and the different spam detection techniques existed in literature.

Spam History

The real origin of the term "SPAM" comes from 1970 Monty Python's Flying Circus skit. In this skit, all the restaurant's menu items devolve into SPAM. When the waitress repeats the word SPAM, a group of Vikings in the corner sing " SPAM, SPAM, lovely SPAM Wonderful SPAM" drowning out other conversation, until they are finally told to shut it.

Although the first spam message had already been sent via telegram in 1864, then it was send as commercial e-mail occurred in 1978, the term spam for this practice had not yet been applied in the 1980s. It was adopted to describe certain users who frequented BB (Bulletin board is a computer system running software that allows users to dial into the system over a phone line or Telnet), who would repeat "SPAM" a huge number of times to scroll other users' text off the screen in early chat rooms services like the early days of AOL (Glasner, 2001).

Spam

Spam is considered to be an unsolicited commercial electronic message (figure 1). It is often a source of scams, computer viruses and offensive content that takes up valuable time and increases costs for consumers, business and governments (Cormack, 2007).

THE DIFFERENT TYPES OF SPAM

The most common spam is of course linked to spam emails. Nevertheless, there are different forms of spam:

Spam Voice Over IP

The spam VoIP also called SPIT or vishing SPLIT is a new kind of spam via the telephone and it's like Anonymous Call issued at any time of day or night, are issued to raise (as phishing technique) personal information (Saberi, 2007).

Figure 1. A model of spam email

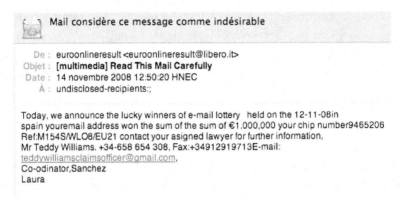

The Spam Messages in the Discussion Forums

This is an advertising message (containing commercial nature hyperlinks) left on some forums the goal is the same as the spam received by email: advertise for free (Saberi, 2007).

Spam in Blogs (SIG)

It is called SPLOG (contraction of spam and blog). It is a very popular technique it's to let Internet users on blogs with links to advertising sites (Fumera, 2007).

Phishing

It is called filoutage or hameçonnage in french as presents the next figure 2. It is a technique by which attackers pose major corporations or financial institutions that are familiar by sending fraudulent e-mails. It retrieves passwords of bank accounts or credit card numbers. In this case the hacker could create a false social network page (Facebook, Twitter, ...etc.) appearance entirely legitimate. Then, when you try to connect the fake page, it saves your information with your user name and password in hand [A3].

Scam

It is based on using a false name or a false quality. It is a technique that abuses the credulity of email recipients to extort money. For e.g. someone proposes to a claim to have a large sum of money and wants to collaborate with him to use an existing

Figure 2. A phishing model (Chirita2005)

bank account to transfer money. Of course in exchange for this person service promises a percentage of the large sum to be channeled through profit account of the recipient (Grier, 2010).

Spammers Activities

There are many ways in which spammers can harvest your email address such as:

Image Spam

The spammers put their spam into the image, they put the text as a GIF or JPEG image like advertisement and business then they send it in email, and it's difficult to detect that kind of spam because they exist different type of images (color modified image, Gray image, multi farm animated, image background, image text image...) (Fumera, 2007).

Zombie Spam

It's a collection of computer system that sends a million of spam messages at once. Nevertheless it can find itself in bed reputation with the spams filters (Sahami, 1998).

Java Script Tricky

It makes the messages more difficult to decode. The spammers' dispatch the contents of the spam message into java script in which will be activated once the message is opened (Firte, 2010).

Spam Creation Process

The different steps to create a spam can be defined as follows:

1. Collection and address verification: sort addresses by groups (targets)
2. Creating platforms for mass mailing (servers and / or individual computers)
3. Writing mass mailing programs
4. Promoting the spammer services
5. Development texts for specific campaigns then t it send the spam

Filtering

It's a program or a source of code that allowed to import or export data where it allow data to pass just if it's matched with the given information and when we speak about the spam filtering we are trying to find a solution to eliminate the spam or put it in the junk mail box it's also called a spam blockers it's configured and based on different and variety of criteria including the email senders and specific words whether in the subject or the message (Krasser, 2007).

I.8-Spam Detection Systems Existed in Literature

The most known spam detection techniques existed in literature are grouped in the next figure 3 and detailed in the next paragraphs:

Figure 3. Different approach of spam detection

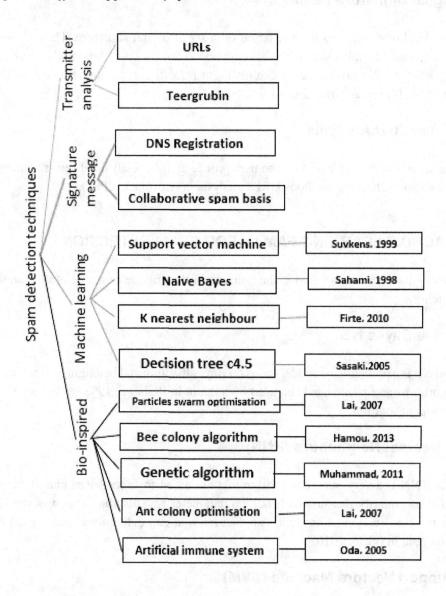

Classical Family for Spam Detection

There are two large families of classical techniques to deal with spammers as detailed in the next titles:

Digital Signature Family

This kind of techniques usually based on a set of digital signature. They need to have a detailed analysis of mails that circulate in the network. Among the methods according to this principle, we can distinguish DNS registration (Chirita, 2005), blacklists (Grier, 2010) and Grey list.

Transmitter Analysis

These techniques are based on the user profile and the analysis of the spammers' behaviour such as the methods URLs analysis in (Cormack, 2007).

MACHINE LEARNING FAMILY FOR SPAM DETECTION

Among the techniques found in the literature following the principle of this family as fellow:

Naive Bayes NB

The NB is a probabilistic model based on Bayes theorem and belonging to the linear algorithms group that has been used by Sahami in (Sahami, 1998) to improve the anti-spam solution.

K-Nearest Neighbours (KNN)

The KNN is a very simple algorithm that allows an instance-based classification using a similarity measure and fixing a parameter K. This algorithm was applied for the construction of an online application that can detect undesirable mail by Firte & al in (Firte, 2010).

Support Vectors Machine (SVM)

SVM is a classification technique that aims to find a function hyper plane based on the supports vector calculated by Lagrange to maximize the margin between classes. Ducker and his collaborators in (Suykens, 1999) used this principle for the categorization of electronic messages (spam and ham).

K-Means

K Means is an unsupervised algorithm based on the initialization of the parameter K. Sasaki and al in (Cormack, 2007) thought to apply this principle with K = 2 (spam and ham) for spam detection problem.

Decision Tree c4.5

After a new form of spamming based on image has appeared. In (Krasser, 2007) the researchers had applied the C4.5 to generate decision rules that will make a choice between the spam image and ham image.

Bio-Inspired Family for Spam Detection

This section is dedicated to the different work done around the spam detection using the bio-inspired techniques.

Genetic Algorithms for Spam Detection (GA-SD)

A very interesting paper was presented (Mohammad, 2011) as a recapitulation of the application of three bio-inspired algorithms (artificial immune system AIS, genetic algorithms and GAs Artificial neural network ANN) for the detection of spam (Holland, 1973).

Particle Swarm Optimization for Spam Detection (PSO-SD)

Lai et al (Mohammad, 2011) had the idea of examining how particle swarm optimization algorithm can help select relevant features for discriminating the classification of solicited and unsolicited messages (Kennedy, 1995).

Ant colony Optimization for Spam Detection (ACO-SD)

Taweessiwate et al (Taweesiriwate, 2012) had the idea to reformulate the principle of ACO for the problem of host spam detection using the webspam-UK2006 dataset for his experimentation (Dorigo, 1996).

Artificial Social Bees for Spam Detection (ASB-SD)

Hamou et al (Hamou, 2013) have formulated a new method inspired from the social life of bees, and their way to ensure the proper functioning of the hive using the filtering principle. Each filter is by ensuring bee workers (supervisor, cleaner and collector). A message is identified as spam if it succeeds spent three filtering (Karaboga, 2007).

Artificial Immune System for Spam Detection (AIS-SD)

To better counter the phenomenon of spamming the researchers considered spam as pathogens that are combated by humans where a spam detection method was introduced by Oda et al (Mohammad,2011) called artificial immune system AIS to effectively protect the email users. This algorithm has been tested on the Spam Assassin corpus and gave satisfactory results (Dasgupta, 1999).

CONCLUSION

It is important for the administrators of electronic mail servers and organizer of information systems to have a better detector of spam. Newly, about 85% of information that exists in the web and the emails exchanged between the users, the business and administrators are in unstructured format (textual data). In order to better control the data and have a best filtering, we must have a better representation of emails to make them interpreted by the machine. This is the context of the next chapter which brings together the different steps of text mining and text pre-processing.

REFERENCES

Chirita, P. A., Nejdl, W., & Zamfir, C. (2005). Preventing shilling attacks in online recommender systems. WIDM'05, 67–74. doi:10.1145/1097047.1097061

Cormack, G. V. (2007). Email spam filtering: A systematic review. *Foundations and Trends in Information Retrieval, 1*(4), 335–455. doi:10.1561/1500000006

Dasgupta, D., & Forrest, S. (1999, July). Artificial immune systems in industrial applications. In *Intelligent Processing and Manufacturing of Materials, 1999. IPMM'99. Proceedings of the Second International Conference on* (Vol. 1, pp. 257-267). IEEE.

Dorigo, M., Maniezzo, V., & Colorni, A. (1996). Ant system: optimization by a colony of cooperating agents. *Systems, Man, and Cybernetics, Part B: Cybernetics. IEEE Transactions on, 26*(1), 29–41.

Firte, L., Lemnaru, C., & Potolea, R. (2010, August). Spam detection filter using KNN algorithm and resampling. In *Intelligent Computer Communication and Processing (ICCP), 2010 IEEE International Conference on* (pp. 27-33). IEEE. 10.1109/ICCP.2010.5606466

Fumera, G., Pillai, I., Roli, F., & Biggio, B. (2007). Image spam filtering using textual and visual information. *Proceedings of the MIT Spam Conference 2007.*

Glasner, J. (2001). *A brief history of spam, and spam.* Retrieved from http://www.wired. com/techbiz/media/news/2001/05/44111

Grier, C., Thomas, K., Paxson, V., & Zhang, M. (2010, October). @ spam: the underground on 140 characters or less. In *Proceedings of the 17th ACM conference on Computer and communications security* (pp. 27-37). ACM 10.1145/1866307.1866311

Hamou, R. M., Amine, A., & Boudia, A. (2013). A New Meta-Heuristic Based on Social Bees for Detection and Filtering of Spam. *International Journal of Applied Metaheuristic Computing, 4*(3), 15–33. doi:10.4018/ijamc.2013070102

Holland, J. H. (1973). Genetic algorithms and the optimal allocation of trials. *SIAM Journal on Computing, 2*(2), 88–105. doi:10.1137/0202009

Karaboga, D., & Basturk, B. (2007). A powerful and efficient algorithm for numerical function optimization: Artificial bee colony (ABC) algorithm. *Journal of Global Optimization, 39*(3), 459–471. doi:10.100710898-007-9149-x

Kennedy, J., & Eberhart, R. (1995). Particle Swarm Optimization. *Proceedings of IEEE International Conference on Neural Networks, 4*, 1942–1948. 10.1109/ICNN.1995.488968

Krasser, S., Tang, Y., Gould, J., Alperovitch, D., & Judge, P. (2007, June). Identifying image spam based on header and file properties using C4. 5 decision trees and support vector machine learning. In *Information Assurance and Security Workshop, 2007. IAW'07. IEEE SMC* (pp. 255-261). IEEE.

Mohammad, A. H., & Zitar, R. A. (2011). Application of genetic optimized artificial immune system and neural networks in spam detection. *Applied Soft Computing, 11*(4), 3827-3845.

Saberi, A., Vahidi, M., & Bidgoli, B. M. (2007, November). Learn to detect phishing scams using learning and ensemble? methods. In *Web Intelligence and Intelligent Agent Technology Workshops, 2007 IEEE/WIC/ACM International Conferences on* (pp. 311-314). IEEE.

Sahami, M., Dumais, S., Heckerman, D., & Horvitz, E. (1998, July). A Bayesian approach to filtering junk e-mail. In *Learning for Text Categorization: Papers from the 1998 workshop* (*Vol. 62*, pp. 98-105). Academic Press.

Suykens, J. A., & Vandewalle, J. (1999). Least squares support vector machine classifiers. *Neural Processing Letters, 9*(3), 293–300. doi:10.1023/A:1018628609742

Taweesiriwate, A., Manaskasemsak, B., & Rungsawang, A. (2012, March). Web spam detection using link-based ant colony optimization. In *Advanced Information Networking and Applications (AINA), 2012 IEEE 26th International Conference on* (pp. 868-873). IEEE. 10.1109/AINA.2012.118

Chapter 11
Security in Wireless Sensor Networks:
Sybil Attack Detection and Prevention

Mekelleche Fatiha
University of Oran 1 Ahmed Ben Bella, Algeria

Haffaf Hafid
University of Oran 1 Ahmed Ben Bella, Algeria

Ould Bouamama Belkacem
University of Lille 1, France

ABSTRACT

A wireless sensor network (WSN) is a special ad hoc network. It consists of a large number of sensors communicating with wireless links to monitor the real-world environment. They have limited energy, computational power, memory, and transmission range. They are widely used in different fields like military operations, environmental monitoring, and healthcare applications. However, the openness and hostility of the deployment space and the resources limitations make these networks vulnerable to several types of attacks and intrusions. So, the WSN security becomes a real challenge. Principally, the attacks in the network aim at damaging the smooth running of the legitimate nodes and cause a dysfunction of the network. Sybil attack is one of the perilous attacks which affects the WSN networks and poses threats to many security goals. This attack makes the sensor node into Sybil node and illegitimately takes and claims multiple identities.

DOI: 10.4018/978-1-5225-7338-8.ch011

INTRODUCTION

In recent years, thanks to advanced technology and more particularly to the evolution of microelectronics and wireless communication, Wireless Sensor Networks (*WSNs*) (Yick, Mukherjee, & Ghosal, 2008) have experienced considerable growth. For that, these networks are considered as an emerging technology resulting from the progress of the different domains. Their main objective is to offer economically interesting solutions for remote control and data processing. So, currently, they are an integral part of our lives, as they allow the user a better understanding of the environment. Indeed, they are generally deployed to monitor a more or less extensive area of interest, to take regular measurements and to send back alarms to certain nodes responsible for relaying information on a large scale. For this, they are widely used in different fields namely, the military, environmental, medical, home automation, and of course the applications related to the monitoring of critical infrastructures.

Wireless sensor networks (WSNs) are considered as a special type of Ad-hoc networks (Perkins, 2001), in which the nodes are smart sensors. These (also called nano-computers) have limited computing capacity, energy and bandwidth. They are powered by a power source (battery) of limited capacity. They bring an interesting perspective: that of devices capable of self-configuration and self-organization. Typically (see Figure 1), WSNs consist of a potentially large number of randomly deployed sensors in the area of interest also known as the sensing area to monitor a phenomenon and collect its data. The latter are then routed, through a multi-hop routing, to a collection point called collector node (*base station* or *sink*) for usual operating purposes. The base station is linked to the network user via the Internet or a satellite.

Figure 1.Typical architecture of a WSN

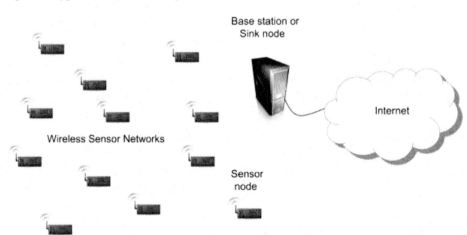

A sensor is a measuring instrument with advanced feel features. It makes it possible to generate data relating to its physical environment. Its main role lies in: the recording of a physical quantity (such as temperature, humidity, speed, motion, pressure, etc.) observed (also called *measurand (M)* in the model of a measure proposed by the electronics engineer Georges Asch (Asch, 2010), which will later be transformed into a physical quantity of electrical nature (electrical signal) (see Figure 2) This transformation must reflect as perfectly as possible these quantities (Noury, 2002). After scanning in an analog / digital representation, the measured value can be stored, processed, transmitted to be used with other information to meet the needs of a specific application, and the sensors can detect real-world events such as forest fires The main advantages of sensor nodes are: their small size, low cost, fault tolerance, self-organizing ability, and especially their ability to communicate wirelessly (usually a radio channel) (which allows great freedom of movement compared to wired nodes).

WSNs network design assumes that all deployed sensor nodes are cooperative and trustworthy. However, this is not the case in real-world deployments, where nodes are exposed to different types of attacks and intrusions that can downright damage the network. Indeed, the sensors are on the one hand endowed with very limited resources in terms of computing capacity, storage space, transmission power and embedded energy (battery) and on the other hand, they are deployed without infrastructure predefined in hostile and hard-to-reach environments, without physical protection (limited physical security) and without the possibility of battery recharging. In addition, the radio communication links are also fragile and their failure can cause partitioning of the network and a change in the topology. These factors make this type of network very vulnerable to disruptive and malicious actions that could compromise the network and hinder its proper functioning. So, these vulnerabilities to malicious attacks are their major drawbacks slowing down their proliferation and are now living up to their promises.

Figure 2. Essential function of a sensor (Noury, 2002)

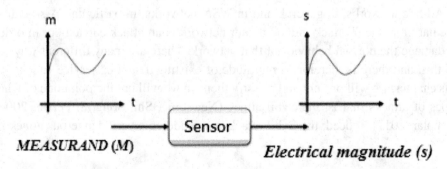

More specifically, the vulnerabilities caused by the physical constraints of the sensor nodes, the nature of the transmission channel as well as the multi-hop communication mode, the nature of the deployment environment, the dynamic topology and the large number of sensors deployed, on the one hand, and the need for real-time assurance, the basic services of a WSN network such as the confidentiality, integrity and availability of collected environmental data on the other hand, make the security of WSNs networks is a real challenge. As a result, the security of WSNs networks is at the source, today, of many scientific and technical challenges.

WSNs networks cannot rely on human intervention to deal with adversaries who attempt to threaten such networks or impede its operational safety. In addition, they cannot use existing security mechanisms, which are very expensive in calculation. Therefore, it is imperative to integrate a security infrastructure dedicated to WSNs networks where each layer, each protocol, each technology used must be secure.

Security in Ad-hoc networks is a quality of the network that is desired, at least to a minimum degree, in all applications (Arampatzis, Lygeros, & Manesis, 2005). A WSN sensor network is a special network that has many constraints. Because of these constraints, it is difficult to put in place mechanisms traditionally deployed in this context. The application of security to WSNs is therefore a specific domain that is addressed in several stages. It is primarily the different components of security that are addressed: privacy, authentication, integrity and other properties (Kraus,2014). In other words, the concept of security in a WSN network is to secure it against external or internal attacks (Ahmed, Huang, & Sharma, 2012) (Li, Zhang, Das, & Thuraisingham, 2009), active or passive (Padmavathi & Shanmugapriya, 2009) and against resource failures (such as the depletion of energy resources). Thus, the captured information must be protected against unauthorized access, disclosure, disruption, modification or destruction. Several types of attacks, therefore, appeared as they generally adopt new strategies, exploiting the characteristics and vulnerabilities of these WSNs networks. To brave them, it is necessary to know the nature, types and classes of attacks (i.e. attackers or adversary) in order to implement appropriate and reliable defense solutions and strategies.

Denial of service attacks (Wood & Stankovic, 2002) are the most common threats in Ad-hoc networks, in general, and in WSN networks, in particular. A so-called "denial of service" attack in a computer network is an attack carried out in order to damage the normal behavior of that network. There are many different ways to do this, and there is therefore a multitude of existing denial of service attacks. In this chapter, we will present and classify them so we will put the point one of what types of attacks that is, the Sybil attack (Newsome, Shi, Song, & Perrig, 2004) (Scholar, 2017). Indeed, the Sybil attack is considered a very dangerous attack in the context of WSNs networks. It is launched when a malicious node participates in the network with multiple identities to destroy the network and disturb it. Our goal in this document is to talk about the concept of security in WSNs networks in general (challenge, available attacks, etc.) then present the Sybil attack in an explicit way (principle, applications, relative works, etc.).

Security in WSN Networks

Computer security is seen as a set of rules or operational measures to be put in place to manage computer risks in a formal way, this is very close to quality management (*QoS*) and hazard management. These rules represent the security policy imposed by the system to ensure certain predefined security levels. In our context, WSN networks, security comes down to the management of risks that threaten the different services imposed by the intended application. i.e. which threaten confidentiality, integrity, data availability, access to resources, etc.

WSNs represent a new perspective for a large number of applications (Arampatzis et al., 2005) related to the environment. They are deployed without a predefined infrastructure and generally left unattended and without physical protection. In addition, their inherent characteristics make them subject to different types of malicious attacks that can ruin network functionality. Security in these networks is one of the major challenges to ensure their availability and dependability throughout their deployment. However, the implementation of existing security measures at these networks is still unrealistic. Hence, the need to implement new mechanisms and protocols that best respect the various constraints dedicated to sensors.

Figure 3. Security concept in WSNs networks

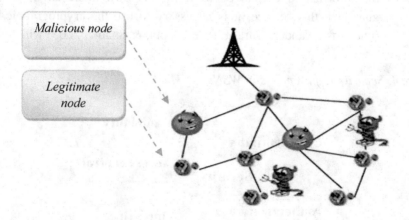

Security Objectives (Security Needs)

In WSNs, as in traditional networks, when we approach the security problem, we aim to achieve certain goals. More specifically, the main guarantees that we seek to provide are illustrated in Figure 4. These objectives are classified in two classes: main (standard) and secondary (Labraoui, 2012) (Chen, Makki, Yen, & Pissinou, 2009).

- **The Main Objectives Are:**
  - **Authentication:** Is to verify the authentic identity of the nodes. Indeed, we cannot ensure the confidentiality and integrity of messages exchanged if, from the outset, we are not sure to communicate with the right node. If authentication is mismanaged, an attacker can join the network and easily inject bad messages.
  - **Data Confidentiality:** It is one of the main security goals of a network. It aims to ensure that the information has not been disclosed, and no adversary can interfere in the communication between two nodes in order to recover the data during their transfer. Today's cryptographic algorithms can provide sufficient privacy by using large keys (symmetric or asymmetric keys). Nevertheless, these algorithms are expensive in terms of memory and calculation, moreover for the WSNs it is necessary to consider the time and the energy which they consume. It is therefore necessary to adapt these algorithms so that they can be a benefit and not a handicap.
  - **Data Integrity:** It is the fact of ensuring that the data are not altered or modified when they are transferred to the network on a voluntary or accidental basis. In fact, we want to prevent an intruder from modifying the information exchanged to fulfill his own interests. In order to guarantee this service, it is necessary to use the cryptographic hash functions (Wander, Gura, Eberle, Gupta, & Shantz, 2005) which make

Figure 4. Security requirements in WSNs

it possible to obtain the digital fingerprint of the data. Then the data is sent with their fingerprint. The recipient can verify the integrity of data by calculating again the print data received and comparing it with the one that was sent.

○ **Availability of Data:** It means that the network is available at all times for its services. This property remains difficult to satisfy in the WSN network because of the intrinsic constraints of these networks, namely dynamic topology, limited node resources, and wireless communications.

- **Secondary Objectives Are:**

○ **Data Freshness:** It implies that the data is recent, and that the attacker has not retransmitted old messages. To solve this problem, a sequence number can be added to the data packets to identify old messages.

○ **Non-Repudiation:** A security system must prohibit repudiation in order to improve the traceability of messages in the network. it is the fact that no node can deny (disavow) the fact of having exchanged information. In other words, the non-repudiation of the origin proves that the data were correctly sent to the recipient, and the non-repudiation of the arrival proves that they were correctly received. This service is not always essential in WSNs networks, but may be useful in identifying the source of malicious behavior in the network.

○ **Location Security:** Location has become valuable information, whether from an economic or military point of view. Indeed, it represents a very important factor in ensuring the operational reliability of WSNs. Indeed, a WSN network must be able to automatically locate its sensor nodes (auto-localization). And that of course to locate various events occurring in the network. This location service requires efficient algorithms to position the nodes in their deployment space with better accuracy (location accuracy). However, a malicious node may falsify the positioning calculation and attempt to compromise the location information to destabilize the operation of the entire network, making location security a very important goal for security systems.

○ **Access Control:** This service is to prevent unauthorized entities from joining the WSN network. Indeed, the network must be able to give and remove access authorization to the nodes to discriminate legitimate authorized nodes from malicious ones.

WSN security can be classified into two broad categories (1) *operational security* and (2) *information security*. The purpose of operation security is to ensure the continued operation of the entire network even if some of its components have been attacked (availability service). On the other hand, the purpose of information security is to ensure that the confidentiality of the information is never divulged and that the integrity and authentication of the information must always be ensured. We note that the security of information is almost always based on the use of cryptographic solutions to be easily completed in the network (Labraoui, 2012).

Challenges of Security in WSNs

Network security depends on the security protocols used. Several mechanisms have been proposed and deployed in Ad-hoc networks to provide certain security guarantees. Nevertheless, because of the constraining specificities of the sensors, these mechanisms are inapplicable in the case of WSNs networks. Therefore, in order to be able to develop a security framework dedicated to this type of network, satisfying the security objectives mentioned above, it is essential to know and understand these constraints mentioned later.

- **Very Limited Resources:** As previously stated, sensors are tiny devices that carry only a limited amount of hardware. So they end up with limited capabilities, especially with regard to: computing power, memory space, radio bandwidth and amount of energy. The biggest challenge in the context of WSNs is to design protocols that optimize the consumption of these resources. For this, the security protocols dedicated to the WSNs must confront the physical limitations of the nodes.
  - ○ **Calculation Capabilities:** Sensors are small devices at low cost. As a result, CPU embedded processors are relatively weak. Therefore, the algorithms executed by the sensors must be of relatively low complexity. This means that a complex security mechanism could have too many instructions and therefore increase the calculation. So, in order to develop an effective security mechanism, the code size of the security algorithm must be as small as possible.
  - ○ **Memory Capabilities:** The sensors have very limited *RAM* memory and a little storage space for the algorithms codes executed at their level. So, they are not at all designed to back up large databases. For this, it is interesting to limit the size of the code and the number of encryption / decryption keys to have a security mechanism that has a small impact on the performance of the network.
  - ○ **Available Energy:** The sensors have a battery that provides them with a finite amount of energy and usually not rechargeable. The failure of sensor nodes is often related to the depletion of their batteries. Therefore, the energy limitation of the sensors is probably the most penalizing constraint. It is therefore essential to have parsimonious

energy management for any program implemented on the sensors in order to extend the life of the network. In particular, when implementing a security mechanism, the energy impact of the code must be taken into consideration. The energy dissipated to provide security functions is used primarily for the calculation, storage and transmission of security keys, encryptions, decryptions, data signatures, signature checks, detection, and storage of security settings .

Currently, securing the basic operations of a WSN becomes a difficult task Indeed, existing security solutions are not desirable because they are often too expensive in terms of resource. For example, public key based encryption algorithms (Gaubatz, Kaps, & Sunar, 2004) are often banned from this type of network because they are very greedy in terms of physical resources. On the other hand, algorithms based on symmetric encryption (Zhang, Heys, & Li, 2010) and hashing functions (Legendre, 2014) are widely used. However, these techniques are not as effective as public-key cryptography, which complicates the design of secure applications. So new security protocols are needed.

- **Wireless Communication:** As indicated by their name, WSNs do not use any physical cable to communicate with each other or with the base station: all transmissions are made over the air (radio). Each sensor is equipped with a radio module used to transmit \ receive data. The wireless environment is open and accessible to everyone. As a result, any transmission can easily be intercepted, corrupted, or returned by an attacker. In addition, a malicious node can cause the loss, loss or modification of security-critical packets such as the encryption key, causing collisions and interference in the transmission channel. This makes it possible to increase the error rate of the channel (Hill et al., 2000).
- **Unsupervised Environment:** As the mission of a WSN is usually unattended, the sensors are left unchecked and unprotected for long periods of time. This introduces the following caveats:
  - **Vulnerability to Physical Attacks:** The sensors are miniaturized low cost devices, deployed in a dense manner in hostile environments and open to adversaries. Therefore, it is difficult to confer inviolable physical protection to all nodes of the network. As a result, they can easily be intercepted and corrupted. Indeed, an attacker can easily take control of a node in the network, which allows to physically damage it, thus rendering it non-functional. It is also able to modify the information captured by the sensor node which allows it to perform a variety of attacks (for example, corrupt communication links or inject erroneous

data). In addition, sensitive information for network security (such as the routing table or cryptographic keys) can be retrieved from the attacked node.

- ○ **Remote Management:** Remote management of the network makes the detection of any physical alteration (compromise of the sensors) and the maintenance of the sensors (replacement or battery recharge) practically impossible. For example, in a military context, there are deployed nodes to perform remote reconnaissance behind enemy lines.

- ○ **No Centralized Management:** The WSN is deployed in an ad-hoc manner to be a distributed network without a central management point. But the absence of any fixed infrastructure increases the vulnerability of the network. Indeed, there is no central controller to monitor the operation of the network and identify intrusion attempts (the Sink collects data and distributes requests, and has no monitoring architecture).

- • **Random Deployment and Large Scale Use:** The topology of a WSN has no fixed structure, for its size as well as its shape. Indeed, the ability to be deployed in large areas with a large number of sensor nodes is one of the most captivating features of WSNs. The physical topology of the WSN depends on the deployment model. Several forms of deployments can be envisaged according to the needs of the applications. Nodes can be deployed in a random or deterministic way. However, in the majority of scenarios, the deployment is done in a random manner without any prior knowledge of node position. This topology requires a permanent reconfiguration of the nodes that must adapt quickly to unforeseen changes such as the addition, the absence (devastation or exhaustion of energy) of the nodes. In this case, an attacker can infiltrate easily and carry out his attacks in order to corrupt the network or hinder his own operations. For this, it is interesting to design more robust security mechanisms to deal with the instability of the environment. In addition, these mechanisms should be adapted so that scalability will not affect their effectiveness.

- • **Data Aggregation:** In WSNs networks, to conserve the energy of the sensors, it is very important to reduce the communication load. To this end, an interesting approach is to aggregate the data (Al-Karaki, Ul-Mustafa, & Kamal, 2004). Data aggregation aims to reduce the amount of data transferred to the base station, eliminating redundant data is useless. This ultimately serves to extend the life of the network. This technique is relatively trivial, but becomes a challenge when one wants to add the security and more particularly the confidentiality (encryption of the messages). Indeed, the intermediate nodes access the exchanged data to perform the data aggregation processing. This makes it easier for malicious nodes to disclose sensitive information and access the content of messages exchanged. As a result, aggregation algorithms represent another barrier for security protocols.

Attacks in WSNs Networks

An attack can be defined as an attempt to unlawfully access a service, information, or system resource. Specifically, an attack (threat, intrusion or anomaly) is a set of computer techniques, aiming at harming the normal functioning of the network by exploiting the faults of it (Han, Chang, Gao, & Dillon, 2006). Attackers who can threaten WSNs are numerous and have multiple goals. They can greatly aggravate security problems. Indeed, the consequences related to these attacks can vary from a simple listening of the traffic until the total stop of the network according to the capacities of the attackers. For example, some attacks are intended to affect the integrity of messages passing through the network, while others aim to reduce the availability of the network or its components. Therefore, to fight them, it is important to know the nature, the technical capabilities and the class of attacks (i.e. attackers) in order to develop and design appropriate and robust defense solutions.

As shown in Figure 5, an attack can affect nodes, protocols (as routing protocols), or the transmission channel.

Attacker: Definition and Model

As we said before, WSNs can be the subject of a large number of attacks, each with its own objectives. These attacks often occur through the integration of intruding elements into the network in order to violate security requirements. There are also attacks against the external environment of the network, which causes deterioration or interference on the transmitted signals.

Figure 5. Possible attacks in WSNs networks

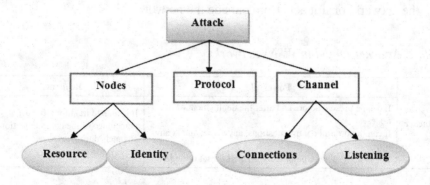

In addition, several attackers can threaten the behavior of the WSN at the same time in an autonomous or coordinated manner, in order to achieve a common attack making the defense arduous. So the more the attacker has resources, the more expensive the defense is. The definition of attackers' technical capabilities is important to know the nature of their threat, for example an attacker can only receive data transmission, but he can also present himself as a legal sensor of the network, and have access to all services network.

The attacker can access the entire network using broadcast, as he can access only a certain region of the network. The target and its importance are key elements of an attack of a service or a layer. Attacking a lower (lower) layer is more important because it affects the other layers above. Several critical services can be attacked, such as localization, synchronization, as well as energy management.

Different types of attacker models can bring the same attack, which makes the modeling of an attacker essential in the study of security. Indeed, it is essential to be able to define the model of an attack to be able to propose adequate countermeasures. The modeling of an attacker depends on the type of attack to be executed, its location in relation to the network, its robustness and also the number of opponents used. In general, according to (Anderson, Chan, & Perrig, 2004), a WSN network can be threatened by two types of attackers: a powerful attacker and a realistic attacker (see Table 1).

CLASSIFICATION OF ATTACKS IN WSNS NETWORKS

In the WSNs networks, several classifications have been planned for the attacks, in our case we will approach the classification illustrated in Figure 6.

- **According to the Origin (the Situation of the Attacker):** A first way to classify attacks is to consider the opponent's situation. Indeed, the attacks can be differentiated according to the origin of the attacker, namely if it is part of the network, or if it acts from outside the network.

Table 1. Attacker model in WSNs networks.

	Powerful	**Realistic**
Attacker	It can be present before and after the deployment of the nodes. It can monitor all communications, anywhere, and at any time. It is able to subvert, potentially, a small subset of nodes.	It is able to monitor a fixed percentage of the communication channels during network deployment.

Figure 6. Classification of attacker in the WSN network

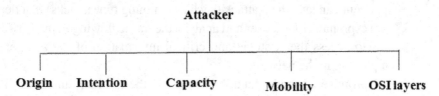

- ○ **External Attack:** It is performed by a node that does not belong to the network. i.e. The attacking node is not allowed to participate or access the network. An external attacker is not necessarily aware of how the network works (communication architecture or protocols used). It can trigger an attack without this information (such as eavesdropping or radio jamming), or just trying to break into the network. Techniques such as cryptography and authentication are needed to protect the network against attacks by this type of attacker.
- ○ **Internal Attack:** It is launched by a legitimate sensor node (belonging to the network) that behaves against its specifications (bad behavior). Typically, an attack from the inside often plays on the parameters of the protocols used. Therefore, it is considered the most stringent threat that can disrupt the smooth operation of the network, and therefore, the most dangerous from the security point of view. Nevertheless, security strategies are often aimed at fighting only external attacks, and there are no longer effective and robust strategies for this type of attack. For this, it is necessary to design and implement other complementary approaches such as monitoring systems (Ioannis, Dimitriou, & Freiling, 2007) (Rajasegarar, Leckie, & Palaniswami, 2008) to facilitate the detection and identification of these attacks in order to eliminate them from the network.
- **According to the Objective:** Another way to classify attacks is to consider the attacker's goal and the security aspect he wants to destabilize. An attacker can operate at two levels: at the level of the information transmitted in the network and at the level of the nodes themselves. The main goals can be:
  - ○ Cornering of resources for the appropriate needs for the attacker, for example, monopolization of the medium of transmission for the sending of the data of the attacker only.
  - ○ Decrease, or outright annihilation, of the network's ability to properly service the services for which it has been deployed, in order to harm the operators of that network. This nuisance can be expressed by financial

losses and sometimes human, for example in a military setting, an opponent can launch an attack (such as jamming type attacks) that deals with espionage for recover and analyze the traffic flowing in the network thus to access the strategic and critical information of the antagonist employing in the network.

○ Compromise of nodes and hijacking of their initial functions. For example, an adversary, during the process of calculating of node positions in the network, can disrupt the localization system used by the falsification of anchor identities and sending erroneous distance estimates.

- **According to the Nature:** The defense mechanisms in the WSN network should not just take into account the origin of the attack, but they must also take into account its nature and its characteristics. Then, an attack can be classified also according to the intention of the attacker:

    ○ **Passive Attack:** It is triggered when a malicious node obtains access to a resource in the network without modifying the data or disrupting the normal operation of the network. During this time, no data packet is sent on the network by the attacker which makes its detection too difficult. It is generally limited to passive listening of messages and analysis of traffic, interception and spying of data (this attack is easier to accomplish, just have a good receiver). Its purpose, on the one hand, is to extract valuable information from data packets such as confidential information in the network, and on the other hand, is to analyze the paths taken by these packets to obtain strategic information about the Network operation such as network topology, base station position, Cluster-Head position, aggregation node identity, and so on. By analyzing this information, the attacker will prepare to launch a specific action that transforms the passive attack into an active attack. Example: the Eavesdropping attack (detailed later).

    ○ **Active Attack:** Unlike the passive attack, the active attack is triggered when a malicious node gains access to a resource to introduce new behaviors into the network. An attacker periodically sends packets of data over the network to destroy its operation in a partial or total way or to trigger a denial of service (Wood, 2002). Several attacks, which will be detailed later, can be performed to achieve this goal. Typically, active threats attempt to delete, modify or reject messages transmitted over the network, compromise communication between nodes, and so on. According to *Stallings* (Stallings, 1995), they belong mainly to four categories:

- **Interruption:** An attack that threatens availability, in which case a communication link becomes lost or unavailable.
- **Interception:** An attack that threatens confidentiality, in which case the attacker may have unauthorized access to the nodes or data exchanged between them.
- **Modification:** An attack that threatens the integrity of the data, in which case the attacker usually targets the application layer. His goal is to manipulate the data in order to change their semantics.
- **Manufacturing:** An attack that threatens the authenticity of data, in this case the attacker aims to infiltrate the network and inject erroneous data to compromise the reliability of communication in the network.

- **According to the Ability (the Power of the Attacker):** The power available to the malicious node is another way of classifying attacks (Alam & De, 2014). Indeed, the definition of the technical abilities of the attackers is important to know the nature of their threat. Therefore, the more the aggressor has resources, the more the defense is expensive.
  - **Strong Attack:** It is led by an attacker who is equipped with extra-resources compared to the other nodes of the network. Indeed, the attacker can have laptop-class attacks, with more powerful devices in terms of computing power, storage capacity, bandwidth, radio coverage, radius of connectivity (he can monitor the entire network) and energy capacity.
  - **Ordinary Attack:** It is conducted by an attacker who uses, during his attack, devices similar to those of the sensor nodes (same characteristics) (mote-class attacks). As a result, he has no privilege over legitimate nodes. For example, an attacker monitors traffic flowing through the network.
- **According to the Mobility:** Attacks can also be differentiated according to the mobility criterion. So, an attacker can be mobile or fixed in the network. Typically, the presence of a mobile attacker in the network is more difficult to detect than that of a fixed attacker.
- **According to the Layers of the OSI Model:** An efficient method of classifying attacks is to proceed by protocol layers (Raymond & Midkiff, 2008). Therefore, attacks in the WSN network can be assigned to the relevant layers of the protocol stack. This ranking allows for an efficient, layer-by-layer review of most known attacks. The protocol stack used by the sensor nodes is recalled in Figure 7.
- **Physical Layer:** Like other traditional wireless networks, the WSN is vulnerable to physical layer attacks. These attacks are few but, at the same

Figure 7. Protocol Stack of WSNs

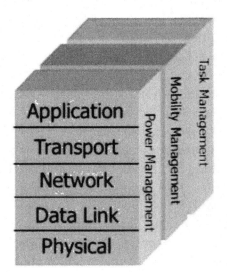

time, may be the most difficult to prevent. For example, an attacker can generate radio jamming (Pelechrinis, Iliofotou, & Krishnamurthy, 2011) to interfere with transmissions and cause a network malfunction.

- **Link Layer:** This data link layer provides the functional and procedural means for the transfer of data between two nodes of the network. It contains two *LLC* sub-layers and *MAC* (Medium Access Control), it's mainly the second one that interests us. At the MAC layer, the protocol used is used to manage access to the transmission channel. Obviously, it aims to provide nodes with equitable access to the communication medium and avoid collisions. Nevertheless, this layer is targeted by several types of attacks. For example, a malicious node may induce a collision in the network, i.e. it sends its own signal when it hears that a legitimate node is transmitting a message to cause interference in order to create a denial of Service attack (*DoS*) (Wood, 2002) (Raymond & Midkiff, 2008).

- **Network Layer:** This is the most interesting layer in the WSN network. Because it serves to connect the nodes of the network and provides the routing service. It is obvious that the routing of data in the WSN is the most important procedure that ensures the routing of information from a collector source node to a destination. However, in this network, each node participates in the routing of the packets and the routing messages pass through the radio waves. Therefore, the protection of communications in these networks is mandatory and requires a high level of security of the sensor nodes in order to prevent any attack aimed at compromising the nodes, recovering their identity, recovering the captured data, altering the network's good by the network. introduction of false information, etc. Several attacks exist at this layer, the most widespread, the attack Backhole (Karakehayov, 2005) where the attacker does not retransmit any packets sent to him and throws all messages.

- **Transport Layer:** This layer helps manage end-to-end connectivity between nodes. It provides the service of segmentation \ collection of packets using sequencing protocols. It splits the data from the application layer into segments for delivery, so it reorders and aggregates segments from the network layer before sending them to the application layer. However, this makes the transport layer very vulnerable to denial of service attacks. These attacks include: Flooding (Raymond & Midkiff, 2008). In this attack, the opponent's goal is to exhaust the memory and energy of a legitimate knot. It can make multiple connection requests until the resources required by each connection are exhausted. If the data link and network layers are secure, the transport layer can be sure that the packets it receives from the network layer are confidential and authenticated.

- **Application Layer:** This layer implements the application used by the WSN at the highest level to provide a particular service. It is vulnerable to different attacks, where their mode of operation is specific to the intended application. For example, attacking erroneous data (Sun et al., 2014). In the latter, a node compromised to the possibility of sending data in perfect contradiction with the measured physical values. The values transmitted at the application level will then distort the final results.

DESCRIPTIONS OF ATTACKS IN WSNS NETWORKS

In the previous section, we saw that there are several ways to categorize security threats in the context of WSNs. A good classification is presented in (Wood, 2002). In this chapter, we present and classify these attacks according to their nature (active or passive) where the active attacks will be, in turn, classified according to the protocol layer (see Figure 8) that they target in the *OSI* model (*classification by layers*).

After classifying the different possible attacks in a WSN network, in this section, we are able to discuss them such as, we will focus on active attacks. In this attack category, an attacker (which is to change the state of the network) attempts to delete or modify the messages transmitted over the network. It can also inject its own traffic or replay old messages to disrupt the operation of the network and cause a denial of service (*DOS*) (Raymond & Midkiff, 2008). In our description, we adopt in

Figure 8. Main attacks in the WSN network: Taxonomy

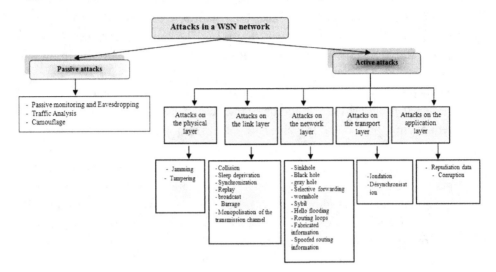

Table 2, where we recapitulate the principle of the most known active attacks (*DoS*) according to the protocol stack and we quote also their countermeasures strategies.

SYBIL ATTACK IN THE WSN NETWORK

WSNs usually communicate sensitive data on which important decisions are based. Thus, the receiver needs to ensure that the data is exchanged in a confidential manner and comes from the right source. Data authentication is one of the services that it should provide to ensure the proper functioning of the network. More concretely, correctly guaranteeing the authentication of the network nodes will prevent an attacker from conducting attacks based on the spoofing of the identity of another node (node replication process). This is mainly to protect the network from the Sybil attack.

- **The Sybil Attack:** (Newsome et al., 2004) (Prabhjotkaur & Singh, 2016) is a dangerous threat in the context of WSNs networks. It consists of creating malicious nodes (Sybil nodes) with false identities (stolen or imaginary). In particular, it targets routing protocols by linking packets to erroneous routes. It can also report non-existent events to ignore the purpose of network deployment. Hence the need to pay special attention to this type of attack. In the remainder of this chapter, we will focus on the Sybil attack such that, first, we will study this attack with the different forms it takes. In the following, we will quote the principles developed to detect and then thwart it.

Table 2. Sensor network layers and active attacks.

Network Layer	Active Attack		Possible Threat	Violated Security Need	Possible Security Scheme
Physical	Jamming		Disrupt the communication in the network (radio interferences, packets collision).	Availability	Lower duty cycle, Spread-spectrum, region mapping, Priority messages.
	Tampering		Physical alteration of node (extract all its information as the cryptographic code).		Tamper proofing.
Link	Collision		Upset the communication in the network (interferences, discarding packets, energy exhaustion).	Availability	Error-correcting code.
	Exhaustion	Sleep deprivation	Energy exhaustion in order to considerably reduce the lifetime of the network.	Availability Integrity	Rate limitation.
		Synchronization			
		Replay			
		Broadcast			
		Barrage			
Network and Routing	Sinkhole		All the traffic circulating in the network passes through the attacker (modify or reject the received packets).	Availability Confidentiality Integrity	Monitoring, Redundancy, Authentication.
	Black hole		Falsify routing information and reject all packets.		Authentication, Monitoring.
	Greyhole		Falsify routing information and reject some packets (ignores only a subset of packets).		Authentication, Monitoring.
	Selective forwarding		Delete selectively some packets received.		Probing, Redundancy.
	Wormhole		Trick routing protocols (create virtual neighbors at legitimate nodes).	Availability Integrity	Authentication, Transmission of Packet by using geographic and temporal information.
	Sybil		Destabilize the operation of routing protocols (create multiple identities).	Availability Authentication Integrity	Probing, Authentication. Test based on random transmission channels.
	Hello flood		Prevent the transmission of messages (flood the network).	Availability Integrity	Verify the bidirectional link, Authentication.
	Spoofed routing information		Disrupt the routing protocols (create routing loops, alter routing tables).	Availability Authentication Integrity	Authentication, Monitoring.
Transport	Flooding		Saturate the limited capacity (several connection requests).	Availability Integrity	Client puzzles, Control of the connection request rate.
	Desynchronization		Falsifying the exchanged messages (interrupt the communication).	Availability	Authentication, Confidence index.

- **Justification:** In this chapter, we are interested in the Sybil attack, our choice is on this attack since:
    - ○ The Sybil attack first, belongs to the threats related to identities. These target the authentication system set up. This significantly reduces the efficiency of fault-tolerant systems such as redundancy mechanisms, distributed storage, multi-hop routing, and topology maintenance. For this, identity attacks in WSNs are considered the most harmful.
    - ○ The Sybil attacks are particularly easy to launch in wireless networks where the communication medium is open. In addition, in WSNs, most communications are in multi-hop way, which facilitates the infiltration of Sybil nodes.
    - ○ The Sybil attack is an attack by which a node presents various identities to represent several fictitious interlocutors of a request and thus to break the availability and the integrity of the network.
    - ○ The Sybil attack is an attack by which a node partially or totally controls the network by presenting multiple identities. Thus the attacker can take advantage of these identities to be selected as a cluster leader, or a data aggregator (thus bypass strategic areas in the network).
    - ○ Several solutions (cited later) have been proposed in the literature to remedy this attack in the WSNs network. However, these solutions remain in their primitive state (the constraints imposed by the WSN network) and they are limited in terms of detection and performance efficiency, which motivated us to investigate in this field of study (Sybil attack) and provide for effective prevention solutions in our future work that detect and prevent Sybil identities.

DEFINITION AND PURPOSE

The Sybil attack is first described by researcher John Douceur in Peer-to-Peer networks (Douceur, 2002) (Karlof & Wagner, 2003). Historically, the name of the attack "Sybil" comes from the title of the eponymous novel written by Flora Schreiber, in 1973 and telling the treatment of a patient suffering multiple personality duplication (multiple personalities). The process of the Sybil attack is, therefore, based on the creation of two or more duplicate entities with a similar identity. Specifically, the Sybil attack is defined as a malicious device illegitimately taking multiple identities. We refer to the additional identities of a malicious device as Sybil nodes (replicated nodes) (Adjoutah & Chelouche, 2013).

In our context of study, WSNs networks, an attacker Sybil (see Figure 9) consists in creating and claiming a large number of identities (multiple identities) by fabricating

Figure 9. General idea(overview) of the Sybil attack

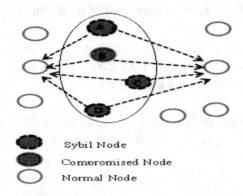

or usurping (stealing) the identities of legitimate nodes (nodes normal). In this case, the base station cannot distinguish the legitimate node from the malicious node. This then makes it possible to disturb the operation of the base station and the other nodes of the network. As a result, the performance of the entire network will degrade or corrupt. The identity (ID) of a Sybil node, generally, can be: (Monnet, 2015).

- Invented (randomly generated), nonexistent nodes.
- Existing nodes, but remote from the corrupt node (malicious or suspect).
- Nodes destroyed and virtually replaced by the corrupted node.

The purpose of this attack is to fill the list of its neighbors by non-existent nodes in order to destabilize the operation of the multi-hop routing protocols and network topology maintenance mechanisms. Indeed, the Sybil attack threatens and scares, mainly, the mechanisms of data transmission as it hacks the redundancy system of paths (failing possible resilience schemes) which ensures the reliability of the network, by creating several routes passing through the adversary and which are actually only one path. Thus, the attacking node can take advantage of these various identities to be selected (or placed in strategic locations in the network so that it can easily manipulate a specific part of the network) as a cluster leader in the Clustering process. or a data aggregator or to create routing paths for its own benefit. In addition, this attack aims to achieve other objectives such a:

- The alteration of the final data retrieved by the legitimate node, transmitting erroneous data from a large number of virtual sensors.
- The exclusion of legitimate nodes from the network in the case where a detection solution is put in place, by simulating irregular behavior on the part of these nodes, or by voting against them under the cover of several

identities in order to receive these votes (the Sybil node can easily determine the outcome of any vote by having all of its multiple identities vote for the same node).

- Resource grabbing, by reserving resources (access to the channel, remaining amount of power, etc.) for multiple virtual nodes, but which will only be used by the single sensor leading the attack.

To better understand the principle of the Sybil attack, we take an example, which is shown in Figure 10, where the malicious node AD is presented by several identities as it appears as:

- Node *F* for *A*,
- Node *C* for *B*,
- Node *A* for *D*,

So when node *A* wants to communicate with *F* it sends the message to *AD* (falsification of the neighborhood information).

The peculiarity of this attack, it does not need any special technical ability so it is executable by a single node. Since the lie about identity is the basis of this attack, authentication is the most obvious way to detect and prevent it.

Characteristics of the Sybil Attack

Different Forms (Types)

Sybil attacks can be classified into three categories (three orthogonal dimensions) depending on the type of communication, identity and their participation in the network. These categories are introduced in (Newsome et al., 2004) as a taxonomy (see Figure 11).

Figure 10. Principle of Attack Sybil

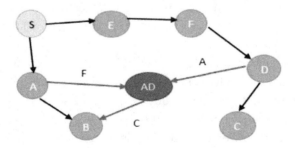

Figure 11. Forms of the attack Sybil: Taxonomy

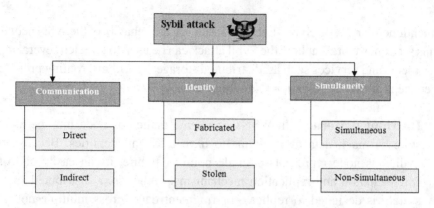

This taxonomy is briefly discussed in the following paragraphs:

- **Communication:** Is done by two types:
  - ○ **Direct Communication:** Sybil nodes communicate directly with legitimate nodes. When a legitimate node sends a message to a Sybil node, one of the malicious devices listens to the message. Similarly, messages sent from Sybil nodes are actually sent from one of the malicious nodes.
  - ○ **Indirect Communication:** In this category of attack, no legitimate node is able to communicate directly with the Sybil nodes. So, one or more malicious nodes can reach the Sybil nodes. Messages sent to a Sybil node are routed through one of these malicious nodes, which are intended to transmit the message to a Sybil node.
- **Identities:** A Sybil node can obtain an identity in two ways:
  - ○ **Fabricated Identities:** The attacker can simply create new arbitrary Sybil identities.
  - ○ **Usurped Identities:** The attacker cannot build new identities. In this case, it must assign other legitimate identities to Sybil nodes (identity theft mechanism). This identity theft may not be detected if the attacker temporarily destroys or disables the spoofed nodes.
- **Participation:** Multiple Sybil identities created by a malicious node can participate in a way:
  - ○ **Simultaneous:** The attacker can participate all his Sybil identities simultaneously in the network. i.e. All identities present themselves at once.
  - ○ **Non-Simultaneous:** The attacker can alternatively present only part of his identities over a given period of time.

Applications of the Sybil Attack

As mentioned earlier, the Sybil attack can influence the behavior of the WSN network. In this section, we present how the Sybil attack can be used to threaten several types of protocols and services such as: distributed storage algorithms, routing protocols, the concept of data aggregation (Newsome et al., 2004).

- **Distributed Storage:** In WSNs, the same malicious node may be able to store as much data as it claims to have different identities. Because this malicious node represents a single point of failure, it can easily undo the fragmentation and replication mechanisms. Although, a distributed storage system is designed to replicate or fragment data across multiple nodes, it could actually store data on Sybil identities generated by the same malicious node.
- **Routing:** Routing protocols in WSNs can be disrupted by Sybil attacks. In particular, multicast routing mechanisms (or multipath routing) where separate paths initially appear disjoint may be vulnerable since malicious nodes may appear at more than one place at a time. On the other hand, in geographic routing (Karp & Kung, 2000) where, instead of having a set of coordinates, a Sybil node could appear at more than one place at a time.
- **Aggregation of Data:** In a WSN network, due to lack of resources (energy), data is often aggregated to a node. A Sybil node can change the entire aggregation read results by contributing many times to aggregating data as a different user. With enough Sybil nodes, an attacker may be able to completely alter aggregate reading.
- **Voting (Falsifying Vote and Reputation of Nodes):** In some cases, WSNs use voting for a number of tasks (for example, choosing the Head cluster in a clustering process). A malicious node may be able to determine the outcome of any vote by having all of its Sybil identities voted for the same entity.
- **Vehicular Network Traffic Congestion (VANET):** A malicious user can create an arbitrary number of non-existent virtual vehicles and transmit false information in the network to give a fake impression of traffic congestion.

Mechanisms of Defenses Against the Sybil Attack

It is obvious that the Sybil attack is one of the most severe attacks in an ad hoc network in general and in WSNs networks in particular. It is an attack in which a malicious node appears in the network with multiple identities, which gives the illusion that there are several legitimate nodes. So, the main goal of the malicious leader node of the Sybil attack is falsification of the neighborhood. Several works were projected in the review of the literature in order to detect it then remove it from the network. In this section, we are able to discuss and summarize the more widespread works.

The authors in (Geetha & Ramakrishnan, 2015), propose an approach to detect the Sybil attack in the static WSN network. To identify this Sybil node, the authors present a TIME-TO-TIME MESSAGE (*TTM*) model. In this model, each node in the network maintains an observation table to store the identity and position of other nodes. First, the authors assume that each node has a unique identity and a position obtained using a Global Positioning System (*GPS*) (Hofmann-Wellenhof, Lichtenegger, & Collins, 2012). When the nodes are deployed, they cannot change their location. This *TTM* model uses a path tracing algorithm to detect the Sybil attack in a network. A message is transmitted from the source to the destination using *AODV* routing protocol to find the shortest paths. The steps of the algorithm are elaborated as follows:

Step 1: During network deployment, each node obtains secret (confidential) information assigned by a server.

Step 2: Each node sends a Hello message to all its neighbors. This Hello message contains the node's id, position, and secret information.

Step 3: Each node maintains an observation table which stores information received from neighboring nodes (registration process).

Step 4: After this registration process, when a new message is received by another node, the entries of the observation table are compared with the previous information stored. If it matches then it is a normal node and the received message will be processed, otherwise it is a Sybil node and the received message will be deleted.

Step 5: If the message is received from a Sybil node, then each time it uses a different identifier and therefore it has different secret information. By comparing this information, the malicious node is easily identified and removed from the network

The authors in (Prasad & Mallick, 2015), propose an algorithm called Sybil Attack Detection Algorithm (SDA) to detect the Sybil attack in the WSN network. This algorithm uses a mobile agent, the threshold value, the random key pre-distribution and the random password generation to identify a Sybil node. the Sybil Attack Detection Algorithm (SDA) is organized in the form of the following steps:

Step 1: Generate a random key and *node_id*. Store this information in the mobile agent in a table called *Ptable*.

Step 2: Assign the *node_id* and the random key to each node.

Step 3: The random password is generated according to the random key.

Step 4: The node sends data via the mobile agent to the Head cluster with the random password.

Step 5: the mobile agent checks the *node_id* received and the *node_id* stored in the table Ptable (if yes).

Phase One: The mobile agent verifies the random password as well as the threshold value stored in Ptable (if yes).

Hypothesis One: The legitimate node is confirmed. The mobile agent sends the data to the Cluster Head (if not).

Hypothesis Two: A Sybil node is detected and blocked by the mobile agent. The information of this node Sybil is stored in this mobile agent in a table called *ctable*. this table is sent to the base station and stored in a table called *btable*.

The authors in (Karuppiah, Dalfiah, Yuvashri, Rajaram, & Pathan, 2014), propose an algorithm to detect the Sybil attack in the WSN network. The special feature of this algorithm is that it accurately detects the Sybil node by spending relatively less energy. Indeed, in WSN, it is imperative to save energy along with the efficiency of the mechanism. In this work, the assumed WSN network is static so all nodes have the same transmission power. The network is organized in clusters to cover the entire area of interest. Each Cluster consists of a Head Cluster (*CH*), four legitimate nodes and a Sybil node. For the detection of Sybil nodes, the authors consider the following cases:

- **Case 1:** The Sybil Node Does Not Respond to the Request Sent by the CH - In this case, the proposed algorithm is implemented with a centralized approach (at CH level). It is based on sending request packets. First, each *CH* contains a table (*CH table*) that stores the identities and positions of its members. This information (identifiers and positions) remains unique for a specific node. When the nodes send their *ACKs* to respond to the *CH's* request, the *CH* checks and compares the received information with the information stored in the *CH* table.

- **Case 2:** The Sybil Node Responds With the Same Identity and Different Positions - The proposed algorithm is also based on sending queries for this case. All legitimate nodes respond to the *CH* with their identities and location coordinates. The Sybil node also provides a response to the *CH* with one of the identities of the nodes and its own position. For example, if a *CH* has 4 member nodes: *x1, x2, x3, x4* with the locations *L1, L2, L3, L4* respectively, the Sybil node must each have these identities (*x1, x2, x3, x4*) and its own location *L5*. If the Sybil node responds to the *CH* with one of these identities and the location L5, it would be easily identified (comparison with the table *CH*).

The authors in (Ho, Liu, Wright, & Das, 2009), propose 3 approaches for the distributed detection of replicated nodes (Sybil) in WSNs, which are based on prior knowledge of node deployment points and assume:

- The nodes are grouped together by the base station, and each group is identified by an ID, the nodes are programmed with group information by the base station, each node is characterized by group ID and a number d identification in his group.
- The nodes are placed in predetermined places according to a well-defined formula.
- Attackers can compromise a large number of nodes in a small area.

Approach 1: The basic idea was that each node only accepts messages from the elements of its group that it trusts, but this prevents intergroup communication. The idea has been extended to consider the deployed nodes near their predetermined deployment points as trusted nodes and the deployed nodes far from their points as non-trusted nodes, so the nodes accept the messages of the trusted nodes which reduces the cost of communication.

Approach 2: This approach allows communication with a non-trusted node with proof that it does not represent the same physical node. This proof includes the location of the node after deployment (this is done by a localization software integrated in the nodes to determine their real points after deployment). If a node U wants to communicate with a node V (a non-trusted node), U sends V an authentication request, V responds with the location query CV indicating whether it is placed in the right place, then U returns CV to the neighbors of V, if the neighbors of V receive two contradictory CVs they deduce that V has been replicated and will be revoked.

Approach 3: This is the same idea as approach 2, but in this approach the node U sends CV to multiple groups rather than a single group (neighbors of V), U chooses groups that are close to the area V deployment (the deployment area of a group is a circle centered at the deployment point of the group with a radius Rz). If groups receive conflicting CVs then node V is replicated.

In (Wen, Li, Zheng, & Chen, 2008), the authors propose to use the difference in *TDOA* (Chen, Li, & Wang, 2008) arrival time between a source node and detector nodes. This solution can detect the existence of Sybil attacks, and locate Sybil nodes. In this proposal, Mi et al. have considered a static network, where all the nodes are randomly deployed and there is synchronization between the source nodes and the detector nodes. Three detector nodes *S1, S2, S3* with known coordinates (*X1, Y1*) (*X2, Y2*) and (*X3, Y3*), respectively, are placed at the boundary of the monitored sector (usually a cluster).Mi et al. have considered that a Sybil node can make many non-existent identities. To detect the Sybil attack they assumed that *S1* is the main detector node, once the three detector nodes hear a message *mi = {data; Dx}* from the source S, these three nodes record their arrival times of the messages, for instance, *t1, t2, t3* to *S1 S2, S3*, the main detector node S1 can calculate the arrival time difference when it receives *t2* and *t3* of *S2* and *S3*. In another transmission, the same process is repeated. If the same *TDOA* value with different *IDs* is received, the receiver detects a Sybil attack. After detecting the attack, the Sybil node is located.

A location algorithm based on *RSSI* (Wang, Yin, Cai, & Zhang, 2008) is proposed in (Demirbas & Song, 2006). The authors base themselves on *Theorem* 5 of (Demirbas & Song, 2006), which assumes that if at least four nodes monitor (called detector nodes or monitoring nodes) the radio signals, no user can hide its location. Instead of calculating the position of each sending node by the four detector nodes and associating this location with its identity included in the message, the proposed approach ignores this calculation and then records compares the *RSSI* report for the received messages to detect a Sybil attack. Taking the following scenario: four monitoring *IDs* have identifiers like: *D1, D2, D3* and *D4* respectively and a Sybil node that forges its *ID* as *S1, S2* and so on with time. Figure 12 shows the topology of the example presented.

At time *t1*, a Sybil node broadcasts messages and its forged *ID* is S1. The four neighboring monitoring nodes receive radio power and falsified identity. Each node transmits messages with its own *ID* and the RSSI received from the Sybil node at the representative node, *D1*. This node *D1* calculates the ratio (ratio) with each node (*D2, D3, D4*) and stores it locally. Similarly, at time t2, the Sybil node broadcasts messages and its forged ID is S2. The four neighboring nodes monitor the radio power of the Sybil node and report it to the *D1* node. The latter calculates each ratio. At this time, this node *D1* can detect the node Sybil by comparing the ratio at time

Figure 12. Example of network topology

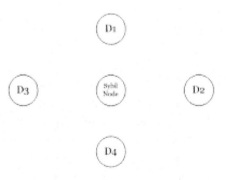

t1 and *t2*. Specifically, node *D1* concludes that there is a Sybil attack that occurs in the region, if the difference between two pieces of information is very close to zero. Indeed, if the received power ratio is the same, it means that the location is the same, but the node broadcasts messages with multiple *IDs*. Otherwise, node *D1* may indicate that there is no Sybil node.

In (Piro, Shields, & Levine, 2006), the authors prove that mobility can be used to improve security, a node can detect a Sybil attack by monitoring traffic for a long enough 30 seconds including data transmission and Hello messages (for neighbor discovery), it records the addresses (*IP* or *MAC*) of all other nodes. After making many observations the node analyzes its results to find the identities that always seem together which leads to the conclusion of probably presence of a Sybil attack. To increase detection accuracy, the authors (Piro et al., 2006) extend collision detection at the *MAC* level to differentiate between an attacker spoofing and a set of mobile nodes in the network. A single node can produce false results, for this purpose they introduced the notion of detection with multiple nodes that analyze traffic and share their observations to increase the detection accuracy of Sybil nodes.

In (Newsome et al., 2004), the authors propose also the use of the test of resources. In this approach, they assume that any physical sensor has only one radio and that this radio is unable to send and receive simultaneously on more than one different channel each verifier assigns a channel. In this paper, the others consider that each check can wait for the message on this channel, it means that this neighbor is a Sybil node. The difficulty of this approach is that we do not always have as many channels as neighbors. In this case if we do not have enough allocated channels, it may take a long time to detect a Sybil attack. It can even remain indented if there are as many or more Sybil nodes as channels.

Synthesis on Security Approaches Against the Sybil Attack

At this stage, we make a comparison between the different approaches (cited above) proposed to fight the Sybil attack, as we will trace their main benefits and limitations (see Table 3).

CONCLUSION

WSNs are designed to work in groups and cooperate to transmit collected data to a central point called base station or Sink. They are fully integrated in the process of monitoring sensitive areas, managing urban traffic, or studying the natural environment. However, like most distributed networks, WSNs are exposed to security threats. Indeed, their special features and communication media make them very

Table 3. Summary of the proposed solutions against the Sybil attack.

Proposed Approach	Advantage	Disadvantage
Detection of Sybil Attack using Neighbour Nodes in Static WSN [37]	Effective and fast detection, No special equipment.	Consume more energy and memory (a large number of messages).
A Mobile Agent based Sybil Attack Detection Algorithm for Wireless Sensor Network [39]	Efficient detection by checking the rate and delivery rate of packets.	Ensure Sybil attack detection with more memory space (random key, random password, node-id.) and too much calculation to perform.
A Novel Energy-Efficient Sybil Node Detection Algorithm for Intrusion Detection System in Wireless Sensor Networks [40].	High accuracy of detection, Consume less energy (*Energy-efficient*). Very handy even with densely deployed networks.	Does not adapt to Irregular Networks. Scalability problem.
Distributed detection of replica node attacks with group deployment knowledge in wireless sensor networks [41]	Average detection rate.	Consume more memory (a large number of messages for communication between nodes). If the number of errors is high the energy consumption increases.
TDOA-based Sybil attack detection scheme for wireless sensor networks [42].	Effective detection, Less storage space and low power consumption (light solution).	Not adapt to asynchronous systems, Several queries used between the source nodes and the detector nodes.
An RSSI-based Scheme for Sybil Attack Detection in Wireless Sensor Networks [43].	Detect the Sybil attack accurately. Robust since it detects all Sybil attack cases with *100%* completeness and less than a few percent false positives. Solution is light (collaboration of another node next to the receiver).	Constraints of *RSSI* measurements (variation over time, radio transmission is non-isotropic). Scalability problem.
Detecting the Sybil Attack in Mobile Ad hoc Networks [44]	High detection with multiple nodes, Solution based on network traffic analysis.	High storage capacity thus overly compute (the nodes store *IP* and *MAC* addresses of all nodes and analyze the results).
The Sybil Attack in Sensor Networks: Analysis & Defenses [11].	Average detection of Sybil nodes based on the resource test.	Problem of number of channels assigned to neighboring nodes.

vulnerable to various malicious attacks. For that, the security of a WSN network is one of the big challenges to make sure it works.

In this chapter, we focus on the issue of security such as, we have identified the challenges and obstacles that make the security of this type of network a difficult task and quite complicated. We also discussed the security needs (issues) required by various protocols. Finally, we have developed a taxonomy of attacks that threaten security.

In the second part of this chapter, after presenting an overview on the problem of security in the WSN network, we highlighted the Sybil attack. We chose to study this attack because it belongs to the most severe attacks in WSNs networks. Indeed, it is an attack in which a malicious node presents itself in the network by using several identities. The goal, among other things, is to falsify the neighborhood to defeat the routing and the topology control mechanisms.

To protect against this attack, several solutions have been proposed in the literature but they are still limited, they cannot completely eliminate the attack. These limitations motivated us to study it and why not propose, in future works, an adequate security solution that detects and locates in an efficient and reliable way this attack.

REFERENCES

Adjoutah, S., & Chelouche, O. (2013). *Sécurité contre l'attaque Sybil dans les réseaux de capteurs sans fils* (Doctoral dissertation). Université Abderrahmane Mira-Bejaia.

Ahmed, M. R., Huang, X., & Sharma, D. (2012). A taxonomy of internal attacks in wireless sensor network. *Memory (Kbytes)*, *128*, 48.

Al-Karaki, J. N., Ul-Mustafa, R., & Kamal, A. E. (2004). Data aggregation in wireless sensor networks-exact and approximate algorithms. In *High Performance Switching and Routing, 2004. HPSR. 2004 Workshop on* (pp. 241-245). IEEE. 10.1109/HPSR.2004.1303478

Alam, S., & De, D. (2014). *Analysis of security threats in wireless sensor network.* arXiv preprint arXiv:1406.0298

Anderson, R., Chan, H., & Perrig, A. (2004, October). Key infection: Smart trust for smart dust. In *Network Protocols, 2004. ICNP 2004. Proceedings of the 12th IEEE International Conference on* (pp. 206-215). IEEE.

Arampatzis, T., Lygeros, J., & Manesis, S. (2005, June). A survey of applications of wireless sensors and wireless sensor networks. In *Intelligent Control, 2005. Proceedings of the 2005 IEEE International Symposium on, Mediterrean Conference on Control and Automation* (pp. 719-724). IEEE. 10.1109/.2005.1467103

Asch, G. (2010). *Les capteurs en instrumentation industrielle-7ème édition.* Dunod.

Chen, H. L., Li, H. B., & Wang, Z. (2008). Research on TDoA-based secure localization for wireless sensor networks. *Journal of Communication*, *29*(8), 11–21.

Chen, X., Makki, K., Yen, K., & Pissinou, N. (2009). Sensor network security: A survey. *IEEE Communications Surveys and Tutorials*, *11*(2), 52–73. doi:10.1109/SURV.2009.090205

Demirbas, M., & Song, Y. (2006, June). An RSSI-based scheme for sybil attack detection in wireless sensor networks. In *Proceedings of the 2006 International Symposium on on World of Wireless, Mobile and Multimedia Networks* (pp. 564-570). IEEE Computer Society. 10.1109/WOWMOM.2006.27

Douceur, J. R. (2002, March). The sybil attack. In *International workshop on peer-to-peer systems* (pp. 251-260). Springer. 10.1007/3-540-45748-8_24

Gaubatz, G., Kaps, J. P., & Sunar, B. (2004, August). Public key cryptography in sensor networks—revisited. In *European Workshop on Security in Ad-Hoc and Sensor Networks* (pp. 2-18). Springer.

Geetha, C., & Ramakrishnan, M. (2015). Detection of SYBIL Attack using Neighbour Nodes in Static WSN. *International Journal on Recent and Innovation Trends in Computing and Communication*, 3(4), 2428 - 2432.

Han, S., Chang, E., Gao, L., & Dillon, T. (2006). Taxonomy of attacks on wireless sensor networks. In *EC2ND 2005* (pp. 97–105). London: Springer. doi:10.1007/1-84628-352-3_10

Hill, J., Szewczyk, R., Woo, A., Hollar, S., Culler, D., & Pister, K. (2000). System architecture directions for networked sensors. *Operating Systems Review*, *34*(5), 93–104. doi:10.1145/384264.379006

Ho, J. W., Liu, D., Wright, M., & Das, S. K. (2009). Distributed detection of replica node attacks with group deployment knowledge in wireless sensor networks. *Ad Hoc Networks*, *7*(8), 1476–1488. doi:10.1016/j.adhoc.2009.04.008

Hofmann-Wellenhof, B., Lichtenegger, H., & Collins, J. (2012). *Global positioning system: theory and practice*. Springer Science & Business Media.

Ioannis, K., Dimitriou, T., & Freiling, F. C. (2007, April). Towards intrusion detection in wireless sensor networks. In *Proc. of the 13th European Wireless Conference* (pp. 1-10). Academic Press.

Karakehayov, Z. (2005). Using REWARD to detect team black-hole attacks in wireless sensor networks. *Wksp. Real-World Wireless Sensor Networks*, 20-21.

Karlof, C., & Wagner, D. (2003, May). Secure routing in wireless sensor networks: Attacks and countermeasures. In *Sensor Network Protocols and Applications, 2003. Proceedings of the First IEEE. 2003 IEEE International Workshop on* (pp. 113-127). IEEE.

Karp, B., & Kung, H. T. (2000, August). GPSR: Greedy perimeter stateless routing for wireless networks. In *Proceedings of the 6th annual international conference on Mobile computing and networking* (pp. 243-254). ACM. 10.1145/345910.345953

Karuppiah, A. B., Dalfiah, J., Yuvashri, K., Rajaram, S., & Pathan, A. S. K. (2014, December). A novel energy-efficient sybil node detection algorithm for intrusion detection system in wireless sensor networks. In *Eco-friendly Computing and Communication Systems (ICECCS), 2014 3rd International Conference on* (pp. 95-98). IEEE. 10.1109/Eco-friendly.2014.94

Kraus, K. (2014). *Security management process in distributed, large scale high performance systems* (Doctoral dissertation). University of Oulu, Finland.

Labraoui, N. (2012). *La sécurité dans les réseaux sans fil ad hoc* (Doctoral dissertation).

Legendre, F. (2014). *Exploitation de la logique propositionnelle pour la résolution parallèle des problèmes cryptographiques* (Doctoral dissertation).

Li, N., Zhang, N., Das, S. K., & Thuraisingham, B. (2009). Privacy preservation in wireless sensor networks: A state-of-the-art survey. *Ad Hoc Networks*, 7(8), 1501–1514. doi:10.1016/j.adhoc.2009.04.009

Monnet, Q. (2015). *Modèles et mécanismes pour la protection contre les attaques par déni de service dans les réseaux de capteurs sans fil* (Doctoral dissertation).

Newsome, J., Shi, E., Song, D., & Perrig, A. (2004, April). The sybil attack in sensor networks: analysis & defenses. In *Proceedings of the 3rd international symposium on Information processing in sensor networks* (pp. 259-268). ACM. 10.1145/984622.984660

Noury, N. (2002). *Du Signal à l'Information: le capteur intelligent* (Doctoral dissertation). Université Joseph-Fourier-Grenoble I.

Padmavathi, D. G., & Shanmugapriya, M. (2009). *A survey of attacks, security mechanisms and challenges in wireless sensor networks.* arXiv preprint arXiv:0909.0576

Pelechrinis, K., Iliofotou, M., & Krishnamurthy, S. V. (2011). Denial of service attacks in wireless networks: The case of jammers. *IEEE Communications Surveys and Tutorials*, 13(2), 245–257. doi:10.1109/SURV.2011.041110.00022

Perkins, C. E. (2001). *Ad Hoc Networks*. Reading, MA: Addison-Wesley.

Piro, C., Shields, C., & Levine, B. N. (2006, August). Detecting the sybil attack in mobile ad hoc networks. In *Securecomm and Workshops, 2006* (pp. 1–11). IEEE. doi:10.1109/SECCOMW.2006.359558

Prabhjotkaur, A. C., & Singh, S. (2016). Review Paper of Detection and Prevention of Sybil Attack in WSN Using Centralizedids. *International Journal of Engineering Science*, 8399.

Prasad, K., & Mallick, C. A Mobile Agent based Sybil Attack Detection Algorithm for Wireless Sensor Network. *International Conference on Emergent Trends in Computing and Communication (ETCC 2015)*.

Rajasegarar, S., Leckie, C., & Palaniswami, M. (2008, May). CESVM: Centered hyperellipsoidal support vector machine based anomaly detection. In *Communications, 2008. ICC'08. IEEE International Conference on* (pp. 1610-1614). IEEE.

Raymond, D. R., & Midkiff, S. F. (2008). Denial-of-service in wireless sensor networks: Attacks and defenses. *IEEE Pervasive Computing, 7*(1), 74–81. doi:10.1109/MPRV.2008.6

Scholar, M. T. (2017). Review on the various Sybil Attack Detection Techniques in Wireless Sensor Network. *SYBIL, 164*(1).

Stallings, W. (1995). *Network and internetwork security: principles and practice* (Vol. 1). Englewood Cliffs, NJ: Prentice Hall.

Sun, F., Zhao, Z., Fang, Z., Du, L., Xu, Z., & Chen, D. (2014). A review of attacks and security protocols for wireless sensor networks. *Journal of Networks, 9*(5), 1103. doi:10.4304/jnw.9.5.1103-1113

Wander, A. S., Gura, N., Eberle, H., Gupta, V., & Shantz, S. C. (2005, March). Energy analysis of public-key cryptography for wireless sensor networks. In *Pervasive Computing and Communications, 2005. PerCom 2005. Third IEEE International Conference on* (pp. 324-328). IEEE. 10.1109/PERCOM.2005.18

Wang, S., Yin, J., Cai, Z., & Zhang, G. (2008). A RSSI-based selflocalization algorithm for wireless sensor networks. *Journal of Computer Research and Development*, 385-388.

Wen, M., Li, H., Zheng, Y. F., & Chen, K. F. (2008). TDOA-based Sybil attack detection scheme for wireless sensor networks [English Edition]. *Journal of Shanghai University, 12*(1), 66–70. doi:10.100711741-008-0113-2

Wood, A. D., & Stankovic, J. A. (2002). Denial of service in sensor networks. *Computer, 35*(10), 54-62.

Yick, J., Mukherjee, B., & Ghosal, D. (2008). Wireless sensor network survey. *Computer Networks, 52*(12), 2292–2330. doi:10.1016/j.comnet.2008.04.002

Zhang, X., Heys, H. M., & Li, C. (2010, May). Energy efficiency of symmetric key cryptographic algorithms in wireless sensor networks. In *Communications (QBSC), 2010 25th Biennial Symposium on* (pp. 168-172). IEEE. 10.1109/BSC.2010.5472979

Chapter 12
Hybridization of Biogeography–Based Optimization and Gravitational Search Algorithm for Efficient Face Recognition

Lavika Goel
Birla Institute of Technology and Science (BITS), India

Lavanya B.
Birla Institute of Technology and Science (BITS), India

Pallavi Panchal
Birla Institute of Technology and Science (BITS), India

ABSTRACT

This chapter aims to apply a novel hybridized evolutionary algorithm to the application of face recognition. Biogeography-based optimization (BBO) has some element of randomness to it that apart from improving the feasibility of a solution could reduce it as well. In order to overcome this drawback, this chapter proposes a hybridization of BBO with gravitational search algorithm (GSA), another nature-inspired algorithm, by incorporating certain knowledge into BBO instead of the randomness. The migration procedure of BBO that migrates SIVs between solutions is done between solutions only if the migration would lead to the betterment of a solution. BBO-GSA algorithm is applied to face recognition with the LFW (labelled faces in the wild) and ORL datasets in order to test its efficiency. Experimental results show that the proposed BBO-GSA algorithm outperforms or is on par with some of the nature-inspired techniques that have been applied to face recognition so far by achieving a recognition rate of 80% with the LFW dataset and 99.75% with the ORL dataset.

DOI: 10.4018/978-1-5225-7338-8.ch012

INTRODUCTION

The history of Automatic Face Recognition dates back to the 1960s (Huang et al, 2007). From then on it has emerged as one of the most extensively studied research topics in computer vision due to its vast application in security systems for surveillance and authentication as it is more robust and secure as compared to other biometric techniques. Several mechanisms have been applied to recognize human faces automatically the most prevalent of which is the Principal Component Analysis (PCA) using Eigen faces (Eigen vectors). PCA is used for dimensionality reduction and feature selection purposes in this work. Another category of algorithms that are widely being applied to Face Recognition includes the nature inspired algorithmic techniques. These algorithms optimize a function by iteratively improving candidate solutions with regard to a given measure of quality or fitness function. Ant Colony Optimization (ACO), Biogeography-Based Optimization (BBO), Genetic Algorithm (GA), Gravitational Search Algorithm (GSA), Neural Networks (NN), Particle Swarm Optimization (PSO) are some among the many nature inspired algorithmic techniques that have been applied to face recognition so far (Dorigo, 2005).

Biogeography-Based Optimization and Gravitational Search Algorithm are relatively new optimization techniques. Biogeography-Based Optimization performs two major operations, they are, migration and mutation. The steps of these two operations include some randomness that apart from making a solution better might lead to it becoming poorer than what it was before as well. This leads to the generation of several infeasible solutions and also delays the convergence of the algorithm. If the replacement of SIVs is done in such a manner that poor SIVs are replaced with good SIVs only, BBO will converge to the optimal solution faster. It might also result in faster generation of better solutions. This work aims to overcome this drawback of BBO by borrowing certain characteristics of the GSA thus leading to a hybridized BBO-GSA algorithm. The hybridized BBO-GSA algorithm is applied to the problem of face recognition by optimizing the Eigen-faces generated by PCA and then a Support Vector Machine (SVM) Classifier is used to classify the faces into different classes.

The organization of the rest of this chapter is as follows, Section 2 provides a brief idea of the related work done in nature inspired algorithms with respect to face recognition, Section 3 provides a review of the major techniques used in this work such as PCA, BBO and GSA, Section 4 explains the BBO-GSA technique proposed in this chapter and its application to face recognition, Section 5 gives the experimental results of this work, Section 6 compares this work with some of the existing approaches to face recognition and Section 7 gives the conclusion and directions for future work.

BACKGROUND

The problem of face recognition has been dealt with by several nature inspired algorithms by employing varying techniques and mechanisms.

Face recognition has been tackled using various techniques as in new model of a Modular Neural Network (MNN) optimized with hierarchical genetic algorithm is proposed for human recognition (Sanchez et la, 2015). In this case the proposed method is tested with the problem of human recognition based on the face information. The work in (Dai et al, 2015) uses neural networks with random weights (NNRWs) to implement such learning scheme in the study of face recognition. Improvement in BBO has been presented in (Du et al, 2009) in which distinctive features from other successful heuristic algorithms are incorporated in BBO and also, a new immigration refusal approach is added to BBO. Face Recognition has been done in (Gupta et al, 2013) using a combination of Biogeography Based Optimization, Principal Component Analysis (Caoa et al, 2003) and Gabor filters. In (Aishwarya et al, 2010), a new approach to face recognition is proposed in which multiple face Eigen subspaces are created, with each one corresponding to one known subject privately, rather than all individuals sharing one universal subspace as in the traditional Eigen face method. Compared with the traditional single subspace face representation, the proposed method captures the extra personal difference to the most possible extent, which is crucial to distinguish between individuals, and on the other hand, it throws away the most intrapersonal difference and noise in the input improving the performance. A comparison of PCA, KPCA and ICA to SVM has been proposed in (Caoa et al, 2003). The experiment shows that SVM by feature extraction using PCA, KPCA or ICA can perform better than that without feature extraction. Furthermore, among the three methods, there is the best performance in KPCA feature extraction, followed by ICA feature extraction. An automatic facial feature extraction algorithm is presented (Lin et al, 1999). In the face region estimation stage, a second chance region growing method is adopted to estimate the face region of a target image. In the feature extraction stage, genetic search algorithms are applied to extract the facial feature points within the face region. It is shown by simulation results that the proposed algorithm can automatically and exactly extract facial features with limited computational complexity. Features are extracted using Principal Component Analysis(PCA) after applying Gabor filters and then BBO is applied to get the most desirable features based on a well-defined fitness function, a hybrid of Biogeography Based Optimization and Particle Swarm Optimization (Mo et al, 2015) where position updating strategy of PSO is applied to increase diversity of population in BBO and then obtained biogeography particle swarm optimization algorithm(BPSO) is used to optimize paths in path network obtained by approximate Voronoi boundary network (AVBN) modelling, a local extrema based Gravitational Search Algorithm has been proposed in (Chakraborti et al, 2014; Chakraborti and Chatterjee, 2014) where two variants of GSA are proposed namely the 2-D version of GSA, in order to cater for the 2-D image data, and the other one is a 2-D randomized local extrema based GSA (RLEGSA), which employs a stochastic local neighborhood based search instead of a global search, as in basic GSA, a Binary Particle Swarm Optimization (BPSO) for feature selection with SVM has been done, feature selection based on a novel Ant Colony Optimization (ACO) based technique has been applied in (Kanan et al, 2008) in this proposed algorithm classifier performance and the length of the selected feature vector are adopted as heuristic information for ACO therefore the optimal feature subset is selected in terms of shortest feature length and the best performance of classifier.

The main aim of this chapter is to overcome the disadvantage of infeasible solution generation and late convergence of BBO by performing migration between solutions only if it leads to a better solution.

A BRIEF REVIEW OF PCA, BBO AND GSA

This section briefly reviews the techniques of PCA, BBO and GSA that are used in this chapter. Hybridization of BBO and GSA is done to form a novel hybridized nature inspired technique and is applied to the Eigen faces (Kanan et la, 2008; Ravi et al, 2013) generated from PCA.

Principal Component Analysis

PCA (Gottumukkal et al, 2004) does feature selection (Ramadan et al, 2009) by extracting the common features that are present between face images and outputs Eigen faces (Aishwarya et al, 2010; Ravi et al, 2013) The working of PCA is described in Fig. 1.

After the 8 steps of PCA described in fig. 1 only those top 'k' Eigen vectors that are noiseless are selected. The k Eigen faces must be mapped back to M images i.e. each face image is represented with some proportion of each

Eigen face which gives us the vector of each face image. For example if we generate k Eigen faces for a training set of M face images, each face image can be made up of "proportions" of all these k "features" or Eigen faces,

$$F_i = [\omega_1, \omega_2, \ldots\ldots, \omega_k] \tag{4}$$

where F_i is the ith face vector in the dataset of M images. Each image will now have a vector associated with it.

Figure 1. Steps of the Principal Component Analysis

1. Each image in the image dataset of M images is represented in the form of a vector I. If the image size is n x n pixels then the dimension of the vector I is n^2 x 1.
2. From all images in the dataset an average face vector X is extracted which represents the common features present in all the faces in the dataset.
3. Each image in the image dataset of M images is represented in the form of a vector I. If the image size is n x n pixels then the dimension of the vector I is n^2 x 1.
4. From all images in the dataset an average face vector X is extracted which represents the common features present in all the faces in the dataset.
5. Then the normalized face vector N is calculated for each person by the formula,

$$N_i = I_i - X \qquad (1)$$

   where i = {1,2,.....M} is the face vector of each person and N is the normalized face vector containing the unique features in each person.

6. To find the Eigen faces we have to calculate the co-variance matrix C, where

$$C = AA^T \qquad (2)$$

   where A = [N_1 N_2 N_3 ..... N_m] a matrix of normalized vectors from (1). The dimension of matrix A is n^2 x M. Therefore the dimension of C becomes n^2 x n^2.

7. To reduce the dimension of C we make (2) as,

$$C = A^T A \qquad (3)$$

   and now the dimension of C becomes M x M which is very small in comparison to its previous dimensions.

8. Finally calculate the Eigenvectors and Eigenvalues of the covariance matrix C in (3). Each Eigenvector has the same dimensionality as the original images, and thus can itself be seen as an image. The Eigenvectors of this covariance matrix are therefore called Eigen faces. They are the directions in which the images differ from the mean image.

Biogeography-Based Optimization

Biogeography (Simon et al, 2008) is the study of geographical distribution of biological organisms. BBO is based on the mathematical models of biogeography. In BBO, habitats are residential areas that represent candidate problem solutions. The variables that characterize habitability are called Suitability Index Variables (SIVs). Good habitats (well suited for residence) have high Habitat Suitability Index (HSI) and poor habitats have low HSI. BBO (Du et al, 2015) optimizes a solution based on two operations, migration and mutation. Habitats with high HSI have high emigration rate and low immigration rate and habitats having low HSI have low emigration rate and high immigration rate. Here original solutions are modified in each iteration as by way of migration of good solutions to poor solution to raise the quality of poor solutions as well as to make good solutions better by randomly selecting solutions for migration. Solutions that are too good are called elite solutions and are left out of the BBO process.

In BBO, each solution has its own emigration rate μ and immigration rate λ. They can be calculated as follows:

Emigration rate $(\mu) = \dfrac{E\ k}{N}$ (5)

Immigration rate $(\lambda) = I\ (1 - \dfrac{k}{n})$ (6)

where E is the maximum emigration rate, I is the maximum immigration rate, k is the solution number in order of goodness; and N is the number of solutions. In the below algorithm for migration and mutation, rndreal (0, 1) is a uniformly distributed random real number in (0, 1), $X_i(j)$ is the jth SIV of the solution X_i, m_i is the mutation rate that is calculated as:

$$m_i = m_{max}\ (\dfrac{1 - Pi}{Pmax})$$ (7)

where m_{max} is an user-defined parameter, and $P_{max} = \text{argmax(Pi)}$ where $i = 1\ldots N$. The probability P_i is computed with the formula,

$$P_i = \dfrac{v}{\sum_{i=1}^{n+1} v_i}$$ (8)

where $v = [v_1, v_2, \ldots, v_{n+1}]^T$

$$V_i\ is\ \begin{cases} \dfrac{n!}{(n-1-i)!(i-1)!} & for\ (i = 1, 2, \ldots i') \\ v_{n+2-1} & for\ (i = i'+1, \ldots, n+1) \end{cases}$$ (9)

$$i' = \text{ceil}\ (\dfrac{n+1}{2})$$ (10)

The probability of immigration and emigration of a solution is calculated using the following formulas, Probability of immigration,

$$(P_{mod}) = \lambda_i / \sum_{i=1}^{N} \lambda_i$$ (11)

Figure 2. Steps of the BBO migration algorithm

```
              for i = 1 to N do

                  Select Xi with probability Pmod

        if rndreal (0, 1) < Pmod then
              for j = 1 to N do
                  Select Xj with probability Pmig
                  if rndreal (0, 1) < Pmig then
                      Randomly select an SIV σ from Xj
                      Replace a random SIV in Xi with σ
                  end if
              end for
          end if
      end for
```

Probability of emigration,

$$(P_{mig}) = \mu_i \Big/ \sum_{i=1}^{N} \frac{1}{4}_i \tag{12}$$

The migration, mutation and BBO algorithm have been described in fig. 2, fig. 3, and fig. 4 respectively.

Figure 3. Steps of the BBO mutation algorithm

1. Initialization of BBO parameters including N, maximum migration rates E and I, maximum mutation rate m_{max}, and an elitism value.
2. Initialization of habitats, each habitat corresponding to a potential solution to the given problem.
3. For each habitat map the HSI to the number of species S, the immigration rate λ and the emigration rate μ.
4. Probabilistically use immigration and emigration to modify each non-elite habitat.
5. Re-compute each HSI.
6. Go to step 3 for the next iteration. This loop can be terminated after a predefined number of generations or after an acceptable problem solution has been found.

Figure 4. Steps of the BBO algorithm

```
for i = 1 to N do
    Compute the probability Pi
    Select SIV Xᵢ(j) with probability α Pi
    if rndreal (0,1) < mᵢ then
            Replace    Xᵢ(j)   with   a    randomly
generated SIV
        end if
end for
```

Gravitational Search Algorithm

This work makes use of only a small part of GSA and hence that alone is explained in this section. GSA is based upon the law of gravity. Here agents are considered as objects and their performance is measured by their masses.

The objects attract towards each other by the force of gravity and this causes a global movement of all objects towards the objects with heavier masses. Every particle is attracted to a particle with a greater mass and as the distance between the particles increases the attraction decreases. Every particle gets attracted to a particle that is closer and has greater mass and moves towards it. A particle with a higher mass is considered to be a better solution to the problem and all other particles get attracted to it. The fitness of each object is its mass which is calculated using the formula below,

$$\text{mass}_i = \frac{fit_i - worst}{best - worst} \tag{13}$$

$$M_i = \frac{mass_i}{\sum_{j=1}^{N} mass_j} \tag{14}$$

where fit_i represents the fitness value of the agent i, worst and best are defined as follows,

$$best = \max fit_j \text{ where } j = 1, 2,...., N \tag{15}$$

$$worst = \min fit_j \text{ where } j = 1, 2,...., N \tag{16}$$

Proposed Methodology for Face Recognition Using the BBO-GSA Algorithm

This section describes the BBO-GSA algorithm proposed in this paper and how it can be applied to the problem of face recognition.

Hybrid BBO-GSA Algorithm

Migration in BBO replaces random SIVs of a solution with random SIVs of another solution. This might lead to a solution becoming a poorer solution than what it was before as well. This leads to the generation of several infeasible solutions and also delays the convergence of the algorithm. If the replacement of SIVs is done in such a way that poor SIVs are replaced with good SIVs only, BBO will converge to the optimal solution and generate better solutions faster. This drawback of BBO can be overcome by borrowing certain characteristics of GSA. The proposed BBO-GSA algorithm replaces SIVs of a solution only with SIVs that are better. Therefore each SIV is also associated with a fitness value that is taken from the mass fitness function of the GSA algorithm. The replacement of SIVs is done only if the mass of the SIV selected for replacement is lesser than the mass of the SIV with which it will be replaced. Two changes are made to the BBO algorithm. They are, after step 3 of the BBO algorithm illustrated in fig. 4 calculate the fitness of every individual SIV of every habitat using the mass equations of GSA described in (10), (11), (12), (13) and changes are made to the migration procedure of the BBO-GSA algorithm as explained in fig.5.

Figure 5. Steps of the migration procedure of the BBO-GSA algorithm

```
for i = 1 to N do
    Select Xi with probability Pmod
    if rndreal (0, 1) < Pmod then
        for j = 1 to N do
            Select Xj with probability Pmig
            if rndreal (0, 1) < Pmig then
                Randomly select an SIV σ from Xi
                Randomly select  an SIV τ from Xj
                If mass(τ)  > mass(σ) then
                    Replace σ with τ otherwise go to step 8
                end if
            end if
        end for
    end if
end for
```

Proposed Methodology for Face Recognition Using BBO-GSA

To the dataset of images the PCA technique explained in fig. 1 is applied. Eigen-faces that result from PCA are the habitats and migration and mutation is done between them in order to increase their quality. Eigen vector elements form the SIVs that will be migrated between habitats. According to the modified migration procedure of BBO explained in fig. 5 the Eigen face vector elements (SIVs) should also be assigned a fitness value such that the migration of Eigen face vector elements between Eigen faces leads only to the betterment of the quality of the Eigen face but does not reduce it. This assignment of fitness value to each Eigen face vector element is done with the GSA algorithm and is explained below.

Eigen faces represent the distinguishing features of the faces in the face dataset. Each Eigen face contributes to a dimension of the face when mapped back to the face images i.e. the face images are mapped back to a space whose number of dimensions equals the number of Eigen faces. This contribution that each Eigen face makes in representing a face image is indicated by a weight value. The weight is calculated by a matrix multiplication of the Eigen vector with the normalized face vector as shown below,

$$\omega_k = \mu_k^T(\Gamma - \psi) \tag{17}$$

where μ_k is a Eigen face and $k = 1,2,..,K$. K is the total number of Eigen faces and Γ is a face image and ψ is the average face of the face dataset.

After mapping back the face images to a reduced space a vector in the form of F shown below is formed for each image,

$$F = [\omega_1, \omega_2, \ldots\ldots, \omega_k] \tag{18}$$

Eqn. 18 is the representation of a face image F in terms of a weight vector where each weight indicates the contribution of each Eigen face in representing the face image. Therefore F is a face vector of length K.

Each Eigen face can be represented with a vector μ as,

$$\mu = [\sigma_1, \sigma_2, \sigma_3, \ldots \sigma_m] \tag{19}$$

The weight value ω which is the contribution of an Eigen face to a face image is high if the Eigen face vector elements (σ_i) have higher values. If the weight becomes high then the amount of contribution that an Eigen face makes in the representation a face increases. Therefore only those Eigen vector elements (σ_i) that have high values are used to replace Eigen vector elements (σ_j) with low values thereby increasing the amount of contribution (ω) that an Eigen face makes to every face in the dataset. Therefore the fitness of each Eigen vector element is the element itself. This property ensures that the migration between the Eigen faces leads only to the betterment of an Eigen face.

The fitness of each Eigen face ($\mu_{i\text{fitness}}$) is calculated as the sum of the contribution that it makes to every face image divided by the total number of face images. This fitness function ensures that those Eigen faces whose contribution to all the face images in the face dataset is high or in other words makes the maximum total contribution in representing the images in the face dataset has a higher fitness value and those Eigen faces whose contribution to the faces in the face dataset is low has a lower fitness value.

$$\mu_{1\text{fitness}} = \omega_{11} + \omega_{12} + \omega_{13} + \ldots\ldots\ldots + \omega_{1M} / M \tag{20}$$

where M is the number of images in the face dataset, ω_{ij} is the contribution of Eigen face i to face image j where i = 1, 2, 3…K and j = 1, 2, 3, … M. Eqn. 20 shows the fitness calculation of Eigen face 1.

The flow of the BBO-GSA algorithm for face recognition is given in fig. 6. The procedure for migration and mutation are repeated a desirable number of times. The steps of the BBO-GSA technique applied to face recognition is shown in fig. 7.

The above flowchart explains the flow of the BBO-GSA algorithm in its application to the problem of face recognition. The flow of the algorithm is similar to the BBO technique but has the additional task of computing the fitness value of each Eigen vector element and also a modification in the migration procedure of the BBO technique where the Eigen vector elements are chosen for migration in such a manner that only if their fitness value i.e there mass is less than the mass of the Eigen vector element chosen for replacement.

The entire algorithm is run a desirable number of times until the required level of refinement of the Eigen faces is reached although it is preferred that the number of iterations of the algorithm is quite less as in the long run the refinement of the Eigen faces could lead to a reduction in the quality of the overall set of Eigen faces.

Figure 6. Flowchart showing the BBO-GSA algorithm for Face Recognition

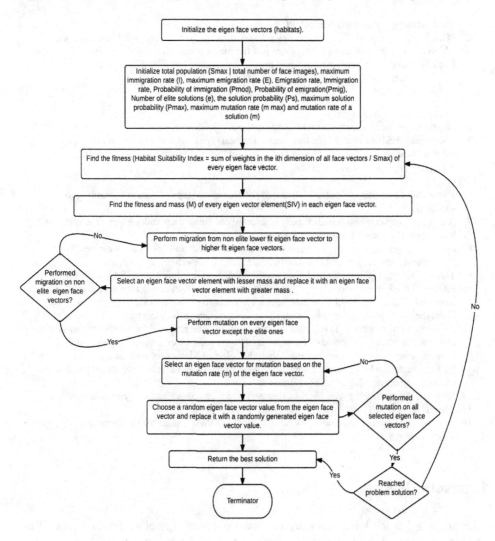

EXPERIMENTAL RESULTS AND COMPARISON WITH EXISTING WORKS

Experimental Results

The BBO-GSA algorithm has been applied to solve the problem of face recognition with LFW and ORL datasets. Experimental results show that the BBO-GSA technique either outperforms or is in par with the existing nature inspired techniques applied to face recognition.

Figure 7. Steps of face recognition using the BBO-GSA algorithm

1. To the training set of images apply PCA.
2. PCA generates a set of Eigen faces, say k lesser than the size of the original training set, which are also face images but represent just the major features of a training set.
3. Each face image is represented as some proportion (weight) of each Eigen face forming a weight vector,

$$F_i = [\omega_1, \omega_2, \ldots\ldots, \omega_k] \tag{21}$$

   where F_i is the ith face vector.
4. On the Eigen faces generated by PCA apply the BBO-GSA technique.
5. The fitness (HSI) of each Eigen face vector (habitat) is calculated as the sum of weights in the ith dimension of all the face vectors divided by the total number of face images.

$$M_{1\,fitness} = \omega_{11} + \omega_{12} + \omega_{13} + \ldots\ldots + \omega_{1M} / M$$
(22)
6. The highly fit habitats (elite) are left out of the following steps as they are already good solutions.
7. An Eigen face vector with high fitness is selected for emigration and a Eigen face vector with low fitness is selected for immigration.
8. From the Eigen face vectors selected for emigration, select an Eigen vector element with high fitness to be replaced with a low fitness Eigen vector element.
9. This replacement is done through the Gravitational Search Algorithm (GSA).
10. Fitness of the Eigen vector elements is the element itself. High Eigen face vector elements have high fitness and low Eigen face vector elements have low fitness.
11. From their fitness values mass of each Eigen vector element is calculated.
12. An Eigen vector element$_i$ is selected for immigration to be replaced by another Eigen vector element$_j$ if mass(Eigen vector element$_j$) >mass(Eigen vector element$_i$) i.e. Eigen vector element$_j$ corresponds to a greater mass than the selected Eigen vector element$_i$.
13. Perform mutation by selecting Eigen face vectors with high mutation rates but replace with randomly generated Eigen vector elements.
14. Now use the modified Eigen faces to represent the face images as face vectors as in step 3.
15. Repeat steps 6 to 15 until a desirable solution is reached.
16. A non-linear, multi-class Support Vector Machine (SVM) is used for the purpose of classification.

Datasets Used

The proposed work has been tested on two datasets, Labelled Faces in the Wild (LFW) people and ORL database of faces, details given in Table 1.

The first dataset to be used is Labelled Faces in the Wild (LFW) people. The dataset contains 13,233 target face images. The dataset contains images of 5749 different individuals. Of these, 1680 people have two or more images in the dataset. The remaining 4069 people have just a single image in the dataset. The images are available as 250 by 250 pixel JPEG images. Most images are in color, although a few are grayscale only. Second dataset to be used is ORL dataset of faces. ORL dataset is acquired at the Olivetti Research Laboratory in Cambridge, U.K. The dataset consists of 400 distinct images that correspond to 40 distinct subjects. Therefore, each subject has 10 facial images and each image has got different illumination,

Table 1. Dataset Details

Dataset	No. of Images	No. of Classes	No. of Images Used	No. of Classes	No. of Elites
LFW	13,233	5749	1827	21	2
ORL	400	40	400	40	2

pose and facial expression. The size of each image is 92 x 112 pixels and has 8-bit grey levels. For some subjects, the images were taken at different times, varying the lighting and facial expressions. All the images were taken against a dark homogeneous background with the subjects in an upright, frontal position (with tolerance for some side movement). Four images per person were used in the training set and the remaining six images were used for testing.

Results

The results of the BBO-GSA technique are analyzed by applying it to face recognition. The Eigen faces generated by applying PCA to the LFW and ORL datasets is shown in fig. 8c and fig. 8d respectively. For the implementation many parameters such as number of Eigen faces, the size of test and train size and the BBO iterations were set. The parameter settings for the implementation are explained in Table 2.The number of Eigen faces generated for both the LFW and ORL datasets is 150 which was found to be optimum, the number of BBO iterations were set to 5. It can be noticed that a very high number of BBO iterations did not improve the results i.e. the size of train and test were in the 90 to 10 ratio. The number of Eigen faces that were left out of the BBO-GSA algorithm were 2.

The performance of the proposed BBO-GSA technique is analyzed by plotting the Receiver Operating Characteristic (ROC) Curve as shown in fig.9 and fig.10 with false positive rate on the X-axis and the true positive rate on the Y-axis.

In addition, the precision, recall and accuracy of the algorithm was also measured. From the results in Table 3 it can be concluded that the proposed algorithm does fairly well for the face recognition application. The prediction results of the algorithm for the two datasets for a sample set of images is given in fig.12 and fig.13. Here the predicted value is the label of the predicted class and the true value is the label of the true class of the image. The predicted results of LFW shows that there is one wrong prediction and the prediction results of ORL dataset shows that all predictions are correct.

Figure 8. A. Representative set of LFW dataset 8B. Representative set of ORL dataset. 8C. Eigen faces extracted from the LFW dataset. 8D. Eigen faces extracted from the ORL dataset

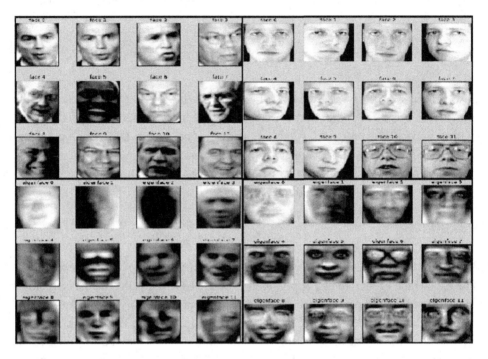

Comparison With Existing Works

Recently many Bio-inspired techniques (Alsalibi et al, 20150 have been proven to be efficient in problem of face recognition. The accuracy of the BBO-GSA technique for the application of face recognition is compared with five different nature inspired techniques combining other techniques in Table 4.

The nature inspired technique that have been used includes Binary Particle Swarm Optimization, Gravitational Search Algorithm (Rashedi et al, 2009), here two variants of GSA are proposed namely the 2-D version of GSA, in order to cater for the 2-D image data, and a 2-D randomized local extrema based GSA (RLEGSA), which employs a stochastic local neighborhood based search instead of global search, as in basic GSA, In (Al-Arashi et al, 2014) Genetic Algorithm is associated with PCA to maintain the property of PCA while enhancing the classification performance. It reconsiders the available training data and tries to find the best underlying distribution for classification. Ant Colony Optimization is used in (Kanan et al, 2008) and a novel algorithm is proposed where classifier performance and the length of the selected feature vector are adopted as heuristic information for ACO. So, the

Figure 9. ROC Curve after applying the BBO-GSA technique on the LFW dataset

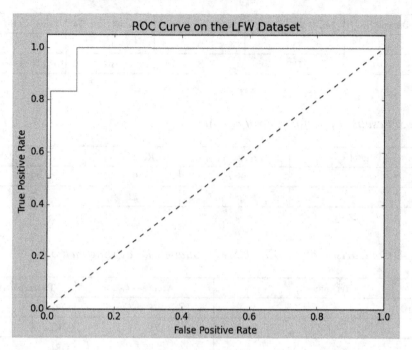

Figure 10. ROC Curve after applying the BBO-GSA technique on the ORL dataset

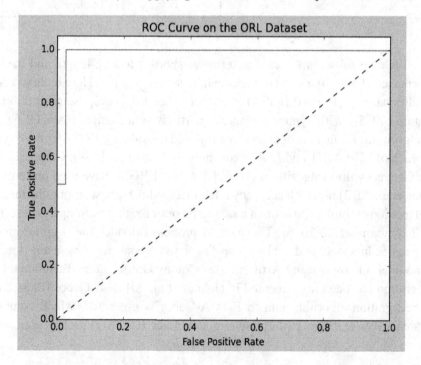

Table 2. Parameter Settings

Dataset	No. of Eigen Faces	BBO Iterations	Test Set Size (%)	Train Set Size (%)
ORL	150	5	10	90
LFW	150	5	10	90

Table 3. Results: Precision, Recall and Accuracy

Dataset	Precision (%)	Recall (%)	Accuracy (%)
ORL	99.75	99	99.75
LFW	80	81	80

Table 4. Comparison of the BBO-GSA technique with existing methods

Technique	Accuracy (%)	Dataset Used
BPSO	95 – 97	ORL
GSA	75 – 77	ORL
GA	97.5	ORL
ACO	99	ORL
GSA	51.5	LFW

optimal feature subset is selected in terms of shortest feature length and the best performance of classifier and Gravitational Search Algorithm, Here binary version of traditional GSA (named BGSA) is further enhanced to propose a novel binary variation of GSA with dynamic adaptive inertia weight (named BAW-GSA). Six new algorithms for face recognition are proposed hybridizing BGSA or BAW-GSA with each of LBP, MCT and LGP algorithms (Preuxa et al, 1999). Comparison of three face recognition algorithms (PCA, LDA, and EBGM) have been presented in (Zhang et al, 2012) in which accuracy rate of EBGM is highest among the three. A novel method of implementation of a stochastic optimization technique is described in (Chakrabarty et al, 2013). The method proposed divides the original images into patches in space, and seeks a non-linear functional mapping using second-order Volterra kernels using Artificial Bee Colony Optimization Technique. Face Recognition has been implemented in (Jakhar et al, 2011). A Gabor filters based face recognition algorithm named POMA-Gabor is presented, which combines comprehensive learning particle swarm optimizer (CLPSO) global search and self-adaptive intelligent single particle optimizer (AdpISPO) local search to select Gabor filter parameters. An Adaptive technique using Firefly Algorithm (Bhanot et al, 2015) where features are extracted using Discrete Cosine Transform (DCT) and Haar wavelets based Discrete Wavelet Transform (DWT) and Bat algorithm is presented for feature selection for face recognition . Here features are extracted using Discrete Cosine Transform and Haar wavelets based Discrete Wavelet Transform. Face recognition using one of the recent optimization algorithm Cuckoo Search Algorithm has been presented in (Tiwari et al, 2012). Its optimization results are better than PSO and ACO. It is based on the principle- new and potentially better solutions (cuckoos) replace a not-so-good solution in the nests, which represents discarding the feature subsets which are least significant (worst feature subset) and these features are dumped from further calculation thus improving features available for face recognition.

CONCLUSION AND FUTURE WORK

This work has proposed a novel hybridized BBO-GSA algorithm that overcomes the infeasible solution generation and late convergence problems of the BBO algorithm. The BBO-GSA technique is tested with face recognition. To the dataset of images PCA is applied. The BBO-GSA algorithm is applied to the Eigen faces extracted from PCA in order to refine the Eigen faces. The refined set of Eigen faces will represent the face dataset more appropriately and thereby improve the accuracy of the classifier. SVM is used for classification due to its robustness and very high accuracy. The performance of the BBO-GSA algorithm is tested on the face recognition application with the LFW and ORL datasets. The experimental results obtained shows that the proposed hybridized algorithm is efficient and optimizes the results of the face recognition system.

FUTURE RESEARCH DIRECTIONS

In future, the BBO-GSA technique can be applied on other problems and its performance on other problems can be tested. It can also be further improved by overcoming the other disadvantages of BBO such as poor exploitation.

REFERENCES

Aishwarya, P., & Marcus, K. (2010). Face recognition using multiple Eigen face subspaces. *Journal of Engineering and Technology Research*, 2(8), 139–143.

Al-Arashi, W. H., Ibrahim, H., & Suandi, S. A. (2014). Optimizing principal component analysis performance for face recognition using genetic algorithm. *Neurocomputing*, *128*, 415–420. doi:10.1016/j.neucom.2013.08.022

Alsalibi, B., Venkat, I., Subramanian, K. G., Lutfi, K. G., & Wilde, P. D. (2015). The Impact of Bio-Inspired Approaches Toward the Advancement. *ACM Computing Surveys*, *48*(1), 1–33. doi:10.1145/2791121

Bhanot, S., & Agarwal, V. (2015). Firefly Inspired Feature Selection for Face Recognition. In *Proceedings of Eighth International Conference* on *Contemporary Computing (IC3)*. Noida, India: IEEE Xplore.

Caoa, L., Chuab, K., Chongc, W., Leea, H., & Gud, Q. (2003). A comparison of PCA, KPCA and ICA for dimensionality reduction in support vector machine. *Neurocomputing*, *55*(1-2), 321–336. doi:10.1016/S0925-2312(03)00433-8

Chakrabarty, A., Jain, H., & Chatterjee, A. (2013). Volterra kernel based face recognition using artificial bee colony optimization. *Intelligence*, *26*(3), 1107–1114.

Chakraborti, T., & Chatterjee, A. (2014). A novel binary adaptive weight GSA based feature selection for face recognition using local gradient patterns, modified census transform, and local binary patterns. *Engineering Applications of Artificial Intelligence*, *33*, 80–90. doi:10.1016/j.engappai.2014.04.006

Chakraborti, T., Sharma, K. D., & Chatterjee, A. (2014). A novel local extrema based gravitational search algorithm and its application in face recognition using one training image per class. *Engineering Applications of Artificial Intelligence*, *34*, 13–22. doi:10.1016/j.engappai.2014.05.002

Dai, K., Zhao, J., & Cao, F. (2015). A novel decorrelated neural network ensemble algorithm for face recognition. *Knowledge-Based Systems*, *89*, 541–552. doi:10.1016/j.knosys.2015.09.002

Dorigo, M., & Blum, C. (2005). Ant colony optimization theory: A survey. *Theoretical Computer Science*, *344*(2-3), 243–278. doi:10.1016/j.tcs.2005.05.020

Du, D., Simon, D., & Ergezer, M. (2009). Biogeography-based optimization combined with evolutionary strategy and immigration refusal. In *Proceedings of IEEE International Conference on Systems, Man and Cybernetics* (pp. 997-1002). San Antonio, TX: IEEE Xplore. 10.1109/ICSMC.2009.5346055

Gottumukkal, R., & Asari, V. K. (2004). An improved face recognition technique based on modular PCA approach. *Pattern Recognition Letters*, *25*(4), 429–436. doi:10.1016/j.patrec.2003.11.005

Gupta, D., & Goel, L., & Abhishek. (2013). An Efficient Biogeography Based Face Recognition Algorithm. In *Proceedings of International Conference on Advances in Computer Science and Engineering, Advances in Intelligent Systems Research* (Vol. 42, pp. 64-67). Los Angeles, CA: Atlantis Press. 10.2991/cse.2013.16

Huang, G. B., Ramesh, M., Berg, T., & Learned-Miller, E. (2007). Labeled Faces in the Wild: A Database for Studying Face Recognition in Unconstrained Environments. University of Massachusetts, Amherst, Technical Report.

Jakhar, R., Kaur, N., & Singh, R. (2011). Face Recognition Using Bacteria Foraging Optimization-Based Selected Features. *International Journal of Advanced Computer Science and Applications*, 106-111.

Kanan, H. R., & Faez, K. (2008). An improved feature selection method based on ant colony optimization (ACO) evaluated on face recognition system. *Applied Mathematics and Computation*, *205*(2), 716–725. doi:10.1016/j.amc.2008.05.115

Lin, C.-H., & Wu, J.-L. (1999). Automatic Facial Feature Extraction by Genetic Algorithms. *IEEE Transactions on Image Processing*, *8*(6), 834–845. doi:10.1109/83.766860 PMID:18267496

Mo, H., & Xu, L. (2015). Research of biogeography particle swarm optimization for robot path planning. *Neurocomputing*, *148*, 91–99. doi:10.1016/j.neucom.2012.07.060

Preuxa, P., & Talbi, E.-G. (1999). Towards hybrid evolutionary algorithms. *International Transactions in Operational Research*, *6*(6), 557–570. doi:10.1111/j.1475-3995.1999.tb00173.x

Ramadan, R. M., & Abdel-Kader, R. F. (2009). Face Recognition Using Particle Swarm Optimization-Based Selected Features. *International Journal of Signal Processing. Image Processing and Pattern Recognition*, *2*(2), 51–65.

Rashedi, E., Nezamabadi-Pour, H., & Saryazdi, S. (2009). GSA: A Gravitational Search Algorithm. *Information Sciences*, *179*(13), 2232–2248. doi:10.1016/j.ins.2009.03.004

Ravi, S., & Nayeem, S. (2013). A Study on Face Recognition Technique based on Eigen face. *International Journal of Applied Information Systems*, *5*(4), 57–62.

Sanchez, D., Melin, P., & Castillo, O. (2015). Optimization of modular granular neural networks using a hierarchical genetic algorithm based on the database complexity applied to human recognition. *Information Sciences*, *309*, 73–101. doi:10.1016/j. ins.2015.02.020

Simon, D. (2008). Biogeography-Based Optimization. *IEEE Transactions on Evolutionary Computation*, *12*(6), 702–713. doi:10.1109/TEVC.2008.919004

Tiwari, V. K. (2012). Face recognition based on Cuckoo search algorithm. *Indian Journal of Computer Science and Engineering*, *3*(3), 401–405.

Zhang, C., Zhou, Z., Sun, H., & Dong, F. (2012). Comparison of Three Face Recognition Algorithms. In *Proceedings of International Conference in Systems and Informatics (ICSAI)*. Yantai, China: IEEE Xplore.

ADDITIONAL READING

Back, T. (1996). *Evolutionary Algorithms in Theory and Practice*. Oxford, UK: Oxford Univ. Press.

Dasgupta, D., & Michalewicz, Z. (2001). *Evolutionary Algorithms in Engineering Applications*. New York: Springer.

Du, D., Simon, D., & Ergezer, M. (2009). Biogeography-Based Optimization Combined with Evolutionary Strategy and Immigration Refusal. In *Proceedings of IEEE International Conference on Systems, Man and Cybernetics* (pp. 1023-1028). San Antonio, TX, USA: IEEE Publications. 10.1109/ICSMC.2009.5346055

Goel, L., Gupta, D., & Panchal, V. K. (2012). Extended species abundance models of biogeography based optimization. In *Proceedings of Fourth International Conference on Computational Intelligence, Modelling and Simulation* (pp. 7-12). Malaysia: IEEE Xplore. 10.1109/CIMSim.2012.30

Goel, L., Gupta, D., & Panchal, V. K. (2012). Hybrid bio-inspired techniques for land cover feature extraction: A remote sensing perspective. *Applied Soft Computing*, *12*(2), 832–849. doi:10.1016/j.asoc.2011.10.006

Kanan, H. R., & Faez, K. (2008). An improved feature selection method based on ant colony optimization (ACO) evaluated on face recognition system. *Applied Mathematics and Computation, 205*(2), 716–725. doi:10.1016/j.amc.2008.05.115

Simon, D. (2011). A Dynamic System Model of Biogeography based Optimization. *Applied Soft Computing, 11*(8), 5652–5661. doi:10.1016/j.asoc.2011.03.028

Turchin, P. (2003). *Complex Population Dynamics: a Theoretical/Empirical Synthesis*. Princeton, NJ: Princeton University Press.

Yao, X., Liu, Y., & Lin, G. (1999). Evolutionary programming made faster. *IEEE Transactions on Evolutionary Computation, 3*(2), 82–102. doi:10.1109/4235.771163

KEY TERMS AND DEFINITIONS

Biogeography-Based Optimization: BBO is an evolutionary algorithm that optimizes a function by stochastically and iteratively improving candidate solutions with regard to a given measure of quality.

Evolutionary: Evolution is change in the heritable characteristics of biological populations over successive generations.

Face Recognition: A facial recognition system is a computer application capable of identifying or verifying a person from a digital image or a video frame from a video source.

Gravitational Search Algorithm: Gravitational search algorithm is an optimization algorithm based on the law of gravity and mass interactions.

Hybridization: Hybridization may refer to the process of combining different varieties of organisms to create a hybrid which is better than the parents.

Nature Inspired: Nature has inspired many researchers in many ways and thus is a rich source of inspiration. Nowadays, most new algorithms are nature-inspired, because they have been developed by drawing inspiration from nature.

Principal Component Analysis: Principal component analysis is a statistical procedure that uses an orthogonal transformation to convert a set of observations of possibly correlated variables into a set of values of linearly uncorrelated variables called principal components.

Recognition Rate: Recognition rate is the total number of correctly identified probe images divided by the total number of probe images.

Compilation of References

Abraham, A., Grosan, C., & Ramos, V. (2007). *Swarm intelligence in data mining* (Vol. 34). Springer.

Accorsi, R., Bortolini, M., Baruffaldi, G., Pilati, F., & Ferrari, E. (2017). Internet-of-things paradigm in food supply chains control and management. *Procedia Manufacturing, 11*, 889–895. doi:10.1016/j.promfg.2017.07.192

Acharya, U. R., Bhat, P. S., Iyengar, S. S., Rao, A., & Dua, S. (2003). Classification of heart rate data using artificial neural network and fuzzy equivalence relation. *Pattern Recognition, 36*(1), 61–68. doi:10.1016/S0031-3203(02)00063-8

Adelsbach, A., Katzenbeisser, S., & Sadeghi, A. R. (2002, September). Cryptography meets watermarking: Detecting watermarks with minimal or zero knowledge disclosure. In *Signal Processing Conference, 2002 11th European* (pp. 1-4). IEEE.

Adjoutah, S., & Chelouche, O. (2013). *Sécurité contre l'attaque Sybil dans les réseaux de capteurs sans fils* (Doctoral dissertation). Université Abderrahmane Mira-Bejaia.

Agrawal, D., & Aggarwal, C. C. (2001, May). On the design and quantification of privacy preserving data mining algorithms. In *Proceedings of the twentieth ACM SIGMOD-SIGACT-SIGART symposium on Principles of database systems* (pp. 247-255). ACM. 10.1145/375551.375602

Ahmed, M. M., & Mohamad, D. B. (2008). Segmentation of brain MR images for tumor extraction by combining k-means clustering and perona-malik anisotropic diffusion model. *International Journal of Image Processing, 2*(1), 27–34.

Ahmed, M. R., Huang, X., & Sharma, D. (2012). A taxonomy of internal attacks in wireless sensor network. *Memory (Kbytes), 128*, 48.

Aishwarya, P., & Marcus, K. (2010). Face recognition using multiple Eigen face subspaces. *Journal of Engineering and Technology Research, 2*(8), 139–143.

Alam, S., & De, D. (2014). *Analysis of security threats in wireless sensor network.* arXiv preprint arXiv:1406.0298

Alam, S., Chowdhury, M. M., & Noll, J. (2010, November). Senaas: An event-driven sensor virtualization approach for internet of things cloud. In *Networked Embedded Systems for Enterprise Applications (NESEA), 2010 IEEE International Conference on* (pp. 1-6). IEEE.

Alam, F., Mehmood, R., Katib, I., & Albeshri, A. (2016). Analysis of eight data mining algorithms for smarter Internet of Things (IoT). *Procedia Computer Science, 98*, 437–442. doi:10.1016/j.procs.2016.09.068

Al-Arashi, W. H., Ibrahim, H., & Suandi, S. A. (2014). Optimizing principal component analysis performance for face recognition using genetic algorithm. *Neurocomputing, 128*, 415–420. doi:10.1016/j.neucom.2013.08.022

Alemdar, H., & Ersoy, C. (2010). Wireless sensor networks for healthcare: A survey. *Computer Networks, 54*(15), 2688–2710. doi:10.1016/j.comnet.2010.05.003

Al-Karaki, J. N., Ul-Mustafa, R., & Kamal, A. E. (2004). Data aggregation in wireless sensor networks-exact and approximate algorithms. In *High Performance Switching and Routing, 2004. HPSR. 2004 Workshop on* (pp. 241-245). IEEE. 10.1109/HPSR.2004.1303478

Alpaydin, E. (2014). *Introduction to machine learning*. MIT Press.

Alsalibi, B., Venkat, I., Subramanian, K. G., Lutfi, K. G., & Wilde, P. D. (2015). The Impact of Bio-Inspired Approaches Toward the Advancement. *ACM Computing Surveys, 48*(1), 1–33. doi:10.1145/2791121

Altınbilek, D. (1995). Water Resources and Environmental Management Plan for Mogan and Eymir Lakes. Final Report prepared by METU Civil Eng. Dept. to The General Directorate of Ankara Municipality Water and Sewage Administration (ASKI), Ankara, Turkey.

Anderson, R., Chan, H., & Perrig, A. (2004, October). Key infection: Smart trust for smart dust. In *Network Protocols, 2004. ICNP 2004. Proceedings of the 12th IEEE International Conference on* (pp. 206-215). IEEE.

Anderson, P. R. (2006). Novel methods improve prediction of species' distributions from occurrence data. *Ecography, 29*(2), 129–151. doi:10.1111/j.2006.0906-7590.04596.x

Anshari, M., Almunawar, M. N., Shahrill, M., Wicaksono, D. K., & Huda, M. (2017). Smartphones usage in the classrooms: Learning aid or interference? *Education and Information Technologies, 22*(6), 3063–3079. doi:10.100710639-017-9572-7

Arai, K., & Barakbah, A. R. (2007). Hierarchical K-means: An algorithm for centroids initialization for K-means. *Reports of the Faculty of Science and Engineering, 36*(1), 25–31.

Arampatzis, T., Lygeros, J., & Manesis, S. (2005, June). A survey of applications of wireless sensors and wireless sensor networks. In *Intelligent Control, 2005. Proceedings of the 2005 IEEE International Symposium on, Mediterrean Conference on Control and Automation* (pp. 719-724). IEEE. 10.1109/.2005.1467103

Arora, S., Sharma, S., Dua, R., & Sharma, A. (2017). Internet of things, artificial intelligence, automation. *Technology*.

Arsénio, A., Serra, H., Francisco, R., Nabais, F., Andrade, J., & Serrano, E. (2014). Internet of intelligent things: Bringing artificial intelligence into things and communication networks. In *Inter-cooperative Collective Intelligence: Techniques and Applications* (pp. 1–37). Berlin: Springer. doi:10.1007/978-3-642-35016-0_1

ASCE Task Committee on Application of Artificial Neural Networks in Hydrology. (2000). Artificial Neural Networks in Hydrology. II, BioComp Systems, I. (1998) NeuroGenetic Optimizer (NGO). Redmond, WA: Hydrologic Applications. *Journal of Hydrologic Engineering, 5*(2), 124–137. doi:10.1061/(ASCE)1084-0699(2000)5:2(124)

Asch, G. (2010). *Les capteurs en instrumentation industrielle-7ème édition.* Dunod.

Ashton, K. (2009). That 'internet of things' thing. *RFiD Journal, 22*(7), 97–114.

Ashworth, P., Bannister, P., & Thorne, P. (1997). Guilty in whose eyes? University students' perceptions of cheating and plagiarism in academic work and assessment. *Studies in Higher Education, 22*(2), 187–203. doi:10.1080/03075079712331381034

Astorga, J., Jacob, E., Huarte, M., & Higuero, M. (2012). Ladon 1: End-to-end authorisation support for resource-deprived environments. *Information Security, IET, 6*(2), 93–101. doi:10.1049/iet-ifs.2010.0259

Atallah, M., Bertino, E., Elmagarmid, A., Ibrahim, M., & Verykios, V. (1999). Disclosure limitation of sensitive rules. In *Knowledge and Data Engineering Exchange, 1999.(KDEX'99) Proceedings. 1999 Workshop on* (pp. 45-52). IEEE.

Atanasova, N. (2006). Computational assemblage of ordinary differential equations for chlorophyll-a using a lake process equation library and measured data of Lake Kasumigaura. In *Ecological Informatics* (pp. 409–427). Springer. doi:10.1007/3-540-28426-5_20

Atzori, L., Iera, A., & Morabito, G. (2010). The internet of things: A survey. *Computer Networks, 54*(15), 2787–2805. doi:10.1016/j.comnet.2010.05.010

Atzori, L., Iera, A., & Morabito, G. (2017). Understanding the Internet of Things: Definition, potentials, and societal role of a fast evolving paradigm. *Ad Hoc Networks, 56*, 122–140. doi:10.1016/j.adhoc.2016.12.004

Aung, M. M., & Chang, Y. S. (2014). Traceability in a food supply chain: Safety and quality perspectives. *Food Control, 39*, 172–184. doi:10.1016/j.foodcont.2013.11.007

Back, T. (1996). *Evolutionary algorithms in theory and practice: evolution strategies, evolutionary programming, genetic algorithms.* Oxford university press.

Baeza-Yates, R., & Ribeiro-Neto, B. (1999). Modern information retrieval (Vol. 463). ACM Press.

Baeza-Yates, R., & Ribeiro-Neto, B. (1999). *Modern information retrieval* (Vol. 463). New York: ACM press.

Balid, W., Tafish, H., & Refai, H. H. (2017). Intelligent Vehicle Counting and Classification Sensor for Real-Time Traffic Surveillance. *IEEE Transactions on Intelligent Transportation Systems*.

Bandara, K. K., Wikramanayake, G. N., & Goonethillake, J. S. (2007, August). Optimal selection of failure data for reliability estimation based on a standard deviation method. In *2007 International Conference on Industrial and Information Systems* (pp. 245-248). IEEE. 10.1109/ICIINFS.2007.4579182

Bandyopadhyay, D., & Sen, J. (2011). Internet of things: Applications and challenges in technology and standardization. *Wireless Personal Communications*, *58*(1), 49–69. doi:10.100711277-011-0288-5

Banerjee, P., Friedrich, R., Bash, C., Goldsack, P., Huberman, B., Manley, J., ... Veitch, A. (2011). Everything as a service: Powering the new information economy. *Computer*, *44*(3), 36–43. doi:10.1109/MC.2011.67

Bartz, J. A., Zaki, J., Bolger, N., & Ochsner, K. N. (2011). Social effects of oxytocin in humans: Context and person matter. *Trends in Cognitive Sciences*, *15*(7), 301–309. PMID:21696997

Basile, C., Benedetto, D., Caglioti, E., Cristadoro, G., & Esposti, M. D. (2009, September). A plagiarism detection procedure in three steps: Selection, matches and "squares". In *Proc. SEPLN* (pp. 19-23). Academic Press.

Begum, S., & Sulegaon, K. (2016). Analysis of various big data techniques for security. *International Journal of Computer Science and Mobile Computing, 5*(3), 54-58.

Bellare, M., Namprempre, C., & Neven, G. (2009). Security proofs for identity-based identification and signature schemes. *Journal of Cryptology*, *22*(1), 1–61. doi:10.100700145-008-9028-8

Bello, O., & Zeadally, S. (2013). Communication issues in the Internet of Things (IoT). In *Next-Generation Wireless Technologies* (pp. 189–219). London: Springer. doi:10.1007/978-1-4471-5164-7_10

Bello, O., & Zeadally, S. (2016). Intelligent device-to-device communication in the internet of things. *IEEE Systems Journal*, *10*(3), 1172–1182. doi:10.1109/JSYST.2014.2298837

Bergman, L. R., Magnusson, D., & El Khouri, B. M. (2003). *Studying individual development in an interindividual context: A person-oriented approach*. Psychology Press.

Berry, M. W. (2004). Survey of text mining. *Computer Review*, *45*(9), 548.

Bhanot, S., & Agarwal, V. (2015). Firefly Inspired Feature Selection for Face Recognition. In *Proceedings of Eighth International Conference* on *Contemporary Computing (IC3)*. Noida, India: IEEE Xplore.

Binitha, S., & Sathya, S. S. (2012). A survey of bio inspired optimization algorithms. *International Journal of Soft Computing and Engineering, 2*(2), 137–151.

Bishop, C. M. (1995). *Neural networks for pattern recognition.* Oxford University Press.

Blum, C., & Roli, A. (2003). Metaheuristics in combinatorial optimization: Overview and conceptual comparison *ACM Computing Surveys, 35*(3), 268–308. doi:10.1145/937503.937505

Bock, W., & Salski, A. (1998). A fuzzy knowledge-based model of population dynamics of the yellow-necked mouse (Apodemus flavicollis) in a beech forest. *Ecological Modelling, 108*(1), 155–161. doi:10.1016/S0304-3800(98)00026-X

Bowden, G. J., Dandy, G. C., & Maier, H. R. (2003). An evaluation of methods for the selection of inputs for an artificial neural network based river model. In *Ecological Informatics* (pp. 215–232). Springer. doi:10.1007/978-3-662-05150-4_11

Boyd, D., & Crawford, K. (2012). Critical questions for big data: Provocations for a cultural, technological, and scholarly phenomenon. *Information Communication and Society, 15*(5), 662–679. doi:10.1080/1369118X.2012.678878

Bredeweg, B., Salles, P., & Neumann, M. (2003). Ecological applications of qualitative reasoning. In *Ecological Informatics* (pp. 15–47). Springer.

Brettel, M., Friederichsen, N., Keller, M., & Rosenberg, M. (2014). How virtualization, decentralization and network building change the manufacturing landscape: An Industry 4.0 Perspective. *International Journal of Mechanical, Industrial Science and Engineering, 8*(1), 37–44.

Brownlee, J. (2011). *Clever algorithms: nature-inspired programming recipes.* Jason Brownlee.

Burnham, K. P., Anderson, D. R., & Huyvaert, K. P. (2011). AIC model selection and multimodel inference in behavioral ecology: Some background, observations, and comparisons. *Behavioral Ecology and Sociobiology, 65*(1), 23–35. doi:10.100700265-010-1029-6

Caoa, L., Chuab, K., Chongc, W., Leea, H., & Gud, Q. (2003). A comparison of PCA, KPCA and ICA for dimensionality reduction in support vector machine. *Neurocomputing, 55*(1-2), 321–336. doi:10.1016/S0925-2312(03)00433-8

Cao, H. (2006). Hybrid evolutionary algorithm for rule set discovery in time-series data to forecast and explain algal population dynamics in two lakes different in morphometry and eutrophication. In *Ecological informatics* (pp. 347–367). Springer. doi:10.1007/3-540-28426-5_17

Capkun, S., Hubaux, J. P., & Jakobsson, M. (2004). *Secure and privacy-preserving communication in hybrid ad hoc networks* (No. LCA-REPORT-2004-015).

Carpenter, G. A., & Grossberg, S. (1987). ART 2: Self-organization of stable category recognition codes for analog input patterns. *Applied Optics, 26*(23), 4919–4930. doi:10.1364/AO.26.004919 PMID:20523470

Caruana, R., & Niculescu-Mizil, A. (2006). An empirical comparison of supervised learning algorithms. In *Proceedings of the 23rd international conference on Machine learning*. ACM. 10.1145/1143844.1143865

Chakrabarty, A., Jain, H., & Chatterjee, A. (2013). Volterra kernel based face recognition using artificial bee colony optimization. *Intelligence*, *26*(3), 1107–1114.

Chakraborti, T., & Chatterjee, A. (2014). A novel binary adaptive weight GSA based feature selection for face recognition using local gradient patterns, modified census transform, and local binary patterns. *Engineering Applications of Artificial Intelligence*, *33*, 80–90. doi:10.1016/j.engappai.2014.04.006

Chakraborti, T., Sharma, K. D., & Chatterjee, A. (2014). A novel local extrema based gravitational search algorithm and its application in face recognition using one training image per class. *Engineering Applications of Artificial Intelligence*, *34*, 13–22. doi:10.1016/j.engappai.2014.05.002

Chandna, D. (2014). Diagnosis of heart disease using data mining algorithm. *International Journal of Computer Science and Information Technologies*, *5*(2), 1678–1680.

Chawla, S., Dwork, C., McSherry, F., Smith, A., & Wee, H. (2005, February). Toward privacy in public databases. In *Theory of Cryptography Conference* (pp. 363-385). Springer Berlin Heidelberg.

Chen, D. G. (2003). Classification of fish stock-recruitment relationships in different environmental regimes by fuzzy logic with bootstrap re-sampling approach. In *Ecological Informatics* (pp. 329–351). Springer. doi:10.1007/978-3-662-05150-4_17

Cheng, X. Q., Jin, X. L., Wang, Y. Z., Guo, J., Zhang, T., & Li, G. (2014). Survey on big data system and analytic technology. *Journal of Software*, *25*(9), 1889–1908.

Chen, H. L., Li, H. B., & Wang, Z. (2008). Research on TDoA-based secure localization for wireless sensor networks. *Journal of Communication*, *29*(8), 11–21.

Chen, X., Makki, K., Yen, K., & Pissinou, N. (2009). Sensor network security: A survey. *IEEE Communications Surveys and Tutorials*, *11*(2), 52–73. doi:10.1109/SURV.2009.090205

Chen, Y. (2017). Integrated and Intelligent Manufacturing: Perspectives and Enablers. *Engineering*, *3*(5), 588–595. doi:10.1016/J.ENG.2017.04.009

Chiang, Y. T., Wang, D. W., Liau, C. J., & Hsu, T. S. (2005, August). Secrecy of two-party secure computation. In *IFIP Annual Conference on Data and Applications Security and Privacy* (pp. 114-123). Springer Berlin Heidelberg.

Chikersal, P., Poria, S., & Cambria, E. (2015). SeNTU: sentiment analysis of tweets by combining a rule-based classifier with supervised learning. In *Proceedings of the 9th International Workshop on Semantic Evaluation (SemEval 2015)* (pp. 647-651). Academic Press. 10.18653/v1/S15-2108

Chirita, P. A., Nejdl, W., & Zamfir, C. (2005). Preventing shilling attacks in online recommender systems. WIDM'05, 67–74. doi:10.1145/1097047.1097061

Chon, T. S. (2006). Non-linear approach to grouping, dynamics and organizational informatics of benthic macroinvertebrate communities in streams by Artificial Neural Networks. In *Ecological Informatics* (pp. 187–238). Springer. doi:10.1007/3-540-28426-5_10

Chung, C. K., & Pennebaker, J. W. (2011). Using computerized text analysis to assess threatening communications and behavior. *Threatening communications and behavior: Perspectives on the pursuit of public figures*, 3-32.

Cios, K. J. (2007). *Data mining: a knowledge discovery approach*. Springer Science & Business Media.

Ciriani, V., Di Vimercati, S. D. C., Foresti, S., & Samarati, P. (2007). Microdata protection. In Secure data management in decentralized systems (pp. 291-321). Springer US. doi:10.1007/978-0-387-27696-0_9

Clough, P. (2003). *Old and new challenges in automatic plagiarism detection*. National Plagiarism Advisory Service. Retrieved from http://ir. shef. ac. uk/cloughie/index. html

Conner, M. K. (2018). *Dynamic Logistics Enabled by IoT*. Academic Press.

Cormack, G. V. (2007). Email spam filtering: A systematic review. *Foundations and Trends in Information Retrieval, 1*(4), 335–455. doi:10.1561/1500000006

Cousin, P., Serrano, M., & Soldatos, J. (2015). Internet of things research on semantic interoperability to address manufacturing challenges. *Enterprise Interoperability: Interoperability for Agility, Resilience and Plasticity of Collaborations (I-ESA 14 Proceedings), 280*.

Craig, T., & Ludloff, M. E. (2011). *Privacy and big data*. O'Reilly Media, Inc.

Crampton, J. (2009). Cryptographically-enforced hierarchical access control with multiple keys. *Journal of Logic and Algebraic Programming, 78*(8), 690–700. doi:10.1016/j.jlap.2009.04.001

Crockford, D. (2006). *The application/json media type for javascript object notation (json)*. Academic Press.

Croft, W. B., Metzler, D., & Strohman, T. (2010). *Search engines: Information retrieval in practice* (Vol. 283). Reading, MA: Addison-Wesley.

Currie, P. (1998). Staying out of trouble: Apparent plagiarism and academic survival. *Journal of Second Language Writing, 7*(1), 1–18. doi:10.1016/S1060-3743(98)90003-0

Da Xu, L., He, W., & Li, S. (2014). Internet of things in industries: A survey. *IEEE Transactions on Industrial Informatics, 10*(4), 2233–2243. doi:10.1109/TII.2014.2300753

Dai, K., Zhao, J., & Cao, F. (2015). A novel decorrelated neural network ensemble algorithm for face recognition. *Knowledge-Based Systems, 89*, 541–552. doi:10.1016/j.knosys.2015.09.002

Dangare & Sulabha. (2012). Improved Study of Heart Disease Prediction System using Data Mining Classification Techniques. *IJCA, 47*(10), 44-48.

Dapper, T. (1998). *Dimensionsreduzierende Vorverarbeitungen für neuronale Netze mit Anwendungen in der Gewässerökologie*. Shaker.

Dasgupta, D., & Forrest, S. (1999, July). Artificial immune systems in industrial applications. In *Intelligent Processing and Manufacturing of Materials, 1999. IPMM'99. Proceedings of the Second International Conference on* (Vol. *1*, pp. 257-267). IEEE.

Das, R., Turkoglu, I., & Sengur, A. (2009). Effective diagnosis of heart disease through neural networks ensembles. *Expert Systems with Applications*, *36*(4), 7675–7680. doi:10.1016/j.eswa.2008.09.013

de Hoon, M. J., Imoto, S., Nolan, J., & Miyano, S. (2004). Open source clustering software. *Bioinformatics (Oxford, England)*, *20*(9), 1453–1454. doi:10.1093/bioinformatics/bth078 PMID:14871861

De Poorter, E., Moerman, I., & Demeester, P. (2011). Enabling direct connectivity between heterogeneous objects in the internet of things through a network-service-oriented architecture. *EURASIP Journal on Wireless Communications and Networking, 2011*(1), 61. doi:10.1186/1687-1499-2011-61

Dean, J., & Ghemawat, S. (2008). MapReduce: Simplified data processing on large clusters. *Communications of the ACM*, *51*(1), 107–113. doi:10.1145/1327452.1327492

Demirbas, M., & Song, Y. (2006, June). An RSSI-based scheme for sybil attack detection in wireless sensor networks. In *Proceedings of the 2006 International Symposium on on World of Wireless, Mobile and Multimedia Networks* (pp. 564-570). IEEE Computer Society. 10.1109/WOWMOM.2006.27

Demuth, H., & Beale, M. (2000). Neural network toolbox user's guide. Academic Press.

Desai, M., & Phadke, A. (2017, February). Internet of Things based vehicle monitoring system. In *Wireless and Optical Communications Networks (WOCN), 2017 Fourteenth International Conference on* (pp. 1-3). IEEE. 10.1109/WOCN.2017.8065840

Devi, S. K., Krishnapriya, S., & Kalita, D. (2016). Prediction of Heart Disease using Data Mining Techniques. *Indian Journal of Science and Technology*, *9*(39).

Dewan, A., & Sharma, M. (2015 March). Prediction of heart disease using a hybrid technique in data mining classification, In *Computing for Sustainable Global Development (INDIACom), 2015 2nd International Conference* (pp. 704-706). IEEE.

Dhariwal, K., & Mehta, A. (2017). Architecture and plan of smart hospital based on Internet of Things (IOT). *Int. Res. J. Eng. Technol*, *4*(4), 1976–1980.

Dharma Rahadi, P. S. A., Shobirin, K. A., & Ariyani, S. (2016). Big Data Management. *International Journal of Engineering and Emerging Technology*, *1*(1).

Dimopoulos, I., Chronopoulos, J., Chronopoulou-Sereli, A., & Lek, S. (1999). Neural network models to study relationships between lead concentration in grasses and permanent urban descriptors in Athens city (Greece). *Ecological Modelling, 120*(2), 157–165. doi:10.1016/S0304-3800(99)00099-X

Dimopoulos, Y., Bourret, P., & Lek, S. (1995). Use of some sensitivity criteria for choosing networks with good generalization ability. *Neural Processing Letters, 2*(6), 1–4. doi:10.1007/BF02309007

Domingo-Ferrer, J., Sebé, F., & Castella-Roca, J. (2004, January). On the security of noise addition for privacy in statistical databases. In *Privacy in statistical databases* (pp. 149–161). Springer Berlin Heidelberg. doi:10.1007/978-3-540-25955-8_12

Dong, L., Mingyue, R., & Guoying, M. (2017). Application of Internet of Things Technology on Predictive Maintenance System of Coal Equipment. *Procedia Engineering, 174*, 885–889. doi:10.1016/j.proeng.2017.01.237

Dong, Z., & Dong, Q. (2003). HowNet: A Hybrid Language and Knowledge Resource. In *Proceedings of International Conference on Natural Language Processing and Engineering* (pp. 820-824). Los Alamitos, CA: IEEE Press.

Dorigo, M., & Blum, C. (2005). Ant colony optimization theory: A survey. Theoretical Computer Science, 344(2-3), 243–278. doi:10.1016/j.tcs.2005.05.020

Dorigo, M., Bonabeau, E., & Theraulaz, G. (2000). Ant algorithms and stigmergy. *Future Generation Computer Systems, 16*(8), 851–871. doi:10.1016/S0167-739X(00)00042-X

Dorigo, M., Di Caro, G., & Gambardella, L. M. (1999). Ant algorithms for discrete optimization. *Artificial Life, 5*(2), 137–172. doi:10.1162/106454699568728 PMID:10633574

Dorigo, M., & Gambardella, L. M. (1997). Ant colony system: A cooperative learning approach to the traveling salesman problem. *IEEE Transactions on Evolutionary Computation, 1*(1), 53–66. doi:10.1109/4235.585892

Dorigo, M., Maniezzo, V., & Colorni, A. (1996). Ant system: optimization by a colony of cooperating agents. *Systems, Man, and Cybernetics, Part B: Cybernetics. IEEE Transactions on, 26*(1), 29–41.

Douceur, J. R. (2002, March). The sybil attack. In *International workshop on peer-to-peer systems* (pp. 251-260). Springer. 10.1007/3-540-45748-8_24

Du, D., Simon, D., & Ergezer, M. (2009). Biogeography-based optimization combined with evolutionary strategy and immigration refusal. In *Proceedings of IEEE International Conference on Systems, Man and Cybernetics* (pp. 997-1002). San Antonio, TX: IEEE Xplore. 10.1109/ICSMC.2009.5346055

Dubelaar, G. B. J., & Gerritzen, P. L. (2000). CytoBuoy: A step forward towards using flow cytometry in operational oceanography. *Scientia Marina, 64*(2), 255–265. doi:10.3989cimar.2000.64n2255

Dubelaar, G. B. J., Gerritzen, P. L., Beeker, A. E. R., Jonker, R. R., & Tangen, K. (1999). Design and first results of CytoBuoy: A wireless flow cytometer for in situ analysis of marine and fresh waters. *Cytometry*, *37*(4), 247–254. doi:10.1002/(SICI)1097-0320(19991201)37:4<247::AID-CYTO1>3.0.CO;2-9 PMID:10547609

Dwork, C., Kenthapadi, K., McSherry, F., Mironov, I., & Naor, M. (2006, May). Our data, ourselves: Privacy via distributed noise generation. In *Annual International Conference on the Theory and Applications of Cryptographic Techniques* (pp. 486-503). Springer Berlin Heidelberg. 10.1007/11761679_29

Ejaz, W., Naeem, M., Shahid, A., Anpalagan, A., & Jo, M. (2017). Efficient energy management for the internet of things in smart cities. *IEEE Communications Magazine*, *55*(1), 84–91. doi:10.1109/MCOM.2017.1600218CM

Elman, J. L. (1990). Finding structure in time. *Cognitive Science*, *14*(2), 179–211. doi:10.120715516709cog1402_1

Espinoza, M., Gómez-Pérez, A., & Mena, E. (2008, June). Enriching an ontology with multilingual information. In *European Semantic Web Conference* (pp. 333-347). Springer.

Etzion, O. (2015, June). When artificial intelligence meets the internet of things. In *Proceedings of the 9th ACM International Conference on Distributed Event-Based Systems* (pp. 246-246). ACM. 10.1145/2675743.2774216

Faure, D., & Nedellec, C. (1999, May). Knowledge acquisition of predicate argument structures from technical texts using machine learning: The system ASIUM. In *International Conference on Knowledge Engineering and Knowledge Management* (pp. 329-334). Springer. 10.1007/3-540-48775-1_22

Fayyad, U. M., Piatetsky-Shapiro, G., & Smyth, P. (1996, August). Knowledge Discovery and Data Mining. *Towards a Unifying Framework in KDD*, *96*, 82–88.

Fayyad, U., Piatetsky-Shapiro, G., & Smyth, P. (1996). From data mining to knowledge discovery in databases. *AI Magazine*, *17*(3), 37.

Feldman, R. (2013). Techniques and applications for sentiment analysis. *Communications of the ACM*, *56*(4), 82–89. doi:10.1145/2436256.2436274

Fernandes, A. C., Cloete, D., Broadbent, M. T., Hayes, R. D., Chang, C. K., Jackson, R. G., ... Callard, F. (2013). Development and evaluation of a de-identification procedure for a case register sourced from mental health electronic records. *BMC Medical Informatics and Decision Making*, *13*(1), 71. doi:10.1186/1472-6947-13-71 PMID:23842533

Fırat, S. Ü. (2016). *Sanayi 4.0 dönüşümü nedir? belirlemeler ve beklentiler*. Global Sanayici: Ekonomi ve İş Dünyası Dergisi ÇOSB Yayını.

Fırat, S. Ü., & Fırat, O. Z. (2017). Dördüncü sanayi devriminde riskler robotlar ve yapay zekanin yönetişim sorunları. *Global Sanayici: Ekonomi ve İş Dünyası Dergisi, 8*(81), 66-70.

Fırat, S. Ü., & Fırat, O. Z. (2017). Sanayi 4.0 Devrimi Üzerine Karşılaştırmalı Bir İnceleme: Kavramlar, Küresel Gelişmeler ve Türkiye. *Toprak İşveren Dergisi*, (114), 10-23.

Firte, L., Lemnaru, C., & Potolea, R. (2010, August). Spam detection filter using KNN algorithm and resampling. In *Intelligent Computer Communication and Processing (ICCP), 2010 IEEE International Conference on* (pp. 27-33). IEEE. 10.1109/ICCP.2010.5606466

Foody, G. M. (2003). Pattern Recognition and Classification of Remotely Sensed Images by Artificial Neural Networks. In *Ecological Informatics* (pp. 383–398). Springer. doi:10.1007/978-3-662-05150-4_20

Foody, G. M., & Arora, M. K. (1997). An evaluation of some factors affecting the accuracy of classification by an artificial neural network. *International Journal of Remote Sensing*, *18*(4), 799–810. doi:10.1080/014311697218764

Fousse, L., Lafourcade, P., & Alnuaimi, M. (2011, July). Benaloh's dense probabilistic encryption revisited. In *International Conference on Cryptology in Africa* (pp. 348-362). Springer Berlin Heidelberg.

Frakes, W. B., & Baeza-Yates, R. (Eds.). (1992). Information retrieval: Data structures & algorithms (Vol. 331). Englewood Cliffs, NJ: Prentice Hall.

Francis, R. I. C. C., Paul, L. J., & Mulligan, K. P. (1992). Ageing of adult snapper (Pagrus auratus) from otolith annual ring counts: Validation by tagging and oxytetracycline injection. *Marine & Freshwater Research*, *43*(5), 1069–1089. doi:10.1071/MF9921069

Frey, C. B., & Osborne, M. A. (2017). The future of employment: How susceptible are jobs to computerisation? *Technological Forecasting and Social Change*, *114*, 254–280. doi:10.1016/j. techfore.2016.08.019

Friederichs, M., Fränzle, O., & Salski, A. (1996). Fuzzy clustering of existing chemicals according to their ecotoxicological properties. *Ecological Modelling*, *85*(1), 27–40. doi:10.1016/0304-3800(95)00009-7

Fuchsbauer, G. J. (2006). An Introduction to Probabilistic Encryption. *Osječki matematički list*, *6*(1), 37-44.

Fumera, G., Pillai, I., Roli, F., & Biggio, B. (2007). Image spam filtering using textual and visual information. *Proceedings of the MIT Spam Conference 2007.*

Gaubatz, G., Kaps, J. P., & Sunar, B. (2004, August). Public key cryptography in sensor networks—revisited. In *European Workshop on Security in Ad-Hoc and Sensor Networks* (pp. 2-18). Springer.

Gedik, B., & Liu, L. (2008). Protecting location privacy with personalized k-anonymity: Architecture and algorithms. *IEEE Transactions on Mobile Computing*, *7*(1), 1–18. doi:10.1109/TMC.2007.1062

Geetha, C., & Ramakrishnan, M. (2015). Detection of SYBIL Attack using Neighbour Nodes in Static WSN. *International Journal on Recent and Innovation Trends in Computing and Communication, 3*(4), 2428 - 2432.

Georgiu, M., & Groza, A. (2011). Ontology enrichment using semantic wikis and design patterns. *Studia Universitatis Babes-Bolyai, Informatica, 56*(2).

Gevrey, M., Lek, S., & Oberdorff, T. (2006). Utility of sensitivity analysis by artificial neural network models to study patterns of endemic fish species. In *Ecological Informatics* (pp. 293–306). Springer. doi:10.1007/3-540-28426-5_14

Giraudel, J. L., & Lek, S. (2003). Ecological Applications of Non-supervised Artificial Neural Networks. In *Ecological Informatics* (pp. 49–67). Springer. doi:10.1007/978-3-662-05150-4_2

Glasner, J. (2001). *A brief history of spam, and spam*. Retrieved from http://www. wired. com/techbiz/media/news/2001/05/44111

Glass, A., McGuinness, D. L., & Wolverton, M. (2008). Toward establishing trust in adaptive agents. In *Proceedings of the 13th international conference on Intelligent user interfaces*. ACM.

Glover, F. W., & Kochenberger, G. A. (2006). *Handbook of metaheuristics* (Vol. 57). Springer Science & Business Media.

Gluhak, A., Krco, S., Nati, M., Pfisterer, D., Mitton, N., & Razafindralambo, T. (2011). A survey on facilities for experimental internet of things research. *IEEE Communications Magazine, 49*(11), 58–67. doi:10.1109/MCOM.2011.6069710

Go, A., Bhayani, R., & Huang, L. (2009). Twitter sentiment classification using distant supervision. CS224N Project Report, Stanford, 1(12).

Goebel, M., & Gruenwald, L. (1999). A survey of data mining and knowledge discovery software tools. *ACM SIGKDD Explorations Newsletter, 1*(1), 20-33.

Goethals, P. (2006). Development and application of predictive river ecosystem models based on classification trees and artificial neural networks. Ecological Informatics, 151–167. doi:10.1007/3-540-28426-5_8

Goldberg, D., Deb, K., & Korb, B. (1989). Messy genetic algorithms: Motivation, analysis, and first results. *Complex Systems, 3*, 493–530.

Goluch, S. (2011). *The development of homomorphic cryptography: from RSA to Gentry's privacy homomorphism*. Academic Press.

Gottumukkal, R., & Asari, V. K. (2004). An improved face recognition technique based on modular PCA approach. *Pattern Recognition Letters, 25*(4), 429–436. doi:10.1016/j.patrec.2003.11.005

Goyal, R., Kumari, A., Shubham, K., & Kumar, N. (2018). IoT and XBee Based Smart Traffic Management System. *Journal of Communication Engineering & Systems, 8*(1), 8–14.

Grier, C., Thomas, K., Paxson, V., & Zhang, M. (2010, October). @ spam: the underground on 140 characters or less. In *Proceedings of the 17th ACM conference on Computer and communications security* (pp. 27-37). ACM 10.1145/1866307.1866311

Gubbi, J., Buyya, R., Marusic, S., & Palaniswami, M. (2013). Internet of Things (IoT): A vision, architectural elements, and future directions. *Future Generation Computer Systems, 29*(7), 1645–1660. doi:10.1016/j.future.2013.01.010

Guellier, A., Bidan, C., & Prigent, N. (2014, November). Homomorphic cryptography-based privacy-preserving network communications. In *International Conference on Applications and Techniques in Information Security* (pp. 159-170). Springer Berlin Heidelberg.

Guellil, I., & Boukhalfa, K. (2015, April). Social big data mining: A survey focused on opinion mining and sentiments analysis. In *Programming and Systems (ISPS), 2015 12th International Symposium on* (pp. 1-10). IEEE. 10.1109/ISPS.2015.7244976

Guerreiro, B. V., Lins, R. G., Sun, J., & Schmitt, R. (2018). Definition of Smart Retrofitting: First steps for a company to deploy aspects of Industry 4.0. In *Advances in Manufacturing* (pp. 161–170). Cham: Springer. doi:10.1007/978-3-319-68619-6_16

Guinard, D., Mueller, M., & Pasquier-Rocha, J. (2010, November). Giving rfid a rest: Building a web-enabled epcis. In Internet of Things (IOT), 2010 (pp. 1-8). IEEE.

Gülbahar, Y. (2017). E-öğrenme. *Pegem Atıf İndeksi*, 1-410.

Gunasekaran, M., & Premalatha, K. (2013). SPAWN: A secure privacy-preserving architecture in wireless mobile ad hoc networks. *EURASIP Journal on Wireless Communications and Networking*, (1): 1–12.

Guo, G., Wang, H., Bell, D., Bi, Y., & Greer, K. (2003, November). KNN model-based approach in classification. In *OTM Confederated International Conferences On the Move to Meaningful Internet Systems* (pp. 986-996). Springer. 10.1007/978-3-540-39964-3_62

Guo, Q., & Zhang, M. (2009). A novel approach for multi-agent-based intelligent manufacturing system. *Information Sciences, 179*(18), 3079–3090. doi:10.1016/j.ins.2009.05.009

Gupta, D., & Goel, L., & Abhishek. (2013). An Efficient Biogeography Based Face Recognition Algorithm. In *Proceedings of International Conference on Advances in Computer Science and Engineering, Advances in Intelligent Systems Research* (Vol. 42, pp. 64-67). Los Angeles, CA: Atlantis Press. 10.2991/cse.2013.16

Ha, K., Cho, E.-A., Kim, H.-W., & Joo, G.-J. (1999). Microcystis bloom formation in the lower Nakdong River, South Korea: Importance of hydrodynamics and nutrient loading. *Marine & Freshwater Research, 50*(1), 89–94. doi:10.1071/MF97039

Hakiri, A., Berthou, P., Gokhale, A., & Abdellatif, S. (2015). Publish/subscribe-enabled software defined networking for efficient and scalable IoT communications. *IEEE Communications Magazine, 53*(9), 48–54. doi:10.1109/MCOM.2015.7263372

Hamou, R. M., Amine, A., & Boudia, A. (2013). A New Meta-Heuristic Based on Social Bees for Detection and Filtering of Spam. *International Journal of Applied Metaheuristic Computing*, *4*(3), 15–33. doi:10.4018/ijamc.2013070102

Han, Z. (2017). Study on safety management information system of coal mine based on internet of things. *Coal Economic Research, 3*, 15.

Han, S., Chang, E., Gao, L., & Dillon, T. (2006). Taxonomy of attacks on wireless sensor networks. In *EC2ND 2005* (pp. 97–105). London: Springer. doi:10.1007/1-84628-352-3_10

Hartigan, J. A., & Wong, M. A. (1979). Algorithm AS 136: A k-means clustering algorithm. *Journal of the Royal Statistical Society. Series C, Applied Statistics, 28*(1), 100–108.

Heath, T., & Bizer, C. (2011). Linked data: Evolving the web into a global data space. *Synthesis Lectures on the Semantic Web: Theory and Technology, 1*(1), 1-136.

Hervé Chabanne, D. H. (2005). *Public Traceability in Traitor Tracing Schemes. Eurocrypt'05*. Aarhus, Denmark: Springer.

Hill, J., Szewczyk, R., Woo, A., Hollar, S., Culler, D., & Pister, K. (2000). System architecture directions for networked sensors. *Operating Systems Review, 34*(5), 93–104. doi:10.1145/384264.379006

Hiromoto, R. E., Haney, M., & Vakanski, A. (2017, September). A secure architecture for IoT with supply chain risk management. In *Intelligent Data Acquisition and Advanced Computing Systems: Technology and Applications (IDAACS), 2017 9th IEEE International Conference on* (Vol. 1, pp. 431-435). IEEE. 10.1109/IDAACS.2017.8095118

Hoang, H. (2006). Elucidation of hypothetical relationships between habitat conditions and macroinvertebrate assemblages in freshwater streams by artificial neural networks. In *Ecological Informatics* (pp. 239–251). Springer. doi:10.1007/3-540-28426-5_11

Hoang, H. T. T. (2001). *Predicting Freshwater Habitat Conditions by the Distribution of Macroinvertebrates Using Artificial Neural Network*. University of Adelaide, Department of Soil and Water.

Hoang, H., Recknagel, F., Marshall, J., & Choy, S. (2001). Predictive modelling of macroinvertebrate assemblages for stream habitat assessments in Queensland (Australia). *Ecological Modelling, 146*(1), 195–206. doi:10.1016/S0304-3800(01)00306-4

Hochachka, W. M., Caruana, R., Fink, D., Munson, A., Riedewald, M., Sorokina, D., & Kelling, S. (2007). Data-mining discovery of pattern and process in ecological systems. *The Journal of Wildlife Management, 71*(7), 2427–2437. doi:10.2193/2006-503

Hofmann-Wellenhof, B., Lichtenegger, H., & Collins, J. (2012). *Global positioning system: theory and practice*. Springer Science & Business Media.

Ho, J. W., Liu, D., Wright, M., & Das, S. K. (2009). Distributed detection of replica node attacks with group deployment knowledge in wireless sensor networks. *Ad Hoc Networks, 7*(8), 1476–1488. doi:10.1016/j.adhoc.2009.04.008

Holland, J. H. (1973). Genetic algorithms and the optimal allocation of trials. *SIAM Journal on Computing, 2*(2), 88–105. doi:10.1137/0202009

Holmes, M. H. (2012). *Introduction to perturbation methods* (Vol. 20). Springer Science & Business Media.

House, W. (2014). *Big Data and Privacy: a technological perspective.* Washington, DC: Executive Office of the President, President's Council of Advisors on Science and Technology.

Hu, X., Shi, Y., & Eberhart, R. (2004). Recent advances in particle swarm. In Evolutionary Computation, 2004. CEC2004. Congress on (vol. 1, pp. 90-97). IEEE.

Huang, G. B., Ramesh, M., Berg, T., & Learned-Miller, E. (2007). Labeled Faces in the Wild: A Database for Studying Face Recognition in Unconstrained Environments. University of Massachusetts, Amherst, Technical Report.

Huda, M., Maseleno, A., Atmotiyoso, P., Siregar, M., Ahmad, R., Jasmi, K. A., & Muhamad, N. H. N. (2018). Big Data Emerging Technology: Insights into Innovative Environment for Online Learning Resources. *International Journal of Emerging Technologies in Learning, 13*(01), 23–36. doi:10.3991/ijet.v13i01.6990

Hui, T. K., Sherratt, R. S., & Sánchez, D. D. (2017). Major requirements for building Smart Homes in Smart Cities based on Internet of Things technologies. *Future Generation Computer Systems, 76*, 358–369. doi:10.1016/j.future.2016.10.026

Huxtable, J., & Schaefer, D. (2016). On Servitization of the Manufacturing Industry in the UK. *Procedia CIRP, 52*, 46–51. doi:10.1016/j.procir.2016.07.042

Index–Forecast, C. V. N. (2008). *Methodology 2007–2012.* Cisco System.

Ioannis, K., Dimitriou, T., & Freiling, F. C. (2007, April). Towards intrusion detection in wireless sensor networks. In *Proc. of the 13th European Wireless Conference* (pp. 1-10). Academic Press.

Ishaq, I., Carels, D., Teklemariam, G. K., Hoebeke, J., Abeele, F. V. D., Poorter, E. D., ... Demeester, P. (2013). IETF standardization in the field of the internet of things (IoT): A survey. *Journal of Sensor and Actuator Networks, 2*(2), 235–287. doi:10.3390/jsan2020235

Jain, A. K. (2010). Data clustering: 50 years beyond K-means. *Pattern Recognition Letters, 31*(8), 651–666. doi:10.1016/j.patrec.2009.09.011

Jakhar, R., Kaur, N., & Singh, R. (2011). Face Recognition Using Bacteria Foraging Optimization-Based Selected Features. *International Journal of Advanced Computer Science and Applications,* 106-111.

Jambu, M., & Lebeaux, M. O. (1978). *Classification automatique pour l'analyse des données* (Vol. 1). Paris: Dunod.

Jeong, K. S., Recknagel, F., & Joo, G. J. (2006). Prediction and elucidation of population dynamics of the blue-green algae Microcystis aeruginosa and the diatom Stephanodiscus hantzschii in the Nakdong River-Reservoir System (South Korea) by a recurrent artificial neural network. In Ecological Informatics. Springer. doi:10.1007/3-540-28426-5_12

Jeschke, S., Brecher, C., Meisen, T., Özdemir, D., & Eschert, T. (2017). Industrial internet of things and cyber manufacturing systems. In *Industrial Internet of Things* (pp. 3–19). Cham: Springer. doi:10.1007/978-3-319-42559-7_1

Ji, Z., & Anwen, Q. (2010, November). The application of internet of things (IOT) in emergency management system in China. In *Technologies for Homeland Security (HST), 2010 IEEE International Conference on* (pp. 139-142). IEEE.

Jiang, L., Yu, M., Zhou, M., Liu, X., & Zhao, T. (2011, June). Target-dependent twitter sentiment classification. In *Proceedings of the 49th Annual Meeting of the Association for Computational Linguistics: Human Language Technologies-Volume 1* (pp. 151-160). Association for Computational Linguistics.

Jo, B. W., & Khan, R. M. A. (2017). An Event Reporting and Early-Warning Safety System Based on the Internet of Things for Underground Coal Mines: A Case Study. *Applied Sciences, 7*(9), 925. doi:10.3390/app7090925

John Lu, Z. Q. (2010). The elements of statistical learning: Data mining, inference, and prediction. *Journal of the Royal Statistical Society. Series A, (Statistics in Society), 173*(3), 693–694. doi:10.1111/j.1467-985X.2010.00646_6.x

Jolliffe, I. T. (1986). Principal component analysis. Springer Verlag.

Kadam, Paikrao, & Pawar. (2013). Survey on Cloud Computing Security. *International Journal of Emerging Technology and Advanced Engineering, 3*(12).

Kahramanli, H., & Allahverdi, N. (2008). Design of a hybrid system for the diabetes and heart diseases. *Expert Systems with Applications, 35*(1), 82–89. doi:10.1016/j.eswa.2007.06.004

Kalish, J. M., Johnston, J. M., Smith, D. C., Morison, A. K., & Robertson, S. G. (1997). Use of the bomb radiocarbon chronometer for age validation in the blue grenadier Macruronus novaezelandiae. *Marine Biology, 128*(4), 557–563. doi:10.1007002270050121

Kalyani, D., & Pooja, K. (2017). Prediction of heart disease using k-means and artificial neural network as hybrid approach to improve accuracy. *International Journal of Engineering and Technology, 9*(4), 3081–3085. doi:10.21817/ijet/2017/v9i4/170904101

Kanan, H. R., & Faez, K. (2008). An improved feature selection method based on ant colony optimization (ACO) evaluated on face recognition system. *Applied Mathematics and Computation, 205*(2), 716–725. doi:10.1016/j.amc.2008.05.115

Karaboga, D., & Basturk, B. (2007). A powerful and efficient algorithm for numerical function optimization: Artificial bee colony (ABC) algorithm. *Journal of Global Optimization*, *39*(3), 459–471. doi:10.100710898-007-9149-x

Karakehayov, Z. (2005). Using REWARD to detect team black-hole attacks in wireless sensor networks. *Wksp. Real-World Wireless Sensor Networks*, 20-21.

Kargupta, H., Datta, S., Wang, Q., & Sivakumar, K. (2003, November). On the privacy preserving properties of random data perturbation techniques. In *Data Mining, 2003. ICDM 2003. Third IEEE International Conference on* (pp. 99-106). IEEE. 10.1109/ICDM.2003.1250908

Karlof, C., & Wagner, D. (2003, May). Secure routing in wireless sensor networks: Attacks and countermeasures. In *Sensor Network Protocols and Applications, 2003. Proceedings of the First IEEE. 2003 IEEE International Workshop on* (pp. 113-127). IEEE.

Karp, B., & Kung, H. T. (2000, August). GPSR: Greedy perimeter stateless routing for wireless networks. In *Proceedings of the 6th annual international conference on Mobile computing and networking* (pp. 243-254). ACM. 10.1145/345910.345953

Karul, C., & Soyupak, S. (2003). A comparison between neural network based and multiple regression models for chlorophyll-a estimation. In *Ecological Informatics* (pp. 249–263). Springer. doi:10.1007/978-3-662-05150-4_13

Karul, C., Soyupak, S., Çilesiz, A. F., Akbay, N., & Germen, E. (2000). Case studies on the use of neural networks in eutrophication modeling. *Ecological Modelling*, *134*(2), 145–152. doi:10.1016/S0304-3800(00)00360-4

Karul, C., Soyupak, S., & Yurteri, C. (1999). Neural network models as a management tool in lakes. In *Shallow Lakes' 98* (pp. 139–144). Springer. doi:10.1007/978-94-017-2986-4_14

Karuppiah, A. B., Dalfiah, J., Yuvashri, K., Rajaram, S., & Pathan, A. S. K. (2014, December). A novel energy-efficient sybil node detection algorithm for intrusion detection system in wireless sensor networks. In *Eco-friendly Computing and Communication Systems (ICECCS), 2014 3rd International Conference on* (pp. 95-98). IEEE. 10.1109/Eco-friendly.2014.94

Kasprzak, J., Brandejs, M., & Kripac, M. (2009, September). Finding plagiarism by evaluating document similarities. In *Proc. SEPLN* (*Vol. 9*, No. 4, pp. 24-28). Academic Press.

Kennedy, J., & Eberhart, R. (1995). Particle Swarm Optimization. *Proceedings of IEEE International Conference on Neural Networks, 4*, 1942–1948. 10.1109/ICNN.1995.488968

Kennedy, J. F. (2001). *Swarm intelligence*. Morgan Kaufmann.

Kephart, J. O., & Chess, D. M. (2003). The vision of autonomic computing. *Computer*, *36*(1), 41–50. doi:10.1109/MC.2003.1160055

Kerschbaum, F., & Oertel, N. (2011). *U. S. Patent No. 8,015,080*. Washington, DC: U. S. Patent and Trademark Office.

Khan, A. Z., Atique, M., & Thakare, V. M. (2015). Combining lexicon-based and learning-based methods for Twitter sentiment analysis. *International Journal of Electronics, Communication and Soft Computing Science & Engineering*, 89.

Khan, M., Wu, X., Xu, X., & Dou, W. (2017, May). Big data challenges and opportunities in the hype of Industry 4.0. In *Communications (ICC), 2017 IEEE International Conference on* (pp. 1-6). IEEE.

Khatoon, M., Banu, W. A., Zohra, A. A., & Chinthamani, S. (2019). Sentiment Analysis on Tweets. In *Software Engineering* (pp. 717–724). Singapore: Springer. doi:10.1007/978-981-10-8848-3_70

Kim, J., & Lee, J. W. (2014, March). OpenIoT: An open service framework for the Internet of Things. In *Internet of Things (WF-IoT), 2014 IEEE World Forum on* (pp. 89-93). IEEE.

King, R., & Brooks, S. P. (2004). Bayesian analysis of the Hector's Dolphin data. *Animal Biodiversity and Conservation*, 27(1), 343–354.

Klir, G., & Yuan, B. Fuzzy sets and fuzzy logic (vol. 4). Prentice Hall.

Klosek, J. (2007). *The war on privacy*. Greenwood Publishing Group.

Kohonen, T., Schroeder, M. R., & Huang, T. S. (2001). Maps, Self-Organizing. doi:10.1007/978-3-642-56927-2

Kortuem, G., Kawsar, F., Sundramoorthy, V., & Fitton, D. (2010). Smart objects as building blocks for the internet of things. *IEEE Internet Computing*, 14(1), 44–51. doi:10.1109/MIC.2009.143

Kostelnik, P., Sarnovsk, M., & Furdik, K. (2011). The semantic middleware for networked embedded systems applied in the internet of things and services domain. *Scalable Computing: Practice and Experience*, 12(3), 307–316.

Kouloumpis, E., Wilson, T., & Moore, J. D. (2011). Twitter sentiment analysis: The good the bad and the omg! *ICWSM*, 11(538-541), 164.

Kowalski, G. J., & Maybury, M. T. (2006). *Information storage and retrieval systems: theory and implementation* (Vol. 8). Springer Science & Business Media.

Ko, Y. (2012, August). A study of term weighting schemes using class information for text classification. In *Proceedings of the 35th international ACM SIGIR conference on Research and development in information retrieval* (pp. 1029-1030). ACM. 10.1145/2348283.2348453

Koza, J. R. (1992). *Genetic programming: on the programming of computers by means of natural selection* (Vol. 1). MIT Press.

Krasser, S., Tang, Y., Gould, J., Alperovitch, D., & Judge, P. (2007, June). Identifying image spam based on header and file properties using C4. 5 decision trees and support vector machine learning. In *Information Assurance and Security Workshop, 2007. IAW'07. IEEE SMC* (pp. 255-261). IEEE.

Kraus, K. (2014). *Security management process in distributed, large scale high performance systems* (Doctoral dissertation). University of Oulu, Finland.

Krink, T., Filipic, B., & Fogel, G. B. (2004). Noisy optimization problems-a particular challenge for differential evolution? In Evolutionary Computation, 2004. CEC2004. Congress on (Vol. 1). IEEE. doi:10.1109/CEC.2004.1330876

Kubat, M., Holte, R. C., & Matwin, S. (1998). Machine learning for the detection of oil spills in satellite radar images. *Machine Learning, 30*(2-3), 195–215. doi:10.1023/A:1007452223027

Kuppusamy, P., Kamarajapandian, P., Sabari, M. S., & Nithya, J. (2018). Design of Smart Traffic Signal System Using Internet of Things and Genetic Algorithm. In *Advances in Big Data and Cloud Computing* (pp. 395–403). Singapore: Springer. doi:10.1007/978-981-10-7200-0_36

Kurgan, L. A., & Musilek, P. (2006). A survey of Knowledge Discovery and Data Mining process model. *The Knowledge Engineering Review, 21*(1), 1–24. doi:10.1017/S0269888906000737

Kushalnagar, N., Montenegro, G., & Schumacher, C. (2007). *IPv6 over low-power wireless personal area networks (6LoWPANs): overview, assumptions, problem statement, and goals* (No. RFC 4919).

Kutner, M. H., Nachtsheim, C., & Neter, J. (2004). *Applied linear regression models.* McGrawHill/Irwin.

Labraoui, N. (2012). *La sécurité dans les réseaux sans fil ad hoc* (Doctoral dissertation).

Lafrate, F. (2018). *Artificial Intelligence and Big Data: The Birth of a New Intelligence.* John Wiley & Sons. doi:10.1002/9781119426653

Lai, C., Doong, S., & Wu, C. (2009). Machine Learning. In *Wiley encyclopedia of computer science and engineering.* John Wiley.

Larson, R. R. (2010). Introduction to information retrieval. *Journal of the American Society for Information Science and Technology, 61*(4), 852–853.

Lasi, H., Fettke, P., Kemper, H. G., Feld, T., & Hoffmann, M. (2014). Industry 4.0. *Business & Information Systems Engineering, 6*(4), 239–242. doi:10.100712599-014-0334-4

Layouni, M. A. (2009). *Privacy-preserving Personal Information Management* (Doctoral dissertation). McGill University.

Lee, I., & Lee, K. (2015). The Internet of Things (IoT): Applications, investments, and challenges for enterprises. *Business Horizons, 58*(4), 431–440. doi:10.1016/j.bushor.2015.03.008

Legendre, F. (2014). *Exploitation de la logique propositionnelle pour la résolution parallèle des problèmes cryptographiques* (Doctoral dissertation).

Lek, S., Belaud, A., Baran, P., Dimopoulos, I., & Delacoste, M. (1996). Role of some environmental variables in trout abundance models using neural networks. *Aquatic Living Resources, 9*(1), 23–29. doi:10.1051/alr:1996004

Lek, S., Delacoste, M., Baran, P., Dimopoulos, I., Lauga, J., & Aulagnier, S. (1996). Application of neural networks to modelling nonlinear relationships in ecology. *Ecological Modelling, 90*(1), 39–52. doi:10.1016/0304-3800(95)00142-5

Leng, K., Jin, L., Shi, W., & Van Nieuwenhuyse, I. (2018). Research on agricultural products supply chain inspection system based on internet of things. *Cluster Computing*, 1–9.

Le-Phuoc, D., Parreira, J. X., Hausenblas, M., Han, Y., & Hauswirth, M. (2010, September). Live linked open sensor database. In *Proceedings of the 6th International Conference on Semantic Systems* (p. 46). ACM.

Li, N., Zhang, N., Das, S. K., & Thuraisingham, B. (2009). Privacy preservation in wireless sensor networks: A state-of-the-art survey. *Ad Hoc Networks, 7*(8), 1501–1514. doi:10.1016/j.adhoc.2009.04.009

Lin, C.-H., & Wu, J.-L. (1999). Automatic Facial Feature Extraction by Genetic Algorithms. *IEEE Transactions on Image Processing, 8*(6), 834–845. doi:10.1109/83.766860 PMID:18267496

Lin, L. J. (1992). Self-improving reactive agents based on reinforcement learning, planning and teaching. *Machine Learning, 8*(3-4), 293–321. doi:10.1007/BF00992699

Li, S., Da Xu, L., & Zhao, S. (2015). The internet of things: A survey. *Information Systems Frontiers, 17*(2), 243–259. doi:10.100710796-014-9492-7

Liu, A., & Ning, P. (2008, April). TinyECC: A configurable library for elliptic curve cryptography in wireless sensor networks. In *Information Processing in Sensor Networks, 2008. IPSN'08. International Conference on* (pp. 245-256). IEEE. 10.1109/IPSN.2008.47

Liu, B., Lee, W. S., Yu, P. S., & Li, X. (2002, July). *Partially supervised classification of text documents* (Vol. 2). ICML.

Liu, C., Chen, C., Han, J., & Yu, P. S. (2006, August). GPLAG: detection of software plagiarism by program dependence graph analysis. In *Proceedings of the 12th ACM SIGKDD international conference on Knowledge discovery and data mining* (pp. 872-881). ACM. 10.1145/1150402.1150522

Liu, M., Ma, J., Lin, L., Ge, M., Wang, Q., & Liu, C. (2017). Intelligent assembly system for mechanical products and key technology based on internet of things. *Journal of Intelligent Manufacturing, 28*(2), 271–299. doi:10.100710845-014-0976-6

Liu, T. Y. (2011). *Learning to rank for information retrieval*. Springer Science & Business Media. doi:10.1007/978-3-642-14267-3

Llopis, F., Ferrández, A., & Vicedo, J. L. (2002, February). Text segmentation for efficient information retrieval. In *International Conference on Intelligent Text Processing and Computational Linguistics* (pp. 373-380). Springer.

Lodhi, H., Saunders, C., Shawe-Taylor, J., Cristianini, N., & Watkins, C. (2002). Text classification using string kernels. *Journal of Machine Learning Research, 2*(Feb), 419–444.

Ludvigsen, L. (1997). Correlating phospholipid fatty acids (PLFA) in a landfill leachate polluted aquifer with biogeochemical factors by multivariate statistical methods. FEMS Microbiology Reviews, 20(3-4), 447–460. doi:10.1111/j.1574-6976.1997.tb00329.x

Lukashenko, R., Graudina, V., & Grundspenkis, J. (2007, June). Computer-based plagiarism detection methods and tools: an overview. In *Proceedings of the 2007 international conference on Computer systems and technologies* (p. 40). ACM. 10.1145/1330598.1330642

Luo, H., Ci, S., Wu, D., Stergiou, N., & Siu, K. C. (2010). A remote markerless human gait tracking for e-healthcare based on content-aware wireless multimedia communications. *IEEE Wireless Communications, 17*(1), 44–50. doi:10.1109/MWC.2010.5416349

Ma, Y. W., Chen, J. L., & Chang, Y. Y. (2016, January). Cloud computing technology for the petroleum application. In *Advanced Communication Technology (ICACT), 2016 18th International Conference on* (pp. 101-104). IEEE.

Machanavajjhala, A., Kifer, D., Gehrke, J., & Venkitasubramaniam, M. (2007). l-diversity: Privacy beyond k-anonymity. *ACM Transactions on Knowledge Discovery from Data, 1*(1), 3, es. doi:10.1145/1217299.1217302

Madakam, S., Ramaswamy, R., & Tripathi, S. (2015). Internet of Things (IoT): A literature review. *Journal of Computer and Communications, 3*(05), 164–173. doi:10.4236/jcc.2015.35021

Maedche, A., & Staab, S. (2000, August). Discovering conceptual relations from text. *ECAI, 321*(325), 27.

Maimut, D. S., Patrascu, A., & Simion, E. (2012). Homomorphic Encryption Schemes and Applications for a Secure Digital World. Journal of Mobile. *Embedded and Distributed Systems, 4*(4), 224–232.

Majeed, A. A., & Rupasinghe, T. D. (2017). Internet of things (IoT) embedded future supply chains for industry 4.0: An assessment from an ERP-based fashion apparel and footwear industry. *International Journal of Supply Chain Management, 6*(1), 25–40.

Majumder, A., Namasudra, S., & Nath, S. (2014). Taxonomy and classification of access control models for cloud environments. In *Continued Rise of the Cloud* (pp. 23–53). Springer London. doi:10.1007/978-1-4471-6452-4_2

Malan, D. J., Welsh, M., & Smith, M. D. (2004, October). A public-key infrastructure for key distribution in TinyOS based on elliptic curve cryptography. In *Sensor and Ad Hoc Communications and Networks, 2004. IEEE SECON 2004. 2004 First Annual IEEE Communications Society Conference on* (pp. 71-80). IEEE. 10.1109/SAHCN.2004.1381904

Malewicz, G., Austern, M. H., Bik, A. J., Dehnert, J. C., Horn, I., Leiser, N., & Czajkowski, G. (2010, June). Pregel: a system for large-scale graph processing. In *Proceedings of the 2010 ACM SIGMOD International Conference on Management of data* (pp. 135-146). ACM.

Manikantan, V., & Latha, S. (2013). Predicting the analysis of heart disease symptoms using medicinal data mining methods. *International Journal of Advanced Computer Theory and Engineering*, 2, 46–51.

Mashey, J. R. (1997, October). Big Data and the next wave of infraS-tress. In *Computer Science Division Seminar*. University of California.

Masters, T. (1995). *Neural, novel and hybrid algorithms for time series prediction*. John Wiley & Sons, Inc.

Matallah, H. (2011). *Classification Automatique de Textes Approche Orientée Agent* (Doctoral dissertation).

Ma, X., Pan, Y. J., Chen, F., Ding, X., & Tseng, S. P. (2017, November). A Constructive Problem-Based Course Design for Internet of Things. In *International Conference on Smart Vehicular Technology, Transportation, Communication and Applications* (pp. 397-402). Springer.

McGregor, S., & Harvey, I. (2005). Embracing plagiarism: Theoretical, biological and empirical justification for copy operators in genetic optimisation. *Genetic Programming and Evolvable Machines*, 6(4), 407–420. doi:10.100710710-005-4804-9

McIntosh, B. S. (2003). Qualitative modelling with imprecise ecological knowledge: A framework for simulation. *Environmental Modelling & Software*, 18(4), 295–307. doi:10.1016/S1364-8152(03)00002-1

Mehrotra, K., Mohan, C. K., & Ranka, S. (1997). *Elements of Artificial neural networks*. The MIT Press. doi:10.1145/1807167.1807184

Memmah, M. M., Lescourret, F., Yao, X., & Lavigne, C. (2015). Metaheuristics for agricultural land use optimization. A review. *Agronomy for Sustainable Development*, 35(3), 975–998. doi:10.100713593-015-0303-4

Metzler, D., & Croft, W. B. (2007). Linear feature-based models for information retrieval. *Information Retrieval*, 10(3), 257–274. doi:10.100710791-006-9019-z

Meyer, F. G., & Shen, X. (2014). Perturbation of the eigenvectors of the graph laplacian: Application to image denoising. *Applied and Computational Harmonic Analysis*, 36(2), 326–334. doi:10.1016/j.acha.2013.06.004

Michalewicz, Z., & Fogel, D. B. (2013). *How to solve it: modern heuristics*. Springer Science & Business Media.

Mihalcea, R., & Radev, D. (2011). *Graph-based natural language processing and information retrieval*. Cambridge university press. doi:10.1017/CBO9780511976247

Miorandi, D., Sicari, S., De Pellegrini, F., & Chlamtac, I. (2012). Internet of things: Vision, applications and research challenges. *Ad Hoc Networks*, 10(7), 1497–1516. doi:10.1016/j.adhoc.2012.02.016

Mo, H., & Xu, L. (2015). Research of biogeography particle swarm optimization for robot path planning. *Neurocomputing, 148*, 91–99. doi:10.1016/j.neucom.2012.07.060

Mohamed, A., Hamdi, M. S., & Tahar, S. (2015, August). A machine learning approach for big data in oil and gas pipelines. In *Future Internet of Things and Cloud (FiCloud), 2015 3rd International Conference on* (pp. 585-590). IEEE. 10.1109/FiCloud.2015.54

Mohammad, A. H., & Zitar, R. A. (2011). Application of genetic optimized artificial immune system and neural networks in spam detection. *Applied Soft Computing, 11*(4), 3827-3845.

Mohanty, S. P., Choppali, U., & Kougianos, E. (2016). Everything you wanted to know about smart cities: The internet of things is the backbone. *IEEE Consumer Electronics Magazine, 5*(3), 60–70. doi:10.1109/MCE.2016.2556879

Monachesi, P., & Markus, T. (2010, May). Using social media for ontology enrichment. In *Extended Semantic Web Conference* (pp. 166-180). Springer.

Monnet, Q. (2015). *Modèles et mécanismes pour la protection contre les attaques par déni de service dans les réseaux de capteurs sans fil* (Doctoral dissertation).

Montori, F., Bedogni, L., & Bononi, L. (2018). A collaborative internet of things architecture for smart cities and environmental monitoring. *IEEE Internet of Things Journal, 5*(2), 592–605. doi:10.1109/JIOT.2017.2720855

Montoya, G. N., Junior, J. B. S. S., Novaes, A. G., & Lima, O. F. (2018, February). Internet of Things and the Risk Management Approach in the Pharmaceutical Supply Chain. In *International Conference on Dynamics in Logistics* (pp. 284-288). Springer. 10.1007/978-3-319-74225-0_38

Moreno, M., Jelenchick, L. Egan, K. Cox, E. Young, H., & Gannon, K. (2011). Feeling Bad on Facebook: Depression Disclosures by College Students on Social Networking Site. *Depression and Anxiety, 28*, 447-455.

Morison, A. K., Robertson, S. G., & Smith, D. C. (1998). An integrated system for production fish aging: Image analysis and quality assurance. *North American Journal of Fisheries Management, 18*(3), 587–598. doi:10.1577/1548-8675(1998)018<0587:AISFPF>2.0.CO;2

Morrall, D. (2003). Ecological applications of genetic algorithms. Ecological Informatics, 35–48. doi:10.1007/978-3-662-05150-4_3

Nasrabadi, N. M. (2007). Pattern recognition and machine learning. *Journal of Electronic Imaging, 16*(4), 049901. doi:10.1117/1.2819119

Newsome, J., Shi, E., Song, D., & Perrig, A. (2004, April). The sybil attack in sensor networks: analysis & defenses. In *Proceedings of the 3rd international symposium on Information processing in sensor networks* (pp. 259-268). ACM. 10.1145/984622.984660

Nigam, K., McCallum, A. K., Thrun, S., & Mitchell, T. (2000). Text classification from labeled and unlabeled documents using EM. *Machine Learning, 39*(2-3), 103–134. doi:10.1023/A:1007692713085

Nothhaft, C. (2018). Understanding China's Consumers. In *Made for China* (pp. 3–20). Cham: Springer. doi:10.1007/978-3-319-61584-4_1

Noury, N. (2002). *Du Signal à l'Information: le capteur intelligent* (Doctoral dissertation). Université Joseph-Fourier-Grenoble I.

O'Sullivan, C., Wise, N., & Mathieu, P. P. (2018). The Changing Landscape of Geospatial Information Markets. In *Earth Observation Open Science and Innovation* (pp. 3–23). Cham: Springer. doi:10.1007/978-3-319-65633-5_1

Okamoto, T., & Uchiyama, S. (1998, May). A new public-key cryptosystem as secure as factoring. In *International Conference on the Theory and Applications of Cryptographic Techniques* (pp. 308-318). Springer Berlin Heidelberg. 10.1007/BFb0054135

OMG. (2015). *Object Management Group*. DDS. Retrieved from http://www.omg.org/spec/DDS/1.4/PDF/

Ornato, M., Cinotti, T. S., Borghetti, A., Azzoni, P., D'Elia, A., Viola, F., & Venanzi, R. (2017). Application system design: Complex systems management and automation. In *IoT Automation* (pp. 317–352). CRC Press. doi:10.1201/9781315367897-10

Öz, E., & Baykoç, Ö.F. (2004). Expert System Approach Supported by Decision Theory on Supplier Selection Problem. *Gazi Univ. Eng. Faculty, 19*(3).

Padmavathi, D. G., & Shanmugapriya, M. (2009). *A survey of attacks, security mechanisms and challenges in wireless sensor networks.* arXiv preprint arXiv:0909.0576

Paganelli, F., Turchi, S., Bianchi, L., Ciofi, L., Pettenati, M. C., Pirri, F., & Giuli, D. (2013). *An information-centric and REST-based approach for EPC Information Services.* Academic Press.

Paliouras, G., Spyropoulos, C. D., & Tsatsaronis, G. (2011). Bootstrapping ontology evolution with multimedia information extraction. In *Knowledge-driven multimedia information extraction and ontology evolution* (pp. 1–17). Springer Berlin Heidelberg. doi:10.1007/978-3-642-20795-2_1

Pang, B., & Lee, L. (2008). Opinion mining and sentiment analysis. *Foundations and Trends® in Information Retrieval, 2*(1–2), 1-135.

Pang, Z., Chen, Q., Tian, J., Zheng, L., & Dubrova, E. (2013, January). Ecosystem analysis in the design of open platform-based in-home healthcare terminals towards the internet-of-things. In *Advanced Communication Technology (ICACT), 2013 15th International Conference on* (pp. 529-534). IEEE.

Pang, Z., Chen, Q., Han, W., & Zheng, L. (2015). Value-centric design of the internet-of-things solution for food supply chain: Value creation, sensor portfolio and information fusion. *Information Systems Frontiers, 17*(2), 289–319. doi:10.100710796-012-9374-9

Pao, Y. (1989). Adaptive pattern recognition and neural networks. Academic Press.

Park, A., Chang, H., & Lee, K. J. (2017). Action research on development and application of Internet of Things services in hospital. *Healthcare Informatics Research*, *23*(1), 25–34. doi:10.4258/hir.2017.23.1.25 PMID:28261528

Patel, A., & Patel, H. S. (2014). *A Study of Data Perturbation Techniques For Privacy Preserving Data Mining*. Academic Press.

Patel, P., Jardosh, S., Chaudhary, S., & Ranjan, P. (2009, September). Context aware middleware architecture for wireless sensor network. In *Services Computing, 2009. SCC'09. IEEE International Conference on* (pp. 532-535). IEEE. 10.1109/SCC.2009.49

Patel, K. K., Patel, S. M., & Professor, P. S. A. (2016). Internet of Things-IOT: Definition, characteristics, architecture, enabling technologies, application & future challenges. *International Journal of Engineering Science and Computing*, *6*(5).

Pawar, V., & Bhosale, N. P. (2017). *SMART local bus transport Management System using IoT*. Academic Press.

Pedregosa, F., Varoquaux, G., Gramfort, A., Michel, V., Thirion, B., Grisel, O., ... Vanderplas, J. (2011). Scikit-learn: Machine learning in Python. *Journal of Machine Learning Research*, *12*(Oct), 2825–2830.

Peet, R. K., & Loucks, O. L. (1977). A gradient analysis of southern Wisconsin forests. *Ecology*, *58*(3), 485–499. doi:10.2307/1938999

Pelechrinis, K., Iliofotou, M., & Krishnamurthy, S. V. (2011). Denial of service attacks in wireless networks: The case of jammers. *IEEE Communications Surveys and Tutorials*, *13*(2), 245–257. doi:10.1109/SURV.2011.041110.00022

Perera, C., Zaslavsky, A., Christen, P., & Georgakopoulos, D. (2014). Context aware computing for the internet of things: A survey. *IEEE Communications Surveys and Tutorials*, *16*(1), 414–454. doi:10.1109/SURV.2013.042313.00197

Perkins, C. E. (2001). *Ad Hoc Networks*. Reading, MA: Addison-Wesley.

Petasis, G., Karkaletsis, V., Paliouras, G., Krithara, A., & Zavitsanos, E. (2011). Ontology population and enrichment: State of the art. In *Knowledge-driven multimedia information extraction and ontology evolution* (pp. 134–166). Springer Berlin Heidelberg. doi:10.1007/978-3-642-20795-2_6

Pineda, F. J. (1987). Generalization of back-propagation to recurrent neural networks. *Physical Review Letters*, *59*(19), 2229–2232. doi:10.1103/PhysRevLett.59.2229 PMID:10035458

Piotrowski, J. A., Bartels, F., Salski, A., & Schmidt, G. (1996). Geostatistical regionalization of glacial aquitard thickness in northwestern Germany, based on fuzzy kriging. *Mathematical Geology*, *28*(4), 437–452. doi:10.1007/BF02083655

Piro, C., Shields, C., & Levine, B. N. (2006, August). Detecting the sybil attack in mobile ad hoc networks. In *Securecomm and Workshops, 2006* (pp. 1–11). IEEE. doi:10.1109/SECCOMW.2006.359558

Polat & Gunes. (2007). A hybrid approach to medical decision support systems: Combining feature selection, fuzzy weighted pre-processing and AIRS. *Computer Methods and Programs in Biomedicine, 88*, 164–174.

Polat, K., & Güneş, S. (2009). A novel hybrid intelligent method based on C4. 5 decision tree classifier and one-against-all approach for multi-class classification problems. *Expert Systems with Applications, 36*(2), 1587–1592. doi:10.1016/j.eswa.2007.11.051

Poniszewska-Maranda, A., & Kaczmarek, D. (2015, September). Selected methods of artificial intelligence for Internet of Things conception. In *Computer Science and Information Systems (FedCSIS), 2015 Federated Conference on* (pp. 1343-1348). IEEE. 10.15439/2015F161

Potthast, M., Eiselt, A., Barrón Cedeño, L. A., Stein, B., & Rosso, P. (2011). Overview of the 3rd international competition on plagiarism detection. *CEUR Workshop Proceedings*.

Potthast, M., Barrón-Cedeño, A., Eiselt, A., Stein, B., & Rosso, P. (2010). Overview of the 2nd international competition on plagiarism detection. *Proceedings of the 4th Workshop on Uncovering Plagiarism, Authorship, and Social Software Misuse*, 1-14.

Prabhjotkaur, A. C., & Singh, S. (2016). Review Paper of Detection and Prevention of Sybil Attack in WSN Using Centralizedids. *International Journal of Engineering Science*, 8399.

Prasad, K., & Mallick, C. A Mobile Agent based Sybil Attack Detection Algorithm for Wireless Sensor Network. *International Conference on Emergent Trends in Computing and Communication (ETCC 2015)*.

Premaratne, U., Samarabandu, J., & Sidhu, T. (2009). A new biologically inspired optimization algorithm. In *Industrial and Information Systems (ICIIS), 2009 International Conference on*. IEEE.

Press, W. H. (1992). *Numerical Recipes in C: The Art of Scientific Computing*. Cambridge Univ. Press.

Preuxa, P., & Talbi, E.-G. (1999). Towards hybrid evolutionary algorithms. *International Transactions in Operational Research, 6*(6), 557–570. doi:10.1111/j.1475-3995.1999.tb00173.x

Punt, A. E., Smith, D. C., Thomson, R. B., Haddon, M., He, X., & Lyle, J. M. (2001). Stock assessment of the blue grenadier Macruronus novaezelandiae resource off south-eastern Australia. *Marine & Freshwater Research, 52*(4), 701–717. doi:10.1071/MF99136

Purao, S., Storey, V., Sugumaran, V., Conesa, J., Minguillón, J., & Casas, J. (2011). Repurposing social tagging data for extraction of domain-level concepts. *Natural Language Processing and Information Systems*, 185-192.

Qin, E., Long, Y., Zhang, C., & Huang, L. (2013, July). Cloud computing and the internet of things: Technology innovation in automobile service. In *International Conference on Human Interface and the Management of Information* (pp. 173-180). Springer. 10.1007/978-3-642-39215-3_21

Qin, T., Liu, T. Y., Xu, J., & Li, H. (2010). LETOR: A benchmark collection for research on learning to rank for information retrieval. *Information Retrieval, 13*(4), 346–374. doi:10.100710791-009-9123-y

Qiuping, W., Shunbing, Z., & Chunquan, D. (2011). Study on key technologies of Internet of Things perceiving mine. *Procedia Engineering, 26*, 2326–2333. doi:10.1016/j.proeng.2011.11.2442

Quinn, T. J., & Deriso, R. B. (1999). *Quantitative fish dynamics*. Oxford University Press.

Rajasegarar, S., Leckie, C., & Palaniswami, M. (2008, May). CESVM: Centered hyperellipsoidal support vector machine based anomaly detection. In *Communications, 2008. ICC'08. IEEE International Conference on* (pp. 1610-1614). IEEE.

Rajkumar, A., & Reena, G. S. (2010). Diagnosis of heart disease using data mining algorithm. *Global Journal of Computer Science and Technology, 10*(10), 38-43.

Ramadan, R. M., & Abdel-Kader, R. F. (2009). Face Recognition Using Particle Swarm Optimization-Based Selected Features. *International Journal of Signal Processing. Image Processing and Pattern Recognition, 2*(2), 51–65.

Rao, Y. R. (2017). Automatic smart parking system using Internet of Things (IOT). *Int J Eng Technol Sci Res, 4*(5).

Rashedi, E., Nezamabadi-Pour, H., & Saryazdi, S. (2009). GSA: A Gravitational Search Algorithm. *Information Sciences, 179*(13), 2232–2248. doi:10.1016/j.ins.2009.03.004

Rathore, M. M., Ahmad, A., Paul, A., & Rho, S. (2016). Urban planning and building smart cities based on the internet of things using big data analytics. *Computer Networks, 101*, 63–80. doi:10.1016/j.comnet.2015.12.023

Ratnaparkhi, D., Mahajan, T., & Jadhav, V. (2015). Heart Disease Prediction System Using Data Mining Technique. *International Research Journal of Engineering and Technology, 2*(08), 2395–0056.

Ravi, S., & Nayeem, S. (2013). A Study on Face Recognition Technique based on Eigen face. *International Journal of Applied Information Systems, 5*(4), 57–62.

Raymond, D. R., & Midkiff, S. F. (2008). Denial-of-service in wireless sensor networks: Attacks and defenses. *IEEE Pervasive Computing, 7*(1), 74–81. doi:10.1109/MPRV.2008.6

Recknagel, F. (2003). Ecological applications of adaptive agents. Ecological Informatics, 73–88. doi:10.1007/978-3-662-05150-4_5

Recknagel, F. (2006). Artificial neural network approach to unravel and forecast algal population dynamics of two lakes different in morphometry and eutrophication. In *Ecological informatics* (pp. 325–345). Springer. doi:10.1007/3-540-28426-5_16

Recknagel, F. (2006). *Ecological Informatics–Scope*. Technique and Applications. doi:10.1007/3-540-28426-5

Reick, C. H., Grünewald, A., & Page, B. (2006). Multivariate Time Series Prediction of Marine Zooplankton by Artificial Neural Networks. In *Ecological Informatics* (pp. 369–383). Springer. doi:10.1007/3-540-28426-5_18

Reinsel, D., Gantz, J., & Rydning, J. (2017). *Data Age 2025: The Evolution of Data to Life-Critical*. Don't Focus on Big Data.

Reis, M. S., & Gins, G. (2017). Industrial Process Monitoring in the Big Data/Industry 4.0 Era: From Detection, to Diagnosis, to Prognosis. *Processes, 5*(3), 35. doi:10.3390/pr5030035

Reynolds, J. H., & Ford, E. D. (1999). Multi-criteria assessment of ecological process models. *Ecology, 80*(2), 538–553. doi:10.1890/0012-9658(1999)080[0538:MCAOEP]2.0.CO;2

Ritter, N., Kilinc, E., Navruz, B., & Bae, Y. (2011). Test review: Test of nonverbal intelligence-4 (TONI-4). *Journal of Psychoeducational Assessment, 29*(5), 384–388.

Robertson, S. E. (1977). The probability ranking principle in IR. *The Journal of Documentation, 33*(4), 294–304. doi:10.1108/eb026647

Robertson, S. G., & Morison, A. K. (1999). A trial of artificial neural networks for automatically estimating the age of fish. *Marine & Freshwater Research, 50*(1), 73–82. doi:10.1071/MF98039

Robertson, S. G., & Morison, A. K. (2003). Age Estimation of Fish Using a Probabilistic Neural Network. In *Ecological Informatics* (pp. 369–382). Springer. doi:10.1007/978-3-662-05150-4_19

Ruiz-Casado, M., Alfonseca, E., & Castells, P. (2007). Automatising the learning of lexical patterns: An application to the enrichment of wordnet by extracting semantic relationships from wikipedia. *Data & Knowledge Engineering, 61*(3), 484–499. doi:10.1016/j.datak.2006.06.011

Rumelhart, D. E., Hinton, G. E., & Williams, R. J. (1985). *Learning internal representations by error propagation. Tech. rep.* DTIC Document. doi:10.21236/ADA164453

Rzevski, G. (1993). On Behaviour and Architectures of Autonomous Intelligent Agents: An Engineering Perspective. First International Round-Table on Abstract Intelligent Agents, Rome, Italy.

Saberi, A., Vahidi, M., & Bidgoli, B. M. (2007, November). Learn to detect phishing scams using learning and ensemble? methods. In *Web Intelligence and Intelligent Agent Technology Workshops, 2007 IEEE/WIC/ACM International Conferences on* (pp. 311-314). IEEE.

Sadowski, B., Nomaler, O., & Whalley, J. (2016). *Technological Diversification of ICT companies into the Internet of things (IoT): A Patent-based Analysis*. Academic Press.

Sahami, M., Dumais, S., Heckerman, D., & Horvitz, E. (1998, July). A Bayesian approach to filtering junk e-mail. In *Learning for Text Categorization: Papers from the 1998 workshop* (Vol. 62, pp. 98-105). Academic Press.

Salles, P., & Bredeweg, B. (2003). Qualitative reasoning about population and community ecology. *AI Magazine, 24*(4), 77.

Salski, A. (2003). Ecological applications of fuzzy logic. In *Ecological informatics* (pp. 3–14). Springer. doi:10.1007/978-3-662-05150-4_1

Salton, G., & Buckley, C. (1988). Term-weighting approaches in automatic text retrieval. *Information Processing & Management, 24*(5), 513–523. doi:10.1016/0306-4573(88)90021-0

Salton, G., Fox, E. A., & Wu, H. (1983). Extended Boolean information retrieval. *Communications of the ACM, 26*(11), 1022–1036. doi:10.1145/182.358466

Sanchez, D., Melin, P., & Castillo, O. (2015). Optimization of modular granular neural networks using a hierarchical genetic algorithm based on the database complexity applied to human recognition. *Information Sciences, 309*, 73–101. doi:10.1016/j.ins.2015.02.020

Santhi, P. (2011). Improving the performance of Data Mining Algorithm in Health Care data. *International Journal of Clothing Science and Technology, 2*(3).

Santoro, G., Vrontis, D., Thrassou, A., & Dezi, L. (2017). The Internet of Things: Building a knowledge management system for open innovation and knowledge management capacity. *Technological Forecasting and Social Change.* doi:10.1016/j.techfore.2017.02.034

Sarkar, C., SN, A. U. N., Prasad, R. V., Rahim, A., Neisse, R., & Baldini, G. (2015). DIAT: A scalable distributed architecture for IoT. *IEEE Internet of Things Journal, 2*(3), 230-239.

Schleiter, I. M. (2000). Prediction of running water properties using radial basis function self-organising maps combined with input relevance detection. In *Second International Conference on Applications of Machine Learning to Ecological Modelling*, Adelaide, Australia.

Schleiter, I. M., & ... . (2006). Modelling ecological interrelations in running water ecosystems with artificial neural networks. In *Ecological informatics* (pp. 169–186). Springer. doi:10.1007/3-540-28426-5_9

Schleiter, I. M., Borchardt, D., Wagner, R., Dapper, T., Schmidt, K.-D., Schmidt, H.-H., & Werner, H. (1999). Modelling water quality, bioindication and population dynamics in lotic ecosystems using neural networks. *Ecological Modelling, 120*(2), 271–286. doi:10.1016/S0304-3800(99)00108-8

Schleiter, I. M., Obach, M., Borchardt, D., & Werner, H. (2001). Bioindication of chemical and hydromorphological habitat characteristics with benthic macro-invertebrates based on artificial neural networks. *Aquatic Ecology, 35*(2), 147–158. doi:10.1023/A:1011433529239

Scholar, M. T. (2017). Review on the various Sybil Attack Detection Techniques in Wireless Sensor Network. *SYBIL, 164*(1).

Schutz, A., & Buitelaar, P. (2005, November). Relext: A tool for relation extraction from text in ontology extension. In *International semantic web conference* (pp. 593-606). Springer. 10.1007/11574620_43

Sen, J. (2013). *Homomorphic Encryption: Theory & Applications.* arXiv preprint arXiv:1305.5886

Sen, A. K., Patel, S. B., & Shukla, D. P. (2013). A data mining technique for prediction of coronary heart disease using neuro-fuzzy integrated approach two level. *International Journal of Engineering and Computer Science, 2*(9), 1663–1671.

Setiawan, N. A. (2009, December). Rule Selection for Coronary Artery Disease Diagnosis Based on Rough Set. *International Journal of Recent Trends in Engineering, 2*(5), 198–202.

Sharma, M. L., Kumar, S., & Mehta, N. (2018). *Internet of things application, challenges and future scope.* Academic Press.

Shelby, Z., Hartke, K., & Bormann, C. (2014). *The constrained application protocol (CoAP).* Academic Press.

Shukla, D. P., Patel, S. B., Sen, A. K., & Yadav, P. K. (2013). *Analysis of Attribute Association Rule from Large Medical Datasets towards Heart Disease Prediction.* Academic Press.

Si, A., Leong, H. V., & Lau, R. W. (1997, April). Check: a document plagiarism detection system. In *Proceedings of the 1997 ACM symposium on Applied computing* (pp. 70-77). ACM. 10.1145/331697.335176

Silva, I., Ribeiro-Neto, B., Calado, P., Moura, E., & Ziviani, N. (2000, July). Link-based and content-based evidential information in a belief network model. In *Proceedings of the 23rd annual international ACM SIGIR conference on Research and development in information retrieval* (pp. 96-103). ACM. 10.1145/345508.345554

Simon, D. (2008). Biogeography-Based Optimization. *IEEE Transactions on Evolutionary Computation, 12*(6), 702–713. doi:10.1109/TEVC.2008.919004

Singh, D., Tripathi, G., & Jara, A. J. (2014, March). A survey of Internet-of-Things: Future vision, architecture, challenges and services. In Internet of things (WF-IoT), 2014 IEEE world forum on (pp. 287-292). IEEE.

Singh, M. P., & Chopra, A. K. (2017, June). The Internet of Things and Multiagent Systems: Decentralized Intelligence in Distributed Computing. In *Distributed Computing Systems (ICDCS), 2017 IEEE 37th International Conference on* (pp. 1738-1747). IEEE.

Sintef, O. V., & Norway, P. F. (2014). *Internet of Things–From Research and Innovation to Market Deployment.* Academic Press.

Soni, J., Ansari, U., Sharma, D., & Soni, S. (2011). Predictive data mining for medical diagnosis: An overview of heart disease prediction. *International Journal of Computers and Applications, 17*(8), 43–48. doi:10.5120/2237-2860

Specht, D. F. (1991). A general regression neural network. *IEEE Transactions on Neural Networks, 2*(6), 568–576. doi:10.1109/72.97934 PMID:18282872

Sreelatha, B., Alakananda, E., Bhavya, B., & Prasad, S. H. (2018). *IoT applied to logistics using intelligent cargo.* Academic Press.

Sriram, B., Fuhry, D., Demir, E., Ferhatosmanoglu, H., & Demirbas, M. (2010, July). Short text classification in twitter to improve information filtering. In *Proceedings of the 33rd international ACM SIGIR conference on Research and development in information retrieval* (pp. 841-842). ACM. 10.1145/1835449.1835643

Stallings, W. (1995). *Network and internetwork security: principles and practice* (Vol. 1). Englewood Cliffs, NJ: Prentice Hall.

Steinbach, M., Karypis, G., & Kumar, V. (2000 August). A comparison of document clustering technique. KDD Workshop on Text Mining, 400(1), 525-526.

Sterritt, R., & Hinchey, M. (2005, August). Autonomicity-an antidote for complexity? In Computational systems bioinformatics conference, 2005. Workshops and poster abstracts (pp. 283-291). IEEE. doi:10.1109/CSBW.2005.28

Storn, R., & Price, K. (1997). Differential evolution–a simple and efficient heuristic for global optimization over continuous spaces. *Journal of Global Optimization, 14*(4), 341–359. doi:10.1023/A:1008202821328

Su, J. P., Wang, C. A., Mo, Y. C., Zeng, Y. X., Chang, W. J., Chen, L. B., . . . Chuang, C. H. (2017, May). i-Logistics: An intelligent Logistics system based on Internet of things. In *Applied System Innovation (ICASI), 2017 International Conference on* (pp. 331-334). IEEE.

Sumathi, S., & Sivanandam, S. N. (2006). *Introduction to data mining and its applications* (Vol. 29). Springer. doi:10.1007/978-3-540-34351-6

Sun, F., Zhao, Z., Fang, Z., Du, L., Xu, Z., & Chen, D. (2014). A review of attacks and security protocols for wireless sensor networks. *Journal of Networks, 9*(5), 1103. doi:10.4304/jnw.9.5.1103-1113

Sutton, R. S., & Barto, A. G. (1998). Reinforcement learning: An introduction (Vol. 1). MIT Press.

Suykens, J. A., & Vandewalle, J. (1999). Least squares support vector machine classifiers. *Neural Processing Letters, 9*(3), 293–300. doi:10.1023/A:1018628609742

Sweeney, L. (2002). Achieving k-anonymity privacy protection using generalization and suppression. *International Journal of Uncertainty, Fuzziness and Knowledge-based Systems, 10*(05), 571–588. doi:10.1142/S021848850200165X

Sweeney, L. (2002). k-anonymity: A model for protecting privacy. *International Journal of Uncertainty, Fuzziness and Knowledge-based Systems, 10*(05), 557–570. doi:10.1142/S0218488502001648

Szarvas, G., Farkas, R., Iván, S., Kocsor, A., & Busa-Fekete, R. (2006). *An iterative method for the de-identification of structured medical text. Workshop on Challenges in Natural Language Processing for Clinical Data.*

Taneja, A. (2013). Heart disease prediction system using data mining techniques. Oriental. *Journal of Computer Science and Technology, 6*(4), 457–466.

Tao, F., Zuo, Y., Da Xu, L., & Zhang, L. (2014). IoT-based intelligent perception and access of manufacturing resource toward cloud manufacturing. *IEEE Transactions on Industrial Informatics, 10*(2), 1547–1557. doi:10.1109/TII.2014.2306397

Taweesiriwate, A., Manaskasemsak, B., & Rungsawang, A. (2012, March). Web spam detection using link-based ant colony optimization. In *Advanced Information Networking and Applications (AINA), 2012 IEEE 26th International Conference on* (pp. 868-873). IEEE. 10.1109/AINA.2012.118

Tesauro, G. (1994). TD-Gammon, a self-teaching backgammon program, achieves masterlevel play. *Neural Computation, 6*(2), 215–219. doi:10.1162/neco.1994.6.2.215

Theodoridis, S., & Koutroubas, K. (1999). Feature generation II. *Pattern Recognition, 2*, 269–320.

Thomas, Fowler, & Hunt. (n.d.). *Programming Ruby 1.9: The Pragmatic Programmers' Guide, Pragmatic Bookshelf*. Tech. rep.

Tien, J. M. (2017). Internet of Things, Real-Time Decision Making, and Artificial Intelligence. *Annals of Data Science, 4*(2), 149–178. doi:10.100740745-017-0112-5

Tiwari, V. K. (2012). Face recognition based on Cuckoo search algorithm. *Indian Journal of Computer Science and Engineering, 3*(3), 401–405.

Toksari, M. D. (2006). Ant colony optimization for finding the global minimum. *Applied Mathematics and Computation, 176*(1), 308–316. doi:10.1016/j.amc.2005.09.043

Topchy, A., Jain, A. K., & Punch, W. (2004). A mixture model for clustering ensembles. In *Proceedings of the 2004 SIAM International Conference on Data Mining*. SIAM. 10.1137/1.9781611972740.35

Townsend, A. M. (2013). *Smart cities: Big data, civic hackers, and the quest for a new utopia*. WW Norton & Company.

Tu, Shin, & Shin. (2009). Effective Diagnosis of Heart Disease through Bagging Approach, study report, 2009. *2009 2nd International Conference on Biomedical Engineering and Informatics*.

Tupa, J., Simota, J., & Steiner, F. (2017). Aspects of Risk Management Implementation for Industry 4.0. *Procedia Manufacturing, 11*, 1223–1230. doi:10.1016/j.promfg.2017.07.248

Uzuner, Ö., Katz, B., & Nahnsen, T. (2005, June). Using syntactic information to identify plagiarism. In *Proceedings of the second workshop on Building Educational Applications Using NLP* (pp. 37-44). Association for Computational Linguistics. 10.3115/1609829.1609836

Vaidya, J., Clifton, C. W., & Zhu, Y. M. (2006). *Privacy preserving data mining* (Vol. 19). Springer Science & Business Media.

Vandaele, H., Nelis, J., Verbelen, T., & Develder, C. (2015, October). Remote management of a large set of heterogeneous devices using existing IoT interoperability platforms. In *International Internet of Things Summit* (pp. 450–461). Cham: Springer.

Velardi, P., Fabriani, P., & Missikoff, M. (2001, October). Using text processing techniques to automatically enrich a domain ontology. In *Proceedings of the international conference on Formal Ontology in Information Systems-Volume 2001* (pp. 270-284). ACM. 10.1145/505168.505194

Venkatesh, A. N. (2017). *Connecting the Dots: Internet of Things and Human Resource Management*. Academic Press.

Verdouw, C. N., Wolfert, J., Beulens, A. J. M., & Rialland, A. (2016). Virtualization of food supply chains with the internet of things. *Journal of Food Engineering, 176,* 128–136. doi:10.1016/j. jfoodeng.2015.11.009

Verykios, V. S., Bertino, E., Fovino, I. N., Provenza, L. P., Saygin, Y., & Theodoridis, Y. (2004). State-of-the-art in privacy preserving data mining. *SIGMOD Record, 33*(1), 50–57. doi:10.1145/974121.974131

Vijayarani, S., & Sudha, S. (2013). An efficient classification tree technique for heart disease prediction. *International Journal of Computer Applications, 201.*

Wander, A. S., Gura, N., Eberle, H., Gupta, V., & Shantz, S. C. (2005, March). Energy analysis of public-key cryptography for wireless sensor networks. In *Pervasive Computing and Communications, 2005. PerCom 2005. Third IEEE International Conference on* (pp. 324-328). IEEE. 10.1109/PERCOM.2005.18

Wang, L., & Luo, H. (2017, December). Design of intelligent vehicle for distribution system based on speech recognition. In *Computer and Communications (ICCC), 2017 3rd IEEE International Conference on* (pp. 2807-2811). IEEE. 10.1109/CompComm.2017.8323044

Wang, Q., Gauch, S., & Luong, H. (2010). Ontology concept enrichment via text mining. In IADIS international conference on internet technologies & society (pp. 147-154). Academic Press.

Wang, S., Yin, J., Cai, Z., & Zhang, G. (2008). A RSSI-based selflocalization algorithm for wireless sensor networks. *Journal of Computer Research and Development,* 385-388.

Wang, S., Wan, J., Li, D., & Zhang, C. (2016). Implementing smart factory of industrie 4.0: An outlook. *International Journal of Distributed Sensor Networks, 12*(1), 3159805. doi:10.1155/2016/3159805

Wang, X., Zhang, C., Ji, Y., Sun, L., Wu, L., & Bao, Z. (2013, April). A depression detection model based on sentiment analysis in micro-blog social network. In *Pacific-Asia Conference on Knowledge Discovery and Data Mining* (pp. 201-213). Springer. 10.1007/978-3-642-40319-4_18

Wasan, Bhatnagar, & Kaur. (2006, October). The Impact of Data Mining techniques on medical diagnostics. *Data Science Journal, 5*(19), 119–126.

Wen, M., Li, H., Zheng, Y. F., & Chen, K. F. (2008). TDOA-based Sybil attack detection scheme for wireless sensor networks [English Edition]. *Journal of Shanghai University, 12*(1), 66–70. doi:10.100711741-008-0113-2

Werner, H. (1993). *Integration ausländischer Arbeitnehmer in den Arbeitsmarkt-Deutschland, Frankreich, Niederlande, Schweden (No. 992967913402676)*. International Labour Organization.

Whigham, P. A., & Recknagel, F. (1999). Predictive modelling of plankton dynamics in freshwater lakes using genetic programming. Academic Press.

Whigham, P. A. (2000). Induction of a marsupial density model using genetic programming and spatial relationships. *Ecological Modelling, 132*(2-3), 299–317. doi:10.1016/S0304-3800(00)00248-9

Whigham, P. A., & Fogel, G. B. (2003). Ecological applications of evolutionary computation. In *Ecological Informatics* (pp. 49–71). Springer. doi:10.1007/978-3-662-05150-4_4

Wilkins, M. F., Boddy, L., & Dubelaar, G. B. J. (2003). Identification of marine microalgae by neural network analysis of simple descriptors of flow cytometric pulse shapes. In *Ecological Informatics* (pp. 355–367). Springer. doi:10.1007/978-3-662-05150-4_18

Witkowski, K. (2017). Internet of Things, Big Data, Industry 4.0–Innovative Solutions in Logistics and Supply Chains Management. *Procedia Engineering, 182*, 763–769. doi:10.1016/j.proeng.2017.03.197

Wood, A. D., & Stankovic, J. A. (2002). Denial of service in sensor networks. *Computer, 35*(10), 54-62.

Wood, S. (2006). *Generalized additive models: an introduction with R*. CRC Press.

Wu, T. F., Lin, C. J., & Weng, R. C. (2004). Probability estimates for multi-class classification by pairwise coupling. *Journal of Machine Learning Research, 5*(Aug), 975–1005.

Yadav, J., Yadav, R., & Monika, M. (2017). A Study on Internet of Things. *International Journal (Toronto, Ont.), 8*(1).

Yamaguchi, T. (2001). Acquiring conceptual relations from domain-specific texts. *Proceedings of the IJCAI 2001.*

Ye, Y., Hu, T., Yang, Y., Zhu, W., & Zhang, C. (2018). A knowledge based intelligent process planning method for controller of computer numerical control machine tools. *Journal of Intelligent Manufacturing*, 1–17.

Yick, J., Mukherjee, B., & Ghosal, D. (2008). Wireless sensor network survey. *Computer Networks, 52*(12), 2292–2330. doi:10.1016/j.comnet.2008.04.002

Yue, X., Cai, H., Yan, H., Zou, C., & Zhou, K. (2015). Cloud-assisted industrial cyber-physical systems: An insight. *Microprocessors and Microsystems, 39*(8), 1262–1270. doi:10.1016/j.micpro.2015.08.013

Yu, J., & Branton, D. (1976). Reconstitution of intramembrane particles in recombinants of erythrocyte protein band 3 and lipid: Effects of spectrin-actin association. *Proceedings of the National Academy of Sciences of the United States of America*, *73*(11), 3891–3895. doi:10.1073/pnas.73.11.3891 PMID:1069273

Zelenkauskaite, A., Bessis, N., Sotiriadis, S., & Asimakopoulou, E. (2012, September). Interconnectedness of complex systems of internet of things through social network analysis for disaster management. In *Intelligent Networking and Collaborative Systems (INCoS), 2012 4th International Conference on* (pp. 503-508). IEEE. 10.1109/iNCoS.2012.25

Zeng, W., Yang, Y., & Luo, B. (2013, October). Access control for big data using data content. In *Big Data, 2013 IEEE International Conference on* (pp. 45-47). IEEE. 10.1109/BigData.2013.6691798

Zhang, C., Zhou, Z., Sun, H., & Dong, F. (2012). Comparison of Three Face Recognition Algorithms. In *Proceedings of International Conference in Systems and Informatics (ICSAI)*. Yantai, China: IEEE Xplore.

Zhang, X., Heys, H. M., & Li, C. (2010, May). Energy efficiency of symmetric key cryptographic algorithms in wireless sensor networks. In *Communications (QBSC), 2010 25th Biennial Symposium on* (pp. 168-172). IEEE. 10.1109/BSC.2010.5472979

Zhang, L., Li, J., Shi, Y., & Liu, X. (2009). Foundations of intelligent knowledge management. *Human Systems Management*, *28*(4), 145–161.

Zhang, Y. C., & Yu, J. (2013). A study on the fire IOT development strategy. *Procedia Engineering*, *52*, 314–319. doi:10.1016/j.proeng.2013.02.146

Zhang, Y., Chen, B., & Lu, X. (2011, August). Intelligent monitoring system on refrigerator trucks based on the internet of things. In *International Conference on Wireless Communications and Applications* (pp. 201-206). Springer.

Zheng, P., Sang, Z., Zhong, R. Y., Liu, Y., Liu, C., Mubarok, K., ... Xu, X. (2018). Smart manufacturing systems for Industry 4.0: Conceptual framework, scenarios, and future perspectives. *Frontiers of Mechanical Engineering*, 1–14.

Zhong, N., Ma, J., Huang, R., Liu, J., Yao, Y., Zhang, Y., & Chen, J. (2016). Research challenges and perspectives on Wisdom Web of Things (W2T). In *Wisdom Web of Things* (pp. 3–26). Cham: Springer. doi:10.1007/978-3-319-44198-6_1

Zu Eissen, S. M., & Stein, B. (2006, April). Intrinsic plagiarism detection. In *European Conference on Information Retrieval* (pp. 565-569). Springer.

About the Contributors

Hadj Ahmed Bouarara received a licence degree in computer Science and Master diploma in computer modeling of knowledge and reasoning from the Computer Science department of Tahar Moulay University of Saida Algeria. Now Hadj Ahmed BOUARARA is a phd student in Web and Knowledge Engineering in Dr. Tahar Moulay University. His research interests Data Mining, Knowledge Discovery, Metaheuristic, Bio-inspired techniques, Retrieval Information, Cloud Computing and images processing.

Reda Mohamed Hamou received an engineering degree in computer Science from the Computer Science department of Djillali Liabes University of Sidi-Belabbes-Algeria and PhD (Artificial intelligence) from the same University. He has several publications in the field of BioInspired and Metaheuristic in many journals as IJAMC, IJIRR, IJAEC, IJALR, IJISP, IJIIT, JITR, IJCINI, IJOCI, IJSIR, IJSI, IJAEIS, IJDSST, IJBRA, Applied Inteligence,.... His research interests include Data Mining, Text Mining, Classification, Clustering, computational intelligence, neural networks, evolutionary computation and Biomimetic optimization method. He is a head of research team in GecoDe laboratory. Dr. Hamou is an associate professor in technology faculty in UTMS University of Saida-Algeria.

Amine Rahmani received a licence degree in computer Science from the Computer Science department of Dr. Tahar Moulay University of Saida-Algeria, received the Master diploma in Network, System and Security Informatics from Djillali Liabes University. Now Amine RAHMANI is a phd student in Web and Knowledge Engineering in Dr. Tahar Moulay University. His research interests include Big Data, Privacy Preserving, Informatics Security, Data Mining, Cloud Computing, Big Data analytics, Access Control, and Cryptography.

* * *

Damian Alberto is a member of the laboratory ITIC in bombay institution. he has a licence degree in computer science and electronics engineer. he has different publication in different conferences and journals.

Abdelmalek Amine received an engineering degree in Computer Science from the Computer Science department of Djillali Liabes University of Sidi-Belabbes-Algeria, received the Magister diploma in Computational Science and PhD from Djillali Liabes University in collaboration with Joseph Fourier University of Grenoble. His research interests include data mining, text mining, ontology, classification, clustering, neural networks, and biomimetic optimization methods. He participates in the program committees of several international conferences and on the editorial boards of international journals. Prof Amine is the head of GeCoDe-knowledge management and complex data-laboratory at UTM University of Saida, Algeria; he also collaborates with the "knowledge base and database" team of TIMC laboratory at Joseph Fourier University of Grenoble.

Yasmin Bourara has got a license diploma in computer network and she's a student in second year master of computer network and distributed system in the department of technology university Dr. Moulay Taher Saida, studies interest spam detection, web designing and protocol communication.

Banu Çalış Uslu is an Instructor Dr. at Marmara University. She graduated from Sakarya University Faculty of Engineering Industrial Engineering Department in 2000. Following the graduation she worked as a planning and project engineer for three years. In 2008, she completed the master's degree program of Marmara University on Engineering Management. In 2015, she received Ph.D title by completing the Ph.D program of Marmara University on Industrial Engineering. After she finalized her doctorate, she went to UK, worked as a Postdoctoral Researcher. Banu Çalış Uslu has scientific publications in internationally and nationally acclaimed journals, in the field of scheduling, optimization, simulation and agent-based systems as well as presentations in international and national scientific congresses on her research areas.

Seniye Umit (Oktay) Firat, PhD, is the Professor of Industrial Engineering at the University of Marmara. She has been carried out many field surveys and projects on Data Mining Applications, Sustainability (energy topics), Productivity Analysis and Performance Measurement, Quality Engineering, TQM and SPC Applications, Multivariate Data Analysis, Risk Analysis, Supplier Evaluation, Six Sigma Implementation, Process Analysis, Marketing Research, Customer Segmentation and BI implementation in the SME and Large Size manufacturing firms, retailing and banking sectors. Recent years, her focus on sustainability issues and Industry 4.0 and its components. She has been worked as researcher and director for several national and international projects that supported by, EPSRC -Engineering and Physical Science Research Council –UK, İKV, SKD Türkiye, İSO, İTO, Italian Foreign Trade Institute, BAP-Marmara University, … She has published over 200 academic papers in national and international journals and conferences, and many edited books and book chapters in international publications on her research areas. She has gave many seminars and trainings in the industrial units and institutes. In addition she has published several informative articles in sector magazines in order to share new scientific developments with industry sectors.

Lavika Goel is currently an Assistant Professor in the Department of Computer Sc. & Information Systems at BITS, Pilani. She had earlier worked as an Assistant Professor at Delhi Technological University (DTU), and also holds a corporate experience working at Oracle India Private Ltd. She is Ph.D., M.E. and B. Tech with distinction in Computer Science & Engineering from Delhi Technological University (formerly Delhi College of Engineering) and holds membership of Machine Intelligence & Research (MIR) Labs. She has always been among the top rank holders of the university – IInd rank holder in M.E., and Ist rank holder in B. Tech batch. She was also the gold medalist in Mathematics (100% marks) and Chemistry in XIIth class (ISC board). During her M.E., she was offered six months internship from ST Microelectronics and a dual campus recruitment by ORACLE India Pvt. Ltd. as well as ARICENT Technologies. During her B. Tech, she was offered recruitment by HCL Technologies as a part of B. Tech Campus Recruitment Program and had also cleared the MICROSOFT Off-Campus recruitment Written Examination. She secured a percentile of 98.7 and an ALL INDIA RANK of 242 in GATE, 2008. She qualified National Eligibility Test (NET) held by CBSE-UGC on 28th June, 2015 for eligibility for Assistant Professor in central organizations. She serves as a reviewer of recognition to many reputed international journals including the Elsevier Journal of Information Sciences and Applied Soft Computing. She has published around 40 research papers in SCI indexed International conferences, journals and book chapters including Elsevier, IEEE, Taylor and Francis, Springer, etc.

Frederic Jack has a master degree in computer science. he is a chef of the society of developing in computer science in France. he has some contribution in datamining, machine learning and security in big data.

Rahmani Mohamed Elhadi received a licence degree in computer Science from the Computer Science department of Dr. Tahar Moulay University of Saida-Algeria, received the Master diploma in Data mining and knowlodge managment from same University. Mohamed Elhadi Rahmani received his PhD in Web and Knowledge Engineering in Dr. Tahar Moulay University. His research interests include Data Mining, Cloud Computing, Big Data analytics, Ecological Issues, Ecosystem.

Souria Ortiga is Engineer in Electronics and Computer Engineering in the University of Mente. She has published in different journals and conference.

Salvia Praga has a PhD in computer science from the university Worcester Poland. She has different publication in journals like IJIRR, JAI, IJBEAD, and different communication in different conferences.

Index

A

artificial intelligence 1, 4, 6, 11-12, 15, 31, 39, 63, 183

B

Big Data 2, 4-7, 104-105, 113, 118, 125, 127-128, 142-145, 147-148, 150, 153, 159, 174, 176
Biogeography-Based Optimization (BBO) 258-259

C

classification 34, 43, 48-51, 72, 76, 109-110, 125-127, 140, 143, 166, 169, 175, 180-184, 186-192, 201, 218-219, 234-235, 239, 272, 275
clustering 35-36, 93, 126, 164-165, 167, 169, 175, 188-189, 209-210, 243

D

data mining 27-29, 31-32, 37, 43, 49, 51-52, 68, 104-106, 109-112, 124-127, 137-138, 140, 142, 159-163, 204
depression 68-70

E

ecological data analysis 52
ecosystem data 46
Enrichment 91-93, 95, 97-100, 102
evolutionary 39-41, 47, 51, 258, 279

F

face recognition 258-260, 266-272, 274-275, 279

G

Gravitational Search Algorithm (GSA) 258-259

H

Hybridization 45-46, 52, 258, 261, 279

I

Industry 4.0 1, 3-5
information retrieval 210
Internet of Things 1, 3, 5

K

Knowledge Discovery 27-28, 32, 104, 125, 163

L

linked data 91-93, 98-100, 102

M

machine learning 2, 11, 30-32, 36-37, 93, 96, 175, 180-181, 183-185, 187, 191-192, 218

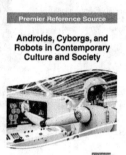

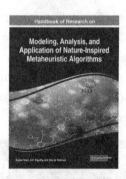

Ensure Quality Research is Introduced to the Academic Community

Become an IGI Global Reviewer for Authored Book Projects

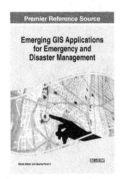
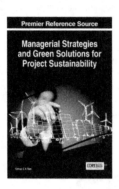

The overall success of an authored book project is dependent on quality and timely reviews.

In this competitive age of scholarly publishing, constructive and timely feedback significantly expedites the turnaround time of manuscripts from submission to acceptance, allowing the publication and discovery of forward-thinking research at a much more expeditious rate. Several IGI Global authored book projects are currently seeking highly qualified experts in the field to fill vacancies on their respective editorial review boards:

Applications may be sent to:
development@igi-global.com

Applicants must have a doctorate (or an equivalent degree) as well as publishing and reviewing experience. Reviewers are asked to write reviews in a timely, collegial, and constructive manner. All reviewers will begin their role on an ad-hoc basis for a period of one year, and upon successful completion of this term can be considered for full editorial review board status, with the potential for a subsequent promotion to Associate Editor.

If you have a colleague that may be interested in this opportunity, we encourage you to share this information with them.

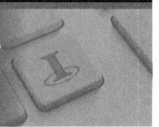

Printed in the United States
By Bookmasters